THE WAITE GROUP®

IMAGE LAB

TIM WEGNER

™

WAITE GROUP
PRESS™

IMAGE LAB

Editorial Director: *Scott Calamar*
Development Editor: *Mitchell Waite*
Managing Editor: *Joel Fugazzotto*
Technical Editor: *Heidi Brumbaugh*
Design and Production: *Pat Rogondino*
Illustrations: *Pat Rogondino*
Cover Design: *Kathy Locke; Locke & Veach*
Production Manager: *Julianne Ososke*

Waite Group Press™ is distributed to bookstores and book wholesalers by Publishers Group West, Box 8843, Emeryville, CA 94662, 1-800-788-3123 (in California 1-510-658-3453).

Printed in the United States of America
92 93 94 95 • 10 9 8 7 6 5 4 3 2 1

Wegner, Tim (Timothy I.)
    Image Lab / Tim Wegner
       p. cm.
    Includes index.
    ISBN 1-878739-11-5 : $39.95
      1. Computer graphics. I. Title.
  T385.W43 1992
  006.6'865--dc20   92-24959
                                           CIP

Dedication

With love to Susan, Dietrich, and Gretchen, who kept the turtle, guinea pigs, fish, and author well fed during the writing of this book.

PREFACE

THE IMAGE LABORATORY: A HOW-TO GUIDE FOR IMAGE PROCESSING

Image Lab is about creating and processing computer graphics images. This is a hands-on book that comes with the Image Lab suite of software—a powerful collection of Shareware programs for generating, painting, manipulating, combining, and viewing computer graphics images. The software suite includes CompuShow, Piclab, Improces, the POV-Ray tracer, and Image Alchemy, and is designed as a companion to the Fractint program that comes with the book *Fractal Creations*. This book guides you through the powerful image-processing features of these programs and provides a comprehensive reference to their capabilities. A beginner can use these tools to create and manipulate images with dazzling effects. Beginners and experts alike can follow the step-by-step reconstruction of the world-class portfolio images and learn from talented graphics artists.

The Image Lab suite includes image-processing software tools and examples on a companion disk, and the book contains software installation instructions, eight chapters, a poster, and 3D glasses.

About the Software

Three of the programs included with this book are distributed as shareware software: CompuShow, Improces, and Image Alchemy. Shareware distribution gives you the opportunity to evaluate the software on your own system and make sure that it meets your needs. The software is included with this book as a convenience for you, and should be registered with the software authors if you decide to use the programs beyond an evaluation period. Several of the authors will provide an enhanced program to those who register. More information about registering is included in the chapters on each program, and in the authors documentation. The POV-Ray program is copyrighted freeware, which you can use for non-commercial purposes without charge. The Piclab program is public domain with no restrictions.

The best way to get support for these software packages is directly from the software authors. All of them provide support on CompuServe in the PICS forum (GO PICS) or the COMART forum (GO COMART.) You can also write the authors at addresses listed in the software documentation files on the distribution disk.

Chapter 1 Installation

The installation chapter tells you how to build the Image Lab directories on your hard disk and install the software suite. Additional software configuration details are provided in the individual software application chapters.

Chapter 2 The Image Laboratory

This chapter describes the computer graphics revolution and explains the concept of turning your computer into an electronic camera and photographic darkroom rolled into one.

Chapter 3 CompuShow

This chapter introduces you to the versatile Cshow program, which allows you to view graphics files on your PC screen and create your own graphics slide shows.

Chapter 4 Piclab

Piclab is a powerful image-processing program that is the heart of your electronic darkroom. If a photographer can do it with chemicals in a darkroom, you can do it on your computer with Piclab. The chapter begins with a step-by-step tutorial of all the image-processing capabilities of Piclab, and concludes with a reference to all of the Piclab commands.

Chapter 5 Improces

The Improces program is part paint program, part image processor. In this chapter you will learn how to use Improces to paint your own images with a rich set of drawing tools, which are explained in a lucid tutorial. You will learn how to apply dozens of special-effect transformations to your images, including some that are not possible with any other piece of software. The chapter concludes with a comprehensive reference to all the functions of Improces.

Chapter 6 Fractint

This chapter is about the fractal-generating program Fractint, which comes with the book *Fractal Creations* and is also widely available on computer bulletin boards and CompuServe. The chapter provides a tutorial on advanced fractal generation techniques, and contains an in-depth investigation of a family of fractals never before published. You will also learn how the central image on the *Fractal Creations* poster was created, and how to create fractal images that you can use with the other Image Lab tools.

Chapter 7 Persistence of Vision Ray Tracer

This chapter leads you into the fascinating world of ray tracing using the Persistence of Vision ray tracing software. A hands-on tutorial will lead you through the steps of making photo-realistic images complete with lighting, shadows, shapes, and textures. You will learn how to build scene description files in POV-Ray's scene description language, and how to bring these scenes to life on your computer screen. Many ready-to-run examples are provided on the companion disk.

Chapter 8 Image Alchemy

The world of computer graphics is blessed and cursed with a plethora of different file formats for storing images. Image Alchemy is a powerful program for converting images from one file format to another. You will learn how to take a bitmapped graphics image from virtually any source format, and convert it to the formats used by the Image Lab suite. This chapter will also show you how to share your Image Lab creations with the world by converting your images to foreign formats.

Chapter 9 Graphics Portfolio

If the earlier chapters are solo software performances, this chapter is an image-processing symphony. You will learn how all the Image Lab software tools work together to create striking images. This chapter guides you through the steps used by talented artists to create their best images.

Color Poster

Attached to this book is a color poster containing high-resolution reproductions of the best of the images described in this book.

ACKNOWLEDGMENTS

. . . .

The author of a book about a half-dozen software programs owes a debt to a great many people. Without the Image Lab applications, there could have been no book. Let's have a hearty round of applause for the software authors for a job well done!

Special thanks to Lee Crocker, whose classic Piclab program was the inspiration for this book, and to John Swenson, the world's number one Piclab user and advisor. The entire Persistence of Vision team provided patient answers to questions at the time they were laboring to get POV-Ray 1.00 out the door. Drew Wells, the POV team leader, directly contributed material for the POV-Ray tutorial. The excitement of the images in this book is a testament to the skill of the artists who contributed them, Lee Skinner, Eli Boyajian, Mike Miller, Dan Farmer, Doug Muir, and Drew Wells. Thanks to Larry Wood, whose graphics forums on CompuServe (GO GRAPHICS) provide an invaluable resource of software and information for anyone interested in graphics. Thanks to STB for providing a Sierra-DAC-equipped STB Powergraph Ergo-VGA graphics board, and to Charles Marslett of STB for valuable technical information and support.

Thanks to Mitch Waite for his vision on this project and his insightful editing, and to Joel Fugazzotto and Juliane Ososke of The Waite Group for very capably shepherding this complex project to a successful conclusion.

Last and definitely not least, thanks to my family for cheerfully keeping the home ship sailing smoothly during the long days of writing!

Tim Wegner
March 1992

About the Author

Tim Wegner is an author of the best-selling book *Fractal Creations*, and is one of the programmers of the internationally acclaimed fractal generating program Fractint. He is a Member of the Technical Staff of the MITRE corporation supporting the NASA at the Johnson Space Center. Mr. Wegner has written shuttle navigation software and designed a scheduling system for NASA aircraft. He holds BA and MA degrees in mathematics.

Dear Reader:

About two years ago, I came across a mesmerizing program that actually changed my life. The program was Fractint, a powerful fractal processor, authored by a "collective" of programmers that reside on the COMART forum of Compuserve, and are known as The Stone Soup Group. Forever fascinated by patterns, I was immediately hooked on Fractint: it lit up my computer with infinitely detailed patterns, ran at what seemed like the speed of light, and required no programming knowledge whatsoever.

I invited the Stone Soup Group to write a book on their program and Fractal Creations. The book took The Waite Group on a course through uncharted waters; it was a leisure-time book that was very different from the programming Primers and Bibles that our reputation had been built on. Yet it became an immediate success.

The response to Fractal Creations was *more, more*. Our readers who sent in their Reader Satisfaction Cards said they wanted to delve deeper into image processing. They wanted to be able to take the fractals they generated and make them into more detailed works of art. "How do I make realistic water, clouds, mountain ranges? How do I open various graphic images, draw on them, change their color palettes, and save them in any of 50 different file formats?" Our readers wished to combine fractal images, ray-trace them, and process them along with other images, and view their work on the fly. I knew of a number of freeware and shareware programs that would turn Fractint users into Picassos. So I asked Fractal Creations author Tim Wegner to write a book that included these tools, explained how to use them, and provided hands-on examples.

WAITE
GROUP
PRESS™

The results of Tim's efforts, Image Lab, exceeded my expectations. It is a one-stop image processing laboratory. It is, I think, the high-tech Fotomat™ of computer books. Right here in your hands is a complete package to create the beautiful masterpieces that you see on the cover of this book and the bound-in poster.

We'd like to hear what you think. Fill out and return our Reader Satisfaction Card at the back of this book to obtain a catalog and see what else is in store!

Sincerely,

Mitchell Waite
Publisher

200 Tamal Plaza   Corte Madera . California   94925   415-924-2575   FAX 415-924-2576

TABLE OF CONTENTS

CONTENTS

INTRODUCTION

This book is a hands-on tutorial and reference for a powerful suite of image-processing software. It has been designed to be read while you try the examples on your computer. The companion disk contain both the Image Lab software packages and the supporting example files. The goal of this book is to enable you to create spectacular graphics images and master the processes needed to combine, modify, and manipulate images.

INSTALLING THE SOFTWARE

Chapter 1 contains the information needed to install the Image Lab software on your hard disk. Each program in the Image Lab suite has its own hardware requirements, and while some of the programs will run fine on older 8088 machines, the practical minimum platform is an 80386 machine, a VGA adapter, and about 10 MB of free disk space. However, each of the Image Lab programs are usable for certain purposes by themselves, and it is not necessary to install the whole suite of software at once to use this book if disk space is at a premium. If you can spare the disk space, the best approach is to install the entire software suite before reading the book, so all the programs are available. Keep in mind that several of the programs require disk space to run, so you should leave anywhere from 1 to 10 MB free, depending on the size of the images you are handling.

You will find a discussion of the hardware needed to support image processing in Chapter 2. If you are thinking of upgrading your hardware, refer to that chapter for graphics considerations to help in planning your purchase.

THE IMAGE LAB SOFTWARE CHAPTERS

Chapters 3 through 8 are about individual Image Lab software packages. Each of these chapters is self-contained, and they do not have to be read in order. The most generally useful programs are introduced first, and the more specialized programs later.

Each of the software chapters provides background material to enhance your understanding of the *whys* of image processing, followed by a hands-on tutorial that guides you through the processes of creating and manipulating images. Sample images provided on the companion disk are used in the tutorials. Each chapter concludes with a reference section that documents all the functions of the piece of software under discussion. The reference sections also contain examples, and can be used to augment the tutorials. For more information, you can also check the software authors' own documentation.

The Fractint chapter (Chapter 6) does not include a reference section because that is provided in the book *Fractal Creations*. It does provide a tutorial, as well as advanced examples of fractal generation for readers who have *Fractal Creations* or who have obtained the Freeware version of Fractint.

THE GRAPHICS PORTFOLIO

When you have become comfortable with the basic operation of the Image Lab software programs, then it is time to look at the advanced examples in Chapter 9. The central theme of the Graphics Portfolio chapter is ray tracing, although all the Image Lab programs are used together to create these examples.

WHERE TO LOOK

The programs that come with this book have been carefully selected to work together and provide different basic functions. In many cases an application will have other functions in addition to the functions for which it was selected as part of the Image Lab suite. Here is a brief guide to different image processing functions that can be done with the software packages.

Converting File Formats

The Image Alchemy program (Chapter 8) is the workhorse file conversion tool in the Image Lab suite. You can also use Piclab (Chapter 4) to convert between Targa, GIF, and Raw, or Improces (Chapter 5) to convert between Targa, PCX, and GIF.

Creating Landscapes

You can create mountain ranges with Fractint (Chapter 6), Improces (Chapter 5), and Persistence of Vision (Chapter 7).

Cutting and Pasting Images

Improces (Chapter 5) allows you to cut and paste using the mouse. Piclab (Chapter 4) does the same job using a command language.

Image-Processing Effects

Piclab (Chapter 4) is the main image-processing tool. Improces (Chapter 5) also has a variety of special transformations that can be applied to images.

Painting and Drawing

See Improces (Chapter 5).

Render Images with Light and Shadows

When it comes to photo-realistic scenes with light and shadow, Persistence of Vision Ray Tracer (Chapter 7) is the tool you need.

Viewing Graphics Files

All the main Image Lab programs have the capability to display images. The one program dedicated to this function is CompuShow (Chapter 3). If you want to view images with rapid color cycling, try Fractint (Chapter 6) or Improces (Chapter 5).

Wrapping Images around Spheres

Both Ray Tracer Persistence of Vision (Chapter 7) and Fractint (Chapter 6) can map images onto spheres.

Printing Images

If you have an HP Laserjet or Deskjet, you can use Piclab (Chapter 4) for printing images. The Fractint program (Chapter 6) has limited printing capabilities for dot matrix and postscript printers. After you register your copy of CompuShow (Chapter 3) you will receive an enhanced version that comes with a large number of printer drivers.

1

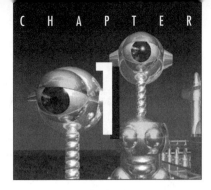

INSTALLATION

T his chapter describes how to install the Image Lab software suite that is bundled with this book. Later in the book you will find chapters about each of the individual software packages containing more details on configuring the programs for your computer.

THE *IMAGE LAB* DISK

This book comes with a 3.5 inch high density disk containing the files shown in Table 1-1.

File	Size Compressed	Size Expanded	Software Package
CSHOWA.EXE	132,005	254,000	CompuShow image viewer
EXAMPLES.EXE	456,355	650,000	Image Lab examples
IMGALC.EXE	375,488	672,000	Image Alchemy conversion program
IMPROC.EXE	188,679	433,000	Improces paint program
PICLAB.EXE	101,736	177,000	Piclab image processor
POV-RAY.EXE	191,814	480,000	POV-Ray Tracer
README.COM	2,844	2,844	Image Lab disk readme file

Table 1-1 Contents of the Image Lab companion disk

The files are contained in compressed form as self-extracting executables. Table 1-1 shows how much free disk space you must have for each package in order to have room for the uncompressed files. Keep in mind that to actually run the software you will want additional free space. The complete suite of software will take up a little less than 3 MB. If your disk space is very limited you can just install one package at a time for use as you read the chapters corresponding to each specific software package. You should also install the EXAMPLES.EXE file which contains example files and images that are used throughout the book.

IMAGE LAB SOFTWARE INSTALLATION

The recommended method of installing the Image Lab software is to install the packages in subdirectories under a single directory called \IMLAB. To make this directory, change to the drive where you wish to install the software suite. In the following instructions, and throughout this book, the system or software prompt is shown in regular type, and what you type in is printed in bold. Type :

```
C:>CD \ (ENTER)
C:>MD IMLAB (ENTER)
C:>CD \IMLAB (ENTER)
```

Now the C:\IMLAB directory will be the current directory. To install each Image Lab software program, run the desired self-extracting executable programs. These instructions assume you are installing the Image Lab disk from drive A:. to drive C: If not, just replace A: or C: in the instructions below with the correct drive letter. To install the entire software suite, type:

```
C:\IMLAB>A:CSHOWA (ENTER) ✓
C:\IMLAB>A:PICLAB (ENTER) ✓
C:\IMLAB>A:IMPROC (ENTER) ✓
C:\IMLAB>A:ALCHEMY (ENTER) ✓
C:\IMLAB>A:POV-RAY (ENTER) ✓
C:\IMLAB>A:EXAMPLES (ENTER)
```

As you run each self-extracting file, a message will appear on your screen telling you what software package is being installed, and how much disk space is needed, and asking you whether you wish to proceed with the installation. This message looks something like:

```
LHA's SFX 2.13L (c) Yoshi, 1991
Cshow will be installed in the CSHOW directory under the
current directory, requiring approximately 254,000 bytes.

Continue?

[Y/N]
```

If you wish to proceed, type:

Y

You will then see a message reporting each file as it is being decompressed and installed on your hard disk.

As a result of the installation process, subdirectories for each software package will be created under the current directory. If you used the \IMLAB directory as recommended, your directory tree is shown in Figure 1-1. In addition to the directories for the software that comes on the *Image Lab* disk, Figure 1-1 shows a recommended directory for the Fractint software that comes with *The Waite Group's Fractal Creations* and is discussed in Chapter 6 of this book.

You will find several batch files used to invoke the programs in the \IMLAB directory, while the remaining software will automatically be installed in directories under the current directory.

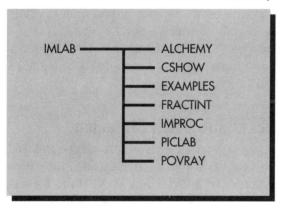

Figure 1-1 Image Lab directory tree

MAKE A \TMP DIRECTORY

Many of the Image Lab programs use a special directory for temporary files. The recommended name of this directory is C:\TMP, but it can be on any drive and have any name as long as the software is told where it is. To make this directory, change to the desired drive (C: in this example) and type:

`C:> MD \TMP` (ENTER)

After you install Piclab (contained in the self-extracting archive PICLAB.EXE on your image lab disk,) you will find a file called SSTOOLS.INI in your IMLAB directory. This file tells piclab where the TMP directory is, and it must match the actual location of \TMP. Start your text editor, and load the file SSTOOLS.INI. This file contains the lines:

```
; This file is a sample of how to set up your SSTOOLS.INI file.
; The values shown here are for use with The Waite Group's Image
; Lab book.
[fractint]
; fractint settings go here
[piclab]
tempdir=c:\tmp
helpfile=c:\imlab\piclab\pl.hlp
display=svga2
```

If you used a directory name other than \TMP or a drive other than C:, then edit the line

```
temdir=c:\tmp
```

to reflect the actual name and location that you used. If you used C:\TMP, then the SSTOOLS.INI file is correct and does not need to be changed.

Other Image Lab programs use the TMP environment variable to determine the location of the temporary directory. To set the TMP variable to C:\TMP, add the following line to your AUTOEXEC.BAT file:

```
SET TMP=C:\TMP
```

Add \IMLAB to the AUTOEXEC.BAT PATH Statement

The Image Lab suite has been set up so that all the software can be invoked from batch files in the \IMLAB directory. Edit your AUTOEXEC.BAT file with a text editor, and look for a line beginning with PATH. Add the C:\IMLAB directory to the list of directories. Each directory name should be separated from the others with a semicolon. A typical PATH statement might look like:

```
PATH=C:\IMLAB;C:\DOS;C:\WIN;C:\BAT
```

If you have another directory where you keep your batch files that is already listed in your PATH, then you can copy the all the files with the .BAT extension to this directory. In this case it is unnecessary to add \IMLAB to your PATH. More instructions of setting up the Image Lab applications are given in the chapters on each software package.

Check the README.COM File

The distribution disk contains a file called README.COM that contains any last minute instructions relating to the installation of the software tools. This file contains its own listing program. To read the notes, type :

```
A:README (ENTER)
```

Use the arrow keys to scroll up and down the file.

CHAPTER 2

THE IMAGE LABORATORY

THE WORLDS OF COMPUTER IMAGING

The use of computers to create and modify images has become a part of our daily lives, whether we are aware of it or not. You turn on the TV, and see the metamorphosis of a car into a tiger. A hospital patient's body is scanned with ultrasound, creating a 3D image on a monitor for the doctor. NASA scientists painstakingly process radar signals from a far-off planet, and you are treated to a high-speed flyby through the canyons of Venus. A tourist takes some photos, and instead of taking the film to the local photo finisher, the camera is plugged into a computer and the pictures shown on the screen.

Beauty and the Beast

All over the world people enjoy watching animated cartoons. The pioneering studio that brought the world such characters as Mickey Mouse and Donald Duck is Disney Pictures. Their recent instant classic, *Beauty and the Beast,* was created largely with traditional hand-painting techniques. In this classical approach, artists paint detailed backgrounds, or in some cases layers of backgrounds, as the backdrop for their animated figures. The opening scenes of the film show a perspective view of a hilly terrain. As the viewer's point of view floats over the landscape, closer trees and hills move in relation to the distant background, giving a 3D effect. The result is charming and artful, but recognizable as the clever combination of several static paintings superimposed and moving with respect to each other to provide an animated perspective.

Later in the film, however, we see a completely different kind of scene. The beauty and the beast dance in a huge and elegant ballroom. The walls are decorated with elaborate moldings, Corinthian columns, and hundreds of candles. A starry sky shows through the upper windows, and an elaborate Renaissance-era painting graces the domed ceiling. Hanging in the center of the ballroom is a blazing candelabra.

Such a scene could have been accomplished with traditional animation techniques — painting such a spectacular backdrop of the romantic dance scene is certainly well within the talents of the skilled Disney artists. The result would have been a scene with a static background and moving dancers. But the makers of the film had a different vision. They wanted a moving perspective that would follow the dancers about the room, giving visual expression to the soaring emotions of the scene.

An elaborate full-scale computer model of the ballroom was built and rendered on high-end 3D computer workstations. The 3D-modeling approach allowed the continuous alteration of perspective as the viewpoint flew about the room. Unlike the static approach, where depth is simulated by moving several fixed scenes in relation to each other, every point of the computer-generated ballroom changes from frame to frame. Even with state-of-the-art graphics workstations, each frame of the scene could take as much as four-and-a-half hours of rendering time. But what a result! You feel like you are flying through the room with the dancers. At one point you sail up to the ceiling and down through the chandelier.

The *Beauty and the Beast* ballroom scene represents an animation first: conventional painted 2D characters overlaid on a 3D computer-animated room. The use of these techniques by the talented but conservative Disney organization demonstrates that computer imaging has come of age in the entertainment world. The best part is that you can create images on your PC in much the same way as Disney created the dance hall for *Beauty and the Beast!*

Digital Photography

Conventional chemical photographic processing will probably be with us for a long time. However, a quiet race is under way, a race between silicon memory and silver halide film. At the moment silver-based photographic technology is ahead, but digital imaging technology is catching up rapidly.

Today's digital cameras have low resolution compared to conventional cameras, but the memory density possible using silicon chips is doubling every few years, making higher resolutions more practical. Although digital cameras may have limited resolution, they also have tremendous advantages. For example, suppose you wanted to insert employee photographs in your company's personnel data base. You could take a conventional photograph, chemically process it, digitize it with a scanner, and place the resulting image in the data base. Or you could take the pictures directly with a digital camera, connect the camera to a computer with a cable, and transfer the images straight into the data base.

Printing color pictures used to be a laborious task. Lighting conditions and film characteristics vary, and correct color balance was obtained only through trial and error. Today's one-hour processing lab, however, has a different approach. A computerized video device contains a mathematical model of the complete process of making a positive color print from a color negative, including the color-correction step. A video camera captures an image of the color negative, and creates a positive image on a video monitor. The lab operator can see a simulation of the final print, and can adjust the color filtration interactively until it looks good — all without the benefit of tests that require chemical processing. Once the image looks good on the monitor, the filtration is set and the picture is exposed and processed.

Digital photography takes the photo lab's technology a step further. Instead of using a computerized image to simulate a chemically produced image, the computer monitor displays the real image, which exists in digital form. All the photographic filtration and chemical processes that can be done to a silver-halide image can be accomplished by digitally processing the electronic image.

The Image Laboratory

The software that comes with this book turns your computer into an image-processing laboratory. Not only can you accomplish traditional photographic darkroom tasks such as lightening, darkening, changing contrast, and enlarging images, but you can achieve effects that would be difficult or impossible with conventional photographic means. But that's not all — your PC can not only process images, it can create them! Figure 2-1 shows a fascinating example.

THE PC GRAPHICS HARDWARE REVOLUTION

An image laboratory on your PC is made possible by a revolution of computer hardware that is bringing the capabilities of high-end workstations into the home. The trend of ever-increasing hardware capabilities at lower prices shows no sign of abating any time soon. This is good news for the graphics worker,

Figure 2-1 Phoon

because computer graphics is very demanding of your PC's capabilities. Let's look at the hardware capabilities that will help you with your graphics projects.

More Pixels on the Screen

One of the attributes of high-end workstations that has set them apart from PCs is their high-resolution graphics. In today's market a minimum of 1024 pixels wide by 768 pixels high has become the norm even for the generic brands. To put this graphics resolution in perspective, remember that the original PC had 64K of random access memory (RAM), and came equipped with CGA 320x200 pixel four-color graphics. The CGA graphics mode requires only 16,000 bytes of memory to store a graphics image. A 256-color image at 1024x768 requires 786,432 bytes, or 49 times more graphics memory, which is larger than the 640K maximum of conventional memory available to

MS-DOS! Even more remarkable, the price of this high resolution is very modest. One of the reasons for this is that memory itself is much cheaper than it was a few years ago. The megabyte of memory that comes with one of these 1024x768 Super VGA boards does not add a great deal to the cost.

This situation of advanced graphics capabilities for modest expenditure has two "gotchas." The first is that a 1024x768 pixel image probably exceeds what a 14-inch monitor can really display. An important distinction to keep in mind is the difference between logical pixel addressability and physical visibility. Your graphics equipment may have the capability to "display" a high-resolution image (that is, it can logically address the pixels at the high resolution), but as a practical matter adjacent pixels may not be distinguishable (are not physically visible). To really see a high-resolution image, a 16-inch or larger monitor is needed, which costs a great deal more money.

The second "gotcha" has to do with vertical frequency. The vertical frequency is the number of times per second that the whole image is drawn. In the past, high-resolution images were displayed at 60 Hz or even slower. At a vertical frequency of 40 Hz, virtually everyone can see an unpleasant flicker. Somewhere around 70 Hz the flicker becomes invisible. At in-between values such as 60 Hz, the visibility of flicker is a very individual matter. Graphics adapters have become available that support these higher vertical frequencies. Once again, the problem is that monitors that can handle the higher frequencies cost more money.

If money is an issue (as it is for most of us), you can compromise. You can upgrade your graphics adapter to a new high-resolution ergonomic model that can support 1024x768 pixels at a flickerless 72 Hz vertical frequency, but keep your old multisync monitor. At high resolutions a slower vertical resolution can be used, and at the more modest 640x480 resolution, the ergonomic 72 Hz refresh rate can be used to eliminate flicker. The reasoning behind this compromise is that flicker is tolerable when viewing occasional high-resolution graphics images, but a high refresh rate should be used for modes that you are likely to use for many hours at a time, such as 640x480 with Windows 3.

A Rainbow of Colors

For many purposes, having plenty of colors available is even more important than high resolution. A critical eye is tolerant of lower resolution in a very colorful image. Here again the PC graphics hardware market has created a bonanza for graphics enthusiasts. This time there is no monitor "gotcha" — an analog monitor is capable of displaying infinite gradations of color, whether it is the latest model or an older multisync.

The original VGA standard had exactly one 256-color graphics mode, namely the 320x200 pixel MCGA mode. These dimensions are not an accident; the graphics memory required to display 256 colors at 320x200 is exactly 64,000 bytes, which fits nicely into one memory segment of the Intel 80X86 chip. The 256 VGA colors can be selected from a large palette of 262,144 different colors, which means that in many cases a 256-color image can look very realistic.

Today the VGA standard started by IBM has been superseded by the VESA Super VGA standard. VESA stands for the Video Electronic Standards Association, a consortium of hardware manufacturers that have agreed on a common way to access Super VGA capabilities. When you buy a graphics adapter, it is a good idea to locate one that supports the VESA standard, since you will be guaranteed to have graphics compatibility with software that supports VESA. All of the software in this book supports the VESA standard, as well as many individual graphics chip sets.

If you have experienced the "good old days" of four-color CGA graphics, you might think that nobody could ask for more than 256 colors. As you will see later in this book, palette-based color, though very powerful and economical, has some limitations for image processing. The VGA standard is like the gasoline engine — everyone agrees that it is obsolete, but refinements keep coming along that extend its life. The latest refinement is the invention of several replacements for the VGA Digital to Analog Conversion (DAC) chip by enhanced versions that supported more colors. The most popular example is the Sierra DAC, which provides 16-bit color capabilities and can allow your graphics adapter to display 32,768 colors simultaneously. This is fewer than the 262,144 possible with regular VGA, but the difference is that all the Sierra colors can be displayed at once, compared to only 256 simultaneous colors on a VGA. When you buy a new VGA graphics board, consider buying one that either has the Sierra chip built in, or one that can be upgraded with a Sierra chip. If your old VGA board has a socketed DAC chip, this may be an easy and inexpensive upgrade. Take your board to your local computer repair shop or dealer to find out. Even if your DAC is not socketed, an upgrade may be possible. If you are the brave type who dares to unsolder a chip from a computer board, you can do it yourself!

The 16-bit color provided by the Sierra chip is not the last word in color graphics. A higher standard is 24-bit true color, which permits 16,777,216 colors. Currently 24-bit graphics boards do exist, but still cost considerably more than Super VGA boards equipped with 16-bit DACS. Keep checking the market, because sooner or later 24-bit boards will become inexpensive commodity items, just as Super VGA boards already have.

All of the software included with this book supports Super VGA resolutions, and most of the software supports 16-bit color with the Sierra DAC.

While you can do a lot with 16-color EGA graphics, some form of VGA is the practical minimum equipment for doing serious image processing. Having 16-bit color capability is a desirable extra.

A final word on graphics adapters. More and more graphics adapters are coming on the market equipped with a CPU on the graphics board that accelerates graphics operations. Some of these emulate the IBM 8514a adapter, and others use newer chips. These boards can make your graphics-based software, such as Windows 3.X, much snappier in interactive performance. As long as they work with software supporting the VGA or VESA standards, these boards will work with the software in this book. For most image-processing activity, the display of images on the screen is fast compared to the underlying computation. Such boards are not really necessary to support your personal image laboratory, although they still may be a good value for you for other purposes.

Giant Hard Disks

Storing graphics images takes space — a lot of space! The calculation we did above to show how much graphics memory was required for a 1024x768 image applies equally to storing images on your hard disk. An uncompressed 1024x768 256-color image will eat up three-quarters of a megabyte of your hard disk space. Fortunately the GIF graphics format used by your Image Lab software contains a compression algorithm that greatly reduces this size. But then again, several of these same software packages create or manipulate images in a 24-bit true color uncompressed format. Use of 24-bit color increases the amount of information and hence the required disk space by three times. Suddenly we are talking 2,359,296 bytes, or 2.3 MB to store one high-resolution image!

If you had a PC a few years ago, you might remember going out and upgrading your two-floppy PC with a state-of-the art 10-MB hard disk for over $1,000, running the CHKDSK program, and being awestruck when you saw a seven-digit number indicating the capacity in bytes of your hard disk! If you still have that old computer, you couldn't store five high-resolution true color images on it!

The good news is that mass storage is getting cheaper every day. Mass storage prices drop approximately 20 percent every year. This is an area where UNIX workstations and PCs are on equal ground; it is no costlier to equip a PC with a large hard disk than a workstation, and is probably much less. There is no such thing as too much disk space when you are doing image processing.

You may also find that a good tape drive for backing up your hard disk is a necessity. As your collection of images increases and your 200-MB hard disk fills up, you can store your images off-line using your tape backup. Keep in mind that tape drives use compression algorithms, and the manufacturers quote capacities for the tape drive that assumes that the contents of your hard disk will compress well. Remember that a hard disk full of GIF files is a hard disk full of files that are already compressed. This means that when considering alternative tape drives for your PC, you should look at the uncompressed capacity. A heavily advertised 120-MB tape backup probably really only handles 60 MB of highly compressed files.

Free Memory

The price of random access memory (RAM) fluctuates with political and economic conditions, but on average it drops 40 percent a year. At the same time, memory density (the amount of memory packed into one chip) goes up. By 1996 the price of memory should reach the dollar-a-megabyte level, which means it will be essentially free!

A few years ago, the way to add memory to a system was to add a memory add-on board. Today this is a poor strategy because the bus of your PC probably operates at a speed of 8 MHz or so, which limits access of your PC to that memory to that speed. Memory located on an add-on board is accessed through the 8 MHz bus. If your PC can run at 33 MHz, you want to be able to access memory at that speed. Today most newer PCs have a lot of memory capacity on the motherboards.

When you buy a PC, you should find out the maximum amount of memory that the motherboard can hold. This is a function of the number of SIMMS (Standard Inline Memory Modules) it holds, and how much memory each SIMM holds. Currently 1-MB and 4-MB SIMMS cost about the same per megabyte, and soon 4-MB SIMMS and 16-MB SIMMS will be the better value. Not every motherboard can take 4 MB or 16 MB SIMMS, so you should check. Buying a motherboard that holds the next generation of SIMMS is good insurance against obsolescence. Many computers on today's market can hold 16 4-MB SIMMS, for a total RAM capacity of 64 MB. You don't need that much now, but installing 8 MB of RAM or even more is not too much for serious image processing. Some of the *Image Lab* software can directly address extended or expanded memory, and other software is very disk intensive and can benefit from a large software cache or RAM disk.

The Latest and Greatest CPU

Image processing does not necessarily need a really fast computer. With a fixed budget, you might be wiser to buy more RAM or a larger hard disk rather than a faster CPU. Having said that, the transition between the 286 and 386 processors was an architectural watershed, and no one buying a new PC should consider anything less than a 386 computer. And while most image processing works fine on slower computers, if you are interested in ray tracing and want to create images with the POV-Ray Tracer, a fast computer will help and a math coprocessor and a 386 CPU are essential.

Your Image Lab Computer

A fast 50 MHz 586-based PC with 1024x768 pixel 16-bit graphics, 16 MB of RAM, and a 200-MB hard disk with a tape backup would be a wonderful platform for creating dazzling photo-realistic images. But maybe your computer isn't quite so new or full featured. If you have a 1-MB 286 with a 40-MB hard disk and an early model VGA, no problem. You'll still be able to make the same high-quality images. You will need to manage your disk space carefully, use a lot of floppy disks to store your images, and run some of the slower projects overnight, but with a little ingenuity and extra patience, you'll be just fine. But be forewarned: Nothing precipitates the decision to upgrade a computer like running powerful graphics software on a low-end PC!

3

COMPUSHOW

THE UNIVERSAL IMAGE VIEWER

CompuShow is a Shareware program that lets you view all types of graphics images on your computer screen. That is a humble purpose, but a critical one for the graphics practitioner. A graphics image viewer is one of those utilities that you take for granted until it doesn't work right, and then you realize how essential it is. CompuShow does its job superbly well, and once you have it installed and have gained familiarity, it will become an automatic part of your imaging tool kit. You think, "I wonder what that file looks like . . ." and before you know it, the image is on the screen and you were hardly conscious of typing "cshow". This is the way all computer software should work!

Most Image Lab programs can display images. Piclab, Image Alchemy, Improces, and Fractint are all able to show image files on your screen. So why a stand-alone image viewer program? There are several answers to this question, but the best one is simply that the other programs have other purposes, and for them displaying images is secondary. CompuShow's only function in life is to display images, so everything about CompuShow is optimized for that task. CompuShow can display image files in many different formats, and can utilize virtually all of the video modes your hardware supports. You really don't need to worry too much about what format an image file is in; if it is a bitmapped image file, chances are CompuShow can read it. And if the image looks best viewed with some unusual mode of your display hardware, chances are CompuShow displays that too. If you want to view an image larger than your graphics adapter can display, Cshow will allow you to scroll the image so that you can see the whole image. The final clincher is that after you send in the modest Shareware registration fee, you will receive an enhanced version that can print images and do slides shows as well.

CompuShow can read the following file formats:

- CompuServe RLE
- MacPaint
- CompuServe GIF 87a and 89a
- PC Paintbrush (PCX)
- PC Paint/Pictor
- Dr. Halo
- Rix ColoRIX and EGA Paint
- Targa uncompressed and run-length encoded, mapped, and true-color
- Electronic Arts DeluxePaint II and DeluxePaint II enhanced
- Microsoft Windows Paint (BMP)
- Tagged Image Format Files (TIFF)

SHAREWARE INFORMATION

The version of CompuShow included with this book is copyrighted by the author. It is bundled with this book as a convenience to you. If you continue to use this program beyond a reasonable trial period, not to exceed 21 days, you must pay for it by registering. This Shareware arrangement lets you try it before you buy it.

Bob Berry, the author of CompuShow, offers some extra incentive for registration. After you send him the registration fee, you will receive the latest revision of an enhanced version of the program, which includes printing and slide-show capabilities. As a registered user, you'll be notified as new versions are released, and may upgrade for a nominal charge.

For your convenience, the author has included an order form in the file ORDRFORM.DOC, with space for all the required information. The basic registration price is $25 for a 5 1/4-inch disk. For more information see the order form.

GETTING CSHOW UP AND RUNNING

This chapter assumes you have installed CompuShow in the directory C:\IMLAB\CSHOW according to the instructions in Chapter 1. If you used a different drive or directory, just substitute the correct drive or directory in the instructions that follow. There are a few additional steps you should take to get the most out of CompuShow.

Invoking Cshow from a Batch File

All the CompuShow files should be on your hard disk in one directory following the installation procedure. The author of CompuShow has experienced difficulty with people who share some of the files of the program with others without giving them the full set. (You are welcome to share CompuShow with friends; just make sure that they get *all* the files.) CompuShow has been designed to require that all the files be present the first time it is run. After that you can delete unneeded files, as described below.

There are two methods to allow the CompuShow program to be run from anywhere on your hard disk. (1) Add C:\IMLAB\CSHOW to the Path statement in AUTOEXEC.BAT; or (2) use a batch file residing in a directory in the Path to execute CompuShow. The second method is recommended. It takes time for your computer to search all the path directories to find your programs, so it is better to run programs from batch files placed in a directory early in your Path statement directory list. Create a batch file in a subdirectory that's already included in the Path statement of AUTOEXEC.BAT. To find out the current setting of your Path variable, execute the Path command without any parameters by typing:

`C:>PATH` (ENTER)

It is a good idea to keep all of your Image Lab batch files in one place, such as in the directory C:\IMLAB. Create a file in C:\IMLAB called CSHOW.BAT that contains the line:

`C:\IMLAB\CSHOW\CSHOW %1 %2 %3 %4 %5 %6 %7 %8 %9`

Then add C:\IMLAB to the Path statement in your AUTOEXEC.BAT file.

These instructions assume that your Cshow directory is C:\IMLAB\CSHOW. If it is different, replace C:\IMLAB\CSHOW with the directory in which your Cshow files are located. Those "%1 %2 . . ." symbols are batch file variables that take on as values the command-line parameters used when the batch file is invoked. They pass on parameters that you want (such as the names of graphics files to view) to CompuShow. This batch file is also a good place to put command-line options that control CompuShow. These options are listed in the reference section at the end of the chapter.

Selecting a Video Driver

CompuShow uses external video drivers to support extended graphics modes on a wide variety of video hardware. The video drivers are files named VIDEOP1.DRV, VIDEOI4.DRV, and so on. You need to locate the video driver that matches your graphics equipment. You also need to create a VIDEO.DAT file to tell CompuShow what video modes work with your hardware. The setup procedure described here takes a few minutes, but it has to be done only once, and then you don't have to think about video modes again.

Table 3-1 shows the list of video drivers and the options required at the command line to use them. Check your display adapter documentation to find which one is right for your computer. If you can't find your computer's driver, check the file DRIVERS.DOC for the latest list. There are many more brands of graphics adapters than there are distinct chip sets used to build them, so if you do not see your brand in the list, try to discover from your documentation or by looking on the board itself what chip set is being used. Also note that many newer boards have built-in support for the VESA standard, which means that the +sV2 driver listed at the bottom of the table should work.

Driver	Cshow Option	Chip set
VIDEOA1.DRV	+sA1	ATI VGA Wonder
VIDEOA2.DRV	+sA2	ATI Graphics Solution
VIDEOA3.DRV	+sA3	Ahead Systems
VIDEOA4.DRV	+sA4	Amstrad PC1512
VIDEOA5.DRV	+sA5	ATI Vga Wonder Plus
VIDEOA6.DRV	+sA6	AT&T 6300
VIDEOC1.DRV	+sC1	Chips & Technologies (Cardinal)
VIDEOC2.DRV	+sC2	Compaq VGA
VIDEOC3.DRV	+sC3	Cirrus
VIDEOD1.DRV	+sD1	DGIS
VIDEOE1.DRV	+sE1	Everex VGAs
VIDEOG1.DRV	+sG1	Genoa 6400
VIDEOH1.DRV	+sH1	Hercules Graphics Station
VIDEOH2.DRV	+sH2	Hercules InColor
VIDEOI1.DRV	+sI1	Generic CGA (any CGA)
VIDEOI3.DRV	+sI3	IBM PGC, Vermont Microsystems
VIDEOI4.DRV	+sI4	IBM 8514/A (Single monitor)

Table 3-1 CompuShow video drivers

Driver	Cshow Option	Chip set
VIDEOI5.DRV	+sI5	IBM 8514/A (8514+VGA monitor)
VIDEOI7.DRV	+sI7	IBM XGA
VIDEON1.DRV	+sN1	NCR VGA
VIDEOO1.DRV	+sO1	Oak Technologies
VIDEOP1.DRV	+sP1	Paradise (AST, Compaq, Dell)
VIDEOP2.DRV	+sP2	Plantronics
VIDEOS1.DRV	+sS1	STB EM16+ (Similar to T4)
VIDEOS2.DRV	+sS2	STB Ergo + Sierra DAC
VIDEOT1.DRV	+sT1	Tseng 3000 (Genoa, STB, Orchid)
VIDEOT2.DRV	+sT2	Tandy 1000SL/TL(ETGA)
VIDEOT3.DRV	+sT3	Trident (Logix, ZyMOS)
VIDEOT4.DRV	+sT4	Tseng 4000 (Orchid ProDesigner II)
VIDEOT5.DRV	+sT5	Tseng 4000 VGAs with Sierra DAC
VIDEOV1.DRV	+sV1	Video 7
VIDEOV2.DRV	+sV2	VBE (VESA Bios Extensions)

Table 3-1 CompuShow video drivers *(continued)*

The +s command-line switch tells CompuShow to load a specific video driver. Find your video driver in Table 3-1, then invoke CompuShow with the +s option for your board. For example, if you have an STB Ergo board with a Sierra DAC, you would use the +sS2 option, and type:

```
C:>CShow +sS2 (ENTER)
```

This loads the S2 video driver (VIDEOS2.DRV).

Change directories to a directory that has a GIF file. (There should be a file called BOB-89A.GIF in your C:\IMLAB\EXAMPLES directory, but any GIF file will do.) Then type in the example above, replacing the +sS2 option with the option for your graphics board. You will then see a list of files in the current directory. Figure 3-1 shows what the File Selection screen looks like. Select the file using the arrow keys and press (ENTER). You will see a screen that looks somewhat like Figure 3-2. The details on the screen will vary with the video driver chosen.

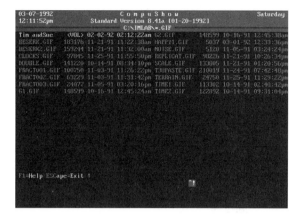

Figure 3-1 The File Selection screen

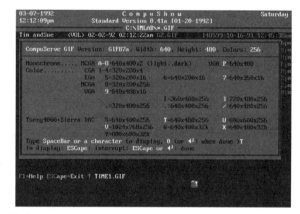

Figure 3-2 The Graphics Information box

Testing Your Video Driver

The real test of your choice of video drivers are the modes attached to the Ⓢ through Ⓨ keys. These keys utilize the extended modes of your graphics hardware. Try them all in turn, and make a note of which ones work. If you press a key from Ⓢ to Ⓨ and the screen stays in text mode (perhaps changing colors), then that mode isn't supported on your adapter. If the same thing happens on all the video driver modes, then you either have the wrong video driver loaded, or your adapter just doesn't have any Super VGA capabilities. (VGA adapters that are built into a system board or bundled with a computer are often low-end adapters without Super VGA capabilities.)

Once you've identified the correct video driver for your system, you can set it up to be loaded automatically whenever the program is started. You'll do this by copying the video driver for your video board to the generic name VIDEO.DRV. For example, if the +sS2 option works for you, then type in:

C:> COPY VIDEOS2.DRV VIDEO.DRV (ENTER)
C:> CSHOW (ENTER)

With no +S switch specified on the CSHOW command line, the program will load a file named VIDEO.DRV. Once you have determined the correct video driver and copied it to VIDEO.DRV, you need no longer be concerned about the video driver options.

Creating a VIDEO.DAT File

CompuShow will select the best video mode for you, which you can use by pressing the (SPACE) bar instead of a letter for a video mode. However, CompuShow doesn't consider extended Super VGA video driver modes when selecting the best mode to display a graphic, unless you tell it which video driver modes work on your adapter and monitor.

For example, assume that modes S, T, U, V, W, X and Y, work on your VGA, but your monitor can't handle mode Y. To tell CompuShow to use modes S, T, U, V, W, X, and Y, create a text (ASCII) file using your text editor, with the characters "STUVWXY". Name the file VIDEO.DAT. Once done, you can press (SPACE) after highlighting a graphics file in the file list, and CompuShow will select the video mode for you that best fits the image you are displaying. This is a tremendous convenience.

Look at Figure 3-2 and notice that there are two 640x480x256 modes. One is marked /: and uses the (/) key, while the other is marked T= and uses the (T) key (the actual keys may be different on your system). The : is your clue that a video mode is a simulated mode and not a genuine mode. The /: mode is a simulated mode that allows 640x480 images to be viewed on graphics hardware that does not support that mode, such as early VGA adapters with only 256K of memory. These boards had 640x400x256 as their top video mode. The simulated 640x480 mode works by throwing out some of the lines in the images, which degrades the image somewhat. This mode is a wonderful convenience if you need it, but if your computer has a real 640x480x256 mode, you definitely should use it instead of the simulated mode. If you don't tell CompuShow that the real 640x480 mode works, by adding the letter T (as in the example) to your VIDEO.DAT file, CompuShow will automatically select and propose the use of the simulated mode. Once again, possible confusion is avoided by properly setting up the VIDEO.DAT file.

Figure 3-2 shows several modes that have 32K (32,768) colors. These modes are made possible by the use of the Sierra DAC (which stands for Digital Analogue Conversion) chip. This 32K color capability is very useful for image processing, and a number of the Image Lab tools support these "hi Color" modes. If your video board has a socketed DAC chip, you may be able to add the Sierra chip for a very modest amount of money. The Sierra chip works particularly well with boards that use the Tseng ET4000 chip set, but it will work with other graphics adapter chip sets as well.

Cleaning Up Your CSHOW Directory

The CompuShow Shareware package includes the program, documentation files, and numerous video drivers. When CompuShow starts for the first time it checks to see that all its files are present, and displays a "missing files" message for 15 seconds if any are missing. If you have a copy of the original disk or archive including all these video driver and documentation files, you don't need to keep them on your hard disk.

After you install CompuShow with *all* the video driver and documentation files in a subdirectory and run it once, the file CSHOW.DAT is created. Once this file is created, it is no longer necessary to have all the video driver files present. After you have copied your video driver to VIDEO.DRV and read or printed out the documentation, you will probably want to delete all the superfluous files. To do so, just type:

`C:>CSHOWDEL` (ENTER)

This command will delete all the nonessential files.

COMPUSHOW QUICK START

Once CompuShow is set up, it is extremely easy to use. The easiest way to view a file is to include the file name as a command-line argument. For example, you can view the file BOB-89A.GIF in your \IMLAB\EXAMPLES directory by typing:

`C:>CD \IMLAB\EXAMPLES` (ENTER)
`C:\IMLAB\EXAMPLES>CSHOW BOB-89A.GIF` (ENTER)

You will then see the File Selection screen with the file BOB-89A.GIF highlighted. Just press (SPACE) to view it with the video mode CompuShow chooses, or (ENTER) to go the Graphics Information screen and select the video mode yourself. When viewing an image, pressing (ESC) allows you to back out to the previous screen. Repeatedly pressing (ESC) will allow you to back out and exit the program. You can also invoke Cshow with no parameters and select the file you wish to view with the arrow keys.

From the File Selection screen, you can get help by using the (F1) key. The Help screen is shown in Figure 3-3. It describes the keystrokes to select files and change directories.

Figure 3-3 The CompuShow
Help screen

WHAT IS A GRAPHICS FILE VIEWER?

CompuShow is a graphics file viewer for bitmapped graphics. A bitmapped graphics file contains color information about pixels, or picture elements, that make up an image on your computer screen. The job of a file viewer is to decode the pixel color information, set your video hardware to the correct video mode, and color each pixel on your screen according to the color encoded in the file. If there is more information in the file than your graphics equipment can handle, the file viewer has the difficult job of approximating the original image as best it can with the available hardware.

Graphics files can be created in many different ways. A paint program allows you to create an image on your computer screen and save it as a graphics file. Ray tracing or fractal programs take mathematical objects and form visual images of them. You can also get graphics files by taking photographs or slides to a scanning service that will digitize them and produce graphics files with the picture encoded in the file. There are many different formats of bitmapped files in the industry today. Most were developed to meet the needs of certain specialized software applications.

Chapter 4 will delve deeper into the questions concerning graphics images and graphics files. This chapter on CompuShow has been placed early in the book because there is one overriding concern about graphics files: Their purpose is to be looked at, so they need a way to be displayed. CompuShow does that job with minimum fuss and maximum effectiveness with a large number of different kinds of files.

COMPUSHOW TUTORIAL

This tutorial will introduce you to the main features of CompuShow. The program will work with just about any kind of PC graphics hardware. This tutorial assumes that you have some kind of VGA. If you have another kind of graphics board, you can still follow along, but the exact steps you take may be different.

Selecting Graphics Files

You can use any of four different methods to select files to view using CompuShow.

The first method is to invoke Cshow with a file name as a parameter. For example, if the file BOB-89A.GIF is in the current directory, you can type:

`C:> CSHOW BOB-89A.GIF` (ENTER)

You will then see the File Selection screen with BOB-89A.GIF highlighted, and can view it by pressing (SPACE).

The second method is to directly type in the name of the file while the File Selection screen is up. There is a text entry field in the lower-right corner of the screen for that purpose. If the file isn't on the current directory screen, you need to include the drive and subdirectory by typing:

`C:\IMLAB\EXAMPLES\BOB-89A.GIF` (ENTER)

When you press (ENTER), the file will be retrieved, or a buzzer will sound if the file is not found.

The third file-viewing method is to select the file from the file list. Press the ⊕ cursor key (or move the mouse up) to move into the directory display. Move the highlight bar around the file directory with the mouse or arrow keys. Table 3-2 shows the effects of various keys. In addition to the file selection keys, there are three handy file management keys listed at the end of the table.

Use these keys to select the file you want to view. You can also use the file list to change directories. To move down a directory in the directory tree, select the desired subdirectory. To move to the next higher directory, select "..".

You can tag files for later viewing with (F7), and then view them one after the other with (F8). Once you have begun viewing a sequence of tagged files, pressing (ENTER) takes you to the next file.

The Graphics Information Box

Pressing (ENTER) rather than (SPACE) after selecting a file causes the Graphics Information box to pop up. This box gives you control over the many possible graphics modes that can be used to view files. Figure 3-4 shows the Graphics Information box.

↓	moves to the next file
↑	moves to the previous file
PGDN	moves to the next screen
PGUP	moves to the previous screen
CTRL-PGDN	moves to the bottom of the column
CTRL-PGUP	moves to the top of the column
CTRL-END	moves to the last file on the screen
CTRL-HOME	moves to the first file on the screen
END	moves to the last file
HOME	moves to the first file
A to Z	moves to the next file starting with that letter
ALT-C	copies the current file
ALT-R	renames the current file
ALT-D	deletes the current file

Table 3-2 File selection keys

The top line of the box identifies the type of graphic, and any other information available, such as the file format version, pixel width, pixel height, and number of possible colors for each pixel. Below the top line you can see a large number of different video modes along with the keys that invoke them. The variety of available modes is a case study in the diversity of the IBM PC-compatible architecture and it is not altogether clear whether this is a blessing or a curse! Be that as it may, CompuShow gives you access to all the modes built in to your graphics adapter, and even some that aren't.

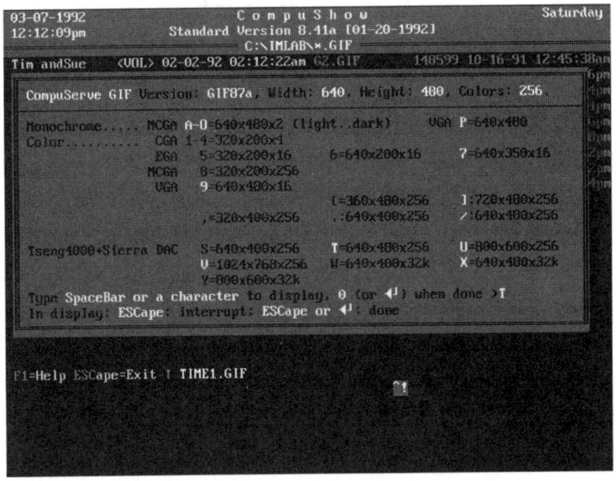

Figure 3-4 The Graphics Information box

Keep in mind that certain video modes have only a limited number of colors available to use for viewing images. For example, the venerable CGA mode has four colors. Therefore, if you display a 256-color image using the CGA mode, CompuShow has to figure out a way to consolidate most of those colors and display the image using only the four available colors. This results in a greatly simplified image, which takes on the character of a poster painted with a few solid colors. The CGA has four different color combinations, or palettes, which can be selected by pressing the keys ⓵ through ⓸. Usually the object of picking a video mode is to display the image as faithfully as possible, which means using a mode with at least as many colors as the image uses; but sometimes it is fun to try different video modes to get different effects. The ability to display images using different video modes is very useful, since it lets you see how your high-resolution images will look at lower resolutions.

You should have a file called BRYCE.GIF in your C:\IMLAB\EXAMPLES directory. You can change directories from the File Selection screen by pressing ⒡⒉. You will see a Log to prompt. To change directories, type:

`Log to C:\IMLAB\EXAMPLES` (ENTER)

Select BRYCE.GIF with the arrow keys or the mouse, and press (ENTER) to get the Graphics Information box. Now you can experiment with some of the modes. Go ahead and try pressing ⓵ to see what the Bryce image looks like with CGA. The Bryce image is 640 pixels wide and 480 pixels high, so you cannot see the whole image with a 320x200 pixel mode. Press the ⓓ key and the ⊖ key in succession, and you will see that you can scroll around the image. Now press (ESC) to return to the Graphics Information box.

Try some of the other modes, such as the simulated 640x480 256-color mode, which is invoked by pressing Ⓢ. This mode gives quite good results. Press (ESC) to return to the Graphics Information box. If your board supports it, compare this mode with the true 640x480 256-color mode by pressing Ⓣ. At first you might think that the image is the same, but you can see that the quality is higher, especially if you examine the pink moon in the sky. The Ⓢ mode does not really have 640x480 pixels; the image is displayed by throwing out some pixels and actually using 640x400. This is useful for video boards with only 256K of memory, which cannot have any video mode with a higher 256-color resolution than 640x400. If your adapter has more than 256K of memory, as most newer boards do, you should always use the Ⓣ mode to get 640x480 resolution. If you include the letter T in your VIDEO.DAT file, CompuShow will select this mode automatically when displaying a 640x480 image and you press (SPACE).

The Graphics Information box gives you the flexibility to control exactly what video mode is used to display an image. If you don't need this flexibility, simply press (SPACE) instead of (ENTER) after selecting a file. CompuShow will automatically pick a mode for you. If the dimensions and color of the image match one of your video modes, and if you have created a VIDEO.DAT file telling CompuShow which of the extended video modes work, then CompuShow's choice will most likely be what you want. If you are viewing an image with odd dimensions or number of colors, you may want to press (ENTER) and try different modes from the Graphics Information screen.

Conducting a Slide Show

After you have created many graphics masterpieces with the Image Lab tools, you will want to show them off to friends. The best way to do this is to create a fully automatic slide show with the enhanced version of CompuShow that you will receive after you register your copy with the author. However, you can create quite a decent manually operated slide show with the unregistered Shareware version included on the Image Lab companion disk.

Place all the images you wish to show in a single directory for convenience. If you want to show the slides in a particular order, you will need to rename the files so they are in alphabetical order. Start CompuShow. If all the files are the same type (let's say they are GIF files for this example) and there are other non-graphics files in the current directory, you may want to start up CompuShow with a file selection mask by typing:

`C:>CSHOW *.GIF` (ENTER)

This limits the files shown on the file selection list to GIF files using the .GIF file name extension. You can also change the file selection mask after starting CompuShow by pressing the (F4) key and typing in the file specification *.GIF. Now move the highlight through the file list, tagging the files you wish to show with the (F7) key. If you accidentally tag a file that you do not wish to show, move the highlight to the file again and press (F7) . The (F7) key toggles the tagging on and off. You can tag all the files with one keystroke by pressing (F9), and untag them all with (F10). If you forget the meaning of all these keystrokes, just remember that (F1) is the Help key! The Help screen contains a reminder of the action of each function key.

When you have tagged all the files you want to show and are ready to start, press (F8) to start the slide show. The first image will display on the screen. To move to the next images, press (ENTER). Each of the tagged graphics files will be displayed one by one on the screen in the sort order, which defaults to sorting by file name. You can change the sort order by pressing (F5) .

CSHOW REFERENCE

This section covers some tables of additional information about CompuShow that may be useful to you. Included are tables of video modes, keystrokes for controlling colors, and command-line switches. For features pertaining to less common video hardware and graphics file types supported by CompuShow, see the author's documentation file, CSHSOW.DOC.

Video Modes

Table 3-3 shows the video modes CompuShow supports on common video hardware. Across the top of the table are the kinds of video boards, and on the left are the various video modes showing the pixel dimensions and number of colors. The chart does not show Super VGA modes, which depend on the specific VGA chip set and BIOS used in your graphics adapter. The meanings of the codes are:

Y = Yes, the mode is supported
O = Optional mode, sometimes supported
M = works on EGAs with a monochrome monitor
P = works on IBM PS/2 and compatible VGA boards.

Mode (width x height x colors)		Herc	CGA	EGA	EGA-480	MCGA	VGA
720x348	monochrome	Y					
640x200	monochrome		Y	Y			
640x350	monochrome			M			
640x480	monochrome					Y	Y
320x200x4	color (4 palettes)		Y	Y	Y	Y	Y
320x200x16	color "PCjr/Tandy"		O	O	O	O	O
640x200x4	color "PCjr/Tandy"		O	O	O	O	O
320x200x16	color EGA			Y	Y		Y
640x200x16	color EGA			Y	Y		Y
640x350x16	color EGA			Y	Y		Y
640x480x16	color EGA				Y		Y
320x200x256	color MCGA					Y	Y
320x400x256	color extended MCGA					P	P
640x400x256	color (simulated)					P	P
640x480x256	color (simulated)					P	P
360x480x256	color extended MCGA					P	P
720x480x256	color (simulated)					P	P

Table 3-3 CompuShow video support

Controlling Color During Display

You can control the color of images displayed on MCGA, VGA, and Super VGA hardware. Table 3-4 shows the effect of various keystrokes when viewing an image.

(F1)	decrease RED
(F2)	increase RED
(F3)	decrease GREEN
(F4)	increase GREEN
(F5)	decrease BLUE
(F6)	increase BLUE
(ALT)-(F10)	save palette to a file (not saved in the image file)
(F9)	show image with original palette
(F10)	show image with adjusted palette
(ALT)-(G)	convert the color image to grayscale
(ALT)-(N)	make a negative of a grayscale image
(PGUP)	lighten a grayscale image
(PGDN)	darken a grayscale image
(ALT)-(C)	return to a color display
(ALT)-(R)	rotates the palette of a color, grayscale, or negated image

Table 3-4 Controlling the color of MCGA/VGA images

CompuShow's color-correction capabilities are useful for experimenting with the effects of changing the color content of your images.

Startup Options

CompuShow requires at least 221K of available memory depending on the startup options specified. If the program displays an "Insufficient memory" message, you need to make more memory available (for example, you could remove some memory-resident programs).

You can control graphics video features through the use of command-line switches. If you invoke CompuShow from a batch file as recommended at the beginning of this chapter, then any command-line switches that you want to regularly use can be added to that file.

Optional Features

A # switch is used to specify optional features. You can use either uppercase or lowercase letters. For example, to turn off sounds, invoke CompuShow with:

`C:>CSHOW #Q` (ENTER)

Table 3-5 lists the switches for optional features.

Switch	Action
#B	Use black and gray screen colors. If you have a laptop or any computer with an LCD screen, this option will provide readable colors.
#D300	This option lets you control the amount of memory reserved for the file directory. The default is 120 files. You may specify any number from 0 to 9999.
#E	EGA display is scrambled. Use this switch to disable horizontal panning.
#J	Enables PC-Junior/Tandy-1000 video modes. The program reserves 32K of memory required for these special video modes.
#K	Keyboard only. Ignore the mouse.
#L	Use this switch if the CompuShow screen goes blank on your Leading Edge IBM-compatible computer.
#MS	Set small file-read buffer (2K).
#MM	Set medium file-read buffer (32K).
#ML	Set large file-read buffer (45K).
#N	Normal memory (ignore EMS memory).
#Q	Turns off the sounds that the program makes.

Table 3-5 Optional features

Super EGA Video Switches

A / switch is used to indicate the presence of a 480-line Super EGA adapter. The program knows about several, which are shown in Table 3-6.

Switch	Action
/A	Ahead Systems
/G	Genoa
/P	Paradise AutoSwitch EGA-480
/T	Tseng
/V	VGA (e.g., the Zenith VGA)
/71	Use mode 71 (decimal)

Table 3-6 Super EGA switches

Video Hardware Identification Override

CompuShow should recognize the type of video adapter present in your computer (Hercules, CGA, EGA, MCGA, or VGA). A + command-line switch can be used to override the automatic detect routine. Keep in mind that it shouldn't be necessary to use one of these switches. If CompuShow doesn't recognize your video adapter, there's probably something unusual with your hardware. Table 3-7 shows the + switches.

Switch	Action
+H	force Hercules mode
+C	force CGA mode
+E	force EGA mode
+B	force EGA (monochrome monitor) mode
+M	force MCGA mode
+V	force VGA mode and disable nonstandard modes

Table 3-7 Video autodetect override switches

4

PICLAB

THE INDISPENSABLE GRAPHICS TOOL

Piclab is the preeminent public domain image-processing program. Behind its modest interface is a powerful set of image-processing and manipulation functions that will enable you to tackle a wide range of graphics tasks. The author, Lee Daniel Crocker, is part of the same Stone Soup Group that created Fractint, and as a result these two programs work well together. Spartan and lean, Piclab presents you with an unassuming text-based interface and a plain prompt that was not written for love at first sight. But as time goes by, and you learn its utility, you will likely develop the same affection for Piclab that a mechanic has for that trusty screwdriver or favorite wrench.

In the Graphics Support Forum on CompuServe (GO GRAPHSUPPORT), where novices and experts mingle to discuss graphics problems and solutions on-line via modem, there is a standard conversation that ends up involving Piclab. Someone will raise a difficulty in converting, combining, or modifying graphics images. Someone else then proposes a solution using Piclab, and gives the exact sequence of Piclab commands needed to solve the problem — often in as few as six or seven simple steps.

This chapter is based on a collection of many Piclab solutions to common graphics problems culled from these on-line conversations. Here are just a few of the things you can do with Piclab (don't worry if you don't know what all these terms mean — we'll cover them shortly):

- Read, write, and display files in CompuServe's GIF format, Truevision's Targa format (8-, 16-, and 24-bit), and a RAW format that contains in order the red, green, and blue color values

- Convert a true-color 24-bit Targa (red-green-blue) image to an 8-bit 256-color GIF file you can display on your VGA screen

- Combine the monochrome left and right images of a stereo pair into one red/blue 3D anaglyph

- Convert a 256-color image to a 234-color image that looks good when viewed under the Microsoft Windows graphical environment

- Correct the color balance of a scanned image

- Reduce a 2048x2048 image to 640x480

- Expand a 640x480 image to 2048x2048

- Convert a colored graphic to a dithered monochrome graphic for use in a desktop publishing program

- Merge separate images into a colorful collage

- Print an image on an HP Laserjet

This list is only the beginning. The biggest challenge in using Piclab is having enough grasp of basic image-processing principles to know what problems it can solve for you. You will have a chance to get on top of the world of image processing as we go through this chapter, because the principles and ideas are discussed in the midst of explanations of how Piclab works. Once problems of modifying and processing graphics files are clearly stated, usually a Piclab solution follows. This chapter will help you in two ways. It is full of practical examples of useful tasks that can be done with Piclab, which you can immediately apply to your situation, and it will help you deepen your understanding of computer graphics. As your prowess with Piclab increases, the pleasure is double: You will gain both skill and knowledge.

GETTING PICLAB UP AND RUNNING

This chapter assumes you have installed Piclab according to Chapter 1. Here are a few pointers you should know about for getting the best use out of Piclab.

To use Piclab you should have an IBM PC-compatible with 640K of memory, preferably at least an 80286-class machine. Piclab does not need any graphics hardware to process images, but a VGA or Super VGA is highly recommended, even though an EGA or even CGA will work. One thing you will need is a lot of disk space. You can get by with less if you restrict yourself to small images, but to really get involved in the kind of graphics processing Piclab can do requires about 4 MB to 5 MB of free disk space. Now is the time to clean up the old hard disk, and maybe compress those seldom-used files!

Piclab is distributed in a self-extracting zip file called PICLAB.EXE. You will find this file on disk containing the following files:

CNVTGA	A Piclab script.
PL.EXE	The program itself.
PICLAB.DOC	Author's documentation.
PL.HLP	Text file for the HELP command.
PICLAB.PIF	Windows 3.0 386 enhanced mode PIF.
PICLAB.ICO	Windows 3.0 icon.
GAMMA1.MAP	Color maps for viewing grayscale.
GAMMA2.MAP	Color maps for viewing grayscale.
PSEUDO.MAP	Color maps for viewing pseudo-color.
READ.ME	

In addition to these files, you will want several of the GIF files provided on your Image Lab disk. These are used in examples to illustrate Piclab commands. They are TIME.GIF, BRYCE.GIF, and T38.GIF. These files are in the EXAMPLES subdirectory; follow the instructions in Chapter 1 to decompress EXAMPLES.EXE

The directory where Piclab resides should be listed in the Path statement of your AUTOEXEC.BAT file. The recommended directory is C:\IMLAB\PICLAB.

The SSTOOLS.INI File

Stone Soup programs share a file for setting the various defaults of all the different programs. This file, called SSTOOLS.INI, which contains settings of variables that Piclab will use unless overridden by commands, should be placed where Piclab can find it. Piclab looks first in a directory whose name is stored in an environment variable called Init. If you wish to use this variable to enable Piclab to find SSTOOLS.INI in a directory called (for example) C:\IMLAB, place this statement in your AUTOEXEC.BAT file :

SET INIT=C:\IMLAB

If Piclab cannot find SSTOOLS.INI using the Init variable, then it searches the directories in your Path variable set in your AUTOEXEC.BAT file. If you are also using the Stone Soup program Fractint, make sure that the directory containing the SSTOOLS.INI file is listed in the Path, because Fractint does not check the Init variable. A good approach would be to place all Stone Soup files and any other Image Lab programs that need to be listed in the Path in the C:\IMLAB directory, and make sure that directory is listed in the Path.

You will find a copy of the file SSTOOLS.INI in the directory above the PICLAB directory with the Piclab files. SSTOOLS.INI looks like this:

```
;  This file is a sample of how to set up your SSTOOLS.INI file.
;  The values shown here are for use with The Waite Group's Image
;  Lab book.

[fractint]

;  fractint settings go here

[piclab]

tempdir=c:\tmp
helpfile=c:\imlab\piclab\pl.hlp
display=svga2
```

The first section following [fractint] contains the settings for Piclab's sister Stone Soup program, Fractint. The commands following [Piclab] set the Piclab defaults, and can contain any Piclab variable that is normally set from within the program. Piclab variables hold various parameters that determine Piclab operation. The variables can also be given values from within Piclab. For more information see the documentation for the Set command in the Piclab Command Reference at the end of this chapter. For now, let's look at the lines in the example one by one.

- **Tempdir=c:\tmp** - This tells Piclab to place its temporary files in the directory C:\TMP. The directory can be wherever you like, on any drive and with any name, but make sure this directory exists! If the specified TMP directory does not exist, Piclab will not work. Since the example gives the directory C:\TMP, if you use this SSTOOLS.INI file unchanged, you must create the directory \TMP on your drive C:. If you use another directory or another drive, edit SSTOOLS.INI accordingly. (See below for more on the uses of the \TMP directory.)

- **Helpfile=c:\imlab\piclab\pl.hlp** - This tells Piclab where to find the help file. If not set, Piclab will look in the current directory. If the PL.HLP file is not found in the specified location, Piclab's on-line help function will not work. Edit this line to reflect the actual location of PL.HLP on your system.

- **Display=svga2** - You can set a video mode that will be used to display files. The value "svga2" in the example is the Super VGA 640 pixel by 480 pixel 256 color mode that requires 512K of video memory. To see what the possible values for the DISPLAY variable are, from the Piclab prompt type in LIST DISPLAYS. If you do not have Super VGA capabilities, set this value to "vga".

The TMP Directory

One of the virtues of Piclab is that all of its functions work quite independently of your computer's graphics display adapter. In fact, Piclab will work on a computer with no display hardware at all. Piclab does this by creating temporary files containing graphics information. The catch is that these files can be quite large.

Piclab puts the temporary files in the directory stored in the TEMPDIR variable, either in the SSTOOLS.INI file, or via the SET TEMPDIR command from within Piclab. If TEMPDIR is not set, then the temporary files go in the directory set in the TMP environment variable in your AUTOEXEC.BAT file. Finally, if neither the Piclab TEMPDIR variable nor the DOS TMP variable have been set, Piclab will place the temporary files in the current directory.

To avoid problems, check how much free disk space there must be in your Tmp directory to handle the size of graphics image you wish to process. In the worst case, each pixel can require 6 bytes of space because there are 2 buffers each containing 3 colors, and each color takes 1 byte. Therefore if you are processing a 640x480 image, the total number of bytes needed for the temporary files is 640*480*6 or 1,843,200 bytes, or almost 2 MB! You must make sure that you have this space. Piclab will warn you when it runs out, but it is inconvenient because the process you are attempting will not work. If you deal with larger images, you will want even more space. To comfortably follow all the examples in this chapter, having lots of hard disk space free is a good idea. Table 4-1 shows how much space you should have to deal with various sizes of images.

Image Size (width x height)	Maximum Disk Space Required (bytes)
320x200	384,000
640x400	1,536,000
640x480	1,843,200
1024x768	4,718,592
2048x2048	25,165,824
4096x4096	100,663,296

Table 4-1: Free disk space needed by Piclab at different resolutions

The version of Piclab that comes with this book has functions that will begin to fail at pixel dimensions of 32763x32763. But as you can see, your disk space will run out long before you reach that resolution, unless you have a truly large hard drive. Future PC versions of Piclab will be limited to 4096x4096 pixels, which Table 4-1 shows, requires up to about 100 MB of free space.

If you are blessed with a computer with lots of RAM (Random Access Memory), you might want to consider making a RAM disk for Piclab's temporary files. Most versions of MS-DOS come with a device driver with a name something like RAMDRIVE.SYS that will create an additional disk drive out of your computer's memory. This will generally involve adding a line something like:

```
DEVICE=C:\DOS\RAMDRIVE.SYS 2048 /E
```

to your CONFIG.SYS file. This example creates a 2048K RAM disk. The /E option causes the use of extended memory. This RAM disk has the virtue that files placed on it can be read and written very rapidly. In the above example, if drive D: was a RAM disk, Piclab's operations would be greatly speeded up. Just make sure that you add a MKDIR D:\TMP command to your AUTOEXEC.BAT so that the subdirectory Tmp exists on the RAM disk. The RAM disk approach only works if you have a *lot* of memory, but fortunately the price of memory is dropping every day, and for many users a 4-MB RAM disk or even greater is a real possibility!

PICLAB SUPER-QUICK TOUR

Now for the acid test to see if everything is OK. Let's start with a quick check and try out a few things in Piclab. You have an SSTOOLS.INI file, which at a minimum has a line like:

```
helpfile=c:\IMLAB\PICLAB\pl.hlp
```

You have placed the SSTOOLS.INI file in a directory listed in your Path, or pointed to by the Init environment variable, and you have moved the PL.HLP file to the Helpdir directory. The program PL.EXE is in a directory in your Path, and the GIF files that come with this book are in your current directory. If all this is not correct, take time to set everything up properly. Let's go!

In what follows, what you type will be in bold type, and the prompt will be in regular type.

Start Piclab

To start Piclab, type at the DOS prompt:

```
C:>PL  (ENTER)
```

You should now see the Piclab prompt, which looks like:

```
PL>
```

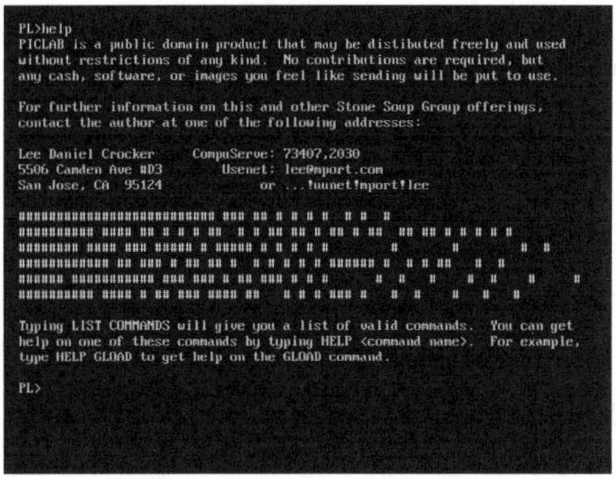

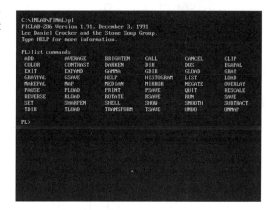

Figure 4-1 The result of the Help command

Figure 4-2 The result of the List Commands command

Get Help

Next enter the following Piclab commands:

PL>**HELP** (ENTER)
PL>**LIST COMMANDS** (ENTER)

Figures 4-1 and 4-2 show the text that will scroll on the screen as a result of these commands.

Load a File

The first step in any Piclab operation is to load a file. You can use the Load command, which applies to whatever file type is set in the Piclab variable Fileformat= statement in your SSTOOLS.INI file. This variable can have the value GIF, Targa, or RAW. You can also set it at the Piclab command prompt with a statement like:

PL>**SET FILEFORMAT GIF** (ENTER)

An alternative command to load a GIF file is Gload, which always works with GIF files even if the Fileformat variable is set to Targa or RAW. It is safer to always use the form of the Load command (like Gload) that works for the kind of file you are loading, rather than depending on the value of the Fileformat variable, but this is a matter of taste.

Now type:

PL>**GLOAD T38.GIF** (ENTER)

You will see some rapidly changing numbers coming on the screen. These numbers count the lines of the GIF file as it is decoded. If the GIF file has 480 lines, the numbers would count from 0 to 479. If you get an error message, type Set, which will show you the values of all the Piclab variables. Make sure Picdir is set for the directory where T38.GIF is located. If Picdir is empty (shown as ""), then T38.GIF should be in the current directory.

Display an Image

Recall that Piclab does not need any graphics hardware to operate. Of course, without any graphics hardware, you could never see the effects of your commands, and that wouldn't be any fun! However, Piclab's independence from your display hardware is not as silly as it seems. This video independence means that you can happily process super-resolution 2048x2048 images in Piclab, images far beyond what your hardware can display. Then you can send the file by modem or by mail to a slide service that can make a high-quality transparency from your image.

To see an image you have loaded into Piclab, type the command

PL>**SHOW** (ENTER)

If an image has been loaded, it should show on the screen, and in our case will look like a more colorful version of the four NASA training jets shown in Figure 4-3.

Figure 4-3 NASA T38 aircraft

The T38.GIF image is a 640-pixel wide by 480-pixel high image. If you have the Piclab variable Display set to SVGA2, you will be able to see the whole image at once. If your computer has regular VGA but not Super VGA capabilities, set Display to VGA1, the standard VGA 320x200 256-color mode. Then the whole image won't show on the screen, but you can still scroll around the image with the cursor keys to see it all. Like other Piclab variables, you can set Display in the SSTOOLS.INI file with the line

`DISPLAY=VGA1`

Or you can set it right now. Press any key, and the T38 image will go away and the Piclab prompt will return. Now type:

`PL> SET DISPLAY VGA1` (ENTER)

and type:

`PL> SHOW` (ENTER)

This time you should see the upper-left part of the image. Use the cursor keys to move around the image. When you are done, if you have a Super VGA graphics board, set the Display variable back to SVGA2 with

`PL> SET DISPLAY VGA2` (ENTER)

The numbers in the display names VGA1, VGA2, SVGA1, and SVGA2 have no special meaning, although they do rank the modes in order of increasing resolution. To see what values the Piclab variable Display can take, type:

`PL> LIST DISPLAYS` (ENTER)

The result is

```
CGA      320x 200   Dithered  CGA  mono
EGA      640x 350   8-color   EGA  dither
VGA1     320x 200   Standard  VGA
VGA2     640x 480   Simulated  on  VGA
SVGA1    640x 400   For  256k  SVGAs
SVGA2    640x 480   For  512k  SVGAs
SVGA3    800x 600   For  512k  SVGAs
HICLR1   640x 480   Sierra  DAC  SVGAs
HICLR2   800x 600   Sierra  DAC  SVGAs
```

The last two display modes work with graphics adapters equipped with a Sierra Digital Analog Conversion chip (DAC). These modes support the display of 32,768 simultaneous colors.

Transform an Image

Before we move on, we really need to try one fun operation to get a feel for the incredible power of this program. If you are viewing the picture, press any key to get back to the Piclab prompt. Now type the following commands:

`PL> NEGATE` (ENTER)
`PL> TRANSFORM` (ENTER)
`PL> SHOW` (ENTER)

Figure 4-4 A negative image

Wow! A color negative image of the T38s! The result is shown in Figure 4-4.

Save an Image

After creating such an unusual image, you will want to save it. As with the Load command, there are different commands for saving images in different file formats, or you can just use Save, and it will apply to the current format in the variable Fileformat. To save as a GIF file, enter:

PL>`GSAVE NEWFILE` (ENTER)

This will save your image as NEWFILE.GIF.

Exit Piclab

Finally, to get out of Piclab, simply type:

PL>`QUIT` (ENTER)

and you will be back to the DOS prompt.

This is the end of our Super-Quick Tour of Piclab. For more hands-on experience, check out the Piclab Tutorial and Command Reference section a little later in this chapter. There you will find all kinds of useful examples of what you can do with Piclab.

PICLAB OVERVIEW

To get the most out of Piclab, you should have a basic grasp of some of the principles behind images and image processing. These concepts are not difficult, and when it comes to graphics, a little understanding goes a long way. So let's dig in!

Images

A computer image is very much like a photograph. A photograph looks like it has continuous shapes; but if you look very closely with a magnifying glass, you will see that in fact the picture is broken up into little dots. A photograph has very good resolution (number of dots per inch) compared to most computer images. A piece of 35mm film can resolve roughly 100 dots per millimeter, which works out to approximately 3750 dots wide and 2500 dots high. An image on your computer screen, by way of comparison, is 640 dots wide and 480 dots high when in the standard 16-color VGA mode. The dots that make up a computer image are clearly visible to the naked eye, whereas the graininess of a photograph is not readily apparent except in large blow-ups. This disparity of resolution is one of the reasons that computer-imaging techniques have not yet replaced conventional photographic film technology; film can record a lot of information in each picture.

Some of the tools discussed in this book, though, can handle resolutions approximating photographic quality. The cover of this book, for example, was made using the Persistence of Vision Ray tracer (covered in Chapter 7) and processed with Piclab. That image is 2048 dots wide and 1536 dots high, which is very close to the amount of information a 35mm slide can hold. (We actually reproduced the cover by making a 4x5-inch transparency from the computer image, because we wanted the best possible quality.) Piclab can deal with even higher resolutions; you will probably run out of disk space long before you run into the limit of Piclab's resolution, which is 32763x32763 pixels. However, unless you want to make book covers or large posters, you will probably find that the top resolution you can show on your computer screen is generally fine. With today's technology, a resolution of 1024x768 dots has become pretty common, and anything more than that requires expensive special equipment.

Pixels

Now we have established that an image is made up of dots. When speaking of computer images, these dots are called *pixels,* which is an acronym for *picture element.* An image, for our purposes, can be defined as a two-dimensional array of pixels. According to the usual convention, these pixels are numbered from

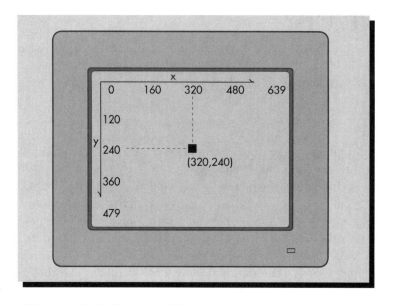

Figure 4-5 The pixel addressing scheme

left to right and from top to bottom, starting with 0. Thus each pixel in an image has a coordinate address, which is the row and column of that pixel, counting from the upper-lefthand corner of the image. Figure 4-5 shows how this addressing scheme works for the 640x480 VGA screen.

There are other systems for describing images besides the approach we are taking in this book. The alternative approaches represent images in terms of *objects* rather than pixels. PostScript is probably the most notable example. The commands sent to a PostScript device tell it to draw lines or boxes or characters and let the device decide how it will perform the commands it gets. The difference between dealing with pixels and objects is the difference between paint programs and draw programs. In a paint program, you can draw a circle; but as soon as you draw it, the circle is merged with the image and can no longer be manipulated as a circle, only as a part of the image as a whole. In a draw program, the circle maintains its identity as a circle, and can be selected and manipulated as a circle. New software is emerging that treats pixels as objects and includes the best of paint and draw programs. There are advantages to both approaches; suffice it to say that none of the software in this book deals with objects. This book deals with pixel-based image processing.

Kinds of Pixel-based Images

There are a number of different kinds of pixel-based images that vary according to how color information is encoded within each pixel. These four kinds of images are called bitmapped, grayscale, color-mapped, and true-color.

In all of these formats, an image is represented as a rectangular array of pixels, but the values contained in these pixels are different and have a different meaning.

Bitmapped Images

Bitmapped images are collections of On/Off dots. That is, each pixel can be turned either On or Off, with no states in between. Figure 4-6 shows how this scheme works. This type of image can be displayed on just about any type of computer, and is especially suited to printer output, because at the most basic level a printer makes a dark dot on the paper. If the pixel is On, a dot of ink is printed; otherwise it is not. Another advantage of bitmapped images is that they are relatively compact when stored in computer disk files. The main disadvantage of bitmapped images is their inability to represent color. However, with large bitmapped images, it is possible to simulate shades of gray by using dot patterns. This process, called halftoning, is used by newspapers to print photographs.

Figure 4-6 Bitmapped image

For years many IBM PC-compatible computers came equipped with a monochrome graphics adapter built to the standard of the original Hercules adapter. In graphics mode the Hercules could show only black-and-white bitmapped images.

Grayscale images represent images by storing the intensity of light for each pixel on a continuous scale with many in-between values, in contrast to bitmapped images in which each pixel is either On or Off. Typically a grayscale image will allow 64 to 256 shades of gray for each pixel. Very high-quality renderings of *black-and-white* photographs can be stored in this format. The term black and white is often used to describe both bitmapped images and grayscale images. Another common term for grayscale is *monochrome*, which is used to describe monitors that can display only shades of one color (often green or amber). The term Monochrome literally means "one color," which is in accordance with popular usage. But from a computer graphics point of view, many shades of gray constitute many "colors," so we have to be careful to avoid confusion. Figure 4-7 shows the scheme of a grayscale image. The bar on the right shows how numbers from 0 to 255 are assigned to shades of gray. For each pixel a number is stored indicating the shade of gray for that pixel.

Color-mapped Images

Color-mapped images are the ones most common on personal computers. Each pixel in an image is represented by a number (called an index) that is

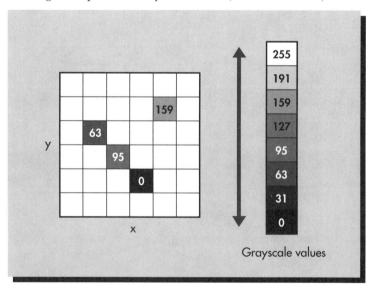

Figure 4-7 How grayscale images work

used to look up the pixel's actual color in a table (called the palette, much like an artist's palette). These images are popular because they can be very colorful, yet they take up less memory than the full-color images that will be described next. The number of colors in the color palette (its length) varies among formats, but is usually either 16 or 256. The original IBM color graphics adapter had a palette with four colors in the 320x200 mode, but let's try not to think about turning back the clock and living under such a restriction! The 640x350 EGA and 640x480 VGA video modes are common examples of video modes with a 16-color palette. The original IBM VGA had exactly one mode with a 256-color palette, namely the 320x200 256-color mode.

The length of the palette of a video mode determines how many colors can be shown on the screen at one time. If the palette has 16 colors, that means that only 16 different colors can be displayed at once. But these 16 colors can usually be selected from a much larger number of colors. For example, each palette entry in the EGA 640x350 16-color mode can be any of 64 different colors obtained by combining four shades of red, four shades of green, and four shades of blue together in different combinations. (Different shades of color are different degrees of brightness of a color. For computer graphics purposes, different shades of a color are considered different colors.) For the VGA color possibilities are much greater, the red, green, and blue components can each have 64 shades, so the total number of possible colors on a VGA is 64x64x64 or 262,144.

Figure 4-8 shows the relationship between pixel indices and palette colors. This scheme is very much like the color-by-numbers coloring books that we played with as kids. Areas in the picture are numbered, and each number is assigned to a color. Depending on what crayons are available or their particular preferences for colors, two different children might assign very different colors to the numbers, resulting in finished pictures with a strikingly different appearance. Using our current terminology, each child might use a different color palette to assign colors to the numbers.

The colors in the color palette are defined according to the amount of each of the three primary colors red, green, and blue. Any color can be represented as a mixture of these three primary colors because of the way the human eye works. If the human eye could directly perceive all the hues of the rainbow, the job of digitally representing colors would be far more difficult. Until the first aliens arrive, basing all our graphics technology on red, green, and blue will work just fine!

True-color Images

True-color images are the highest-quality representation, and when stored on your disk result in the largest files as well. Each pixel contains the complete

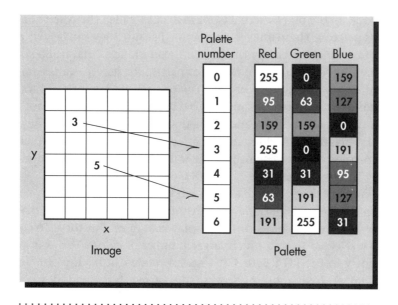

Figure 4-8 Color-mapped images: paint by numbers

color information for that pixel, usually expressed as the intensity of the red, green, and blue color components of the light at that location. Different true-color formats have different numbers of possible shades of red, green, and blue, as you'll see below, so don't take the "true" in true-color as an absolute.

Bits, Bytes, and Color

The number of colors possible with a true-color image format depends on the number of bits that are used to represent the color. The term *bits* is based on the binary number system, where numbers are represented as 1s and 0s. If there are 8 bits of computer memory storage used to store a color value, then there are 2^8 or 256 different possible color values. For true-color formats that have equal storage for the red, green, and blue components of the color, the number of bits of storage will generally be a multiple of three. Computer storage is usually given in terms of 8-bit chunks called *bytes*, and memory sizes are often not multiples of three. In such cases the extra bits can be used for something else. For example, 16-bit color is really 15-bit color with a bit left over.

32-Bit True Color

Some high-end workstations use 32-bit color, which allows the use of up to 10 bits to represent each of the primary colors red, green, and blue. This permits 2^{10} or 1024 shades of each primary color, which may be mixed to form 2^{30} or

1,073,741,824 (more than 1 billion) separate colors! However, most 32-bit graphics formats are really 24-bit formats in disguise. The Apple Macintosh 32-bit color format, for example, reserves 8 bits for advanced features like animation, which leaves 24 bits for the actual color information, with 8 bits for each primary color component. This is the first and last time we will mention 32-bit graphics in this book, since hardware to handle it is unusual and expensive, and since in many cases, from an image-processing perspective, there are only 24 bits to worry about anyway. And as we are about to see, the possibilities of using a mere 24 bits are astounding indeed!

24-Bit True-Color

Piclab stores true-color images using three 8-bit bytes per pixel, as shown in Figure 4-9. These images are stored in three separate files containing a red image, and green image, and a blue image, each with eight bits per pixel. These primary color images are called color planes. With 8 bits or 1 byte for each primary color, there are 2^8 or 256 shades for each color plane. The total number of red-green-blue color combinations is therefore 256*256*256 = 16,777,216 possible colors! This is quite enough, thank you, so you see why we needn't feel sorry for ourselves for lack of 32-bit color.

Before you conclude that such a huge number of colors is totally absurd, remember that in the present context different shades of the same color count

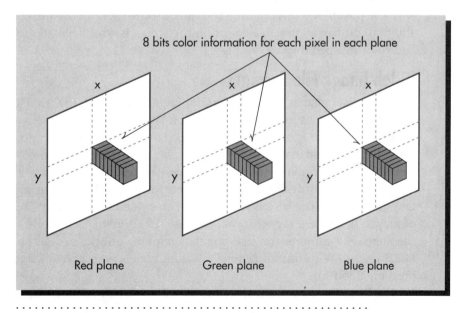

Figure 4-9 How Piclab stores true-color images

as different colors. Photographs may have few colors in the usual sense, but still have many gradations of light and dark shades of color. For example, if the red, green, and blue components of a color are equal, then the color is a neutral shade of gray. With a bit of thought, you will see that a 24-bit true-color format can display 256 distinct shades of gray. Suppose we represent colors as RGB triple (three numbers giving the red, green, and blue brightness values). Then the 256 shades of gray range from a bright white (255, 255, 255) to a medium gray (128, 128, 128) to a dark black (0, 0, 0). That many shades of gray is enough for just about any computer graphics purpose, although it does fall short of what the human eye can discern. For practical computer purposes, 24-bit true-color definitely qualifies as "true color."

16-Bit True-Color and the Sierra DAC

Recently an exciting development in video hardware has put a true-color format within the reach of many home computer users. Inexpensive Super VGA adapters have come on the market that make use of the Sierra High Color DAC (Digital Analog Conversion) chips. These chips allow 16 bits to be stored for each pixel, of which 15 bits store color information. This works out to 2^5 or 32 shades of red, 32 shades of green, and 32 shades of blue, or 32x32x32 = 32,768 possible colors. Note that this is *fewer* colors than the 262,144 colors available for the VGA palette, but the difference is that with the Sierra chip *all* of these colors can be displayed at the same time. With an ordinary Super VGA, there are more possible colors, but only 256 can be shown at once on the screen. The ability to display all possible colors on the screen is what separates true-color and color-mapped display systems.

Piclab Image File Formats

Piclab can load images in any of the GIF, Targa, RAW, PPM, RIX, or IP formats, and can save images in the GIF, Targa, or RAW formats.

The GIF format is only for color-mapped images. One byte per pixel holds the color index for that pixel, which can therefore be one of 256 colors, and the GIF header contains the actual image palette. Even though a grayscale image is not technically a color-mapped format, GIF files can also store grayscale images. The trick is to use a 256-color palette to represent 256 shades of gray. GIF files are very compact because the format specification includes the same LZW compression that popular archiving utilities such as Phil Katz's PKZIP use. (LZW stands for Lempel, Ziv, and Welch, who developed the compression algorithm.)

The Targa format is really three formats. The 8-bit Targa files store grayscale images or color-mapped images. The 16- and 24-bit Targa files store 15- and

24-bit true-color. If you load a GIF file into Piclab and immediately save it as a Targa, you will be saving it as an 8-bit Targa file. The Targa format is often mistakenly thought of as only a true-color format. In fact, the Targa specification encompasses all the varieties of images that Piclab can handle: true-color, color-mapped, and grayscale.

The RAW format stores 8- and 24-bit images directly as a series of bytes. Color images are stored in three files, 1 byte per pixel, with extensions R8, G8, and B8. RAW files do not contain palette information. You can save the palettes separately as MAP files, which are text files containing the red, green, and blue values for each palette color, one per line. The RAW format is also the format that Piclab uses internally to store images.

The PPM format is Jeff Poskanzer's Portable Pixmap format. Piclab supports gray (PGM) and color (PPM) formats, but not bitmaps (PBM).

The RIX256 format is the uncompressed 256-color file format from ColoRix. The file extension must be specified when loading. The SAVE command is not supported for this format.

The IP format is the Amiga DigiView's Raw storage format. It consists of nothing but three planes of data, 1 byte per pixel, followed by 12 bytes not associated with the image. The Save command is not supported for this format.

Why All These Image Formats?

If you are like most of the readers of this book, you probably have some kind of Super VGA graphics adapter on your PC. Since Super VGA graphics modes are color-mapped, why bother with true-color graphics?

The answer to this question casts light on the nature of Piclab. True-color images are ideal for use with image processing because each pixel contains the full color information in a form useful for computation. Piclab was first designed for true-color image manipulation. Color-mapped images are awkward for image processing because the colors are not directly stored, but are only accessible by looking up color values in a palette. But color-mapped devices are currently very popular, and many images can be found in that format. Color-mapped images are compact and convenient, and are capable of very high quality. But, as we said, color-mapped images are difficult to manipulate.

Piclab provides a way out of this dilemma. Given a color-mapped image, the flow of processing with Piclab often takes the following form:

1. Load a color-mapped 256-color image into Piclab.

2. Convert the image to the 24-bit true-color format.

3. Apply various image transformations to the image.

4. Convert the image back to a color-mapped image.

5. Save the resulting color-mapped image.

Step 4 — converting the image from true-color back to color-mapped requires a bit of magic. Piclab analyzes the colors of all the pixels in the image, and comes up with the best set of 256 colors that match the original true-color image as closely as possible. Because this process can often be done effectively, the results are very satisfying, despite the limitation to "only" 256 colors.

You might think that having image data more accurate than your computer can display is wasteful, but it is not. We have already made the point that the 24-bit true-color format is useful for doing many kinds of image processing, even if the final image is a normal VGA 256-color image. Another reason is that images get passed around to users of different machines, and the more accurate the image data, the better each machine will be able to display it. You can also do things like print color images to a color printer even though you have no color display on your computer. Finally, hardware to display images as accurately as Piclab stores them does exist, and is becoming more affordable every day. If you keep your images stored in their full accuracy, you will be better able to take advantage of any new hardware you may get.

A PICLAB TUTORIAL

Command Overview

This section introduces you to the Piclab commands. You will learn not only what the commands are and what they do, but when to use them and how to put sequences of commands together to achieve different effects.

Piclab is a command-driven program. After starting Piclab, you may enter any of a number of commands at the Piclab prompt. The complete command does not have to be spelled out, but only enough of it to distinguish it from other commands. In most cases three letters is sufficient. For example, if you type in CO, that is not unique, since both the Color command and the Contrast command start with CO. But typing in COL has the same effect as typing Color, while CON means the same as Contrast. Each command is generally performed immediately, although the point process commands do not take effect until the Transform command is issued.

Table 4-2 lists all these commands alphabetically.

Add	Combine images by color addition
Average	Combine images by color averaging
Brighten	Brighten colors
Call	Call external program
Cancel	Cancel (undo) last operation
Clip	Clip image dimensions
Color	Color grayscale image
Contrast	Adjust image contrast
Darken	Darken colors
Dir	List files
DOS	Run DOS Shell
EGApal	Make an EGA palette
Exit	Exit Piclab
Expand	Expand image dimensions
Gamma	Adjust image color linearity
Gdir	List GIF files
Gload	Load image from GIF file
Gray	Display as grayscale
Graypal	Load palette for grayscale display
Gsave	Save image as GIF file
Help	Access on-line help
Histogram	Plot color distribution
List	Display lists
Load	Load image from default file type
Makepal	Make a palette
Map	Map colors to palette
Median	Apply median transform to image
Mirror	Reflect image horizontally
Negate	Invert image colors
Overlay	Overlay image on top of another
Pause	Wait for keystroke
Pload	Load palette from a MAP file
Print	Send image to printer
Psave	Save palette as a MAP file
Quit	Exit Piclab
Rescale	Alter image resolution
Reverse	Reverse storage order
Rload	Load image from RAW file

Table 4-2 Alphabetical listing of Piclab commands

. . . .

Rotate	Rotate image
Rsave	Save image as RAW file
Run	Run Piclab command file
Save	Save image as default file type
Set	Set a Piclab variable
Sharpen	Apply Laplace transform to image
Shell	Run DOS shell
Show	Display image on screen
Smooth	Apply averaging transform to image
Subtract	Combine images by color subtraction
Tdir	List Targa files
Tload	Load image from Targa file
Transform	Apply pending transformations
Tsave	Save image as Targa file
Undo	Cancel (undo) last operation
Unmap	Convert color-mapped to true-color

Table 4-2 Alphabetical listing of Piclab commands (*continued*)

Piclab's commands are easier to understand if they are broken into categories by the function the command carries out. Table 4-3 lists the commands again by categories. This tutorial will discuss each of these command groupings one by one. More detail on each command is available in the Command Reference section.

Setting and Displaying Piclab Variables

Commands:

Set	Set a Piclab variable
List	Display lists
Help	Access on-line help

Piclab uses internal variables to control many of its operations. Variables that hold values appropriate for your hardware and software should be defined in your SSTOOLS.INI file. Other variables may be set while you are using Piclab to achieve the results you want. The Set command can be used to give these variables a value or to determine the current status of the variables. The List and Help commands are placed in this group because they give you access to information about the state of Piclab and how it works. For a complete discussion of all the variables and what they do, refer to the Set entry in the Piclab

Setting and displaying the values of Piclab variables and status
Set, List, Help

Accessing the operating system and miscellaneous
Call, Dir, Gdir, Tdir, DOS, Shell, Reverse, Exit, Quit

Loading and saving images and palettes from files
Load, Gload, Tload, Rload, Pload, Save, Gsave, Tsave, Rsave, Psave

Displaying images on your screen
Show

Using Piclab buffers
Cancel, Undo

Modifying images with point processes
Brighten, Darken, Contrast, Gamma, Negate, Transform, Histogram

Modifying images with area processes
Median, Sharpen, Smooth

Converting to and from color-mapped images
Makepal, EGApal, Map, Unmap, Color, Graypal, Gray

Printing images
Print

Clipping, expanding, and rotating images
Clip, Expand, Rescale, Mirror, Rotate

Combining images
Add, Average, Subtract, Overlay

Running Piclab programs
Run, Pause

Table 4-3 Piclab commands grouped by function

Command Reference. Here we will discuss how variables are set and how to get information about Piclab.

To see a list of all the Piclab variables and their current settings, type:

PL> SET (ENTER)

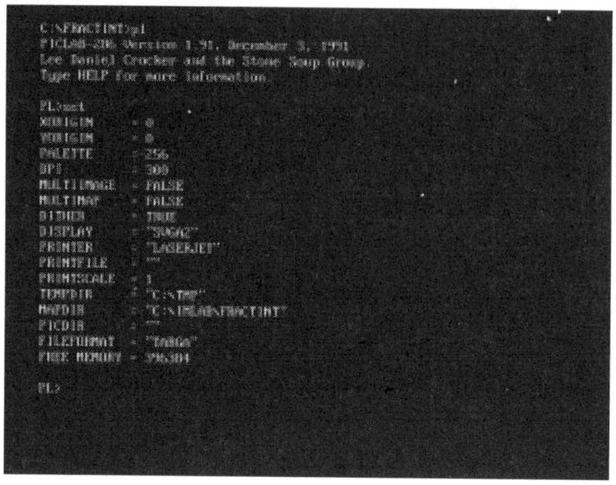

Figure 4-10 Result of the Set Command

The result is shown in Figure 4-10.

The variables Tempdir, Mapdir, and Picdir tell Piclab where to look for and to put temporary files, palette map files, and image files, respectively. The variable Printer determines which kind of printer Piclab expects.

The Tempdir variable should point to a directory on a drive with plenty of disk space, preferably at least 4 MB to 5 MB. Alternatively, for speed, it could point to a directory on a RAM disk.

If you are also running the Fractint program as well as Piclab, you will probably want to keep all palette-map files for both programs in one place. Map files are files that store the colors used by color-mapped displays. Fractint and Piclab can use the same map files, and Fractint has excellent facilities for editing these files. In the example above, the Mapdir variable is set for the C:\IMLAB\FRACTINT directory.

Unless you want to keep all your image files in one place, it is most convenient to leave Picdir empty (set to ""), which is the default. An empty value of Picdir causes Piclab to look for images in the current directory.

The possible values for Printer are Laserjet and Paintjet. These variables are best set in the SSTOOLS.INI file because you will not want to change them often. The lines in the SSTOOLS.INI file to set their values to the values in Figure 4-10 above are:

```
[PICLAB]
PRINTER=LASERJET
TEMPDIR=C:\TMP
MAPDIR=C:\IMLAB\FRACTINT
PICDIR=
```

Of the remaining variables, you will find that Palette and Display are two that you may want to change during a Piclab session. The variable Palette determines how many color entries the Map command uses when converting a true-color image to a color-mapped image; normally it is 256. The Display variable sets the video mode used to display images on your monitor. The syntax for giving a variable a value using the Set command is a little different than the SSTOOLS.INI file syntax. To set the values of Palette and Display from the Piclab command line to the values listed in Figure 4-10, you can start Piclab and type:

```
PL>SET PALETTE 256 (ENTER)
PL>SET DISPLAY SVGA2 (ENTER)
```

The List command gives all kinds of different information. To see the possibilities for arguments for List, type in List with no parameters. The result is:

```
PL>LIST (ENTER)
Listable items:
VARIABLES
COMMANDS
BUFFERS
PRINTERS
FORMATS
DISPLAYS
```

Try all of these to see what they do.

```
PL>LIST VARIABLES (ENTER)
```

gives the identical result as the Set command with no parameters. It shows you all the variables and their current values.

```
PL>LIST COMMANDS (ENTER)
```

shows you all the possible Piclab commands.

```
PL>LIST BUFFERS (ENTER)
```

shows you the status of the Old, New, and Temp image buffers. The image buffers will be discussed a little later in this tutorial.

```
PL>LIST PRINTERS (ENTER)
```

shows you the possible values for the Printer variable.

```
PL>LIST FORMATS (ENTER)
```

shows you all the possible values for the Fileformat variable. This list shows several formats that are not yet supported by Piclab. The legal values are GIF, Targa, and Raw.

```
PL>LIST DISPLAYS (ENTER)
```

shows you all the possible values for the Display variable, including the resolutions of the various possible modes and the number of colors.

Accessing the Operating System and Miscellaneous

Commands:

Call	Call external program
Dir	List files
Gdir	List GIF files

Tdir	List Targa files
DOS	Run DOS shell
Shell	Run DOS shell
Reverse	Reverse storage order
Exit	Exit Piclab
Quit	Exit Piclab

The Exit and Quit commands are used to get out of Piclab once you have started it. There is no difference between these commands; which you use is a matter of taste.

The Shell and DOS commands are another pair of synonyms. These let you drop to DOS with Piclab still resident in memory. You might want to do this to check your disk space, copy a file that Piclab couldn't find to the current directory, or delete some files. It is also interesting to have a look at the your \TMP directory in the middle of some Piclab operations and see what sort of files Piclab put there, and how big they are. You can return to Piclab by typing

`C:> EXIT` `(ENTER)`

You can also use DOS or Shell with a parameter to run a DOS program or command. For example, if you have a series of commands that creates a temporary GIF file called TMP.GIF, you can delete the file within Piclab by typing

`PL> DOS DEL TMP.GIF` `(ENTER)`

Call works similarly to DOS, except that it cannot be used to call a DOS internal command like Del or Dir, but can only be used to run executable files.

The Tdir and Gdir give directory listings of the files in the current directory, or in the directory set in your Picdir directory, if it is set. These display useful images about the type of file, its dimensions, and the number of colors, and the size of the file. Tdir lists Targa files, and Gdir lists GIF files. These are particularly useful with the Load and Save commands that are discussed next.

Reverse can be used to change a Targa file stored in bottom-up order to top-down. The GIF and RAW formats store images row by row, starting at the top. Targa files can store images in either top-down or bottom-up order. If you load a bottom-up Targa file, you will have to issue the Reverse command before converting to GIF.

Loading and Saving Images and Palettes from Files

Commands:

Load	Load image from default file type
Gload	Load image from GIF file
Tload	Load image from Targa file
Rload	Load image from RAW file
Pload	Load palette from MAP file

Save	Save image as default file type
Gsave	Save image as GIF file
Tsave	Save image as Targa file
Rsave	Save image as RAW file
Psave	Save palette as MAP file

The first and last steps of any use of Piclab include loading an image from a file and saving an image to a file. You can either use the generic Load and Save commands, which act on whatever format is stored in the Fileformat variable, or you can use the variations of these commands that are specific to a format. Piclab supports the storage of images in the GIF, Targa, or RAW formats. Gload and Gsave assume the GIF format, Tload and Tsave the Targa format, and Rload and Rsave the RAW format.

The GIF Format

The GIF format stands for Graphics Interchange Format. The specification for GIF was developed by CompuServe for use in displaying on-line graphics, and was not originally intended to be a file format at all. The popularity of GIF stems from the fact that the images are small, since they are compressed with the same algorithm as the popular Arc and Pkzip file compression utilities. The other reason for the popularity of GIF is that the specification has been carefully written in such a way that it can be implemented on many computers. GIF decoder software is available on a wide variety of small computers and workstation platforms. This means that GIF files that you create can be shared with many others, whether or not they have an IBM-compatible PC.

The GIF format can store color-mapped images with up to 256 colors. These colors can be selected from a palette that allows 24 bits for each color, or 256 shades each of red, green, and blue mixed together. Super VGA hardware can support 256 colors, but the palettes are limited to a total of 18 bits per pixel, or 64 shades each of red, green, and blue. This means that the GIF standard actually supports finer gradations of coloring than VGA can display. GIF files can also store grayscale images by using a 256-color palette to represent 256 shades of gray.

GIF files come in two flavors, GIF87a and GIF89a, according to which GIF features are used. The later GIF89a standard allows comments to be stored in a GIF file, provides a mechanism for storing other information, and has other enhancements. (For an example of these advanced features, view the file BOB89a.GIF on your companion disk using CompuShow, the program discussed in Chapter 3.) Piclab can read GIF89a files, but only uses the image information. If a comment is stored in the file, you will see it on the screen before the image itself is decoded. Piclab saves images only in GIF87a format.

The Targa Format

The Targa format was developed by Truevision for use with its Targa graphics boards. Piclab supports three variations of Targa files. The 8-bit Targa files store grayscale and color-mapped images. The 16- and 24-bit Targa files store 15- and 24-bit true-color images. If you load a GIF file into Piclab and immediately save it as a Targa, you will be saving it as an 8-bit Targa file. The 24-bit and 16-bit Targa formats are useful for Piclab because they support true-color. Their disadvantages are that they are not highly compressed, and that they are not as prevalent on non-PC platforms as GIF. There is no point in archiving GIF files with a file compression program because they are already compressed, but you can save a lot of disk space by archiving your Targa files.

The RAW Format

The RAW format stores 8- and 24-bit images directly as a series of bytes in a disk file. RAW files do not contain palette information, or even resolution information. For this reason the Rload command requires you to type in the resolution dimensions as parameters. If a true-color file is saved in RAW format, each primary color is saved in a separate file. Grayscale images are saved in a single file. The RAW format is most useful for experts who want to directly manipulate images with other software. The RAW format is also used internally by Piclab.

Loading and Saving Experiments

Now let's try some experiments. These examples will use the file T38.GIF that is on your book disk. Make sure that file is in the directory pointed to by the Piclab Picdir variable; or, if you haven't set that variable, make sure that T38.GIF is in the current directory.

First, set a VGA or SVGA mode appropriate for your hardware, such as

PL> SET DISPLAY SVGA2 (ENTER)

Next, load the GIF image.

PL> GLOAD T38 (ENTER)

Display the image on the screen to make sure everything is working all right. (We'll discuss the Show command in more detail shortly.)

PL> SHOW (ENTER)

You should now see the NASA jets flying through the clouds in glorious color. Press any key to return to the Piclab prompt. Now try

PL> TSAVE T38 (ENTER)

This causes the T38 image to be saved as an uncompressed 8-bit Targa file with a color map. Now save it as a RAW file.

`PL>`**`RSAVE T38`** (ENTER)

Since the T38 image is color-mapped and not true-color, a single RAW format file is created. You can look for the files you just created by typing

`PL>`**`DOS DIR T38.*`**

You should see the following files:

```
T38     GIF    127500 10-14-91   7:50p
T38     TGA    307986 11-03-91   6:05p
T38      R8    307200 11-03-91   6:06p
     3 file(s)     836171 bytes
              5330944 bytes free
```

As you can see, the GIF file is the smallest. The Targa and RAW files are about the same size. The Targa is an 8-bit uncompressed file with a color map; the color map accounts for the extra space. Notice that there is only one RAW file. You should compare this method of listing files with the Gdir and Tdir commands. The two differences are that these commands only show one type of file, and they show additional image characteristics, such as image dimensions and number of colors.

Now load the newly saved files and view them to see if they are all right.

`PL>`**`TLOAD T38`** (ENTER)
`PL>`**`SHOW`** (ENTER)
`PL>`**`RLOAD T38 640 480 mono`** (ENTER)
`PL>`**`SHOW`** (ENTER)

Note that when loading the RAW file, some extra parameters are needed, since the dimensions of the file are not stored as part of the file. The Targa file should look fine, but the RAW file looks very strange. This is because the RAW file contains indices to a color map that is now gone. Loading the file back in with the mono option causes Piclab to interpret the color numbers as grayscale values. The Rsave command is good for true-color or grayscale images, but not non-grayscale color-mapped images. Using the Gray or Unmap command before saving as RAW would have given different results.

Displaying Images on Your Screen

Command:

    Show   Display image on screen

The Piclab Show command displays the image you have loaded on the screen. Show uses the video mode set in the Piclab Display variable. You can see the possible Display values by typing:

`PL>`**`LIST DISPLAYS`** (ENTER)

The result is

```
CGA       320x 200 Dithered CGA mono
EGA       640x 350 8-color EGA dither
VGA1      320x 200 Standard VGA
VGA2      640x 480 Simulated on VGA
SVGA1     640x 400 For 256k SVGAs
SVGA2     640x 480 For 512k SVGAs
SVGA3     800x 600 For 512k SVGAs
HICLR1    640x 480 Sierra DAC SVGAs
HICLR2    800x 600 Sierra DAC SVGAs
```

If you have a Super VGA with at least 512K of video memory, then SVGA2 is a good overall choice. This mode will display color-mapped images accurately, but will display true-color images only in grayscale. The reason for this is that to display a true-color image in color using a Super VGA video mode, Piclab would have to convert the image to a color-mapped image first by doing the equivalent of a Makepal and a Map command. This would be too slow and would add a lot of complication, so Piclab doesn't attempt it. However, you can always do this conversion yourself, as you will see a little later in this tutorial. Piclab's solution is showing true-color images in grayscale in VGA modes.

Sierra Hicolor and VGA Compared

If your VGA board has the Sierra Hicolor DAC chip, then you can directly view true-color images in color using HICLR1 and HICLR2. These modes display images using 15-bit true-color graphics. However, even if your hardware will support HICLR1 and HICLR2, for viewing grayscale images or color-mapped images, one of the VGA or SVGA modes will be more accurate. The reason is that even though 15-bit color can display 32,768 colors at one time, the 5 bits for each of red, green, and blue allows 32 shades each of the primary colors, compared to the 64 shades possible with VGA. A VGA can show fewer colors on the screen at once, but these colors can be selected from more shades than are possible with 15-bit true-color. In fact, a 256-color VGA mode can display smoother gradations of monochrome color than a 15-bit true-color mode. Use the Sierra Hicolor modes to view true-color images, which Piclab would otherwise show you in monochrome. But use one of the VGA modes when viewing grayscale or color-mapped images such images stored in GIF format.

Here are a few examples to give you the idea of how the different display modes work. First, set a SVGA mode appropriate for your hardware with

PL>**SET DISPLAY SVGA2** (ENTER)

Next, load the GIF image.

PL>**GLOAD T38** (ENTER)

Display the image on the screen to make sure everything is working all right.

PL>**SHOW** (ENTER)

You should now see the NASA jets flying through the clouds in glorious color. Now try a different video mode.

```
PL>SET DISPLAY VGA1 (ENTER)
PL>SHOW (ENTER)
```

Now you will not be able to see the whole image at one time, but you can scroll around the image with the cursor keys. As an experiment, try some of the other modes. For example, try

```
PL>SET DISPLAY CGA (ENTER)
PL>SHOW (ENTER)
```

You will see a grainy-looking black-and-white dithered image of a portion of the whole image. Piclab does its best to represent images on whatever video hardware you have, but what you see on the screen may only be a poor representation of the real image if your video mode is not fully capable. Be glad you are no longer limited to CGA!

Now convert the image to true-color and display again using Super VGA.

```
PL>SET DISPLAY SVGA2 (ENTER)
PL>UNMAP (ENTER)
PL>SHOW (ENTER)
```

You will now see a grayscale version of the image, because Piclab displays true-color images in grayscale on VGA equipment. If you have a Sierra DAC-equipped video board, type:

```
PL>SET DISPLAY HICLR1 (ENTER)
PL>SHOW (ENTER)
```

Now you will see the image in true-color! It looks good, but no better than it did with a Super VGA mode. The benefits of true-color are subtle, and not immediately obvious for all images.

Using Piclab Buffers

Commands:

| Cancel | Cancel (undo) last operation |
| Undo | Cancel (undo) last operation |

Piclab keeps two copies of the image you are working on. These two copies are called the Old and New buffers. Commands generally operate on these two internal picture buffers. Most commands start by deleting Old and renaming New to Old. They then perform some transformation on Old storing the result in New. Since the original image is kept in the Old buffer, it is possible to reverse operations on images. The Undo command swaps New and Old buffers, effectively reversing the last operation. Undo and Cancel are exactly equivalent; they are synonyms for one another.

A good way to learn about Piclab's use of buffers is to use the List Buffers command. Try the following sequence of commands. If you are in Piclab, exit and start again so you are starting with a clean slate as far as the buffers are concerned. Comments beginning with the ";" character are used to annotate the commands. What you type is in bold; the rest is Piclab output or annotations.

```
C:>PL (ENTER)              Load Piclab

PICLAB-286 Version 1.91, December 3, 1991
Lee Daniel Crocker and the Stone Soup Group.
Type HELP for more information.

PL>LIST BUFFERS (ENTER)    Program just started, buffers empty
Buffer    Size         Type    Raster
OLD       <EMPTY>
NEW       <EMPTY>
TEMP      <EMPTY>
```

The first List Buffers reports that all the buffers are empty.

```
PL>GLOAD T38 (ENTER)
Reading T38.GIF...
 Screen: 640 x 480, 256 of 2M colors
  Image: 640 x 480 at (0,0)
Done.


PL>LIST BUFFERS (ENTER)    T38 loaded in NEW buffer, OLD empty
Buffer    Size         Type    Raster
NEW       640 x 480    Mapped  Top-down
OLD       <EMPTY>
TEMP      <EMPTY>
```

After loading the GIF file, the second List Buffers (above) reports that the color-mapped image is in the New buffer, while the others are still empty.

```
PL>UNMAP (ENTER)                 creates a true color image in NEW
Working...
Done.


PL>LIST BUFFERS (ENTER)    color-mapped T38 is now in OLD
Buffer    Size         Type    Raster
OLD       640 x 480    Mapped  Top-down
NEW       640 x 480    Color   Top-down
TEMP      <EMPTY>
```

After Unmap, which creates a true-color image, the buffer with the color-mapped file is renamed to Old, and the true-color image is in the New buffer.

```
PL>CANCEL (ENTER)                UNDO what we did


PL>LIST BUFFERS (ENTER)    color-mapped T38 is back in OLD
Buffer    Size         Type      Raster
NEW       640 x 480    Mapped  Top-down
OLD       640 x 480    Color   Top-down
TEMP      <EMPTY>
```

72

After the Cancel command, the third List Buffers shows that the Old and New buffers have been swapped.

PL> **EXIT** (ENTER)

Modifying Images with Point Processes

Commands:

Brighten	Brighten colors
Darken	Darken colors
Contrast	Adjust image contrast
Gamma	Adjust image color linearity
Histogram	Plot color distribution
Negate	Invert image colors
Transform	Apply pending transformations

Point processes are transformations of images that work one pixel at a time. The effect of a point transformation on a pixel depends on the process being accomplished and the color content of that pixel. The color values of neighboring pixels are not taken into account. In Piclab the results of point processes are not stored in the New buffer until the Transform command is issued. However, the Show command displays the image, including the effect of any pending point processes.

Point processes are where the fun begins in Piclab. They give you the same kind of capability with your computer images that photographers have in the darkroom with their prints. You can make your images darker or lighter, you can increase or decrease the contrast, or you can even turn the image into a negative. The color can be balanced, color casts removed or added. The point process capabilities of Piclab are what really put a darkroom in your computer!

Even though it is not a point process command, the Histogram command is included with this group because it is indispensable for evaluating images. A bit of contemplation of a histogram can help you to decide exactly how to apply one of these point processes to your image. The Histogram command also includes the effect of any pending point process.

What the Histogram Plot Does

Take a look at Figure 4-11 as you read this. Imagine you have 64 bins arranged in a row. Suppose each bin is assigned a brightness range for one of the primary colors, for example, red. Since in Piclab color brightness values range from 0 to 255, each bin is assigned to four color brightness values. Suppose we look at each pixel of an image in turn, and decide which bin corresponds to the red content of that pixel. We then put a checker piece in that bin. After this process is done, there will be as many checker pieces distributed among

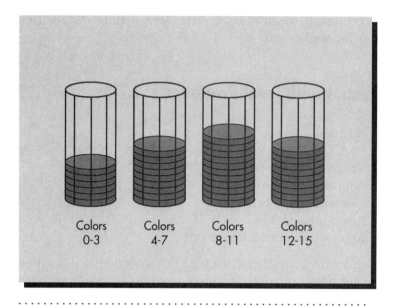

Figure 4-11 A histogram as a collection of bins

the 64 bins as there are pixels in the image. A histogram is a graph showing how many checker pieces are in each bin. It is a picture of how frequently different brightness values of a primary color appear in an image, ranging from darkest to lightest. True-color images have three histograms, one for each primary color; grayscale images have one.

To see a histogram of the T38 image, type the commands:

```
PL>GLOAD T38 (ENTER)      load t38 image
PL>GRAY (ENTER)           convert to grayscale
PL>HISTOGRAM (ENTER)      plot histogram
```

Figure 4-12a shows the histogram for the T38 image converted to grayscale. Since the image has been converted to grayscale, it has one histogram. For true-color images, Piclab will show you the red, green, and blue histograms in turn. The numbers on the horizontal axis are the brightness ranges in hexadecimal notation, ranging from 0 to 255 (FF in hexadecimal), counting in increments of 4. You don't need to know anything about hexadecimal numbers to use a histogram, but you do need to understand that the columns represent light values counting by 4s. The lefthand side of the histogram shows how many pixels have the darker colors, and the right side of the histogram shows how many pixels have lighter colors. The actual pixel count corresponding to each X varies for different images; Piclab scales the histogram so the most frequent brightness value uses 20 Xs. (For the mathematically inclined: The

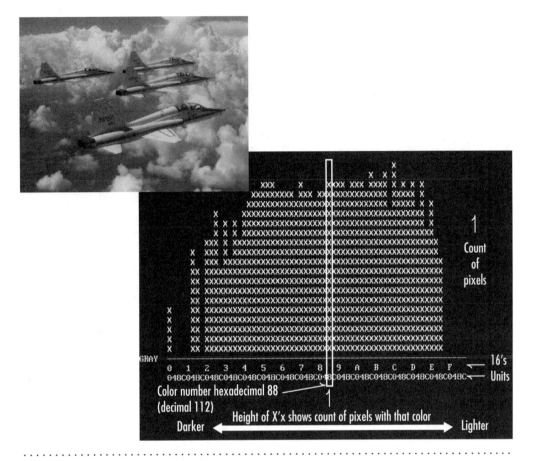

Figure 4-12a Histogram for the grayscale T38.GIF

plot uses a logarithmic scale that exaggerates lower counts and deemphasizes higher counts.) An image with good contrast will have a distribution of both lighter and darker colors.

Here is a series of examples that show the effect of the various point process commands on a histogram. They use somewhat extreme parameter values in order to make the effect more visually obvious in the histogram and figures. Rather than use a parameter value like 64, you should try values closer to 8 or 16 when you are optimizing your images. These examples are a continuation of the previous example, and assume that you have already loaded and grayed the T38 image.

After each of the command sequences are figures that show the results of all of these point process applied to a grayscale version of T38.GIF, along with the histograms.

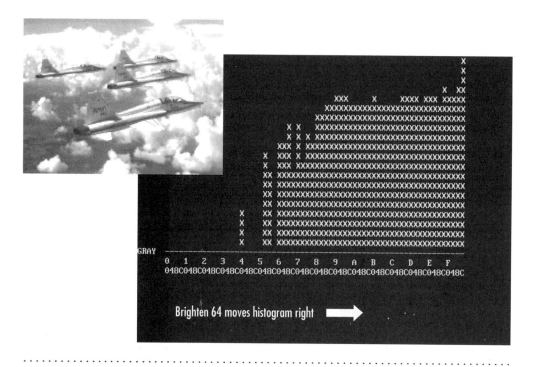

Figure 4-12b Histogram and image after Brighten 64

PL>**BRIGHTEN 64** (ENTER)   brighten image 64 units
PL>**HISTOGRAM** (ENTER)   plot histogram
PL>**SHOW** (ENTER)   display image

This moves the histogram to the right 16 columns. (See Figure 4-12b.)

PL>**CANCEL** (ENTER)   cancel previous point process
PL>**DARKEN 64** (ENTER)
PL>**HISTOGRAM** (ENTER)   plot histogram
PL>**SHOW** (ENTER)   display image

This moves the histogram to the left 16 columns. (See Figure 4-12c.)

PL>**CANCEL** (ENTER)   cancel previous point process
PL>**CONTRAST 64** (ENTER)   increase contrast
PL>**HISTOGRAM** (ENTER)   plot histogram
PL>**SHOW** (ENTER)   display image

This moves column 16 to column 0, and column 47 to column 63, stretching the histogram. (See Figure 4-12d.)

PL>**CANCEL** (ENTER)   cancel previous point process
PL>**CONTRAST -64** (ENTER)   decrease contrast
PL>**HISTOGRAM** (ENTER)   plot histogram
PL>**SHOW** (ENTER)   display image

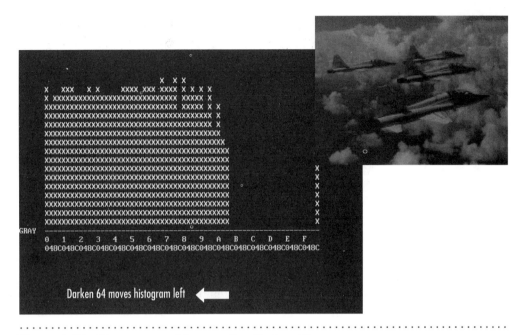

Figure 4-12c Histogram and image after Darken 64

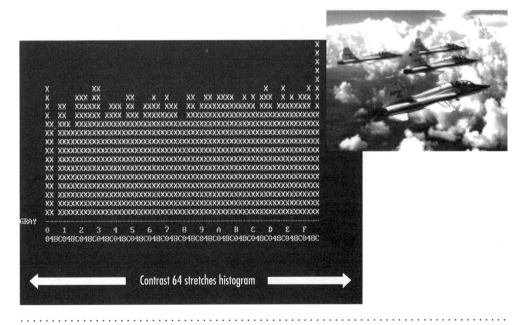

Figure 4-12d Histogram and image after Contrast 64

This moves column 0 to column 16, and column 63 to column 47, compressing the histogram. (See Figure 4-12e.)

PL> **CANCEL** (ENTER)   cancel previous point process
PL> **NEGATE** (ENTER)   make negative of image
PL> **HISTOGRAM** (ENTER) plot histogram
PL> **SHOW** (ENTER)   display image

This makes a mirror image of the histogram. (See Figure 4-12f.)

Brighten and Darken are the easiest to understand. They simply add or subtract to the brightness values of the image, in effect shifting the histogram to the left or right.

Contrast is a little trickier. Imagine the histogram printed on a sheet of rubber. Applying the command Contrast 64 is like grabbing both ends of the histogram and stretching it so the bin corresponding to 64 gets pulled left to 0, and the bin corresponding to 191 (which is 64 less than 255) is pulled right to 256. The original values in bins 0 through 64 and 192 through 255 are lost. This makes the whites whiter and the blacks blacker. A negative parameter has the opposite effect, compressing the histogram and moving all the columns toward the center. This reduces the contrast, darkening the whites and lightening the blacks.

Negate swaps the light and dark areas of the image, converting the histogram to its left-right mirror image.

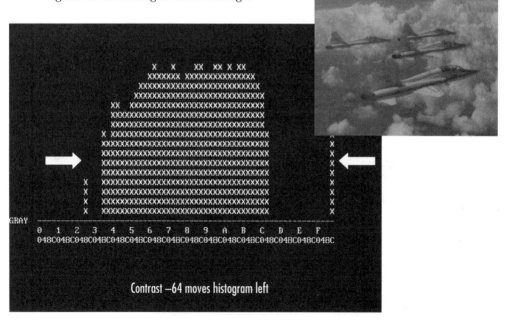

Figure 4-12e Histogram and image after Contrast -64

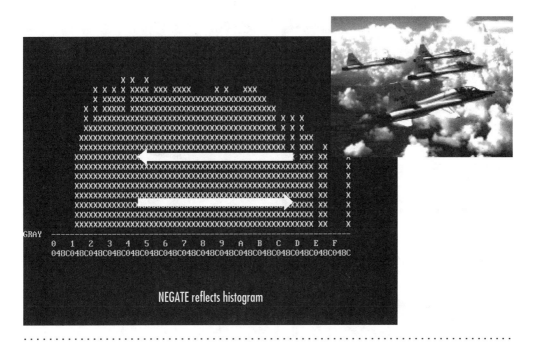

```
                X  X  X
          X X X X  XXXX XXX XXXX         X X    XXX
          X XXXXX XXXXXXXXXXXXXXXXXXXXXXXXXXXXXX
          X X XXXXX XXXXXXXXXXXXXXXXXXXXXXXXXXXX
          X XXXXXXXXXXXXXXXXXXXXXXXXXXXXXXXX X X X
          XXXXXXXXXXXXXXXXXXXXXXXXXXXXXXXX  X X X
          XXXXXXXXXXXXXXXXXXXXXXXXXXXXXXXXXX X XXX
          XXXXXXXXXXXXXXXXXXXXXXXXXXXXXXXXXXXX X XXX  X
          XXXXXXXXXXXX                    X XXX XX   ^
          XXXXXXXXXXXXXXXXXXXXXXXXXXXXXXXXXXXXXXX XX   X
          XXXXXXXXXXXXXXXXXXXXXXXXXXXXXXXXXXXXXXX XX   X
          XXXXXXXXXXXXXXXXXXXXXXXXXXXXXXXXXXXXXXX XX   X
          XXXXXXXXXXXX                     XXXX XX    X
          XXXXXXXXXXXXXXXXXXXXXXXXXXXXXXXXXXXXXXX XX   X
          XXXXXXXXXXXXXXXXXXXXXXXXXXXXXXXXXXXXXXX XX   X
          XXXXXXXXXXXXXXXXXXXXXXXXXXXXXXXXXXXXXXX XX   X
GRAY  ------------------------------------------------------
      0   1   2   3   4   5   6   7   8   9   A   B   C   D   E   F
      048C048C048C048C048C048C048C048C048C048C048C048C048C048C048C

                        NEGATE reflects histogram
```

Figure 4-12f Histogram and image after Negate

Histograms are particularly helpful for use with the Contrast command because the stretching or shrinking action of that command is relative to the center of the histogram. Best results are usually achieved by centering the histogram first with the Brighten and Darken commands, then applying Contrast.

Understanding Gamma

Gamma requires some explanation. It is all well and good to represent true-color pixels as triples of numbers that vary from 0 to 255. In a perfect world, a color value of 254 would be twice as bright as a color value of 127. Unfortunately the phosphors of a CRT tube do not respond proportionally to input. As the colors become brighter, the phosphors become saturated and output proportionally less light. A graph of the input color brightness value versus the actual phosphor light output has a shape that looks like Figure 4-13a. The gamma value of an image is a measure of the nonlinearity of the color-value-to-real-brightness curve. The electronic image has to have nonlinearity that is the reverse of the characteristic of the CRT, so that they cancel out and the colors show with the correct brightness. The shape of the correction applied by the command Gamma .6 is shown in Figure 4-13b. Finally the curve after the application of gamma correction is shown in Figure 4-13c. The relationship between the original color values and the phosphor brightness is a straight line after correction is applied.

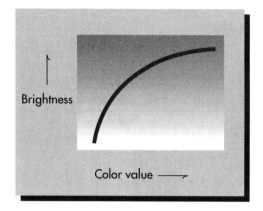

Figure 4-13a Screen phosphor color value/brightness curve

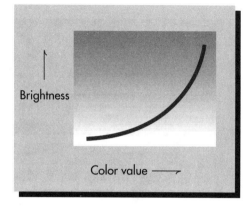

Figure 4-13b Brightness curve of gamma .6 correction

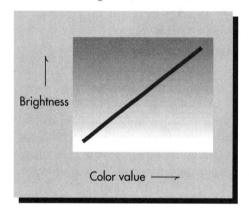

Figure 4-13c Brightness curve of screen phosphors after gamma correction

The Gamma command is the only command that alters the shape of the histogram. All the other commands shift the histogram, stretch it, shrink it, or even flip it, but the shape is the same.

Gamma correction is almost always needed to make images created by electronic scanners look reasonable. The T38 image that comes on this books companion disk was created by scanning a NASA photograph. The image was given to the author as a 24-bit Targa file. Figure 4-14a shows how this image looked before gamma correction and Figure 4-14b shows how it looked after applying

```
PL> TLOAD T38 (ENTER)     Targa file direct from scanner
PL> SHOW (ENTER)          Figure 4-14a
PL> GAMMA .6. (ENTER)     gamma correction applied
PL> SHOW (ENTER)                   Figure 4-14b
```

Figure 4-14a T38 image before gamma correction

Figure 4-14b T38 image after gamma correction

You can see that the uncorrected image is dark and contrasty. The corrected version is lighter, with much more satisfying highlights.

In principle, all point processes should be used with images that have not been gamma-corrected. (In practice, whatever works is fine!) Point processes (besides Gamma) are linear commands and assume that the color numbers are proportional to the brightness of the image. A gamma-corrected image has this relationship skewed. Therefore, when starting with a gamma-corrected image, the processing sequence is:

1. Undo gamma correction (Gamma 1.8).

2. Apply point processes.

3. Reapply gamma correction (Gamma 0.6).

Suppose you wanted to brighten the T38 image by 10. That image is already gamma-corrected, so the correction should be undone first. The steps are:

PL>**GLOAD T38** (ENTER)	load T38.GIF
PL>**GAMMA 1.8** (ENTER)	undo gamma correction
PL>**BRIGHTEN 10** (ENTER)	brighten colors by 10
PL>**GAMMA .6** (ENTER)	reapply gamma correction
PL>**SHOW** (ENTER)	check results
PL>**TRANSFORM** (ENTER)	incorporate pending point processes in image
PL>**GSAVE T38A** (ENTER)	save altered image

If you do much image processing of pictures originating from a scanner, the effort spent understanding the concept of gamma will pay off in your ability to improve images. No matter what your understanding, you'll find that a little experimentation will be required to get good results. For more information see the Gamma command in the Piclab Command Reference section later in this chapter.

Modifying Images with Area Processes

Commands:

Median	Apply median transform to image
Sharpen	Apply sharpening transform to image
Smooth	Apply averaging transform to image

Area processes apply transformations to an image in such a way that what happens to a pixel depends not only on the color value of that pixel, but on the color values of neighboring pixels. Unlike the point process commands, which are deferred until the Transform command is done, the area process commands are executed immediately.

Median and Smooth commands both have the effect of blurring over small imperfections but also making images more fuzzy. They are useful for making images with spot noise look better, at the cost of reduced sharpness. Spot noise is like dust on a negative — it consists of isolated pixels of the wrong color. Suppose, for example, you scanned an old photograph; and because the photo was in poor condition, the resulting electronic image had a lot of dust spots. The Median or Smooth command can clean up the spots. They work by basing the transformation of a pixel on the colors of the eight surrounding pixels plus the pixel itself. The Median command recolors the pixel using the median color of the colors of the nine pixels. The median is calculated separately for each of red, green, and blue. The color values of the nine pixels are sorted, and the median is the middle value of the nine color values. The calculation for Smooth is very similar. Instead of using the median of the nine points, the average value is used. Figure 4-15 shows how the Median and Smooth commands work.

You will find a 320x240 version of the T38 image stored as a grayscale Targa image in the file NOISY.TGA on the companion disk. This image has some spots added. (The spots are actually a starfield created from a Mandelbrot set in Fractint and combined with T38.GIF using the Piclab Add command!) In the example below, the parameter Weighted reduces the power of the Median command somewhat. Since the application of Median blurs the image, you should use the Weighted parameter if it will do the job. The Smooth command has a similar but more powerful effect. Here is how to clean up the spots.

```
PL> TLOAD NOISY  (ENTER)
PL> SHOW  (ENTER)               now you see the spots
PL> MEDIAN WEIGHTED  (ENTER)
PL> SHOW  (ENTER)               now you don't!
```

The Sharpen command causes details to stand out better, and is useful for enhancing the outlines in an image. It works by amplifying the differences between each point and its neighbors.

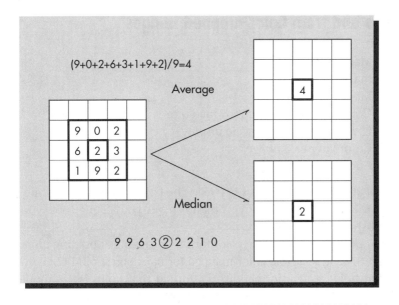

Figure 4-15 How the Median and Smooth commands work

Try Sharpen with the T38 image. The result is less realistic than the original, but the sharpening causes the image to take on an interesting texture. Figure 4-16 shows the result of applying sharpen with no parameters. The steps to create this image are:

```
PL> GLOAD T38  ENTER
PL> SHOW  ENTER           before sharpen
PL> SHARPEN  ENTER
PL> SHOW  ENTER           after sharpen
```

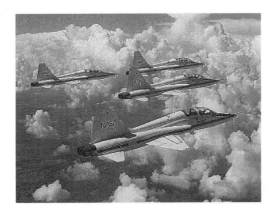

Figure 4-16 Result of applying Sharpen to T38.GIF

Converting to and from Color-mapped Images

Commands:

Makepal	Make a palette
EGApal	Make an EGA palette
Map	Map colors to palette
Unmap	Convert color-mapped to true-color
Graypal	Load palette for grayscale display
Color	Color grayscale image
Gray	Convert to grayscale

Piclab is good at converting images between the color-mapped, grayscale, and true-color formats. This group of commands gives you all the tools you need to accomplish these conversions.

First a word of philosophy. The true-color format is capable of holding more information than the grayscale and color-mapped formats. You should not convert a format that holds *more* information to a format that holds *less* without good reason. It is a good idea to keep permanent copies of your images in a true-color format. You can always reduce the information content of an image, but a conversion cannot add information that is not there. However, many people have graphics hardware such as the VGA and Super VGA graphics adapters that can only display color-mapped images. Thus Piclab renders a valuable service by making the high-quality color-mapped conversions of true-color images so you can enjoy the images without having true-color hardware. Piclab may make excellent conversions, but keep the high-quality original. When you make photocopies, you want to avoid making copies of copies of copies of successively poorer quality; the same principle applies to format conversions.

Table 4-4 shows possible conversions between various image formats and whether information is lost in the process. Each conversion type is numbered for easy reference in the discussion that follows.

	From	To	Information lost?	Piclab Commands
1.	Color-mapped	24-bit true-color	No	Unmap
2.	Color-mapped	16-bit true-color	Maybe	Unmap
3.	Color-mapped	Grayscale	Maybe	Gray
4.	24-bit true-color	Color-mapped	Yes*	Makepal, Map
5.	16-bit true-color	Color-mapped	Yes*	Makepal, Map
6.	Grayscale	Color-mapped	No	Color

* Information is lost if the number of colors is reduced.

Table 4-4 Piclab image format conversions

Color-mapped to 24-bit True-Color

Consider conversion 1 in Table 4-4. (Remember that this discussion is relative to how Piclab handles images. The general situation outside the world of Piclab is somewhat more complex.) A color-mapped image in Piclab can have up to 256 colors. These colors are stored in a palette. Each color in the palette has a red, green, and blue component that can have any of 256 possible shades. A 24-bit true-color image is made up of pixels that also have red, green, and blue components with 256 possible shades. Therefore no information is lost in the conversion.

To convert the color-mapped image stored in T38.GIF to true-color, type:

```
PL> GLOAD  T38 (ENTER)
PL> UNMAP (ENTER)
PL> LIST BUFFERS (ENTER)
PL> TSAVE T38 (ENTER)
```

The List Buffers command will report that

```
Buffer    Size           Type      Raster
OLD       640  x  480    Mapped    Top-down
NEW       640  x  480    Color     Top-down
TEMP      <EMPTY>
```

The true-color version of T38 is in the New buffer, and the color-mapped version is in the Old buffer. The Tsave command saves the true-color version as a 24-bit Targa file.

Color-mapped to 16-bit True-Color

The situation for conversion 2 in Table 4-4, from color-mapped to 16-bit true-color, is very similar. The difference is that 16-bit true-color only has 5 bits to represent each primary color component, which allows for only 32 shades of color. Suppose, for example, that you had a color-mapped image that had 256 possible shades of red. After conversion to 16-bit true-color, these shades would be consolidated into 32 shades, causing a loss of information. Piclab does not internally store 16-bit true-color files, but you can force an image to be stored as a 16-bit file using a parameter with Tsave.

```
PL> GLOAD  T38 (ENTER)
PL> UNMAP (ENTER)
PL> TSAVE T38 16 (ENTER)            save as a 16-bit Targa file
```

The degradation of image quality when making this conversion depends a lot on the image, and whether it has very subtle shades of color. In many cases the conversion is visually indistinguishable from the original.

Color-mapped to Grayscale

With conversion 3 in Table 4-4, a conversion from color-mapped to grayscale, the color information is lost if the image does not have a grayscale palette to begin with. If the color-mapped image was already using a grayscale palette, no information is lost. A color-mapped image with a grayscale palette, and a grayscale image that has no palette, have the identical information, and can be converted from one to the other with the Gray and Color commands. The usefulness of the conversion accomplished by the Gray command is that certain Piclab operations such as rescaling can only be done with true-color or grayscale and not color-mapped images. This conversion is accomplished by typing:

```
PL>GLOAD  T38  (ENTER)
PL>GRAY  (ENTER)              converts colors to gray
PL>TSAVE  T38  (ENTER)        save as a 8-bit monochrome Targa
```

True-Color to Color-mapped

Conversions 4 and 5 in Table 4-4, from true-color to color-mapped, almost always result in information loss because of reduction of the number of colors. The single exception is that if the true-color images have a small number of colors to begin with, or were originally color-mapped and then converted to true-color, then they can be converted to color-mapped with no loss. For example, a true-color image that was created from a color-mapped image with Unmap has no more than 256 different colors, and can therefore be successfully converted back with Map. Here are the steps for converting from true-color to color-mapped.

```
PL>TLOAD <true color Targa file>  (ENTER)
PL>MAKEPAL  (ENTER)            make a palette best fitting the colors
PL>MAP  (ENTER)               convert to color-mapped
PL>TSAVE <new file>  (ENTER)   8-bit Targa file with palette
```

Notice that two commands are needed to effect the conversion. This is because a true-color image does not have a palette, so one has to be created. The Makepal command analyzes all the colors in the true-color image, and comes up with a palette best approximating the colors in the true-color image. The number of colors in the new palette is the value of the Piclab variable Palette.

Rather than have Piclab figure out a suitable color palette, you can load in a palette from a preexisting MAP file with the Pload command. MAP files are text files defining color palettes. Each line defines a palette color using three numbers from 0 to 255 that specify the brightness of the red, green, and blue components of that color. See the discussion of the Pload command in the reference section below for more information.

The last step in the example, saving the file, uses Tsave rather than Gsave, just to make the point that Piclab supports various formats of Targa files. The Tsave command saves the image in whatever Targa format is appropriate for the image in the New buffer. In this case the image is saved as an 8-bit Targa file with a color palette because the image is a color-mapped image. The Gsave command could also be used to create a GIF file instead.

Grayscale to Color-mapped

The last conversion is from grayscale to color-mapped. This is accomplished by the Color command. A grayscale image has no palette; the color index is also the color value. The Color command creates a grayscale palette of 256 shades. After the color command, the image has exactly the same image information. The difference is that Color has converted the image to color-mapped form.

Printing Images

Command:

Print	Send image to printer

Piclab supports the Laserjet and Paintjet printers. Use the Printer variable to set the default printer and the variable Dpi to set what resolution in dots per inch will be used by the printer. An example of printing an image is given in the next command group, since printing it requires the Rescale command.

Clipping, Expanding, and Rotating Images

Commands:

Rescale	Alter image resolution
Clip	Clip image dimensions
Mirror	Reflect image horizontally
Rotate	Rotate image
Expand	Expand image dimensions

Piclab provides tremendous power for altering and manipulating the dimensions and resolution of images. Of all the commands in this group, Rescale is probably the most essential and the most used, so we'll deal with it first.

Images can come from different sources that have different pixel dimensions. The most common reason for rescaling an image is to adjust the dimensions to fit your display hardware. Printers also have limitations in the dimensions of the images they can accept, so you will often want to rescale an image before printing. Rescaling is the process of increasing or decreasing the pixel dimensions of an image, expanding or contracting it so it fits within the new dimensions. Another reason for rescaling images is if you want to combine several large images on one screen.

You might think that there is nothing tricky about rescaling an image. In some cases it can be very simple. For example, suppose you have a 640x480 image that you need to reduce to 640x240. The target size has exactly half the vertical dimensions of the original, so rescaling is just a question of throwing out every other row. All the lines of the rescaled image are already in the original; rescaling is just removing surplus lines and leaving others. But suppose that you want the final image to be 640x400 pixels. This poses a problem. Most of the rows in the 640x400 image are not in the original, but are in between. Throwing out every sixth row would work after a fashion, but would introduce some "jaggies," because the rows aren't in exactly the correct position.

Piclab provides a solution to this problem. When Piclab is calculating the colors of a pixel in one of these in-between rows in the rescaled image, it figures out a weighted average of the colors' values of the nearest pixels in the original image. The "jaggies" problem is greatly reduced, at a cost of slightly increased fuzziness of the image. This averaging process can generate colors not in the original image, and as a result rescaling can only be done with true-color or grayscale images. Therefore, in order to rescale a color-mapped image, it must first be converted to true-color or grayscale.

Now for some examples. To rescale the 640x480 SVGA image T38.GIF to the VGA 320x200 resolution, type:

```
PL> GLOAD T38 (ENTER)
PL> SET DISPLAY SVGA2 (ENTER)        set 640 x 480 video mode
PL> SHOW (ENTER)                     high resolution version
PL> UNMAP (ENTER)                    convert to true color
PL> RESCALE 320 200 (ENTER)
PL> SET DISPLAY VGA (ENTER)          set 320 x 200 VGA mode
PL> SHOW (ENTER)                     low resolution version
```

When you make an image smaller, information is lost. Figure 4-17 shows the 640x480 original and 320x200 rescaled version side-by-side. The 320x200 version was rescaled back to the same size as the original, but the lost detail

Figure 4-17 Effect of rescaling on image clarity

was not regained, although Piclab smoothes over the digitized appearance of the smaller image in the process of rescaling.

Another good use for rescaling is to scale up for printing. Suppose you want to print the T38 image on a full page on an HP Laserjet printer. The Laserjet supports 300 dots per inch; but at 150 dots per inch, Piclab fills a page with an image of 800x600. (Piclab uses a 2x2-dot cell to print 1 pixel in this case, so 600 pixels wide is 1200 dots wide, taking up 8 inches.)

PL> **GLOAD T38** (ENTER)	
PL> **GRAY** (ENTER)	convert to grayscale
PL> **ROTATE** (ENTER)	turn on side for landscape
PL> **RESCALE 600 800** (ENTER)	height and width reversed
PL> **SET PRINTER LASERJET** (ENTER)	
PL> **SET DPI 150** (ENTER)	printer resolution
PL> **PRINT** (ENTER)	print it

Notice in this script that Unmap was not needed before Rescale. The reason is the Gray command, which converted the image to a grayscale image. A grayscale image may be thought of as a "true-color" image. The Rescale command works fine with grayscale images. Also notice the use of Rotate to turn the image on its side so that it is printed in landscape mode instead of portrait mode. Rotate is one of the few Piclab commands that is done in computer memory. Doing Rotate after scaling the image up will run into memory limitations for larger images. This is avoided by applying Rotate while the image is still small.

You can use Clip to cut out pieces of an image. The clipped-out rectangle has the upper-left corner specified in the Piclab variables Xorigin and Yorigin. The two parameters of the Clip command specify the dimensions of the clipped piece. The following script clips the face out of the image TIME.GIF and scales it up to 640x480.

PL> **GLOAD TIME** (ENTER)	
PL> **SET XORIGIN 320** (ENTER)	upper left corner
PL> **SET YORIGIN 240** (ENTER)	center of the screen
PL> **CLIP 80 60** (ENTER)	clip out 80 x 60 piece
PL> **SHOW** (ENTER)	small sunny face
PL> **UNMAP** (ENTER)	convert to true color
PL> **RESCALE 640 480** (ENTER)	scale up
PL> **SHOW** (ENTER)	enlarged sunny face

Figure 4-18 shows the result.

Mirror does just what its name implies. It reverses the left and right of an image, creating the mirror image of the original.

The Expand command technically belongs to this group of commands, but its real purpose is to work with the commands of the next group, which have to do with combining images. Expand increases the dimensions of an image

Figure 4-18 The enlarged sunny face from TIME.GIF

by adding pixels to the right and below the current image. For an example, read on to the next section.

Combining Images

Commands:

Add	Combine images by color addition
Subtract	Combine images by color subtraction
Average	Combine images by color averaging
Overlay	Overlay image on top of another

All of the commands in this group combine the images in the Old and New buffers. The only difference between them is how the colors of the two images are combined where they overlap.

With the Add, Average, and Subtract commands, a new image is formed by applying the mathematical operation of the command's name to the colors. They only work on true-color images because new colors can be created by the operation that might not be in the color palette. Both images must be the same size.

These three commands combine images in such a way that both images show through. The Add command is exactly like a photographic double-exposure; the images are superimposed on top of each other. Where the images overlap, the result is brighter — the sum of the brightness values in the original image. Average has a similar effect, except the overall image is not brighter because the resulting colors are an average rather than a sum of the original colors. Subtract is like adding the negative of an image. You can use these commands to blend together elements of your images.

The Overlay command is much more commonly used than Add, Average, and Subtract, and is different in several respects. Overlay works fine with color-mapped images. The image in the New buffer may be smaller than the image in the Old buffer. In fact, if it is not smaller, this command will do nothing, because the image in the New buffer will completely cover the image in the Old buffer. The other difference is because Overlay and Expand work well together. They can be used to make a large image tiled with smaller images.

This example makes a tiled image out of four small TIME.GIF images.

```
PL>GLOAD TIME.GIF (ENTER)      load the image
PL>UNMAP (ENTER)               convert to true color
PL>RESCALE 320 240 (ENTER)     make half size image
PL>EXPAND 640 480 (ENTER)      small image in upper left
PL>SHOW (ENTER)
PL>UNDO (ENTER)                swap OLD and NEW buffers
PL>OVERLAY 320 0 (ENTER)       overlay to top right
PL>SHOW (ENTER)
PL>UNDO (ENTER)                swap OLD and NEW buffers
PL>OVERLAY 0 240 (ENTER)       overlay to bottom left
PL>SHOW (ENTER)
PL>UNDO (ENTER)                swap OLD and NEW buffers
PL>OVERLAY 320 240 (ENTER)     overlay to bottom left
PL>SHOW (ENTER)
```

This sequence of commands shows a surprising but very helpful use of the Undo command. Undo swaps the Old and New buffers. The normal purpose of this command is to undo the previous action. The use of Undo here makes use of swapping the buffers, and doesn't use it for the purpose of undoing anything. The advantage of using Undo for this purpose is that swapping buffers is fast. The alternative, saving buffers and restoring them using Tsave and Tload, is much slower. You can study this example carefully in order to gain an understanding of how Piclab uses buffers. You might want to insert some List Buffers commands before and after the Undo statements to help you see what is happening.

After the Rescale command, the small version of the clock is in the New buffer. After the Expand command, the small version is in the Old buffer, and the large expanded image is in the New buffer. The Overlay command requires the smaller image (the one that is to be overlayed on top) to be in the New buffer. So swapping the Old and New buffers is exactly what is needed. After each Overlay, the larger expanded image ends up in the New buffer, and the small clock image is changed to the Old buffer again, so another Undo is

Figure 4-19 Using Piclab to tile images

needed to swap them back. Figure 4-19 shows the result of tiling four rescaled copies of TIME.GIF.

Running Piclab Programs

Commands:

Run	Run Piclab command file
Pause	Wait for keystroke

A great convenience of Piclab is that you can place a series of commands in a file and execute the commands in the file by invoking Piclab with the name of the file as an argument. For example, suppose you put the following commands in a file called V2E:

```
GLOAD T38
UNMAP
RESCALE 640 350
EGAPAL
MAP
GSAVE T38ega
```

This script converts the 256-color VGA resolution GIF file called T38.GIF to a 16-color EGA resolution GIF file called T38EGA.GIF. These commands are executed if you type at the DOS prompt:

```
C:>PL V2E (ENTER)
```

If the expressions %1, %2, %3, and so forth appear in the file, they are treated as variables that are replaced by additional Piclab command-line arguments that appear after the file name. If our script is modified to read

```
GLOAD %1
UNMAP
RESCALE 640 350
EGAPAL
MAP
GSAVE %2
```

with this program in the current directory, typing

`C:>`**PL V2E T38 T38EGA** (ENTER)

will load T38.GIF, convert it to 16-color EGA, and save that to T38EGA.GIF. In the script the command-line parameter T38 replaces the Piclab program variable %1, and the command-line parameter T38EGA replaces the variable %2. This facility is very useful, because files like V2E can contain programs that can be used over and over. Without the variable capability, you would have to edit the file and explicitly add the names of the GIF files to be read in and saved each time you used the file.

The words in the command line that begin with the % character are replaced as follows: If the remainder of the word is a number, the word is replaced with the argument to the PL command in that position (starting with 0, which means that %0 is replaced by the name of the program file itself). Otherwise the word is replaced with the value of the DOS environment variable named by the word.

Piclab programs can also be run from within Piclab. To accomplish the same conversion example, start Piclab and type:

`PL>`**RUN V2E T38 T38EGA** (ENTER)

The Pause command can be added to Piclab programs to interrupt the flow of command processing until the user presses a key.

PICLAB COMMAND REFERENCE

This section documents what each of the Piclab commands does. The heading gives the command itself. The remaining sections of each command explanation are as follows:

- *Syntax:* The format of the command and any arguments. Parameters in brackets are optional. For example:

Syntax Pload file [offset [count]]

means that the command PLOAD may have two arguments, offset and count. The brackets mean that "offset" and "count" are optional. Since "count" has its own brackets, even if "offset" is present, "count" is optional.

- *Description:* This tells what the command does, its effect on the Old and New buffers, and when you might want to use it. This section also goes into the background of the command and how it works with other commands.

- *When to Use:* This tells you the circumstances when this command is useful.

- *Limitations:* Here is where you will find what kinds of images the command works with, doesn't work with, or certain argument values that should be avoided.

- *Example:* In this section the command is shown within an example containing a sequence of commands to do a particular job. You can type these examples in at the PL> prompt, or you can type them into a file with your text editor and run them indirectly as

C:> PL EXAMPLE (ENTER)

where EXAMPLE is the name of the file containing Piclab commands. The examples are liberally sprinkled with comments in the style of other Stone Soup software such as Fractint. These comments begin with a ";". The examples usually illustrate several commands working together, and will help you to rapidly get a feel for how Piclab works.

- *See Also:* This is a pointer to other related commands.

....

Add

Combine images.

Syntax Add [Wrap]

Description: The Add command allows you to superimpose two images. The color value of overlapping pixels is obtained by adding together the color values of the two images. This is exactly the effect you would get if two slide projectors projected two images on the same screen.

The Add command adds the Old and New edit buffers, storing the result in the New buffer. If the only argument to the command is Wrap, then values that are taken out of the 0 to 255 range by the addition are taken mod 255 (the remainder after dividing by 255); otherwise, values are clamped. For example, if a pixel in the Old buffer has a red value of 127 and the same pixel in the New buffer has a red value of 200, then the Add command assigns the value

127+200=327. If the Wrap argument is present, this value is "wrapped" to 327 mod 255, or 68. If the Wrap argument is not present, the value 327 is clamped at the maximum red color value of 255.

When to Use: Add is one of several facilities for merging images in Piclab. It works well for doing things like adding planets to dark skies.

Limitations: Add only works on true-color or grayscale images. Use Unmap or Gray first for color-mapped images. Works best if areas of one image are black; otherwise the two images may mix as in a double-exposure.

Example: This example shows how to combine two images with pictures of planets (PLANET1.GIF and PLANET2.GIF). If the backgrounds of both images are black, and the planets are in different positions so that they don't overlap, then this procedure will work well. The result is saved in the file 2PLANETS.GIF. Figure 4-20 shows the result.

```
PL>GLOAD PLANET1.GIF (ENTER)    load the first planet
PL>UNMAP (ENTER)                convert to true color
PL>TSAVE TEMP (ENTER)           save true color version
PL>GLOAD PLANET2.GIF (ENTER)    load second planet
PL>UNMAP (ENTER)                convert to true color
PL>TLOAD TEMP (ENTER)           load in first planet again
PL>ADD (ENTER)                  combine images
PL>MAKEPAL (ENTER)              build a palette
PL>MAP (ENTER)                  map onto new palette
PL>GSAVE 2PLANETS.GIF (ENTER)   save as GIF
```

Figure 4-20
Combining planets with Add

See also: Subtract
Overlay

....

Average

Combine images by averaging.

Syntax Average

Description: The Average command averages color values in Old and New buffers, storing the result in the New buffer. This can be used to reduce random digitizer noise by averaging the results of different samplings. Average can also be used to produce a double-exposure effect when two different images are averaged. No arguments.

When to Use: The results of Average are similar to Add, but with this difference: With Add the two images combine to form a lighter image, which may be washed out if the color values are clamped to color value 255. By averaging the two images, the resulting colors are guaranteed to be in the 0 to 255 range.

Limitations: Average only works on true-color or grayscale images. Use Unmap or Gray first for color-mapped images.

Example: In this example, the files FIRST.GIF and SECOND.GIF are combined with Average and saved as AVERAGE.GIF.

```
PL>GLOAD FIRST.GIF (ENTER)        load first GIF
PL>UNMAP (ENTER)                  convert to true color
PL>TSAVE TEMP (ENTER)             save temporarily
PL>GLOAD SECOND.GIF (ENTER)       load second GIF
PL>UNMAP (ENTER)                  convert to true color
PL>TLOAD TEMP (ENTER)             reload first
PL>AVERAGE (ENTER)                average the two images
PL>MAKEPAL (ENTER)                build a palette
PL>MAP (ENTER)                    convert back to color-mapped
PL>GSAVE AVERAGE.GIF (ENTER)      save as GIF file
```

See Also: Add
Subtract

....

Brighten

Brighten a color.

Syntax   Brighten [[red | green | blue] value]...

Description: The Brighten command adds a constant value to each point in the color planes specified. If only one argument is given, all color planes are brightened by that amount. Otherwise arguments are interpreted in order, and any arguments that specify planes determine which plane the next numerical argument will affect. For example, Brighten red 10 blue 15 would add 10 to the values in the red plane and 15 to those in the blue. Any values that would be taken out of the 0 to 255 range by the transform are clamped.

Because this brightening is a linear operation, the image to be brightened or darkened should be encoded with a gamma of 1.0. That is, there should be a linear relationship between values in the image and intensities on the display. If this is not the case, gamma correction may be applied with the Gamma command before adjusting brightness. See the Gamma command for more about display linearity.

When to Use: Use Brighten when images are too dark. You can also use it to remove color casts by selectively lightening the complementary colors of the color cast.

Example: Try viewing your favorite GIF file before and after Brighten.

```
PL>GLOAD FAVORITE.GIF (ENTER)
PL>SHOW (ENTER)
PL>BRIGHTEN 30 (ENTER)
PL>SHOW (ENTER)
```

See Also: Darken
Gamma

....

Call

Call external program.

Syntax Call program [args]...

Description: The Call command allows you to invoke an external program from within Piclab. The Call command calls the external program named by its first argument, and passes along any subsequent arguments to that program.

When to Use: The Call command is useful when you want to include other programs along with Piclab in image-processing scripts.

Example: `PL>Call Chkdsk (ENTER)`   check available disk space

Limitations: Many programs do not release all of the memory given to them when they terminate, so Piclab will reserve a large portion of memory for itself before calling a program. If you do not have much more memory than Piclab reserves, or if the program you want to run uses a lot of memory, this may result in the program not being able to run in the memory left.

If this is a problem, you can use the DOS or Shell commands, which will give you about 100K more memory to work with. If there simply isn't enough memory available to run your program, you can exit to DOS with all of the free memory available.

Call only works with executable programs, not with DOS internal commands like Dir.

See Also   Run
               Shell
               DOS

Cancel

Cancel (undo) last operation.

Syntax   Cancel

Description: The Cancel command undoes the most recent operation. If there are point transformations pending that have not yet been saved with the Transform command, these are canceled and no changes are made to the edit buffers. Otherwise the New and Old buffers are exchanged.

There are some operations (like Save) that do not alter the edit buffers. If one of these operations was the last one performed, Undo will undo the operation before that. No arguments.

When to Use: Use Cancel when the result of the last command or the last untransformed point process is not as you wish. The Show command gives you an idea of the current status of the image, and includes the result of the application of any pending transforms.

Example:

```
PL>GLOAD BRYCE (ENTER)          load a GIF file
PL>BRIGHTEN RED 120 (ENTER)     brighten Red by 120
PL>SHOW (ENTER)                 check result - UGH!
PL>CANCEL (ENTER)               Undo the damage!
PL>SHOW (ENTER)                 back to before the BRIGHTEN command!
```

Limitations: Cancel can return the New buffer to its former state, but it generally cannot also restore the Old buffer.

See Also: Undo is a synonym for Cancel.

······················

Clip

Clip image.

Syntax Clip [*x*-size *y*-size]

Description: The Clip command cuts out the edges of an image, leaving a central rectangle. A rectangular part of the image is retained after clipping. The upper-left corner is determined by the variables Xorigin and Yorigin. The lower-right corner is determined by the two arguments to the command; it is Xorigin+*x*-size and Yorigin+*y*-size. Figures 4-21 and 4-22 illustrate how the clipping works. (Note that for bottom-up images, the two points defining the saved piece are the lower-left and upper-right corners.)

When to Use: The effect of Clip is analogous to cropping a photograph. Use it when you want to make an image smaller by cutting out extraneous pieces rather than by scaling it down and losing resolution.

Figure 4-21 Clipping coordinates

. . . .

Figure 4-22 Airplane clipped and rescaled

Example:

```
PL>GLOAD T38 ENTER          Load T38 image (Figure 4-21)
PL>GRAY ENTER               grayscale for printing
PL>SET XORIGIN 30 ENTER     upper left corner
PL>SET YORIGIN 60 ENTER
PL>CLIP 248 186 ENTER       clip out small airplane
PL>RESCALE 640 480 ENTER    blow it up
PL>SHOW ENTER               Figure 4-22
```

See Also: Set Origin

. . . .

Color

Color grayscale image.

Syntax Color [mapfile]

Description: The Color command converts a grayscale image into a color-mapped image. If the argument is the name of a MAP file, the image is pseudo-colored with that map, otherwise the color map will contain the original grays. The command works by assigning colors to shades of gray according to the new palette.

The command

```
PL>COLOR CHROMA.MAP ENTER
```

has the same effect as the two commands

```
PL>COLOR (ENTER)
PL>PLOAD CHROMA.MAP (ENTER)
```

The palette-map file must be in the current directory or in the directory stored in the Mapdir variable.

When to Use: This command is useful for colorizing grayscale images to better show off gradations of shading. An example would be applying color to electron microscope images to better show off features visible with contrasting shades.

Example:

```
PL>GLOAD T38.GIF (ENTER)
PL>GRAY (ENTER)                    convert to grayscale
PL>COLOR CHROMA.MAP (ENTER)
```

You will now see the T38 jet in psychedelic color!

See Also: Gray

....

Contrast

Adjust image contrast.

Syntax Contrast [[red | green | blue] value]...

Description: The Contrast command stretches or squeezes the contrast of an image. Arguments are interpreted like those in Brighten. If a given value is positive, the image contrast is stretched so that values that were equal to the given value become 0, and those that were equal to (255-value) become 255. If the given value is negative, the inverse operation is performed. Because contrast is always stretched equally around the midpoint of the range (128), it is a good idea to brighten or darken an image as necessary to center its histogram before performing a contrast stretch. Use the Histogram command to judge how balanced the colors are about the middle value of 128. Figure 4-23 shows the BRYCE.GIF image and Histogram before the application of Contrast. Notice that all the colors are humped around the middle of the histogram, which means that there are many grays but few whites and blacks. Figure 4-24 shows the histogram and image after applying Contrast 60. The histogram is more spread out; all the color values less than 80 hex (128 decimal) have been decreased, and those greater have been increased. The image has more contrast and "snap."

The contrast stretching formula operates on color values assuming a linear relationship between these values and the intensities they represent (as do the Brighten and Darken commands). Therefore, if an image has been scanned

Figure 4-23 Before Contrast

Figure 4-24 After Contrast

with a device with a gamma value not equal to 1.0, the image should be gamma-corrected before contrast stretching.

When to Use: Use Contrast with a positive parameter when an image looks too flat, without strong light or dark colors. Use Contrast with a negative parameter if the lights and darks of an image are too extreme.

Example: The first example is the script used to generate Figures 4-23 and 4-24. Note that this example uses grayscale for simplicity, since a grayscale image has one histogram. The very same idea works in true-color. In that case it could be necessary to inspect the histograms and make contrast adjustments for each color separately.

```
PL>GLOAD BRYCE (ENTER)      load BRYCE.GIF
PL>GRAY (ENTER)             convert to grayscale
PL>HISTOGRAM (ENTER)        This is Figure 4-23
PL>CONTRAST 60 (ENTER)
PL>TRANSFORM (ENTER)
PL>HISTOGRAM (ENTER)        this is Figure 4-24
```

This script illustrates how you might use the Histogram and Brighten commands to center brightness values before applying Contrast. The Transform command is needed to make all the changes take effect before saving.

```
PL>GLOAD TOOFLAT.GIF (ENTER)
PL>HISTOGRAM (ENTER)        check whether histogram is centered
PL>SHOW (ENTER)
PL>BRIGHTEN 20 (ENTER)      center histogram
PL>HISTOGRAM (ENTER)
PL>SHOW (ENTER)
PL>CONTRAST 10 (ENTER)      now apply contrast
PL>TRANSFORM (ENTER)
PL>GSAVE OK_NOW.GIF (ENTER)
```

See Also: Lighten
Darken
Gamma

....

Darken

Darken a color.

Syntax Darken [[red | green | blue] value]...

Description: The Darken command subtracts a constant value to each point in the color planes specified. If only one argument is given, all planes are darkened by that amount. Otherwise arguments are interpreted in order, and any arguments that specify planes determine which plane the next numerical argument will affect. For example, Darken red 10 blue 15 would subtract 10 from the values in the red plane and 15 from those in the blue. Any values that would be taken out of the 0 to 255 range by the transform are clamped.

Because this darkening is a linear operation, the image to be brightened or darkened should be encoded with a gamma of 1.0. That is, there should be a linear relationship between values in the image and intensities on the display. If this is not the case, gamma correction may be applied with the Gamma command before adjusting brightness. See the Gamma command for more about display linearity.

When to Use: Use Darken when images are too light. You can also use it to remove color casts by selectively darkening predominant colors.

Example: Try viewing your favorite GIF file before and after Darken.

```
PL>GLOAD FAVORITE.GIF (ENTER)
PL>SHOW (ENTER)
PL>DARKEN 30 (ENTER)
PL>SHOW (ENTER)
```

See Also: Lighten
Gamma

....

Dir

List files.

Syntax Dir [directory]

Description: Dir lists all files in the Picdir directory in the current file format. If an argument is given, files in that directory are listed. No other file specifications can be given. If Fileformat is set to GIF or Targa, statistics on the files will be listed as well.

Limitations: File statistics are only correctly given for the file type set in the Fileformat variable. For example, if Fileformat is set for Targa, then Dir *.GIF reports incorrect statistics.

Example:

```
PL>DIR (ENTER)
```

See Also: Gdir
Tdir

....

DOS

Syntax DOS [command]

Description: The DOS command calls up the DOS command line. All available memory is released to DOS when this command is given, and is reclaimed upon exit. For this reason, some programs that cannot be run with the Call command may be run from using DOS.

Any arguments to this command will be passed to the system as a DOS command line, and will cause the return to Piclab immediately after the command is done.

When to Use: Use DOS to run an external program or drop to DOS. You might use it, for example, if you are afraid that the Piclab temporary files are using up your disk space. You can use the DOS command to temporarily return to DOS and clean up unneeded files.

Example: One particularly useful possibility for the DOS command is

`PL>DOS COPY /B PDAT PRN` (ENTER)

which copies the print file PDAT. to the printer. Similarly

`PL>DOS DIR` (ENTER)

can be used to view file directories when you want to see all files, not just pictures.

Limitations: More memory is available to programs run with DOS than with Call, but available free memory will still be less than 500K, depending on your computer's configuration. If this is not sufficient, you will have to exit Piclab to run your external program.

See Also: Shell is a synonym for DOS.

....

EGApal

Make an EGA palette.

Syntax EGAPAL

Description: The EGApal command is a special case of Makepal. The EGA graphics adapter supports a palette of 16 colors selected from the 64 possible colors. The EGApal command analyzes the true-color image in the New buffer and selects the 16 best colors from the 64 colors available.

When to Use: The EGApal command is designed primarily for reducing full-color images to a form better suited for display on an IBM EGA. Keep in mind that the EGA mode on a VGA is not limited to 64 colors. If you want to convert an image to the EGA 640x350x16 format for display on a VGA, you should use Makepal instead of EGApal; use EGApal only if the image will be displayed on a real EGA board. The reason for this is the number of colors that the 16-color palette can use is much greater than the 64 allowed on a true-blue EGA.

The Map command must be used to map the image onto the palette.

Limitations: EGApal only operates on true-color images; if you attempt to execute this command when a color-mapped image is in the New buffer, an error message will result.

Example: This Piclab script converts a Super VGA 640x480x256 image to an EGA 640x350x16 image.

```
PL>GLOAD TIME (ENTER)          load the Super VGA image GIF file
PL>UNMAP (ENTER)               convert to true color
PL>RESCALE 640 350 (ENTER)     rescale the image to EGA
PL>EGAPAL (ENTER)              build palette appropriate for EGA
PL>MAP (ENTER)                 convert to color-mapped
PL>GSAVE TIME1 (ENTER)         save EGA image as a GIF file
```

Note: the effect of this example is completely different depending on whether the Dither variable is True or False. If True, the colors of the original image will be approximated by using patterns of colored dots. This renders colors better at the expense of resolution. If Dither is False, only solid colors from the EGA palette are used. To see the difference, try **Set Dither True** or **Set Dither False** before the Map step. Figure 4-25 shows the clock tower printed using 256 colors. Figure 4-26 shows the same image reduced to the 16 EGA colors with dithering. The dithering simulates more gray shades at the expense of adding some graininess to the image. Figure 4-27 shows the same image once again reduced to 16 colors without dithering. This image shows the fewest gradations of tone.

See Also: Map
> Makepal
> Set Dither

....

Exit

Exit (Quit) Piclab.

Syntax Exit [flag]

Description: The Exit command exits Piclab. If there is a point transformation pending, it must be canceled or saved before exiting. If the Exit command is given any arguments, it exits immediately regardless of pending transformations.

Inside a program Exit merely sets a flag so that Piclab will exit after the program is complete.

When to Use: Use Exit when you want to exit Piclab. It is also useful for automated Piclab programs called from DOS batch files.

Example: To brighten the image TOODARK.GIF, type:

```
PL>GLOAD TOODARK.GIF (ENTER)
PL>BRIGHTEN 10 (ENTER)      transformation is now pending
PL>EXIT (ENTER)             doesn't work - pending transform
```

Figure 4-25 Clock with 256 colors

Figure 4-26 Clock reduced to 16 colors with dithering

Figure 4-27 Clock reduced to 16 colors without dithering

PL>**EXIT PHOOEY** (ENTER)   now it works! - any parameter will
cause Piclab to quit
despite the pending transformation

See Also: Quit is a synonym for Exit.

Expand

Expand image size.

Syntax Expand *x*-size *y*-size [(black | white | value) [value]...]

Description: The Expand command increases the size of the image to the width and height specified by its first two arguments by adding extra rows and columns of pixels. If a third argument is given, it can be either Black or White to indicate what color the extra pixels should be. If three numeric arguments are given after the bounds arguments, they are taken as the red, green, and blue value of the extra pixels. For color-mapped images, the third argument is treated as a color map index rather than a color value.

After Expand, the original image is in the upper-left corner of the new larger image.

When to Use: Use Expand when you want to tile several images together to form a larger image. You first use Expand to create the larger image, then use Overlay to add a new image to the empty parts.

Example: Suppose you have four 320x240 images that you want to tile to make a single 640x480 image. The script would be:

```
PL>GLOAD <upper_left_image> (ENTER)      load first image
PL>EXPAND 640 480 (ENTER)                image now upper left
PL>GLOAD <upper_right_image> (ENTER)     load 2nd image
PL>OVERLAY 320 0 (ENTER)                 top right
PL>GLOAD <lower_left_image> (ENTER)      load 3rd image
PL>OVERLAY 0 240 (ENTER)                 bottom left side
PL>GLOAD <upper_right_image> (ENTER)     load 4th image
PL>OVERLAY 320 240 (ENTER)               bottom right
PL>GSAVE <tiled_image> (ENTER)
```

See Also: Overlay

....

Gamma

Adjust color linearity.

Syntax Gamma [[Red | Green | Blue] value]...

Description: The Gamma command adjusts the linearity of the color brightness values. It works like the Brighten and Darken commands, in that it applies to all color planes uniformly unless the keywords red, green, or blue appear before numeric values. The command adjusts brightness linearity so that values encoded for display on a monitor with a gamma value equal to the argument become linear.

For example, images encoded for display on PCs usually expect a monitor with a gamma near 2.0. The Gamma 2.0 command will convert these values to a linear scale.

Images encoded on Macintoshes and similar equipment have linear values already. Such images can be adjusted for display on PCs with the inverse transformation, that is, Gamma 0.5.

Gamma refers to the nonlinear transfer function of CRT screens. This means that the actual brightness on the screen is not in direct linear proportion to the number stored in video memory. This transfer function (color number to screen brightness) is a curve, which when mathematically represented has a constant that defines how "curvy" (how far away from a straight line) it is, which is commonly called the *gamma number*. Common VGA screens have numbers from 1.6 to 2.0.

Suppose you have a photograph converted to a GIF file with a scanner. Typically the color values generated by the scanner are proportional to the color of the original. In order for a "raw" scanned image to display correctly on the CRT, it must be transformed with the inverse of the CRT's transfer function, thus canceling it out when you view the image. This is called a *gamma correction* and is very critical when processing image scanner output for display on a CRT. Fortunately, since the image from a TV camera is already designed to be displayed on a CRT (the TV set), the TV camera performs a standard gamma correction.

Since the Gamma command is just applying a transfer function, it is relative to what the picture already is. Thus an image that is already gamma-corrected will look washed out if it is gamma-corrected again. If an image looks good on the screen, it has already had gamma correction applied. Thus to get something that already looks good into the gamma 1.0 state you need to apply Gamma 1.8, do the processing, then do the Gamma 0.6 to get it back to viewable condition again.

If you have a grayscale image or true-color image, the gamma of the final viewed image can also be controlled with the palette set using Graypal. Suppose you have a non-gamma-corrected image created by scanning. The palette map GAMMA1.MAP is designed to apply implicit gamma correction that allows the image to display properly on a monitor. It does this not by altering the color values in the image, but by the choice of colors in the palette. This means that even though the image displays well, it has not actually been gamma-corrected. Therefore the result of applying

PL>**MAKEPAL** (ENTER)
PL>**MAP** (ENTER)
PL>**SHOW** (ENTER)

will not look satisfactory without applying the Gamma command first.

The palette GAMMA2.MAP is for proper display of images that have already been gamma-corrected.

When to Use: Use the Gamma command to process scanned images that look too contrasty. You can also apply a gamma adjustment before applying linear transforms like Brighten or Darken.

Example: Suppose you want to significantly lighten an image that looks like it has the proper contrast, and thus has already been gamma-corrected. By undoing the gamma correction before applying the linear lightening, the effect of the lightening will be more uniform.

```
PL>GLOAD CORRECT.GIF (ENTER)
PL>GAMMA 1.5 (ENTER)       undo gamma correction
PL>BRIGHTEN 30 (ENTER)     apply linear brighten function
PL>GAMMA .6 (ENTER)        reapply gamma
PL>SHOW (ENTER)            see result
```

See Also: Lighten
Darken
Contrast

....

Gdir

List GIF files.

Syntax GDIR [directory]

Description: The Gdir command lists only GIF files from Picdir or from the directory given as sole argument. Statistics are listed from each file as well.

Example:

```
PL>GDIR (ENTER)
```

See Also: Dir
Tdir

....

Gload

Load GIF file.

Syntax Gload file

Description: The Gload command loads a GIF file regardless of the current setting of variable Fileformat. The file is loaded into the New buffer, moving the current contents of the New buffer to Old.

Example:

```
PL>GLOAD T38.GIF (ENTER)
```

See Also: Load
Tload
Rload

....
Gray

Convert to grayscale.

Syntax Gray

Description: Gray converts true-color or color-mapped images to grayscale. The formula used for conversion to grayscale is the same as used by black-and-white televisions and is designed to mimic the eye's response: gray = (.299 × red) + (.587 * green) + (.114 * blue).

When to Use: Gray is useful for converting images that will be printed or imported into desktop publishing packages as grayscale images. Apply early in a script, especially when dealing with images at high resolutions because the storage needed by Piclab is 1 byte per pixel rather than the 3 bytes needed for true-color images.

Example: Here is the printing example. Without the Gray command, the memory requirements of this script would be very large.

```
PL>GLOAD T38.GIF (ENTER)
PL>GRAY (ENTER)
PL>ROTATE (ENTER)
PL>SET DPI 300 (ENTER)
PL>RESCALE 600 800 (ENTER)
PL>PRINT (ENTER)
```

See Also: Color
Graypal

....
Graypal

Syntax Graypal file [offset [count]]

Description: When you view a monochrome or true-color image on a VGA, Piclab uses a default palette. The default colors are equivalent to GAMMA1.MAP, but GAMMA2.MAP and PSEUDO.MAP can be useful in some situations, depending on the particular characteristics of your hardware. The Graypal command allows you to change the default map to the values in a palette-map file.

Suppose you have a non-gamma-corrected image created by scanning. The palette map GAMMA1.MAP is designed to apply implicit gamma correction that allows the image to display properly in grayscale on a monitor. It does this not by altering the color values in the image itself, but by the choice of colors in the palette used to display the image on color-mapped hardware. This means that even though the image displays well, it has not actually been gamma corrected. Therefore the result of applying

```
PL>MAKEPAL (ENTER)
PL>MAP (ENTER)
PL>SHOW (ENTER)
```

may not look satisfactory without first applying the Gamma command.

The palette GAMMA2.MAP is for proper display of images that have already been gamma-corrected.

The second and third parameters of the Graypal command have the same meaning that they do for the Pload and Psave commands. The parameter *offset* is the first palette index that will be overwritten. The *count* parameter is the number of colors read in.

When to Use: The Graypal command provides advanced control for those with a particular reason to change the default map used for viewing non-color-mapped images with the Show command. However, it is also useful for the experimenter who wants to try adding a little color to Show's rendition of true-color images. Try experimenting with different maps, such as CHROMA.MAP, just be aware that no single color map can do justice to all possible true-color images.

Example: If you found that another map file more accurately displays grayscales on your hardware setup than the default, you might want to place something like this in your SSTOOLS.INI file:

```
[Piclab]
GRAYPAL GAMMA2.MAP
```

See Also: Psave
Pload

....

Gsave

Save image as GIF.

Syntax Gsave file [Interlace]

Description: Saves the New buffer to the file named by the first argument in GIF format regardless of the current setting of variable Fileformat. If the second argument is the word Interlace, image is interlaced, which means that odd lines are encoded first, then even.

Example: This example converts a 24-bit Targa to a GIF file.

```
PL>TLOAD T38.TGA (ENTER)
```

```
PL>MAKEPAL (ENTER)
PL>MAP (ENTER)
PL>GSAVE T38.GIF (ENTER)
```

See Also: Save
　　　　　 Tsave
　　　　　 Rsave

....

Help

Access on-line help.

Syntax Help [subject]

Description: Piclab's on-line help gives you access to succinct descriptions of all the commands. Entering Help by itself gives a description of how the help facility works. To list all the possible commands, type List Commands at the Piclab prompt. Then, for example, if you wanted to know more about Rescale, you would type Help Rescale.

　　　The Help command also can give you information about the Piclab variables. To see what these variables and their current values are, use the Set command with no parameters. Then you can find out more about a particular variable by invoking the Help command with that variable name as a parameter. For example, to get help on the Palette variable, type in Help Palette.

　　　The help information is held in a plain text file. The Help command causes this file to be searched for the keyword. You can edit the PL.HLP file and add your own favorite scripts and additional information.

When to Use: Use Help when you need to be reminded how a command works or what a variable does.

Example: Figure 4-28 shows the result of the following commands:

```
PL>LIST COMMANDS (ENTER)
PL>HELP GDIR (ENTER)
PL>SET (ENTER)
PL>HELP PALETTE (ENTER)
```

Limitations: In order for Piclab to find the help information, the Help file PL.HLP must either be in the current directory or in the directory stored in the Helpdir variable. The best approach is to set that directory in your SSTOOLS.INI file with an entry like

```
[Piclab]
HELPFILE=C:\IMLAB\PICLAB\PL.HLP
```

See Also: List Commands
　　　　　 Set

Figure 4-28 Results of Help commands

....

Histogram

Plot color distribution.

Syntax Histogram [Red | Green | Blue]

Description: A histogram is a graph of frequencies that shows different values. In Piclab the Histogram command counts and graphs how many pixels in the image have each of 256 values of red, green, blue. If no arguments are given, Histogram plots histograms for all color planes; if one or more arguments are given, a histogram is plotted for each color plane specified as an argument. The histograms plotted reflect the image as it would be after any pending transformations, so you can look at the results of many processes before saving or canceling them.

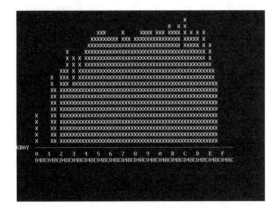

Figure 4-29 A histogram

Figure 4-29 shows an example of a histogram. Each vertical bar of the histogram represents the total number of pixels in the image with values in the range beginning with the value listed below the histogram in hexadecimal. Each bar covers a range of four values and there are 64 bars. The height of each bar is in logarithmic proportion to the frequency of occurrence of values in the range it represents. The bars are automatically scaled so that the tallest one is made 20 characters high.

When to Use: The Histogram command gives you an objective measure of the effect of various commands on image color to augment your subjective color assessment. Certain Piclab commands, such as Contrast, have an effect that depends on where colors fall relative to a middle value of 128 (80 hex). Before applying Contrast it is important to center the distribution of colors around the middle brightness value. This centering can be done with Brighten and Darken. The Histogram command is a powerful tool in assessing the effect of the adjustment. Use Histogram whenever a graphical analysis of the distribution of colors will help in deciding image-processing strategy.

Example: This script shows the effect of the Brighten command

```
PL>GLOAD T38.GIF (ENTER)   load a GIF file
PL>HISTOGRAM (ENTER)       plot histogram
PL>BRIGHTEN 40 (ENTER)     brighten colors
PL>HISTOGRAM (ENTER)       histogram plot is shifted to the right
```

See Also: Contrast
Brighten
Darken

List
Display lists.

Syntax List [item]

Description: If the List command is given without an argument, it shows the possible items that may be listed. The possibilities are Variables, Commands, Buffers, Printers, Formats, Displays. Here is a brief explanation of each.

List Variables shows all the Piclab variables and the variables' contents. This is exactly the same as entering Set with no parameters.

List Commands shows all the possible Piclab commands. This is particularly helpful in conjunction with Help, or when you can't quite remember the name of a command.

List Buffers shows the status of the New, Old, and Temp buffers and what kind of image they currently hold.

List Printers shows the kinds of printers supported by Piclab. The printer can be specified with the Set Printer command.

List Formats shows the kinds of formats supported by Piclab.

List Displays shows the possible video modes available for the Show command.

When to Use: Use List when you have forgotten command or variable names.

Example:

```
PL>LIST VARIABLES (ENTER)
PL>LIST COMMANDS (ENTER)
PL>LIST BUFFERS (ENTER)
PL>LIST PRINTERS (ENTER)
PL>LIST FORMATS (ENTER)
PL>LIST DISPLAYS (ENTER)
```

See Also: Help
Set

....

Load

Load file.

Syntax Load file [args]...

Description: The Load command loads a file in the current file format into the New buffer, moving the current contents of the New buffer to Old. Any arguments are passed along to the function that handles loading for the current format and are interpreted by that routine. The first argument is always the file to be loaded, but other arguments vary with the format.

List Formats will give you a list of all the available file formats, and Help is available for each.

Limitations: The effect of Load depends on the Fileformat variable.

Example:
```
PL>SET FILEFORMAT GIF (ENTER)
PL>LOAD T38.GIF (ENTER)
```

See Also: Tload
Gload
Rload

....

Makepal

Make a palette.

Syntax Makepal

Description: Makepal analyzes all the colors of the true-color image in the New buffer, and determines the palette colors that best fit all the colors in the image. The length of the created palette is the value of the Piclab Palette variable. For example, suppose the Palette variable is set to 256 colors. You can set this by typing:

```
PL>SET PALETTE 256 (ENTER)
```

Now suppose your true-color image has 800 different colors in it. The Makepal command causes Piclab to build a 256-color palette with a set of colors that allows each of those 800 colors to be closely approximated by some palette color. This command is often followed by a Map command, which converts the true-color image in the New buffer to a color-mapped image using the new palette.

When To Use: Eventually color-mapped formats may give way to true-color formats. Since many images are in color-mapped format, an extremely useful operating process of Piclab is to convert color-mapped images to true color, do image processing, and convert back. The Makepal command, along with the Map command, are the commands that do the convert-back part of that process. Use this command whenever you want to convert a true-color image back to a color-mapped (EGA/VGA) image. Be aware that this mapping process can cause a loss of color information, because a color-mapped image can generally display fewer simultaneous colors than a true-color format.

Limitations: Makepal only operates on true-color images; if you attempt to execute this command when a color-mapped image is in the New buffer, an error message will result.

The number of colors in the original image reported by Makepal is not the actual number of colors, but the number of colors converted to 5 bits per primary color, which means that there are 32 possible gradations of each color. Suppose you have loaded in a grayscale image that contains all the possible shades of gray from 0 to 255, and you type:

```
PL>COLOR (ENTER)
PL>UNMAP (ENTER)
PL>MAKEPAL (ENTER)
```

Then only 32 colors will be reported. This is not a problem with the way Makepal works, but only with the way the number of colors found is reported.

Example: Just about every Piclab example illustrates the Makepal command. The following simple Piclab script converts a Targa file to a GIF file. The key to this example is to understand that the GIF format is inherently a color-mapped format that requires a palette.

```
PL>TLOAD <targafile> (ENTER)      load the Targa file
PL>SET PALETTE 256 (ENTER)        build a 256-color palette
PL>MAKEPAL (ENTER)                create palette
PL>MAP (ENTER)                    convert to palette indices
PL>GSAVE <gif_file> (ENTER)       save the GIF file
```

See Also: Map
          EGApal

....

Map

Map colors to a palette.

Syntax Map

Description: The Map command converts each red, green, and blue color of the true-color image in the New buffer to the palette index of the closest color match from the palette. Figure 4-30 shows how this process works. On the left you can see the RGB values of the pixels in true-color format. In the middle you see the colors in the color palette. The Map command causes Piclab to look through the complete palette, comparing each palette color to the RGB value of the true-color pixel, looking for the best match. The palette index of the best match becomes the *color value* for that same pixel in color-mapped format. On the right you see the color index assigned to that pixel in the color-mapped version of the file.

Color information is almost always lost in this process because there are usually more colors in the true color image than there are palette colors; hence some colors cannot be exactly mapped. That is why this Map process is called

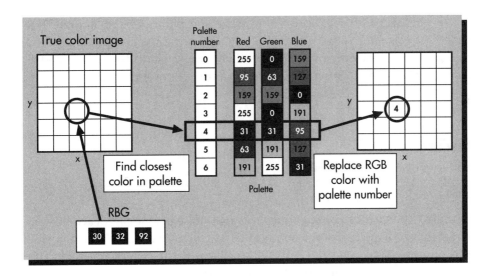

Figure 4-30 The Color-map process

color reduction. However, with 256 colors to work with, Piclab can usually do a pretty good job.

Note: In most cases you will want to build a new palette with the Makepal command rather than using the existing palette.

When to Use: Use the Map command whenever you want to convert a true-color image to a color-mapped image, and you already have the palette you want to use.

Limitations: Map only operates on true-color images; if you attempt to execute this command when a color-mapped image is in the New buffer, an error message will result.

Example: In this example a GIF image is loaded and unmapped, then another palette loaded, and the imaged mapped to that new palette. In this way an image can be forced to use a different palette, with the colors matched to the closest colors in the new palette.

PL>**GLOAD BRYCE** (ENTER)	load a GIF file
PL>**UNMAP** (ENTER)	convert to true color
PL>**PLOAD CHROMA.MAP** (ENTER)	load a new palette
PL>**SET DITHER TRUE** (ENTER)	turn on dithering
PL>**MAP** (ENTER)	convert to color-mapped
PL>**SHOW** (ENTER)	

Try this also with Set Dither False. The colors will not be so accurate, but sharpness is greater without the dithering. Dithering is a method of creating more apparent colors by using the fact that the eye blends the colors of adjacent pixels together. Dithering always has a cost of lower resolution.

See Also: Unmap

....

Median

Reduce noise via median method.

Syntax Median [weighted]

Description: The Median command reduces spot noise in an image. Each point is replaced by the median of the points in its 3x3 area. That is, the nine points in this area are sorted and the fifth one is taken. If the one argument to this routine is weighted, then the center point is added twice more to the list and the sixth of the 11 points is taken. Figure 4-31 shows how this transformation works.

The median filter results in some smoothing, but not as much as with the Smooth command. This effect is a little less drastic with the weighted median filter. Repeated application of this operation will result in an oil-paint texture appearing on the image.

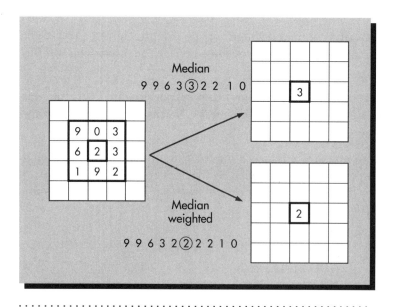

Figure 4-31 The Median process

This filter will not help reduce periodic or other noise — only small spot noise, such as from dust on a lens.

When to Use: Use the Median command to smooth over spot noise and other random imperfections in an image. The price of this smoothing is some loss of detail.

Limitations: The Median command applies only true-color images or grayscale images. Use Unmap or Gray first if you start with a color-mapped image such as a GIF file.

Example:

```
PL>TLOAD NOISY.TGA (ENTER)
PL>MEDIAN (ENTER)
```

See Also: Sharpen
Smooth

Mirror

Reflect horizontally.

Syntax Mirror

Description: The Mirror command flips the image horizontally, reversing left and right. There are no arguments.

When to Use: Mirror is a special-effects kind of command. Use it to have fun playing with images! In the example a file is made that reflects itself. The result is shown in Figure 4-32.

Example:

```
PL>GLOAD TIME.GIF (ENTER)      load the clock tower
PL>UNMAP (ENTER)               convert to true color
PL>RESCALE 320 480 (ENTER)     aspect ratio is squished
PL>MIRROR (ENTER)              reverse left and right
PL>TSAVE TEMP (ENTER)          save reversed image
PL>UNDO (ENTER)                unreverse
PL>EXPAND 640 480 (ENTER)      expand to original dimensions
PL>TLOAD TEMP (ENTER)          load reversed image
PL>OVERLAY 320 0 (ENTER)       overlay over right-hand side
PL>MAP (ENTER)                 using original GIF palette
PL>GSAVE DOUBLE.GIF (ENTER)    save it - See Figure 4-32
```

See Also: Overlay

··

Figure 4-32 Mirrored clocks

····················

Negate

Invert image colors.

Syntax Negate [Red I Green I Blue]...

Description: The Negate command converts the image in the New buffer to its negative. The relationship between an image before and after Negate is very much like the relationship between a photographic negative and a positive color print. All three color planes are negated unless an argument is given to the Negate command specifying one of red, green, and blue, in which case just one color is negated. This can be used after digitizing a negative or for special effects.

The mathematical action of Negate is to subtract the red, green, and blue colors from 255. For example, if the RGB values of a pixel are red=23, green=128, and blue=240, then the color of that pixel in the negated image is red=255-23=232, green=255-128=127, and blue=255-240=15.

When to Use: The Negate command is useful for special color effects. It is also useful for converting text between white-on-black and black-on-white.

Example: Try viewing your favorite GIF file before and after Negate. Figures 4-33 and 4-34 show the results before and after Negate corresponding to the two Show commands in this example.

```
PL>GLOAD TIME (ENTER)
PL>SHOW (ENTER)
PL>NEGATE (ENTER)
PL>SHOW (ENTER)
```

See Also: Brighten
Darken

Figure 4-33 Before Negate

Figure 4-34 After Negate

Overlay

Overlay image on top of another.

Syntax Overlay [x-offset y-offset [threshold]]

Description: The Overlay command overlays the image in the New buffer on top of the Old buffer. If two arguments are given, they are used as the horizontal and vertical position in the base image at which the overlay image is to be placed. Otherwise the Xorigin and Yorigin variables are used. The threshold value allows colors with a lower value than the threshold to be transparent and show through.

When to Use: Use Overlay (as opposed to Add, Subtract, or Average) to combine images when you don't want the overlayed image to look double-exposed with the base image, but want the overlayed image to be completely opaque so the base image doesn't show through where it is covered.

Limitations: The image in the New buffer must not be larger than the image it is to overlay. The threshold parameter is unpredictable with true-color images because it is applied separately to each color plane.

Example: In this example TIME.GIF is rescaled to 320x240, expanded back to 640x480, and the small version is overlayed three times to make a tiled image with four clocks. Figure 4-35 shows the result.

```
PL>GLOAD TIME.GIF (ENTER)      load the clock
PL>UNMAP (ENTER)               convert to true color
PL>RESCALE 320 240 (ENTER)     rescale to half size
PL>TSAVE TMP (ENTER)
PL>EXPAND 640 480 (ENTER)      expand it back
PL>TLOAD TMP (ENTER)           load miniature clock image
PL>OVERLAY 320 0 (ENTER)       overlay in top right
PL>TLOAD TMP (ENTER)           load again
PL>OVERLAY 0 240 (ENTER)       overlay in bottom left
PL>TLOAD TMP (ENTER)           load again
PL>OVERLAY 320 240 (ENTER)     overlay in bottom right
PL>MAP (ENTER)                 convert back to color-mapped
PL>GSAVE TIME2.GIF (ENTER)
```

See Also: Add
Subtract
Average

Figure 4-35 Tiled clocks

....

Pause

Pause for keystroke.

Syntax Pause   [time]

Description: With no arguments, Pause causes Piclab to wait for a key to be pressed before continuing. If one argument is given, Piclab waits for that number of seconds (but will break early if a key is pressed).

When to Use: Use Pause to provide user interaction in automated Piclab scripts.

Example: This example demonstrates that among its other talents, Piclab is the poor person's slide-show program! Type the following into a file called slides.

GLOAD <gif_file1> (ENTER)	load GIF file
SHOW (ENTER)	display file
PAUSE 10 (ENTER)	give user 10 seconds to view
GLOAD <gif_file2> (ENTER)	load GIF file
SHOW (ENTER)	display file
PAUSE 10 (ENTER)	give user 10 seconds to view

Then type:

```
C:>PL SLIDES E
```

....

Pload

Load the current palette from a MAP file.

Syntax Pload file [offset [count]]

Description: Color-mapped files always have a color palette, even if it is only the default palette provided by the IBM PC graphics standard. Piclab can save and load palettes as an ordinary editable map file using the Pload and Psave commands. The format of these MAP files, which is also used by Fractint, is very simple. Each palette entry is a line in the file. Each entry has three numbers, ranging from 0 to 255. These numbers indicate the brightness of the red, green, and blue components of the color, respectively. For example, suppose that the first few lines of the MAP file looked like this:

10	200	30
100	0	0
34	34	34

The first line represents color 0, which is important because on normal PC video hardware, color 0 is the color of the border around the screen. This color in our example is mostly green, because the green component has the bright value of 200, and the other two components are low. The second color (color number 1, since we started counting from 0) is pure red, although a fairly dim shade, since the value 100 is less than half the full brightness value of 255. Color number 2 is a very dark shade of gray, since the red, green, and blue components are equal.

The Pload command replaces the current palette of the color-mapped image in both the Old and New buffers with the palette stored in the MAP file. Two optional numeric parameters are also possible along with the required name of the MAP file, allowing just an initial segment of the new palette to be read in. The parameter *offset* is the first palette index that will be overwritten by the loaded palette. The *count* parameter is the number of colors read in. The default count is the value of the Piclab Palette variable. The palette numbers not included in this range are left unchanged. Note that Piclab will look for MAP files in the directory stored in the Mapdir variable. If this variable is not set, Piclab looks in the current directory. If you want to place all your MAP files in the c:\IMLAB\FRACTINT directory, place the following line in your SSTOOLS.INI file:

```
[PICLAB]
SET MAPDIR=C:\IMLAB\FRACTINT
```

When to Use: There are two very different reasons for loading in a new palette. One is simply to try a completely different color scheme for a color-mapped image. An example of this would be to color a fractal with some of the MAP files bundled with Fractint or Piclab. The other reason is when you are forced to use a particular palette, such as when you intend to combine two color-mapped images. In order for the colors to look right when two color-mapped images are combined, they must have the same palette. In this case the object is not to change the color, but to preserve it as much as possible; so the Map command is used to match the image colors as closely as possible to the new palette. Both of these two purposes are illustrated in the examples below.

Limitations: Palettes are limited to 256 colors.

Example: The first example shows how to simply load in a new palette for the purpose of changing the colors.

```
PL>GLOAD BRYCE (ENTER)            load the GIF file
PL>SHOW (ENTER)                   display on the screen
PL>PLOAD CHROMA.MAP (ENTER)       load in a new palette
PL>SHOW (ENTER)                   Wow! The colors have changed!
PL>GSAVE BRYCE1 (ENTER)           save with the new palette
```

For the second example, let's suppose you have two GIF files, GIF1.GIF and GIF2.GIF, and you want to make GIF2 use the same palette as GIF1. Here's how:

```
PL>GLOAD GIF1.GIF (ENTER)         load the first GIF file
PL>PSAVE GIF1.MAP (ENTER)         save the palette
```

```
PL>GLOAD GIF2.MAP (ENTER)     load the second GIF
PL>UNMAP (ENTER)              convert to true color
PL>PLOAD GIF1.MAP (ENTER)     load palette from the first GIF
PL>MAP (ENTER)                map onto the new palette
PL>GSAVE GIF2A.GIF (ENTER)    save GIF2 with new palette
```

Note that forcing a color-mapped image to use a different palette, as in the second example, may cause the colors to look different if the new palette does not have colors close enough to the original image. The Map command causes Piclab to do its best to match the real image colors to palette colors.

See Also: Psave

....

Print

Print image.

Syntax Print [x-offset [y-offset]]

Description: Print outputs the image in the New buffer into the file specified by the Printfile variable. If the variable is empty, Piclab directs print output to the default printer port. Redirections of the printer port made with the DOS Mode command will affect Piclab. The current setting of the Printer variable determines what codes are sent to the file.

If arguments are given, the first two are used as the x and y offsets of the first dot to print on the first page of output.

When to Use: Use to print images.

Example: Suppose you have a 640x480 image TOPRINT.GIF that you want to print nearly full size on an HP Laserjet with at least 1 MB of memory. Also note that Piclab prints in portrait rather than landscape, so the image needs to be turned on its side. Here is the script to perform all this magic:

```
PL>GLOAD TOPRINT.GIF (ENTER)
PL>GRAY (ENTER)
PL>ROTATE (ENTER)
PL>SET DPI 300 (ENTER)
PL>RESCALE 600 800 (ENTER)
PL>PRINT (ENTER)
```

Limitations: Piclab allows the use of a device name such as Prn in the Printfile variable, but some versions of DOS will not work properly with it. The only printers supported are the HP Laserjet and HP Paintjet.

See Also: Set Printfile
Set Printer

Psave

Save a palette-map file.

Syntax Psave file [offset [count]]

Description: The Psave command saves the current palette as a MAP file. The arguments have the same meaning as the Pload command. The first argument is the name of the MAP file, which is assumed to be in the Mapdir directory. If a second argument is given, the palette is saved starting at that index. If a third argument is given, only that many colors are saved.

This can be used to save a palette created with Makepal so that it need not be calculated again, or so that it can be used with other images. MAP files are plain text files that contain the RGB values for each palette index on one line.

When to Use: Use Psave to avoid having to re-create the palette again later with Makepal, or just to store it for future use.

Limitations: Palettes are limited to 256 colors.

Example: Here is the world's simplest Piclab command script. Do this to discover what the default Piclab palette is.

```
PL>PSAVE PICLAB.MAP (ENTER)
```

Now look at the file PICLAB.MAP with your text editor. You will see that the colors form a continuous grayscale from 000 to 255 255 255. This is Piclab's the default palette.

See Also: Pload

Quit

Quit (Exit) Piclab.

Syntax Quit [flag]

Description: The Quit command exits Piclab. If a point transformation is pending, it must be canceled or saved before exiting. If the Quit command is given any arguments, it exits immediately regardless of pending transformations.

Inside a program, Quit merely sets a flag so that Piclab will exit after the program is complete.

When to Use: Use Quit when you want to exit Piclab. It is also useful for auto-mated Piclab programs called from DOS batch files.

Example:

```
PL>GLOAD T38.GIF (ENTER)
PL>BRIGHTEN 10 (ENTER)        this transformation now pending
PL>QUIT (ENTER)               doesn't work because of xform
PL>TRANSFORM (ENTER)          do the point transformation
PL>QUIT (ENTER)               now it works!
```

See Also: Exit is a synonym for Quit.

....

Rescale

Alter image resolution.

Syntax Rescale value | (x-size y-size)

Description: Resamples the image at a different resolution. This is useful for scal-ing images up to a larger size for printing, or for scaling them down for display. It is recommended that image data always be saved at its original sampling resolution to preserve as much data as possible and only scaled when neces-sary to conform to hardware.

If only one argument is given, horizontal and vertical resolution are both increased in the given proportion. For example, if a 320x240 image is in the New buffer when the command Rescale 1.5 is given, the New buffer will con-tain the same image at 480x360.

More useful, though, is the case where two arguments are present. In this case, the arguments are treated directly as the new horizontal and vertical reso-lution of the image. The transformation above could be expressed as Rescale 480 360. This is most often used to compensate for differing aspect ratios. For example, a 320x400 image from an Amiga can be rescaled to 320x200 to be viewed on a VGA, or to 720x540 for printing on the HP Paintjet.

When to Use: Use Rescale when you want to convert an image to a size with different pixel dimensions.

Limitations: Because Rescale interpolates color values, it cannot be used on color-mapped images, but only on true-color or grayscale images. To use with a color-mapped image, first apply Unmap.

Example: In this example the 640x480 T38.GIF image is rescaled to 320x200.

```
PL>GLOAD T38 (ENTER)           load GIF file
PL>UNMAP (ENTER)               convert to true color
PL>RESCALE 320 200 (ENTER)     shrink image
PL>MAP (ENTER)                 convert back to color-mapped
PL>GSAVE T38a.GIF (ENTER)      save
```

See Also: Expand

....

Reverse

Reverse storage order.

Syntax Reverse

Description: The Reverse command changes the storage order of an image from top-down to bottom-up or vice versa. Targa files can be stored either in bottom-up or top-down format, and contain information in the header specifying which way they are stored.

When to Use: Quite a few Targa files seem to use the bottom-up format. Use Reverse to change to the more common top-down.

See Also: Tload
Tsave

....

Rload

Load RAW file.

Syntax Rload file x-size y-size [Color | Mono]

Description: The Rload command loads an image in RAW format regardless of the current setting of variable Fileformat. The width and height of the image must be specified as the second and third arguments to Rload. A fourth argument may be either of the words Color or Mono to specify the number of planes. Color is the default.

Color-mapped RAW files must be loaded as Mono, then colored with the Color command after the palette is loaded with Pload.

Example:

```
PL>RLOAD IMAGE.R8 640 480 MONO (ENTER)
```

See Also: Load
Tload
Gload
Pload

....

Rotate

Rotate image.

Syntax Rotate value

Description: Rotate rotates the image in 90-degree increments. Possible arguments are 90, 180, or 270 degrees.

When to Use: Use Rotate to change an image from portrait to landscape mode for printing.

Limitations: Rotate is one of the few Piclab commands that uses computer memory rather than disk space to do its magic. Because this operation requires large amounts of memory for large images, you should rotate the image before scaling it up to size for printing.

Example: This example shows how to print an image on an HP Laserjet at nearly full size in landscape mode.

```
PL>GLOAD T38 (ENTER)
PL>GRAY (ENTER)
PL>ROTATE (ENTER)
PL>SET DPI 300 (ENTER)
PL>RESCALE 600 800 (ENTER)
PL>PRINT (ENTER)
```

See Also: Mirror

....

Rsave

Save image as RAW.

Syntax Rsave file

Description: Saves image in RAW format regardless of the current setting of variable Fileformat. No arguments.

Limitations: RAW format does not save palette.

Example:

```
PL>GLOAD T38 (ENTER)
PL>UNMAP (ENTER)
PL>RSAVE T38 (ENTER)
```

See Also: Save
Gsave
Tsave

....

Run

Run a Piclab command file.

Syntax Run program [args...]

Description: The Run command has one required argument — the name of a text file containing Piclab commands. These are interpreted as if they had been typed from the command line, but they are not echoed, and messages are turned off while a program runs. Additional arguments are passed to the Piclab program, to fill in the variables %1, %2, and so forth.

Example: Make a file called V2E containing the commands:

```
GLOAD %1
UNMAP
RESCALE 640 350
EGAPAL
MAP
GSAVE %2
```

To convert a 256-color VGA file called VGA.GIF to an EGA file called EGA.GIF, enter the following Piclab command:

```
PL>RUN V2E VGA.GIF EGA.GIF (ENTER)
```

See Also: Piclab programs

. . . .

Save

Save image.

Syntax Save file [args]...

Description: Saves the image in the New buffer to the file specified by the first argument. Subsequent arguments are passed along to the file save routine of the current file format.

List Formats will give you a list of all the available file formats, and Help is available for each.

Limitations: The effect of the Save command depends on the Fileformat variable.

Example:

```
PL>SET FILEFORMAT TARGA (ENTER)
PL>GLOAD T38.GIF (ENTER)
PL>UNMAP (ENTER)
PL>SAVE T38.TGA (ENTER)
```

See Also: Tsave
Gsave
Rsave

....

Set

Set Piclab variable.

Syntax Set [variable [value]]

Description: The Set command, without any arguments, lists all Piclab variables and their current values. Piclab variables can hold numbers, character strings, or True/False. Variables set system defaults and control the specifics of how many commands perform.

If the Set command is given one argument, the variable named is cleared. For example, the command

PL>SET PALETTE (ENTER)

clears the variable Palette to 0. Numeric variables are cleared to 0, string variables to " ", and True/False variables to False.

If Set is given with two arguments, the variable named by the first is set to the value specified by the second. If a numeric variable is given a string value, it is set to 0. String values should not be put in quotes. True/False values may be set by the keywords True/False, Yes/No, On/Off, or by the numeric values 1/0.

Within the SSTOOLS.INI file, the syntax to accomplish the same effect as the Set command is <variable>=<value>.

Help on individual variables is available by typing Help <variable>.

Table 4-5 shows the Piclab variables and a brief description of each.

. . . .

Xorigin	*x* coordinate of upper left for clipping
Yorigin	*y* coordinate of upper left for clipping
Palette	Number of colors in the palette
Dpi	Resolution of printer in units of dots per inch
Multiimage	Support for multiple image GIF files if True
Multimap	Support for multiple MAP GIF files if True
Dither	Dither when reducing colors if True
Display	Which display resolution to use for Show command
Printer	Name of printer
Printfile	Name of print file
Printscale	Image-size multiplier for printing
Tempdir	Directory for temporary files
Picdir	Default directory for images
Mapdir	Default directory for map files
Fileformat	Default file format

Table 4-5 The Piclab variables

Example: The following command sets the directory where Piclab looks for MAP files.

```
PL>SET MAPDIR C:\FRACTINT (ENTER)
```

See Also: List Variables

....

Sharpen

Sharpen image.

Syntax Sharpen [value]

Description: Sharpen applies what is called a Laplace transform to the image. The effect is that edges in the image are sharpened as if the image had been refocused. Unfortunately it also increases the amount of noise in the image, making it appear more grainy.

The command can be given a single numerical argument, which specifies the severity of the transform. Changing the value of the argument results in a tradeoff between sharpness and noise. The default value is 1.0, which provides a noticeable increase in both sharpness and noise, and is about the best value for sharpening when the purpose is to bring out information. For many images, a less severe value of 0.2 to 0.5 is often better. Values greater than 1.0 should be used only when trying to locate specific objects in an image. They produce too much noise for accurate reproduction.

This function works by amplifying the differences between each point and its neighbors. This has the effect of amplifying high spatial frequency details such as edges and noise.

When to Use: If you don't know what a Laplace transform is, you are not at a disadvantage. Just try this to see what it does. Figures 4-36 and 4-37 show the Bryce image before and after the application of Sharpen 0.5. You can see that the craggy canyon-like features stand out in sharp relief, and that the painted sky breaks down.

Example: This is the script that was used to print the two Bryce image in Figures 4-36 and 4-37

```
PL>GLOAD BRYCE (ENTER)      load Bryce image
PL>GRAY (ENTER)
PL>PRINT (ENTER)            Figure 4-36
PL>SHARPEN .5 (ENTER)       apply sharpen area process
PL>PRINT (ENTER)            Figure 4-37
```

The above example was oriented toward printing so the figures could be reproduced, and so was done in grayscale. The sharpen command also has

Figure 4-36 Image before Sharpen

Figure 4-37 Image after Sharpen

striking effects with color images. In this case the color-mapped image must be unmapped. Try the following:

PL>**GLOAD BRYCE** (ENTER)   load Bryce image
PL>**UNMAP** (ENTER)   make true color image
PL>**SHARPEN .5** (ENTER)   apply sharpen area process
PL>**MAKEPAL** (ENTER)   build a new palette
PL>**MAP** (ENTER)   map image to palette
PL>**SHOW** (ENTER)   look at the result

See Also: Smooth
          Median

Shell

Shell to DOS.

Syntax Shell [command]

Description: The Shell command calls up the DOS command line. All available memory is released to DOS when this command is given, and is reclaimed when DOS is exited. For this reason, some programs that cannot be run with the Call command may be run from using Shell.

Any arguments to this command will be passed to the system as a DOS command line, and will cause the return to Piclab immediately after the command is done. If no arguments are given, the DOS prompt appears, and control will be returned to Piclab when the DOS Exit command is typed in.

When to Use: Use Shell to run an external program or drop to DOS. You might use it, for example, if you are afraid that the Piclab temporary files are using up your disk space. You can use the Shell command to temporarily return to DOS and clean up unneeded files.

Example: One particularly useful action of this program is

`PL>SHELL COPY /B PDAT PRN` (ENTER)

which copies the print file PDAT to the printer. Shell Dir can be used to view file directories when you want to see all files, not just pictures.

Limitations: More memory is available to programs run with Shell than with Call, but available free memory will still be less than 500K, depending on your computer's configuration. If this is not sufficient, you will have to exit Piclab to run your external program.

See Also: DOS is a synonym for Shell.

....

Show

Display image on screen.

Syntax Show [x-offset [y-offset]]

Description: The Show command displays as much of the image in the New buffer as will fit on the computer's display screen. If arguments are given, the first is used as a horizontal offset into the image buffer and the second as a vertical offset. This can be used to look at different parts of an image that is too big for the screen. All video modes allow scrolling with the cursor keys to allow you to see images larger than the display mode's dimensions. If no arguments are given, the current values of the Xorigin and Yorigin variables are used.

If any point transformations are pending, the image you see on screen reflects the image as it would be after the pending transformation. This can be used to look at the effect of a transformation before saving or canceling it.

Because Piclab often stores data more accurately than the display can render it, what you see on the screen is only an approximation of the actual image. In particular, unless you are using one of the 16-bit true-color display modes, true-color images will be shown in grayscale on displays capable of it, or in 8-color dither on others.

The video mode used by the Show command can be set with the Set Display command. You can see the list of possible modes with List Displays. Table 4-6 shows this list of modes.

CGA   320x200 dithered CGA mono
EGA   640x350 8-color EGA dither
VGA1   320x200 standard VGA
VGA2   640x480 simulated on VGA
SVGA1   640x400 for 256k SVGAs
SVGA2   640x480 for 512k SVGAs
SVGA3   800x600 for 512k SVGAs
HICLR1   640x480 Sierra DAC SVGAs
HICLR2   800x600 Sierra DAC SVGAs

Table 4-6 Piclab's video modes

Example:

```
PL>GLOAD BRYCE (ENTER)
PL>SET DISPLAY VGA1 (ENTER)      use 320 x 200 mode
PL>SHOW (ENTER)
```

See Also: Set

Smooth

Smooth by averaging colors.

Syntax Smooth [value]

Description: Smooth replaces each point with the average of the values of the nine points in its neighborhood. This has the effect of smoothing the image and blurring intricate details, somewhat like a photographer's soft-focus lens. If an argument is given, it is taken as a value of the severity of the transform as with the Sharpen command. An argument of 1.0 is calculated using a straight average of the nine points. Values less than 1.0 change the center value less than if a straight average had been done, giving a less pronounced smoothing effect. Values greater than 1.0 are not recommended. If more smoothing is desired, perform Smooth more than once rather than with a high value.

When to Use: Use Smooth to blend contrasty details and give your image a soft, blurred look. Figures 4-38 and 4-39 show BRYCE.GIF before and after applications of Smooth 1.0.

Figure 4-38 Image before
Smooth

Figure 4-39 Image after
Smooth

Limitations: Smooth works only with true-color or grayscale images. If you want to apply Smooth to a color-mapped image, you have to first apply Unmap or Gray.

Example:

```
PL>GLOAD BRYCE.GIF (ENTER)
PL>GRAY (ENTER)
PL>SHOW (ENTER)            Figure 4-38
PL>SMOOTH 1.0 (ENTER)
PL>SMOOTH 1.0 (ENTER)
PL>SHOW (ENTER)            Figure 4-39
```

See Also: Sharpen
Median

Subtract

Subtract images.

Syntax Subtract [Wrap]

Description: The Subtract command allows you to superimpose two images together. The color value of overlapping pixels is obtained by subtracting the color value in the New buffer from the corresponding color value in the Old buffer. If the only argument to the command is Wrap, then values that are taken out of the 0 to 255 range by the addition are taken mod 255 (that is, taken as the remainder after dividing by 255); otherwise, values are clamped.

When to Use: When to use Subtract — this is a tough question. In the absence of an obvious example, here is a unusual one. Photographers with a technical bent and a love of darkroom tricks are familiar with a technique called *solarization.* It involves exposing film to light halfway through development. The result is a strangely colored photograph that is half-negative and half-positive. Exposing the film to light halfway through makes the whole exposure/development process highly nonlinear. The idea of photography is usually to have a linear relationship between the light in the original scene and the lightness of the final picture, which means both are proportionally light and dark in the same places. What we are proposing here is the image lab equivalent of solarization, and to do it we need a nonlinear process.

The idea is to start with an image, apply the Gamma transform to it, and subtract the result from the original. The reason for using Gamma is that it is a nonlinear transformation. You don't need to know more about it than that — the rest is all experimentation. See the example below for the steps. Figures 4-40 and 4-41 show a beautiful ray-traced image of a clock tower before and after our nonlinear tricks. The after image looks like a negative — but is it? You really need to try this and see the result in color.

Limitations Subtract only works on true-color or grayscale images. Use Unmap or Gray first for color-mapped images.

Example: Here is the solarization example. The Brighten and Contrast commands at the end were added to make the result less dim. The values chosen were figured out using the Histogram command. As with true photographic solarization, nothing about this is cut and dried. Experiment to your heart's content!

Figure 4-40 Normal clock tower

Figure 4-41 Solarized clock tower

```
PL>GLOAD TIME.GIF (ENTER)      load clock tower image
PL>UNMAP (ENTER)               convert to true color
PL>GAMMA 2 (ENTER)             apply non-linear transform
PL>BRIGHTEN 30                 increase difference between images
PL>TRANSFORM (ENTER)           apply GAMMA and BRIGHTEN
PL>SUBTRACT (ENTER)            subtract non-linear version
PL>BRIGHTEN 110 (ENTER)        center the histogram (move up)
PL>CONTRAST 110 (ENTER)        increase contrast
PL>TRANSFORM (ENTER)           apply BRIGHTEN and CONTRAST
PL>GSAVE TIME1.GIF (ENTER)     save result (see Figure 4-41)
```

See Also: Subtract
           Overlay

....

Tdir

List Targa files.

Syntax Tdir [directory]

Description: The Tdir command lists only Targa files from Picdir or from the directory given as sole argument. Statistics are listed from each file as well.

Example:

PL>TDIR (ENTER)

See Also: Gdir
           Dir

....

Tload

Load Targa file.

Syntax Tload file

Description: The Tload command loads a Targa file regardless of the current setting of the variable Fileformat. The file is loaded into the New buffer, moving the current contents of the New buffer to Old.

Example:

PL>TLOAD T38.TGA (ENTER)

See Also: Load
           Gload
           Rload

....

Transform

Apply pending transformations.

Syntax Transform

Description: The Transform command saves the result of a series of point process transformations to the edit buffer. A point process is a transformation that alters the color value of a pixel based only on the existing color value of that pixel, and not the value of adjacent pixels or other pixels.

If you wish to cancel the pending transformations without saving them, use Undo or Cancel.

The point transformations that Transform applies to are: Negate, Brighten, Darken, Contrast, and Gamma.

When to Use: Use the Transform command after you are satisfied that the pending point transformations are having the desired effect. The Show command renders the image as though the pending transformations have taken effect, giving you the opportunity to visualize the results beforehand.

Example: The following script brightens an image. Without the Transform command, the Brighten command would not take effect and the Gsave command would result in an error message.

```
PL>GLOAD T38.GIF (ENTER)
PL>BRIGHTEN 20 (ENTER)
PL>TRANSFORM (ENTER)
PL>GSAVE <gif_file1> (ENTER)
```

See Also: Color
Graypal

....

Tsave

Save image as Targa.

Syntax Tsave file [bits]

Description: Saves the New buffer to the file named by the first argument in Targa format regardless of the current setting of variable Fileformat. If the second argument is 16, 24, or 32, it is used as the number of bits per pixel stored in the file.

Example: This example converts a GIF file to a 24-bit Targa file.

```
PL>GLOAD T38 (ENTER)     GIF extension is implied
PL>UNMAP (ENTER)         Convert to true color
PL>TSAVE T38 (ENTER)     TGA extension and 24 bits implied
```

See Also: Save

Gsave

Rsave

....

Undo

Cancel (undo) last operation.

Syntax Undo

Description: Cancels the most recent operation. If there are point transformations pending that have not yet been saved with the Transform command, these are canceled and no changes are made to the edit buffers. Otherwise, the New and Old buffers are exchanged.

There are some operations (like Save) that do not alter the edit buffers. If one of these operations was the last one performed, Undo will undo the operation before that. No arguments.

When to Use: Use Undo when the result of the last command or the last untransformed point process is not as you wish. The Show command gives you an idea of the current status of the image, and includes the result of the application of any pending transforms.

Example:

```
PL>GLOAD <gif_file> (ENTER)     load a GIF file
PL>BRIGHTEN RED 40 (ENTER)      brighten Red by 40
PL>SHOW (ENTER)                 check result - UGH!
PL>UNDO (ENTER)                 undo the damage!
PL>SHOW (ENTER)                 back to before the BRIGHTEN command!
```

See Also: Cancel is a synonym for Undo.

....

Unmap

Convert to true-color.

Syntax Unmap

Description: Unmap converts a color-mapped image to a 24-bit RGB true-color image. It is the opposite of the Map command, but what it does is considerably easier to understand. For each pixel, Piclab looks up the RGB value for the color index stored for that pixel and writes the red, green, and blue color values to the buffer. When done, the original color-mapped image is in the Old buffer and the true-color conversion is in the New buffer.

When to Use: Use Unmap before applying true-color transformations such as rescaling. After transformations have been performed in true-color, the image may be reduced to a color-mapped one again with the Makepal and Map commands.

Example: In this example, besides showing how Unmap is used, we also illustrate how to gain an understanding of how the Piclab buffers are used. The List Buffers commands in this script don't do anything except show you what image is in each buffer.

This Piclab script shows how to rescale an image to a new resolution.

PL>**GLOAD T38** (ENTER)	Load GIF file
PL>**LIST BUFFERS** (ENTER)	Color-mapped image is in NEW buffer
PL>**UNMAP** (ENTER)	Make true color image
PL>**LIST BUFFERS** (ENTER)	Color-mapped now in OLD;
	True color in NEW
	Transformation commands go after UNMAP.
PL>**RESCALE 100 100** (ENTER)	can only rescale a true color image
PL>**LIST BUFFERS** (ENTER)	Original dimensions in OLD
	100x100 in NEW
PL>**MAP** (ENTER)	map colors to palette
PL>**LIST BUFFERS** (ENTER)	100x100 mapped in NEW
	100x100 true color in OLD

Limitations: Unmap only applies to color-mapped images; it gives an error message otherwise.

See Also: Map

5

IMPROCES

The Paint Program Plus

Improces is a powerful shareware painting and image-editing program for Super VGA PCs that has some very useful image-processing extras as well. An image editor allows you to alter details of an image, while image processing applies transformations globally to the whole image. Improces can do both. Hence the name: Improces is short for Image Process.

Improces is distinguished by an easy-to-use graphical interface that lets you access all its features using a mouse. Be not deceived by this friendly exterior; Improces is a very powerful program with an unusually strong mix of features. With Improces you can:

- Edit your computer images — retouch, cut, paste.
- Use drawing tools — ovals, squares, brushes, pens, fills.
- Add text to images.
- Create kaleidoscopes and montages.
- Manipulate color palettes, rotate colors (color cycle).
- Apply image-processing functions — contrast, make negative, solarize.
- Read and write GIF and PCX files.

A bit later in this chapter, a step-by-step tutorial will lead you through the main functions of Improces. The end of this chapter contains a reference of all of the functions of Improces.

Shareware Information

Improces is a Shareware program that may be freely distributed in unmodified form for evaluation purposes. If you decide to keep it and use it, you are obligated to pay for it. A registration fee of $25 is required if you wish to continue to use Improces after you try it. A single registration is all it takes, and you will be registered for life. When you consider the power and usefulness of the program, this is a bargain.

There are no differences in functionality between the registered version of Improces and the unregistered version. Registration disables the opening and the ending screen so the program will start running without delay and you will not be required to press a key to exit. To register, send the $25 registration fee to the program's author:

John Wagner
6161 El Cajon Blvd.
Suite B-246
San Diego, CA 92115

California residents, please add the appropriate sales tax. For more information on the Shareware arrangement, see the IMPROCES.DOC file on the disk.

Getting Improces Up and Running

Installation

The installation instructions are given in Chapter 1. The rest of this chapter assumes that the Improces Files are installed in the recommended directory C:\IMLAB\IMPROC.

System Requirements

Memory

You need at least 512K RAM of conventional memory free after loading DOS and TSR (Terminate and Stay Resident) programs. The more memory you have over 512K before starting the program, the better. Improces can also use extended or expanded memory (the memory over the conventional 640K) to improve performance if your system has it, but it is not required. You have EMS memory if you have a memory add-on board for your computer that supports the EMS specification, or if you are running an 80386 machine with a memory manager such as QEMM386, 386 to the Max, or the Windows EMM386.SYS, which converts your extended memory to expanded memory. Note that for extended memory to be usable to Improces, Microsoft's HIMEM.SYS driver or equivalent must be loaded from your CONFIG.SYS file with a line similar to DEVICE=C:\DOS\HIMEM.SYS.

Processor

Improces will run on any MS-DOS machine, from an 8088 to an 80486 or greater. Improces can run on a 4.77 MHz 8088 (the same speed and processor as the original IBM PC). A math coprocessor chip (8087, 80287, 80387, or the coprocessor built in to the 80486) will be utilized if one is available, but it is only utilized to speed up a few of the advanced image-processing functions, so it is optional.

Video

Improces supports from regular 320x200x256 color VGAs to Super VGA graphics adapters with 1024x768 pixels and 256 colors. *A VGA card and monitor is a requirement to run the program.* Make sure your monitor as well as your video card supports the modes you try to use. Improces supports VGA adapters using the Ahead, ATI, Chips & Tech, Everex, Paradise, Trident, Tseng (both ET3000 and ET4000 chip sets) and Video7, as well as any card supporting the new VESA standard. Which modes are supported depend both on the chip set your adapter uses and how much memory it has. Table 5-1 shows how much video memory is required for different video modes. This is memory on your graphics board, not your regular computer memory.

Video Mode	Video Memory Required
320x200 256 colors	64K
640x400 256 colors	256K
640x480 256 colors	512K
800x600 256 colors	512K
1024x768 256 colors	1024K

Table 5-1 Memory requirements of video modes

The question of video support is not as complicated as it sounds. The list of chip sets covers virtually all the VGA boards currently on the market, and new ones are likely to support the VESA standard. Improces automatically detects which chip set you are using, so you don't have to worry about it.

Mouse

A Microsoft-compatible mouse and mouse driver are required. Improces will not run if no mouse is installed. Make sure your mouse driver is installed in your CONFIG.SYS or AUTOEXEC.BAT file.

DOS

Improces requires that you are running MS-DOS 3.0 or greater. It runs fine under DOS 5.0 or DR-DOS 6.0.

Hard Disk

Improces requires a hard disk with at least 1.5 MB of free space at run time. (It could probably be made to work on a two-floppy system, but this is not recommended.) The reason for this large free space requirement is that Improces creates temporary files for some operations. Temporary files are placed in the same directory that Improces is stored in, or on the drive and directory that is specified by a TMP or TEMP variable SET in your environment.

Improces has a virtual screen capability that lets you edit very large images. This capability can require as much as 5 MB of additional disk space.

Setting the Temp Variable

The installation of Improces is covered in Chapter 1. All the Improces files should be unzipped from the companion disk and placed in one directory. You can either add that directory to your Path statement in your AUTOEXEC.BAT file, you can change your Improces directory before starting Improces, or you can invoke Improces using the IMPROC.BAT batch file.

Improces, like Piclab, looks for an environment variable called *Temp* to tell it where to put temporary files. Piclab and Improces can use the same setting for this variable. The variable should contain the name of a directory with at least 1.5 MB free. You can set it with the statement

```
SET TEMP=C:\TEMP
```

in your AUTOEXEC.BAT file.

Improces Quick Start

This quick tour will get you started with Improces, and will test that the installation is correct and the hardware and software of your system is working right. Improces is a menu-driven program, and you can learn a lot just by following the various menus and trying out the functions. But don't forget to come back to this chapter, because as with much advanced software, there are features that may not be readily apparent to you as you explore the program on your own.

Launching Improces

First, change to the drive where Improces resides. Assuming that Improces is stored on your C: drive, and your current drive is some other drive, type:

`:> C :` (ENTER)

Next, change to the directory where Improces is stored. If Improces is stored in the directory as recommended \IMLAB\IMPROC, type:

`:> CD \IMLAB\IMPROC` (ENTER)

These first two steps are not necessary if the Improces drive and directory are listed in your Path statement in your AUTOEXEC.BAT file, or you run Improces using the IMPROCES.BAT batch file.

To run the program, type:

`> IMPROCES` (ENTER)

If all is well, you will see the Shareware announcement inviting you to register your copy of Improces with the author. (If your mouse driver is not installed, Improces will not start. If so, install your mouse driver and try again.) After clicking the mouse, you should see a screen that looks like Figure 5-1.

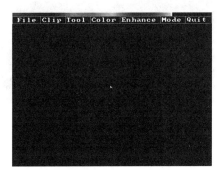

Figure 5-1 The opening Improces screen

At the top of the screen, you will see the menu items File, Clip, Tool, Color, Enhance, Mode, and Quit. You can select menu items by pointing at them with the mouse cursor and clicking the left mouse button. The right mouse button works as an escape key that lets you back out of nested pull-down menus. When you are at the very top-level menu, the right mouse button hides and unhides the menu. For many purposes you will not want the menu in the way of the image, so you will find the right mouse button handy for getting the menu out of the way, and then retrieving it when you need it. To *click on* something (usually a menu item) means to point the mouse cursor at the item, press the left mouse button, and release it.

Setting Improces Defaults

The first order of business is to set the Improces defaults. Click on the File menu item, and the File submenu will drop down. Figure 5-2 shows the screen with the File submenu showing. Select the bottom item, Set Pref, and click on it with the left mouse button. Figure 5-3 shows the Set Preferences screen.

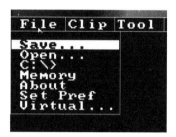

Figure 5-2 The File submenu

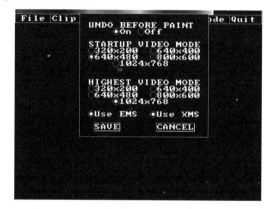

Figure 5-3 The Set Preferences submenu

There are five options in the Set Preferences screen: Undo Before Paint, Screen Startup Mode, Highest Video Mode, Use EMS, and Use XMS.

Undo Before Paint

When Undo Before Paint is set to On, the on-screen image is saved before you enter the Paint menu. Setting this On is a good idea, because it will let you undo changes that you don't want when you use the Paint menu. The only reason to turn this Off is if you have limited XMS or EMS memory, so that Improces has to save the screen to disk, and you are short of disk space. If this option is turned On, Improces will always ask if you want to keep the changes you made when you exit the Paint menu.

Screen Startup Mode

This controls the video mode that the program starts with. The 640x480 mode is a good choice if your graphics board supports it. See the tutorial later in this chapter for more on video modes.

Highest Video Mode

This option controls the highest video mode that shows in the Mode menu. Look at your video board documentation to see what video modes your board supports. This is a safety feature for people whose video card does not support all of the modes that Improces can support.

Use EMS and Use XMS

Click on the appropriate button to toggle the use of either type of memory on or off. EMS is expanded memory that is made available if you have an expanded memory add-on board or if you are using an expanded memory manager such as QEMM386, 386Max, or the EMM386.SYS driver that comes with DOS 5.0. XMS memory is extended memory that is made available using the HIMEM.SYS driver in your CONFIG.SYS. The main purpose of these options is to turn off one or both of these memory options if you are experiencing problems. You can keep them both on and Improces will attempt to use both EMS and XMS.

Clicking on Save will save the default parameters you set up in a file called IMPROCES.CFG. The settings will then take effect each time you use Improces.

Drawing a Picture

You should be back to the Main menu now. From the Main menu click on op-down menu select Paint. You should now see the Paint Tools menu, which looks like Figure 5-4.

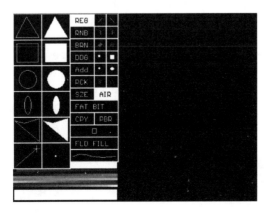

Figure 5-4 The Paint Tools menu

The paint tools include geometric shapes like the usual squares and circles that you expect to see in a paint program, but it also has some less familiar items. These will all be explained in the tutorial later in this chapter. For right now, let's try one spectacular option. Click on Fld Fill (which stands for Flood Fill) near the lower-right corner of the Paint Tools box. You will then see the Flood Information box, which is shown in Figure 5-5.

This box has two sets of radio buttons. *Radio buttons* are named after the kind of buttons found in car radios a few years ago. These buttons were mechanically linked so only one could be pushed in at a time to select a station. When you pushed in a new button, the old one popped out. This style of radio may have vanished, but radio buttons will be with us for a long time in connection with computer graphical user interfaces!

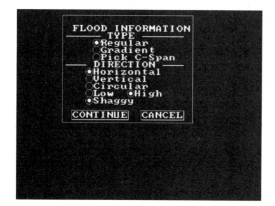

Figure 5-5 The Flood Information box

Click on the Gradient and Circular buttons, and then click on Continue. All menus will vanish, and you will be left with the mouse cursor. The flood fill option works by your clicking on the inside of a geometric figure you want to fill. If you have been following these instructions, your screen will now be blank, so position the mouse somewhere near the center and click the left mouse button. Magically your screen will fill up with a circular pattern with a rainbow of brilliant colors. A black-and-white reproduction can't do the picture justice, but your screen should look like Figure 5-6.

If you enjoy exploring on your own, go ahead now and try out the other tools in the Paint Tools menu. One hint is that you can always clear the screen by selecting a video mode (even the same one that is currently active) from the Mode item on the Main menu.

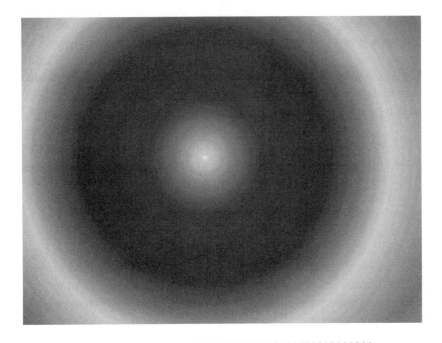

Figure 5-6 The result of the circular gradient fill

Pixel Painting

What makes Improces fun is its unusual features which combine traditional paint program capabilities with image processing and even fractal-generation abilities. Improces has some of the image-processing functions of Piclab and even a few of the fractal-creating features of Fractint. The strong point of Improces is that these features are very accessible and interactive, giving you immediate visual feedback. Both Piclab and Improces, for example, can cut and paste pieces of images. Improces does this in a highly visual way with the mouse, and Piclab uses a less interactive approach that requires entering the coordinates of the pieces to be cut and pasted. On the other hand, the mechanisms of Improces are tied to your computer's graphics capabilities, while Piclab's approach is independent of your graphics hardware, allowing Piclab to deal with just about any size or number of colors. As you get familiar with all the Image Lab tools, you will discover that these programs complement each other very well.

What's a Paint Program?

A graphics image, for our purposes, may be considered a two-dimensional array of pixels. Each pixel of the image you see on the screen is mapped to memory locations of the memory on your graphics adapter. For the kinds of 256-color VGA images that Improces supports, this mapping is very simple. Each pixel corresponds to 1 byte of graphics memory. The contents of that byte of memory is a number from 0 to 255 that is used to look up the color of the pixel in the current palette. The palette assigns colors to each of the 256 different color numbers.

A paint program allows editing the pixels of a graphics memory. It contains tools for adding different shapes to the image, and mechanisms for cutting, copying, and pasting pieces of the image. It also allows control of colors in the palette. A paint program is pixel oriented. This means that once a shape has been added to an image, that shape ceases to have any independent existence, but becomes a part of the overall image. A draw program, by way of contrast, maintains the existence of shapes and parts of the image as objects that can be independently manipulated. If you add a circle to an image using a draw program, later you can select and manipulate that same circle. With a paint program, you can draw the same circle, but it can thereafter only be manipulated as the pixels that make it up, not as a coherent object. Both kinds of programs have advantages. A paint program allows artistic control of the image down to the last pixel. A draw program works better if the image has well-defined parts whose arrangement is not fixed but must be realigned.

Improces is a paint program. If you like, you can magnify and then adjust each individual pixel of the whole image to any color value you want. Improces can take images created or modified in the other Image Lab programs and add text or drawings to them, and modify them.

More Than a Paint Program

Improces is first and foremost a paint program, but it doesn't stop there. Improces is also a capable image-processing program that can adjust contrast, brightness, and other attributes of images. Improces also has some fractal image-generation features that allow you to make color patterns and landscapes to place in your images.

AN IMPROCES TUTORIAL

This section is a tutorial that will lead you through the main functions of Improces. You'll learn how to load and save images in several formats, use powerful drawing tools to paint images, cut and paste parts of images, and access some unusual and intriguing image-process functions. The best way to use this tutorial is to follow along with all the steps on your computer. Along the way we'll build and modify colorful images, and by the end you will understand how Improces works and how to make spectacular images with it.

To begin the tutorial, change directories to your Improces directory and start Improces by typing:

```
C:>cd \IMLAB\IMPROC (ENTER)

C:>IMPROCES (ENTER)
```

Improces comes up with a Shareware announcement. After clicking the mouse, you will see the opening screen. If you do not have a mouse driver loaded, Improces will not start.

Navigating Menus with the Mouse

Improces uses a mouse-driven interface. In some contexts you also use the keyboard to perform an action, and in a few contexts (such as typing in the name to use for saving an image) you must use the keyboard. But most actions in Improces can be performed completely with the mouse. The left and right mouse buttons have a consistent meaning throughout the Improces menus. Clicking the left mouse button while pointing the mouse cursor at a menu item selects that item. There is no notion of double-clicking in Improces; a single click suffices to select a menu item. If you are used to the Windows style of using the mouse, you will find Improces's approach a little different. The right mouse button is used to perform an *escape* function. It lets you back out of the sequence of actions. If you repeatedly click the right mouse button, you can back out all the way to the Main menu. If you click the right mouse button once, Improces will give you a chance to repeat your last action. For example, in order to copy a piece of an image to the clipboard, you have to click on the spot in the image where you want the corner of the copied region to be, then move the mouse to the opposite corner and click again. Suppose you have fixed the first corner by clicking the left button, and as you move the mouse in order to place the opposite corner, you realize that the first corner is not where you want it. Then you can click the right mouse button to cancel the previous click (which set the first corner), move the mouse to the correct position, and click the left mouse button again to reset the corner. You can try out these mouse actions for yourself in a moment.

Improces uses drop-down menus. This means that if you click on a menu item that has submenus, the submenu will drop down and stay down even after you release the mouse button. When you see instructions to *click on* a menu item, in Improces this always means to point the mouse cursor at the item and click the left mouse button. When you first start Improces, you will see the menu items File, Clip, Tool, Color, Enhance, Mode, and Quit.

Loading and Saving Files

You can use Improces in two ways: to modify existing graphics image files, or as a paint program to make entirely new images. This tutorial will begin by loading an existing file to give you a fast start.

Click on File at the top left menu. The File submenu will drop down, as shown in Figure 5-7. Notice that the Open and Save items on the menu end with three dots. The dots are your indication that those menu items have

Figure 5-7 The File submenu

submenus. Click on Open and you will see another submenu, with the choices Open GIF, Open PCX, Open TGA, and Open Prf. Click on Open GIF. You will now see the *file picker* tool, which enables you to select files and navigate the directory tree of your hard disk. Figure 5-8 shows the file picker. The file picker shows all the files in the current directory with GIF extensions. Subdirectory names are listed in <> symbols; "\" and ".." designate the root directory and the directory above the current directory, respectively. You can change to another directory by clicking on its name. Clicking on ".." will take you up one directory in the tree. Use the file picker to change directories to the

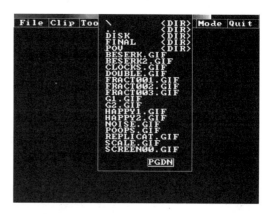

Figure 5-8 The file picker

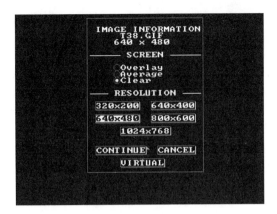

Figure 5-9 The File Information screen

directory where the file T38.GIF is (probably \IMLAB\EXAMPLES), and click on it.

You should now see the File Information screen, as shown in Figure 5-9. This is used to control what video mode to use for loading in the GIF file. At the top of the screen is the name of the file (in this case T38.GIF) and its resolution (640x480). Below that are three options that control how the file you are about to load is to be combined with the current image. Click on Clear. The bottom of the screen gives you some alternative video modes. The current video mode shows under the word Resolution. If you select a mode with a lower resolution than the current video mode, such as 320x200, Improces will throw away alternate pixels of the higher resolution T38.GIF (640x480) and scale the image to fit. If you select a larger resolution, such as 1024x768, Improces will load the image into a corner of the screen with a black space around its borders. If your video adapter supports this mode, select 640x480; otherwise select 320x200. Click on Continue.

You should now see the T38.GIF image displayed on the screen along with the File menu. Notice that the image has some white speckles that do not look correct. Click the right mouse button several times, and both the speckles and the menu will vanish. The reason for the speckles is that Improces needs several colors in the palette to draw the menus. While the menus are showing, two colors in the image may be incorrect. This is not really a problem, because the speckles will not show in the final saved image. You can get rid of this effect by clicking on Colors on the Main menu, and then clicking on Menu Adjust. If Improces can locate colors in the image palette close to its menu colors, then it will not have to change two of your palette colors and the speckles will go away.

While you have the full image on the screen with no menus, click the left mouse button. Notice that the mouse arrow cursor disappears. If you want to use screen capture software (such as VGACAP) to capture a screen, you might want to hide the mouse cursor in this way.

Now click the right mouse button until you see the Main menu. At any time, you can return to the Main menu, click on File, click on Save, and then Save GIF to save your image as a GIF file. Alternatively you can use Save PCX and save your image as a PCX file. All of the Image Lab tools read and write GIF files, so GIF is the best choice, unless you wish to move your image to other software that supports PCX but not GIF.

Using the Clipboard

Basic Clipboard Operation

From the Main menu, click on Clip. Improces has a clipboard that is independent of any particular image. You can copy parts of images to the clipboard and paste them back on top of other images. After you click on Clip, you will see a submenu that looks like Figure 5-10. The options are Cut, Paste, Save, Open, View, and Remap Pal. The Cut option copies parts of images to the clipboards. You can use Paste to place the contents of the clipboard in an image. Save and Open allow you to save or restore the clipboard to disk. You can use this facility to build your own clip art library. View lets you check the contents of the clipboard before Pasting to make sure all is well. Remap Pal lets you adjust the palette of the clipboard image in case it was cut from an image with a different palette, so that it will look good when pasted onto your current image.

Click on Cut with the left mouse button. The menus will vanish. Copy the leftmost T38 aircraft to the clipboard. To do this, place the mouse cursor above and a little to the left of the aircraft and click the left mouse button. Then drag the mouse cursor to the lower-right corner. A box will appear as you move the mouse. (If you decide the fixed corner of the box is not in the correct position, you can click the right mouse button to cancel and start over.) Frame the box around an aircraft and click the left mouse button. The image has now been

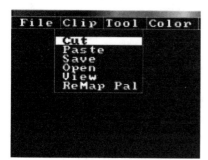

Figure 5-10 The Clip
submenu

copied to the clipboard. To verify this, return to the Main menu, select Clip, and click on View. The contents of the clipboard will appear in the upper-left corner of the screen temporarily, until you click either mouse button.

The other way to load an image into the clipboard is to open a previously saved clipboard file. Try this by clicking on Save from the Clip submenu, and typing in a file name when prompted. No extension is needed; Improces will add the .CLB extension.

More Advanced Clipping: Overlay and Average

Improces has other methods of cutting and pasting besides the functions in the Clip menu, but the use of the clipboard has the advantage that you can copy parts of one image and paste them to another image. To illustrate this, return to the Main menu and click on Mode. Select the same mode you have been using. The Mode menu has two functions: to change video modes, and to clear the screen. Select 640x480 to clear the screen. Now click on Clip and then Paste. You will now see an Options screen with Copy, Average, Overlay, Fringe, Spray, Pattern, and Rain. These options determine how the pasted image is combined with the underlying image. Copy and Overlay are almost the same; the pasted image covers what is underneath. The only difference is that color number 0 (black background) is transparent when you use the Overlay option, so that the underlying image will show through. The Average option calculates the color by averaging the color of the original image with the color of the pasted image. This only makes sense for images that have a grayscale palette or other palette that has continuous shades of color. Click on Copy. A box will appear. Move this box to the position where you would like to place the airplane, and click the left mouse button. A copy of the airplane, which is still on the clipboard, will appear. The box will still be there, and you can move it and click to make more copies as often as you like. Each time you will have to click on a Copy/Average/Overlay option.

Just to experiment, paste an aircraft half over another aircraft using the Average option. The overlapping area will look nonsensical. Figure 5-11 shows the result. That is because the T38.GIF does not use a continuous palette. A bit later in this tutorial you will learn how to remedy this. But first let's cover the Overlay option.

Clear the screen again by setting a video mode using Mode under the Main menu. Click on Clip and Paste and paste a single aircraft onto the blank screen. Now click the right mouse button (to clear the pasting box) and select Cut again. This time cut an area including the T38 jet but also including a bit of the black background. Return to the Main menu, click on File, Open, Open GIF, and load the T38.GIF again using the Clear option. Now click on Clip and

Figure 5-11 Paste with Average
using a noncontinuous palette

Paste and paste the little T38 using the Copy option. Repeat the Paste, this time using the Overlay option. The difference should be clear. The black background that was copied to the clipboard along with the airplane shows when it is pasted back using the Copy option, but not when pasted back using the Overlay option. This is because when using the Overlay option with Paste, the color 0 background is transparent and allows the underlying image to show through. The wording of the previous statement is not accidental. What makes a color transparent for Overlay is that it is color 0, not that it is black.

Using Color Palettes

Now return to the Main menu and select File, Open, Open GIF, and click on T38.GIF. (If you loaded the image at 640x480 the previous time, you might try 320x200 this time so you can see the result of scaling the image to a lower resolution. As you can see, a lot of detail is lost.) Improces displays the palette colors in a strip on the top of the Main menu. Have a look at the palette strip at the top. The palette is made up of colors in a random order.

Return to the Main menu and select Color. The Color menu gives you access to a number of tools for manipulating color palettes. Click on Palettes, and then Col2Gray. Click on Yes to accept the changes. This will convert the color T38 image to grayscale. Many Improces functions that do not work with images that have random-looking palettes like the original colored T38.GIF work just fine in grayscale. The palette strip at the top of the Main menu now looks like a continuous streak of gray graduated from dark to light. The Palettes menu should still be on the screen. If it is not, go back to the Main menu using the right mouse button, click on Color and then Palettes. Try out some of the built-in palettes of Improces. They are called Default, Ice, Heat, Green, and Sun. Notice what they do to the grayscale T38 image. The result should look quite reasonable because these palettes have colors that go from dark to light.

Try repeating the Cut and Paste exercise above on the grayscale image T38.GIF. Cut out an airplane, and paste it back on top of the original image. Try the Average option again. This time it makes sense. The result of pasting the airplane looks rather like a double exposure. This effect is useful in the same circumstances where a double exposure might be used by a photographer; to have semitransparent ghostly objects in an image.

Improces has a palette-sorting option that will allow you to keep the colors of your images and still use the image-processing functions of Improces without having to convert the image to grayscale first. This option sorts the colors in the palette from dark to light. The image will look the same, but the order of the colors in the palette will look different.

Return once again to the Main menu and select File, Open, Open GIF, and click on T38.GIF. Notice the palette shown at the top of the screen is made up of colors in a random order. Click on Color and then Sort. Improces will report to you that it is sorting the palette. When it is done after a few seconds, the image will look the same, but the palette strip at the top of the screen will now show an orderly progression from dark to light colors. After sorting the palette, the effects under the Enhance menu will work quite well for most images. Sorting the palette also makes color cycling (rapidly rotating the colors in the image palette) look better. Color cycling is discussed a little later in this tutorial.

The Paint Tools

The Tool menu of Improces is a whole universe by itself. This menu includes a full set of painting tools for starters, and other fun features like the ability to rotate and reflect parts of images and create fractal landscapes.

To begin, reset the video mode using Mode from the Main menu to clear the screen. Setting the mode does not clear out the palette. If you still have the color palette from the T38.GIF file showing (you can tell by looking at the color bar on top of the Main menu), click on Color, Palettes, and then Default to select the colorful default palette. Finally, from the Main menu, again click on Tool and then Paint. You should now see the Paint Tool Icon menu shown in Figure 5-12.

Drawing Geometric Shapes

Near the bottom of the Icon menu is the color selector. Clicking on a color changes the current color. Refer to Figure 5-12 to help you find it. The current color is shown right under the Curve icon, which looks like a wavy line. The current color is used to draw the filled and unfilled geometric figures.

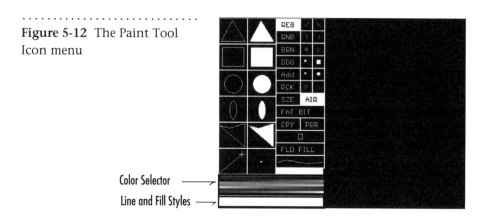

. . . .
Figure 5-12 The Paint Tool
Icon menu

Color Selector ———→
Line and Fill Styles ———→

Click on the Circle icon, and move the mouse cursor to where you want the center of the circle. Moving the mouse then increases the radius of the circle. Click the left mouse button to incorporate the circle in the image, or click the right mouse button to cancel and mark a new circle center. At any point you can get back to the Paint Tool Icon menu by clicking the right mouse button several times. Try a solid circle, and try clicking on the color selector before creating each circle to set its color. You should be able to make circles of different sizes and colors.

The other geometric shape drawing tools work in a similar way. The mouse action for drawing a rectangle is identical to the action required to clip a rectangular region on the screen, as discussed earlier in the tutorial. Click on the Rectangle icon, click where you want one corner to go, move the mouse to the other corner, and click.

The line tool keeps drawing connected line segments until told to stop by clicking the right mouse button. The action of the polygon tool is identical, except that the first and last points are connected for you when you click to stop.

At the very bottom of the Icon menu, the current line styles and fill styles show. If you click on this area, you can select various line styles (patterns and colors) and fill styles from a submenu. Figure 5-13 shows what this submenu looks like. The fill style will work with the filled shapes, and the line style works with the line and polygon tools. There are three broken-line styles and two solid-line styles. When the leftmost line style is selected, that means that one of the two solid lines on the right side will be used. The best way to understand this is to repeatedly click on the current styles to get the line and full style selector, then click the right mouse button to get back to the Tool Icon menu and draw a line to see the result.

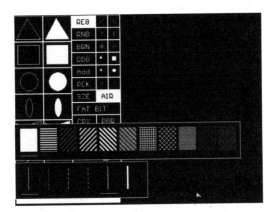

Figure 5-13 Line and fill styles

By this time you probably have created a great work of art that looks something like Figure 5-14. OK, maybe it's not art — but playing with the tools is an excellent way to learn!

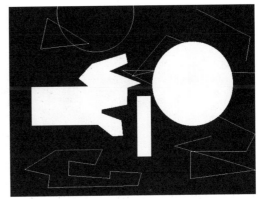

Figure 5-14 Result of the use of the geometric shape drawing tools

Flood Fill

Go back out to the Main menu and clear the screen using the Mode menu. Come back to the Paint Tool Icon menu by clicking on Tool and Paint. Make two fairly large unfilled objects, say a square and a rectangle. Make them overlap so the screen is divided into four total regions, counting the outside. (Just how you do this is not critical.) For some real fun, click on the Flood Fill icon, which is the word Fld Fill. The Flood Fill options menu will come up. This menu is shown in Figure 5-15. The Regular flood fill is useful but is a lot less fun than Gradient, so go ahead and select Gradient. Then select Circular. The Gradient option causes the flood fill to fill with a whole rainbow of colors. The Circular direction means that the colors will change outward from the seed point of the fill. The Shaggy option adds irregularities — try it with and without and see how you like it. Click on Continue and the flood fill options menu will vanish. Then click inside one of the regions defined by the objects you drew. That region should then fill up with a rainbow of colors. If you click on any more regions, they will fill up the same way. Rather than do that, click the right mouse button to get back to the Paint Tools Icon menu, click on Fld Fill again, and try the vertical option. Then repeat with the horizontal option.

Keep in mind that once a circle, square, fill, or other effect has been painted, it can no longer be independently manipulated. While there is an eraser tool, some of these are impossible to really undo. If you have turned on Undo Before Paint in Set Preferences under File, then every time you exit the Paint Tools Icon menu, you will be asked whether you want to keep the image. With a bitmap type paint program, it is possible to invest a lot of time on a complex image and destroy it all in an instant, so periodically, when your image is as you want it, you can exit from the paint tools, click Yes, and return. Of course an even more conservative approach would be to periodically save the image using the File menu.

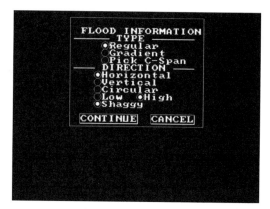

Figure 5-15 Flood Fill options

Paintbrushes

In the upper-right corner of the Paint Tools Icon menu are 12 boxes containing paintbrush shapes. Just to the left of them are four coloring modes that work with these brushes. These are named Regular, Rainbow, Burn, and Dodge. First, clear the screen to make yourself some room to work after saving your previous image (if you wish). Then, from the Main menu, click on Tool and Paint. Make sure the Reg box is turned on (reverse video — black letters on white) and the Air box is turned off. Click on one of the brushes. Move the mouse cursor to where you want to paint. Click and drag the mouse. Notice that the speed of moving the mouse makes a difference. What Improces is doing is repeatedly writing the brush pattern on the screen, so if you move the mouse fast enough, you will get separated brush marks. Click the right mouse button to lift the paintbrush off the canvas, and the left mouse button to resume painting. Click the right mouse button twice to return to the Icon menu. The brush you are using is not remembered when you go back to the menu; the brush icons are switches that turn on their brushes. Returning to the menu turns the brush off.

Try the different brush options. Burn and Dodge increase and decrease pixels that are painted over. Rainbow changes colors with time as you paint. Then try turning on the Airbrush option, which adds some random spray effect to the brush strokes.

CPY

The Paint Icon menu contains a function that is very much like copying and pasting to and from the clipboard, except that the clipboard is not involved and it can only be done within an image. This is the Cpy icon, just below the Fat Bits editor. Just to the right is the Paint icon; make sure this is turned off.

Once again, clear the screen with the Mode command and return to the Paint Tools Icon menu by clicking on Tool and Paint. Do your best to draw a small happy face. The author's attempt is shown in Figure 5-16. Click on Cpy and use the mouse exactly as you did when using the Cut command to select a rectangular area around the happy face. Then, as you move the mouse, a happy face moves with it, and every time you click the mouse a happy face is pasted. You will notice right away the absence of the Overlay option that comes with the clipboard Paste. With Cpy, the rectangular black background is pasted along with the face. If two faces are pasted too close together, the black background cuts into the face. As long as you paste images far enough apart, this is not a problem, and it is much faster than the same operation using the Paste facility under Clip. Figure 5-17 shows the result of pasting happy faces. The faces near the edge were pasted using the Cpy command. The faces near the center were placed there by using Clip→Cut to copy to the

Figure 5-16 Happy face drawn with Improces tools

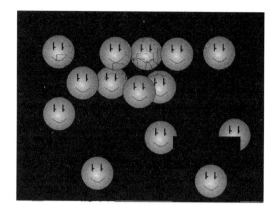

Figure 5-17 Result of pasting faces

clipboard and Clip→Paste to place in the picture using Overlay. In the lower-right corner is an example of the lack of transparency of the black background when using Cpy. You can see how the black background covers part of two happy faces.

Making Terrains

Now for something really different. Go back to the Main menu by clicking the right mouse button several times. Clear the screen using the Mode menu. Click on Tool and select Terrain. The screen will go blank. You should now define a rectangle by clicking somewhere near the upper-left corner of the screen and dragging the mouse to the lower-right and clicking again. Leave some room on the right. Now you will see a tool called the color bar that is used in a number of different Improces commands. The purpose of the color bar is to select two colors. Improces is about to create a wire-frame mountain-like image called a terrain. The first color is the "water" color, and the second color is the "mountain" color. Figure 5-18 shows the color bar you use for

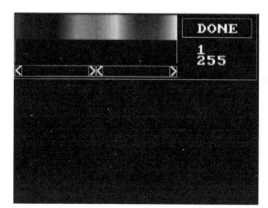

Figure 5-18 Color bar

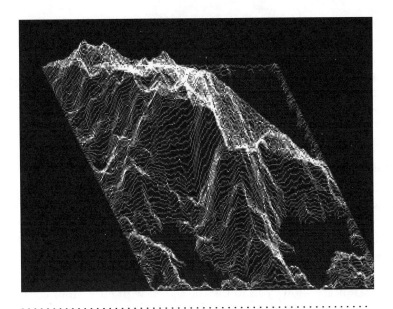

Figure 5-19 Terrain

selecting these two colors. At the top is a color-filled bar that shows the palette. The two selected colors are shown as vertical white lines in the color bar. They are initially set at the two extreme ends of the palette, 0 and 255. Under the color bar are two boxes with arrows at the ends. Holding down the left mouse button while the mouse cursor is pointing at these arrows moves the selected colors. Alternatively, you can click on either box to pick up one of the selected colors, and click the left mouse button to put it down. A pair of numbers next to the Done box let you see exactly what the selected endpoints are. When satisfied, click on Done. You will now see Improces draw the terrain. Figure 5-19 shows the result.

Making Plasma Patterns

The Plasma tool makes interesting cloud-like patterns and works exactly the same way as terrain. After clicking on Plasma, you define a rectangle with the mouse, and then select two colors. Try defining a rectangle to fill the whole screen. Once again the color bar will appear, enabling you to select two colors. In this case the two colors are the endpoints of the range of colors in the palette that will be used to make the plasma image. It works fine with the whole palette. When you click on Done, the magic begins.

You will see a grid of points plotted on the screen, and then colors will begin filling up the grid. The screen fills with a peculiar winding algorithm, which subdivides quadrants of the screen into subquadrants and is fascinating

169

to watch. The result is a very colorful cloud pattern. Now you should try cycling the colors. To do this, click the right mouse button to get back to the Main menu. Click on Color and then Cycle. You will see yet another use of the color bar. This time the two colors determine the endpoints of the range of colors that will be cycled. Once again, the effect is fine with the whole palette included. Click on Done. The colors magically ooze as you watch.

Making Wallpaper Patterns

The Enhance section of the Main menu gives you access to a number of image-processing special effects. For the most part, these require use of Improces's built-in palettes or grayscale, although you can make them work with almost any image by sorting the color palette first (load the image, then click on Color and then Sort).

To start off, try Rplcate (short for replicate), which is the last item under Enhance. Rplcate allows you to tile the screen with either four copies or two copies of the current image. When you select two copies, each copy is squished in the horizontal direction, resulting in a skinny image with an altered aspect ratio. The four-way tiling does not have this problem, since both the horizontal and vertical dimensions are halved.

To try this function, go to the File menu, click on Open, then Open GIF, and use the file picker to locate the file TIME.GIF. Load this image. Use the 640x480 mode if it is supported on your board. Now click on Enhance and Rplcate. You will see a submenu with the choices 2X and 4X. Click on 4X. There will be a short pause while Improces calculates. Then four smaller versions of the clock tower will appear. Repeat this several times. Each time the number of little images is squared, and the size of each image is reduced by half the width and half the height.

You can find a lot of really fun and interesting effects to try in the Effects submenu under Enhance. These effects show a delightful creativity on the part of the Improces author, and most of them are found only in this program.

From the Main menu, load TIME.GIF again. Remember that the Enhance effects depend on the image palette having a continuous range of colors from dark to light. Since TIME.GIF has a randomly ordered palette, you must first sort the palette. To do this, click on Color from the Main menu, and then Sort. You can also experiment with the Effects menu without first sorting the palette if you are curious to see what happens; just be forewarned that the results are somewhat unpredictable.

Now click on Enhance and then Effects. Your choices are Relief, Reverse, Solarize, Melt, Bentley, Oil, and Jiggler. You can try all of these in rapid succession. Improces will let you undo the results of each one, so you do not have to keep reloading TIME.GIF.

First click on Relief. You will see a transformation run from the top to the bottom of the image. When it is complete, you will be asked if you want to accept the image, and be given the options Yes, No, and View. Click on View to see the result, which looks as though the image were molded in sand. Then click the right mouse button to get the Yes, No, and View options back, and press No. The original TIME.GIF will be restored and you can try the other options. Try them all. Reverse makes a negative; Solarize is a half-negative, half-positive; Melt looks like water dripping down the image like rain on a window; Bentley is pseudo-3D effect; and Oil breaks the image up into patches that look a lot like an oil painting. These effects are shown in Figure 5-20.

Finally there is Jiggler. This effect is unique to Improces, and can be very amusing. While viewing TIME.GIF, click on Jiggler in the Effects menu. You will be prompted to select five small areas on the screen. Click on the spot just above and to the left of the clock face, and drag the mouse to the lower right, framing the face. Click on the left mouse button. Repeat this step for four other areas of the image. You might try the Roman numerals on the clock. When done, click the right mouse button. (If you select all five possible areas of the image, the effect will begin by itself.) The selected parts of the image will start to vibrate in an animated dance on your computer screen!

Relief

Negative

Figure 5-20 The results of various effects

Solarize

Melt

Bentley

Oil

Figure 5-20 (*continued*) The results of various effects

IMPROCES COMMAND REFERENCE

The File Menu

Save GIF

Save image as GIF file.

Menu Access: File→Save→Save GIF

Description: Enter the file name to save as, which may include the full path. Press (ENTER) or the left mouse button. Press (ESC) or the right mouse button to abandon the save. If the file already exists, Improces will ask if you want to overwrite it.

The .GIF extension will automatically be used, even if you enter another file extension. The image is saved in the resolution of the current video mode.

When to Use: Save your image as a GIF file when you want to process the file in one of the other Image Lab programs. Since Improces can load PCX files, this function can be used to convert from PCX to GIF.

Limitations: The GIF file can only be one of the resolutions supported by the Improces video driver. If Save GIF is used as part of a procedure to convert a PCX file to GIF as in the example below, and the PCX file is an odd resolution, Improces cannot convert it to a GIF file of the same resolution.

Example: The following actions will convert a PCX file to GIF. From the Main menu, click on File, click on Open, click on Open PCX, and use the file picker to select a PCX file. Click on the file name. You will then see the Image Information screen. Click on Clear (to make the image replace any current image on the screen), and click on the desired resolution. The image will then be displayed. Click the right mouse button to return to the Main menu. Then click on File, Save, and Save GIF. Enter the GIF file name and press (ENTER) or the left mouse button.

See Also: Save PCX
    Save PRF
    Open GIF

....

Save PCX
Save image as PCX file.

Menu Access: File→Save→Save PCX

Description: Enter the file name to save as, which may include the full path. Press (ENTER) or the left mouse button. Press (ESC) or the right mouse button to abandon the save. If the file already exists, Improces will ask if you want to overwrite it. The .PCX extension will automatically be used, even if you enter another file extension. The image is saved in the resolution of the current video mode.

When to Use: Save your image as a PCX file when you want to process the file in other software that supports that format. Since Improces can load GIF files, this function can be used to convert from GIF to PCX.

Limitations: The PCX file can only be one of the resolutions supported by the Improces video driver. If Save PCX is used as part of a procedure to convert a GIF file to PCX, as in the example below, and the GIF file is an odd resolution, Improces cannot convert it to a PCX file of the same resolution.

Example: The following actions will convert a GIF file to PCX. From the Main menu, click on File, click on Open, click on Open GIF, and use the file picker to select a GIF file. Click on the file name. You will then see the Image Information screen. Click on Clear (to make the image replace any current image on the screen) and click on the desired resolution. The image will then be displayed. Click the right mouse button to return to the Main menu. Then click on File, Save, and Save PCX. Enter the PCX file name and press (ENTER) or the left mouse button.

See Also: Save GIF
Save PRF
Open PCX

....

Save PRF

Save image as PRF file.

Menu Access: File→Save→Save PRF

Description: This is an option included for programmers who wish to use Improces to draw images and save them for use with the Fastgraph Programmers Library from Ted Gruber Software.

After entering the name of the file to save, define the area to save by rubber-banding a rectangle around the region to save and then clicking the left mouse button to continue or the right mouse button to abandon the save. Improces will then show you the dimensions of the image (Fastgraph requires you to have this, so be sure to write it down) and then gives you the option of micro-adjusting the width and length. Click the Done button to save the image or click Cancel to abort the save.

When to Use: The PRF format is for programmers who want to include image files created by Improces in programs they write that utilize the Fastgraf graphics library from Ted Gruber Softw are.

Limitations: Only registered users may use images created by Improces in their Fastgraph programs.

See Also: Save GIF
Save PCX
Open PCX

....

Open GIF

Open a GIF file.

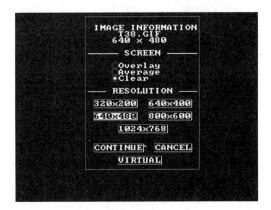

Figure 5-21 The Image
Information control panel

Menu Access: File→Open→Open GIF

Description: After you click on Open GIF, the Improces file picker window will open. This window displays the file names of GIF files in the current directory, as well as subdirectory names. You can navigate up or down your disk's directory tree by clicking on directory names. Select the GIF file you wish to open by clicking on the file name.

After you select a file to load, you will be presented with an Image Information Control Panel that will give you the Image name, Image dimensions, Current Screen Resolution, and the Overlay and Average options. Figure 5-21 shows this window.

You have four options that control how the image is loaded: Overlay, Average, Clear, and Resolution.

1. Overlay does not clear the image on the screen. Color 0 (which is usually black in the palette) is treated as a transparent color. Parts of the overlayed image of color 0 allow the underneath image to show through. Use this option if you want to do things like overlaying planets with black backgrounds on top of landscapes.

2. Average does not clear the image on the screen. Instead it takes an average of the pixel being loaded with the one on the screen as the image is loaded. The palette is loaded from the incoming image.

3. Clear will clear the screen and load the new image fresh.

4. The Resolution options will let you change video modes before you load the image. You may display any resolution image in any of the available resolutions. If the image you want to display is larger then the screen size, it will be scaled to fit as it is loaded.

Click on Continue to continue with loading the image, or click on Cancel to cancel the loading of the image or click on any of the Resolution options.

Click on Virtual to load the image into a virtual screen. (See the the Move/ Create command below for more about virtual screens.)

When to Use: The GIF format is a good medium of exchange between the different Image Lab programs. You can use Open GIF to load in and edit images saved from the other programs. You can also use the Overlay feature to make composite images.

Limitations: No matter what their original dimensions, files must be converted to the dimensions of one of the supported video modes. Opening images larger than the dimensions of the selected video mode will cause a loss of information. The image is rescaled as it is loaded.

When using the Average and Overlay options, the palette of the overlayed image replaces the previous palette, altering the colors of the original image. The Average option only makes sense when using palettes with continuously varying colors.

Example: The following actions will convert a PCX file to GIF. From the Main menu, click on File, click on Open, click on Open PCX, and use the file picker to select a PCX file. Click on the file name. You will then see the image information screen. Click on Clear (to make the image replace any current image on the screen) and click on the desired resolution. The image will then be displayed. Click the right mouse button to return to the Main menu. Then click on File, Open, and Open GIF. Enter the GIF file name and press (ENTER) or the left mouse button.

See Also: Open PCX
Open TGA
Open PRF
Save GIF

....

Open PCX

Open image as PCX file.

Menu Access: File→Open→Open PCX

Description: Open PCX works exactly like the Open GIF format above, except that it opens PCX files instead of GIF files.

See Also: Open GIF
Open TGA

Open PRF
Save PCX

....

Open TGA

Open image as Targa file.

Menu Access: File→Open→Open TGA

Description: Open TGA works exactly like the Open GIF format above, except that it opens TGA files instead of GIF files. Improces supports the Type II uncompressed Targa format. Since this is a true-color format, Improces analyzes the image and creates a color palette. Once loaded in Improces, some of the color information is lost, and the image cannot be resaved as a Targa file.

See Also: Open GIF
Open PCX
Open PRF

....

Open PRF

Open image as PRF file.

Menu Access: File→Open→Open PRF

Description: Loading a PRF file is slightly different than the other formats. After the file to load is selected, a check is made to see if the image has a header file (if it was it was saved by Improces). If so, the image dimensions will then be checked. If it is too wide or too long for the current video mode, it will not be loaded. If no header file is found, you will be prompted for the image dimensions (only the width is actually used) and the format the image is saved in. The image will then load from the bottom-left corner of the screen without clearing the screen first.

When to Use: This option is included for programmers who wish to open images saved in the PRF format used by the Fastgraph Programmers Library from Ted Gruber Software.

Limitations: The Overlay and Average options are not supported for PRF files.

See Also: Open GIF
Save PRF
Open PCX

....
Set Current Drive
Set the default disk drive.

Menu Access: File→C:>

Description: Right after Open on the File menu, Improces reports the current disk drive that applies for Load and Save operations. If you click on the disk drive letter, you will see a drop-down list of drives. Click on one of these to change drives.

When to Use: Use this option before saving or loading files to or from a drive other than the current default drive.

Limitations: The list of possible drives may include drives that do not exist on your computer. If you select one of these, Improces will report an error.

....
Memory
Display current memory status.

Menu Access: File→Memory

Description: This command shows the status of three kinds of memory in your computer: base memory, EMS memory, and XMS memory. The base memory is conventional memory below 640K. The number of EMS pages available indicates whether there is any expanded memory that Improces can access. Expanded memory was originally made available through memory add-on boards that supported the Lotus-Intel memory specification. Now that 80386-based computers are common, you are more likely to have expanded memory available as the result of the use of a 386 memory manager such as QEMM386, 386Max, or the EMM386.SYS driver that comes with DOS 5. XMS memory is memory above 1 MB that is made available by the Microsoft HIMEM.SYS driver or equivalent.

Improces can use these kinds of memory to store images in the clipboard and to preserve copies of images so that operations can be undone.

When to Use: Use the Memory command to monitor the status of your memory when you are setting up your computer configuration and tuning the Improces settings for optimum results.

Limitations: The amount of available XMS memory is not shown, but only whether the XMS driver is detected.

Example: Figure 5-22 shows the results of the Memory command when running Improces in a DOS window under Windows 3.0. In this case the EMS pages are provided by Windows' own memory manager.

. . . .

Figure 5-22 The Memory status
report

See Also: Set Preferences

. . . .

About

Access information about Improces.

Menu Access: File→About

Description: Click on About to see the Improces author's address, registration information, and technical information about Improces.

When to Use: The About screen is handy when you would like to register the software or contact the author.

Limitations: The About screen does not report the version of Improces you are using.

See Also: Save PCX

. . . .

Set Pref (Set Preferences)

Set Improces defaults.

Menu Access: File→Set Pref

Description: The Set Preferences command allows you to control whether or not images are saved, so you can undo changes; what video modes are shown in video mode menus; and what kind of memory Improces uses. Figure 5-23 shows the Preferences screen.

Undo Before Paint
The first option is to turn On or Off Undo Before Paint. When this is set On, the on-screen image is saved before you enter the Paint menu. Setting this On is a good idea, because it will let you undo changes that you don't want when

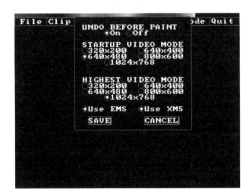

File Clip · de Quit

Figure 5-23 The Set Preferences options

you use the Paint menu. The only reason to turn Off Undo Before Paint is if you have limited XMS or EMS memory so that Improces has to save the screen to disk, and you are short of disk space. If this option is turned On, Improces will ask if you want to keep the changes you made when you exit the Paint menu, giving you a chance to back out if you have made alterations in the image that you not want to keep.

Startup Video Mode

The next option lets you set the startup video mode. This controls the video mode that the program sets when it is started. The 640x480 mode is a good choice if your graphics board supports it. It is very common and has square pixels, which means that the number of pixels per unit length on your monitor is the same horizontally and vertically. The normal default mode is the 320x200 256-color mode that is present on every VGA board. If you accidentally set the startup mode to a value illegal for your hardware, and you can't run Improces, just delete the file IMPROCES.CFG and the startup mode will revert to the default value.

Highest Video Mode

This option controls the highest video mode that shows in the Modes menu and in the Load File menus. Look at your video board documentation to see what video modes your board supports. This is a safety feature for people whose video card does not support all of the modes that Improces can support.

Use EMS and Use XMS

Click on the appropriate button to toggle the use of either type of memory On or Off. EMS is expanded memory that is made available if you have an expanded memory add-on board or if you are using an expanded memory manager such as QEMM386, 386Max, or the EMM386.SYS driver that comes with DOS 5.0. XMS memory is extended memory that is made available using the HIMEM.SYS driver in your CONFIG.SYS file. You can click on Memory under

File to see what kind of memory Improces has detected on your system. The main purpose of these options is to turn Off one or both of these memory options if you are experiencing problems. You can keep them both On, and Improces will attempt to use both EMS and XMS. Improces will create temporary files if neither XMS or EMS memory is available. The advantage of using either EMS or XMS memory is faster program operation, as well as freeing up disk space not needed for temporary files.

Clicking on Save will save the parameters you set up in a file called IMPROCES.CFG. The settings will then take effect each time you use Improces.

When to Use: Use the Set Preferences menu when you first run Improces. Once you have set the options to fit your computer setup to your satisfaction, there is no reason to change them unless your computer hardware or software configuration changes. If you purchase a new video graphics adapter or install a 386 memory manager, you should check to see if any of the preferences you have set need to be changed.

Limitations: Even though you set the maximum video mode properly, it does not mean that all the listed video modes are legal. For example, not all video boards support the 640x400 mode even though they support higher-resolution modes. You should not attempt to select modes not supported by your hardware. While this will not generally cause any problem, attempting an illegal video mode could conceivably cause damage to your monitor.

Example: Suppose you have a Super VGA graphics board with 512K of memory, and an 80386 computer with 4 MB of RAM and 3 MB of disk space free. You should turn Save Before Paint On, because you have plenty of RAM and disk space. The 1024x768 256-color mode is not supported by your board, since that mode requires 1 MB of graphics memory; so the maximum video mode should be set for 640x480. If you have DEVICE=HIMEM.SYS in your CONFIG.SYS file, XMS memory should be available, so you should turn On XMS. You should also turn On EMS if you have a 386 memory manager, or run Improces under Windows 3.0, which makes EMS available in DOS windows.

See Also: Memory

....

Move/Create

Move or create a virtual screen.

Menu Access: File→Virtual→Move/Create

Description: Normally the images you edit with Improces are the exact dimensions of one of the supported video modes, such as 640x480. You can load an

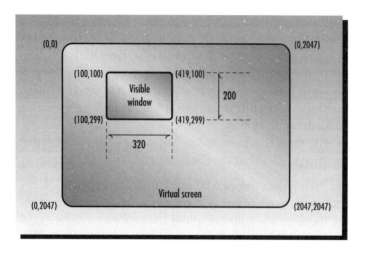

Figure 5-24 The relationship between the virtual screen and the visible window

image using a virtual screen instead of a regular video mode. A virtual screen is memory area that can store an image larger than your video screen. You can see and edit a 320x200 section of the virtual screen. Using this feature you can edit images as large as 2048x2048 pixels. Figure 5-24 shows the relationship between the virtual screen and the visible window.

The Move/Create option lets you convert from a normal video mode to a virtual screen video mode. Once you are using a virtual screen, the Move/Create function allows you to move the 320x200 pixel window so that you can view and edit different parts of the virtual screen.

Creating a Virtual Screen

If you are not currently using a virtual screen, you will see the prompt Not in a Virtual Mode. Switch to a virtual mode? The options are Yes, View, and No. If you click on the View option, the dialog box will disappear and let you see the current image. You can return to the Yes/View/No dialogue box by clicking the right mouse button. If you click on the No option, you are returned to the previous menu.

If you click on the Yes option, and you are in a high-resolution mode, you will see the prompt Save current screen to virtual mode or clear screen? The options are Save, Clear, and View. If you select Save, a virtual screen will be created that is the same size as the current image, which will then be copied to the virtual screen. If you select Clear, the current image is erased and you will be prompted to select the size of the virtual screen. Table 5-2 shows the possible sizes for your virtual screen and the amount of disk space needed for each size.

. . . .

Virtual Screen Size	Amount of Free Disk Space Required
512x512	262,144 bytes — 256K
640x400	256,000 bytes — 250K
640x480	307,200 bytes — 255K
800x600	480,000 bytes — 469K
1024x768	786,432 bytes — 768K
1024x1024	1,048,576 bytes — 1 MB
2048x2048	4,194,304 bytes — 4 MB

Table 5-2 Virtual screen sizes and disk space requirements

After you are done editing in virtual mode, you can change back to a video mode the same size as or larger then the virtual screen and continue editing.

Moving around the Virtual Screen

When you are using a virtual screen, you can apply Improcess editing functions to the visible 320x200 window of the larger virtual screen. You can move this window and edit a different part of the virtual screen using the Move/Create option. If you select Move/Create when you are using a virtual screen, you are asked if you want to "Save the changes made to this portion of the Virtual Screen." If you click on Yes, the changes will be saved. If you click on No, the changes won't be saved, and the virtual screen will be returned to its original state. After you answer, Improces will change to a mode that allows you to move the visible 320x200 window to view a different section of the virtual screen. The current coordinates of the physical screen's top-left corner are shown at the top of the screen. Press the left mouse button or (ENTER) key when the area you want to edit shows on the screen. Rolling the mouse will move you 20 pixel rows or columns at a time. You can also use keystrokes shown in Table 5-3.

When to Use: Virtual screens are useful for making detailed changes to images. If you have a 1024x768 image you wish to edit, you could use a 1024x768 video mode. By using a 1024x768 virtual screen instead, you will see a small 320x200 portion of the image magnified to fill your computer screen. This will allow you to make detailed edits. You can also use virtual screens to edit images much larger than the highest resolution video mode possible with your graphics adapter.

Key	Action
(←)	1 column left
(→)	1 column right
(↓)	1 row down
(↑)	1 row up
(CTRL) - (←)	20 columns left
(CTRL) - (→)	20 columns right
(CTRL) - (↓)	20 rows down
(CTRL) - (↑)	20 rows up
(PGUP)	200 rows up
(PGDN)	200 rows down
(HOME)	top left of screen
(END)	bottom right of screen
(CTRL) - (END)	320 columns left
(CTRL) - (PGDN)	down 320 columns right

Table 5-3 Keystrokes for moving the visible window around the virtual screen

Limitations: Not all Improces functions work with virtual screens, and other commands are limited to the visible window.

Under the Color menu, the commands Re-Align, Sort, Menu Adjust, Reduce, Make 8/16/32/64/128, Palette, Col2Grey, and Grayscale do not work with virtual screens. These color commands require Improces to scan the entire image, which is not all available in memory at one time.

The Halftone command under the Color menu and all the options under Effects do work, but are limited to the visible window.

See Also: Virtual→Clear
Virtual→View

View

View a virtual screen.

Menu Access: File→Virtual→View

Description: View will scale the entire virtual screen into 320x200 so that you can view it in its entirety. Press the right mouse button when done viewing.

When to Use: Use View to get an impression of the effects of your edits on the whole image when using a virtual screen.

Limitations: View always uses the 320x200 video mode, so your image will be viewed at a lower resolution with much less detail than is actually contained in the image.

See Also: Virtual→Move/Create
Virtual→Clear

....

Clear

Clear a virtual screen.

Menu Access: File→Virtual→Clear

Description: The Clear command will clear the virtual screen and move the 320x200 physical screen window to the top-left corner of the virtual screen.

When to Use: Use Clear to wipe out the current image in the virtual screen and begin work on a new virtual screen image.

See Also: Virtual→Move/Create
Virtual→View

The Clip Menu

The next set of commands ia accessed under the Clip menu item in the Main menu. Improces includes a clipboard for cutting and pasting between images. You can cut pieces of images, which are stored in the clipboard, and then paste them back into the same image or into other images. The cut-and-paste operations use the mouse and are very easy to control. The pasting operation has Overlay and Average options that give you alternative ways the pasted image is combined with the underlying image.

....

Cut

Copy part of image to clipboard.

Menu Access: Clip→Cut

Description: This command is really a Copy command rather than a Cut, since the area copied is not erased. Suppose you want to copy a rectangular area of the current image to the clipboard. After you click on Cut to activate this command, move the mouse cursor to a corner of the area of the image that you wish to copy, and click the left mouse button. The cursor will disappear, and you will see a rectangle as you move the mouse. One corner of the rectangle is fixed to the spot where you clicked, and the other moves as you move the mouse. When the rectangular box covers the area that you want to copy to the clipboard, click the left mouse button to copy the framed area, or click the right mouse button to cancel the operation. If you clicked the left button, then the selected area has been copied to the clipboard and is available to be pasted back. If you canceled by clicking the right mouse button, then you can reset the first corner in a new location and click the left button.

When to Use: Use Cut to save parts of images that you wish to combine with other images. The Tool→Paint→Cpy command is very similar to Cut. Use Cut when you want to copy pieces of one image to another image, or when you want to paste with the Overlay or Average options. Cpy is much more convenient for copying part of an image to other places in the same image.

Limitations: No color palette information is saved with the clip file. If you cut a piece from an image and then load an image with a different palette, and then paste from the first image, the clip image will most likely look a little different then expected because the palette is different.

Example: Load the file TIME.GIF and clip out the clock face. To do this, back out to the Main menu (if it is not showing) by clicking the right mouse button as many times as necessary. Click on File, Open, Open GIF, and use the file picker to select TIME.GIF. (You may need to use the file picker to change directories, depending on where you placed the TIME.GIF file that comes with the companion disk.) Then click on Cut, and place the mouse above the clock face and to the left of it. Click the left mouse button, and move the mouse down and to the right until the framing rectangle covers the clock face. Click the left mouse button and the clock face will be copied to the clipboard. Your next step would be either to save the clipboard to a file or paste it onto an image. This is a good way to create your own library of clip art.

See Also: Tool→Paint→Cpy
　　　　　　Clip→Paste
　　　　　　Clip→Save

．．．．．．．．．．．．．．．．．．．．

Paste

Paste clipboard image onto an image.

Menu Access: Clip→Paste

Description: The Paste command allows you to combine a clipboard image onto an image. (You can use the Cut command to copy an image into the clipboard, or the Open command to load the clipboard from a file.) After clicking on Paste to activate the Paste command, a box will appear, corresponding to the size of the image in the clipboard. Use the mouse to position this box over the

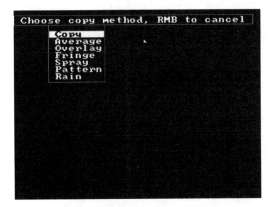

Figure 5-25 Paste options

area where you want to paste the clipboard image, and click the left mouse button. You will then have a choice as to what type of paste you want to do, Copy, Overlay, or Average. Figure 5-25 shows the submenu with these choices as it appears over the underlying image. Copy will replace all pixels in the covered area with the clipboard image. Average will average all noncolor 0 pixels in the clip image with the area it is going to copy over, in effect merging the clipboard image with the underlying image. Overlay will copy all pixels except those of color 0. This means that areas of the clipboard image that have color 0 are transparent, and will allow the underlying image to show through.

When to Use: The Tool→Paint→Cpy command is very similar to Cut and Paste. Use Cut and Paste when you want to copy pieces of one image to another image, or when you want to paste with the Overlay or Average options. Cpy is much more convenient for copying part of an image to other places in the same image.

Use the Overlay option to paste objects that are not rectangular by making use of the transparency of color 0. Use the Copy option to paste rectangular images. Use the Average option to merge the pasted image with the background.

Limitations: The clipboard does not save the palette, so the palette of the underlying image is used. This means that the pasted image might look very different than it did originally. The effect of the Average option is particularly sensitive to the underlying palette. It works best with continuously varying palettes, such as the built-in palettes you can set with the Color-Palette command. You can tell if a palette is continuous or not by looking at the palette strip at the top of the Main menu. If the colors in that strip merge smoothly into one another, then the Average option will probably work well.

Figure 5-26 The result of the three Paste options

Example: Figure 5-26 shows the result of using the Copy, Overlay, and Average options when pasting a clipboard image. The clipboard image is a sphere on a black background of color 0. The Copy option pastes the ball with the rectangular background. The Overlay option allows the plasma image to show through the background. Finally the Average option merges the ball into the plasma background so that it is barely perceptible. The effect of Average is very dependent on the color of the ball and the color of the area where the ball is pasted.

See Also: Tool→Paint→Cpy
Clip→Cut
Clip→Save
Clip→Open

Save

Save the current contents of the clipboard to a file.

Menu Access: Clip→Save

Description: This command copies the clipboard to a file in the current directory with the .CLB extension.

When to Use: Use Clip→Save to create your own clip art collection to use for pasting into your images.

Limitations: The clipboard does not contain a palette, so the appearance of the saved image may look different when it is restored to the clipboard and pasted onto an image.

See Also: Clip→Cut
Clip→Open
Clip→Paste

....

Open

Copy the contents of a previously saved file to the clipboard.

Menu Access: Clip→Open

Description: This command copies a *.CLB file into the clipboard, after which it can be pasted into images.

When to Use: Use Clip→Open to use your own clip art collection for pasting into images.

Limitations: The clipboard does not contain a palette, so the appearance of the saved image may look different when it is restored to the clipboard and pasted onto an image.

See Also: Clip→Cut
Clip→Save
Clip→Paste

....

View

View the clipboard contents.

Menu Access: Clip→View

Description: The View command will display the contents of the clipboard in the upper-left corner. After displaying the clipboard, click either the left mouse button or the right mouse button to return to the menu.

When to Use: Use View when you want to see how the clipboard image will look with the current palette, since the clipboard does not have its own palette. This allows you to preview the effect of the Paste command.

See Also: Clip→Open
           Clip→Save
           Clip→Cut
           Clip→Paste
           Clip→ReMap Pal

The Tool Menu

Improces includes many standard and a few nonstandard drawing tools. The functions you can access under the Tool menu range all the way from standard painting tools to fractal plasma and landscape generators.

....

Paint

Access Paint tools.

Menu Access: Tool→Paint

Description: The Paint command brings up an Icon menu that gives you access to a whole collection of painting tools. Figure 5-27 shows the menu with a key to what each section of the menu does. The menu allows you to:

1. Access filled and unfilled triangle, rectangle, circle, ellipse, polygon, line, and point tools.

2. Set a switch to select regular, rainbow, burn, or dodge brushes.

3. Access a text tool and set font controls.

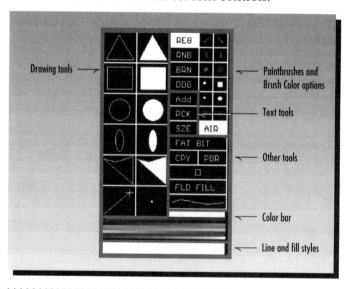

Figure 5-27 Paint Tools Icon menu

190

4. Turn on or off the air brush.

5. Toggle between regular copy and paintbrush.

6. Access the Fat Bit editor.

7. Use an eraser.

8. Generate curves.

9. Select colors, line styles, and fill patterns.

Each of these will be explained in detail below. As you can see, the Paint Tool menu allows you to access the features of a whole paint program from just this one menu!

Drawing Tools

The drawing tools allow you to draw filled or unfilled geometric shapes. In addition, you can set fill types and line styles that apply to the shapes. For each tool, the name of the tool is given, then the icon used to access the tool, and then a description of the procedure for using the tool. Figure 5-28 shows the Paint Tools Icon menu with the drawing tool icons highlighted.

Current Fill Pattern and Line Style

Set the current fill pattern and line style.

Menu Icon: **Current fill pattern and current line style (bottom of menu)**

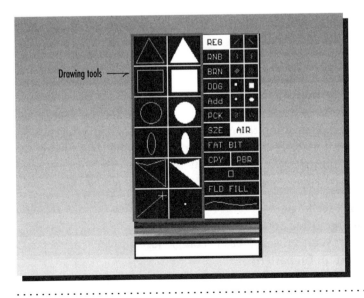

Figure 5-28 Drawing tool icons

Procedure: At the bottom of the Paint Icon menu, you can set the fill pattern and line style. The filled drawing tool shapes use the fill pattern that is shown on the bottom of the menu. The line and the polygon tools both use the line style shown just below the current fill pattern.

To change the current fill pattern or the current line style, click in the current pattern box at the bottom of the menu. Two windows will appear, one with all of the possible fill patterns and one with the possible line styles. The current fill pattern and the current line style will be underlined. The line style has four possible patterns and two possible thicknesses. Click on a new pattern or line style to change them. Click the right mouse button to return to the icon menu.

Triangle
Draw an unfilled triangle.

Menu Icon: **Large unfilled triangle**

Procedure: Move the mouse to where you want one side of the triangle to begin, and press the left mouse button. Reposition the side until it is where you want it and click the left mouse button (or right mouse button to cancel). Now define the other two sides of the triangle by moving the mouse until the triangle is the desired size, and click the left mouse button. Either draw another triangle as before, or click the right mouse button to return to the menu.

Filled Triangle
Draw a filled triangle.

Icon: **Large filled triangle**

Procedure: Works the same as Triangle (see above). The triangle is filled with the current fill pattern.

Rectangle
Draw an unfilled rectangle.

Icon: **Large empty square**

Procedure: Move the mouse to a corner of the rectangle and click the left mouse button. Reposition the rectangle until it is where you want it, and click the left mouse button. Either draw another rectangle (as before) or click the right mouse button to return to the menu.

Filled Rectangle
Draw a filled rectangle.

Icon: **Large filled square**

Procedure: Works the same as Rectangle (see above). The rectangle is filled with the current fill pattern.

Circle
Draw a circle.

Icon: **Large empty circle**

Procedure: Move the mouse to the spot you want to be the center of the circle, and click the left mouse button. Resize the circle until it is the desired size, and click the left mouse button or the right mouse button to cancel. Either draw another circle (as before), or click the right mouse button to return to the menu.

Filled Circle

Draw a circle.

Icon: **Large filled circle**

Procedure: Works the same as Circle (see above). The circle is filled with the current fill pattern.

Ellipse

Draw an ellipse.

Icon: **Large empty ellipse**

Procedure: Move the mouse to the spot you want to be the center of the ellipse, and click the left mouse button. Resize the ellipse until it is the desired size, and click the left mouse button or the right mouse button to cancel. Either draw another ellipse (as before), or click the right mouse button to return to the menu. Note: An ellipse differs from a circle in that its x and y radius can be different.

Filled Ellipse

Draw a filled ellipse.

Icon: **Large filled ellipse**

Procedure: Works the same as Ellipse (see above). The ellipse is filled with the current fill pattern.

Poly

Draw a polygon.

Icon: **Large rhombus**

Procedure: Move the mouse to where you want the line to begin, and click the left mouse button. Reposition the line until it is where you want it, and click the left mouse button (or right mouse button to cancel). You can continue drawing from where you left off, or click the right mouse button to stop drawing and reposition the cursor to draw another line or click the right mouse button to go back to the menu. When you finish, the last point is automatically connected to the first.

Filled Poly

Draw a filled polygon.

Icon: **Large filled rhombus**

Procedure: Works the same as Polygon (see above). The polygon is filled with the current fill pattern.

Line

Draw a series of connected line segments.

Icon: **Diagonal line with a + at the end**

Procedure: Move the mouse to where you want the line to begin and click the left mouse button. Reposition the line until it is where you want it, and click the left mouse button (or right mouse button to cancel). You can continue drawing from where you left off, or click the right mouse button to stop drawing and reposition the cursor to draw another line or click the right mouse button to go back to the menu.

Point

Fills the pixel the mouse is pointing to with the current color.

Icon: **Point in center of box**

Procedure: Click the left mouse button to start drawing. Keep drawing until you click the right mouse button. Click the right mouse button again to return to the menu, or click the left mouse button to start drawing again.

Paintbrushes and Brush Color Options

A brush is a pattern that can be moved with the mouse on the screen, leaving a colored trail. The action of a brush depends on the brush pattern selected, on four switches that control how the colors applied by a brush are determined, on the current color, and on the Airbrush toggle. Painting with brushes is also sensitive to the speed of moving the brush with the mouse. The best way to get a feel for what the brushes and brush options do is to try them out and see for yourself. There are a lot of combinations to try out. Consider yourself lucky — some of these effects would be very difficult to achieve with real brushes and paint!

Brushes and brush switches are selected by clicking on the appropriate icons. Switches are highlighted when they are turned on. Figure 5-29 shows the location of the brush selection icons, the paintbrush option switch icons, the Airbrush toggle icon, and the color selector area.

Brushes

Select brush type.

Icon: **12 icons in upper-right corner of Paint Tools Icon menu**

Procedure: Click on the desired brush, then click the left mouse button to begin drawing. Keeps drawing until the right mouse button is clicked. Click the right mouse button again to return to the menu, or click the left mouse button to start painting again. The colors applied by the brush are altered by the different toggles which are discussed next.

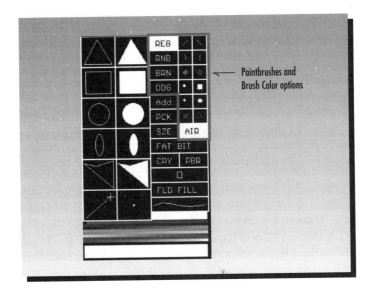

Figure 5-29 Brush selection, brush switch icons, and color selector

Airbrush Switch

Turn Airbrush action On or Off.

Icon: **Air**

Procedure: When the Airbrush switch is On (the Air icon will be in reverse video — black on white background), the brush you use will not color every brush point on the brush. Instead random points will be colored, like a spray can. Click on the Air button to toggle the switch.

Regular Brush Switch

When On, brush applies the current color.

Icon: **Reg**

Procedure: Click the Reg icon to turn this toggle on, then select a Brush icon (see Brushes above) and paint. The painting action will leave a pattern based on the brush you selected, and using the current color.

Rainbow Brush Switch

When On, changes the color as the brush is moved.

Icon: **Rnb**

Procedure: Click the Rnb icon to turn this switch On, then select a Brush icon (see Brushes above) and paint. The color will start with the current color, and increment one color at a time through the palette as the brush moves.

Burn Brush Switch
When On, increments the color as the pixels are repainted.
   Icon: **Brn**
   Procedure: Click the Brn icon to turn this switch On, then select a brush icon (see Brushes above) and paint. When you paint over the same area, the color number is incremented, having the effect of burning in the area if the palette has darker colors assigned to lower palette numbers. This has the opposite effect from the Dodge Brush switch. The result is very dependent on the current palette. You can get an idea of the effect by looking at the color selector at the bottom of the Paint Tools Icon menu. The colors of the palette are laid out in order in the color selector. Multiple brush strokes with the Burn Brush switch On will have the effect of moving the color to the right along the color selector.

Dodge Brush Switch
When On, decrements the color as the pixels are repainted.
   Icon: **Ddg**
   Procedure: Click the Ddg icon to turn this switch On, then select a Brush icon (see Brushes above) and paint. When you paint over the same area, the color number is decremented, having the effect of fading or dodging the area if the palette has darker colors assigned to lower palette numbers. This has the opposite effect from the Burn Brush switch. The result is very dependent on the current palette. You can get an idea of the effect by looking at the color selector at the bottom of the Paint Tools Icon menu. The colors of the palette are laid out in order in the color selector. Multiple brush strokes with the Dodge Brush switch On will have the effect of moving the color to the left along the color selector.

Adding Text to Images
With Improces you can add text to images. You can select a font style and font size, as well as change the color.

The Add Text mode, font style, and font size are selected by clicking on the appropriate icons. Figure 5-30 shows the location of these icons.

Add Text
Turns on Add Text mode.
   Icon: **Add**
   Procedure: Click on the Add icon. Position the cursor to where you want to start entering text and press the left mouse button. A vertical text cursor will

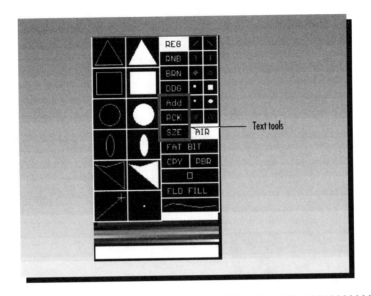

Text tools

Figure 5-30 Text control icons

appear. Enter your text. You may use the (BACKSPACE) key to back up, and the (ENTER) key to advance one line down. Press the (ESC) key (or right mouse button) to quit entering text. Then you can either add more text or press the right mouse button to return to the menu. Once you advance to the next line, you may not go back up, so make sure what you enter on the line is what you want before you press (ENTER) or (ESC).

Font Style
Select font style.
   Icon: **Pck**
   Procedure: Click on the Pck icon, and you will see a Font Styles menu that looks like Figure 5-31. To select a new font style, click in the desired fonts box. Press the right mouse button to return to the menu.

Font Size
Select font size.
   Icon: **Sze**
   Procedure: Click on the Sze icon, and you will see a Font Size menu that looks like Figure 5-32. To select a new font size, click in the desired size box. Press the right mouse button to return to the menu.

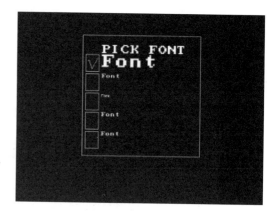

Figure 5-31 The Font Styles menu

Figure 5-32 Font Size menu

Other Tools

The remaining tools are accessed using the icons in the lower-right corner of Paint Icon menu. They include the Fat Bits editor, copy and paint facilities, eraser, flood fill, and a curve drawer. Figure 5-33 shows where the icons for these tools are located.

Fat Bits

Access Fat Bits editor.

Icon: **Fat Bit**

Procedure: The Fat Bits editor lets you edit each individual pixel of your image to make detailed corrections in your image. If you are very patient, you can build any image you want with just this one tool! The term "fat bits" comes from the ability of the editor to magnify the pixels and make them "fat" so they are easy to manipulate.

Click on the Fat Bits icon to access the editor. A rectangle will appear on the screen. Select an area to edit by moving the rectangle over the area you wish to edit using the mouse and clicking the left mouse button. Figure 5-34 shows

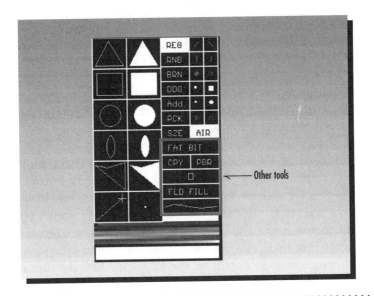

Figure 5-33 Other tools

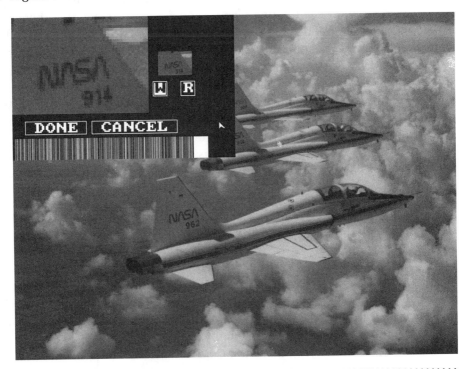

Figure 5-34 Fat Bits editor screen

what the editor screen looks like when the NASA name on an airplane in T38.GIF is selected. The area you are editing is shown twice. The larger version is the edit area, where you can alter individual pixels by pointing and clicking the mouse. The smaller version shows you the appearance of the selected area at the normal magnification. At the bottom of the Fat Bits screen is a bar that shows all the colors of the current palette. On the right end of this bar is a rectangle that is colored according to the current color. This color will be used to color any pixels you want to change. There are two edit modes, which can be set by clicking on the W and R buttons on the screen. The W stands for Write (default) and the R stands for Read. The purpose of the Read mode is to allow you to select the current color from the image itself. Click on R to change to Read mode, then point to a pixel in the edit area that has the color you want. Point to that pixel with the mouse cursor and click the left mouse button. The current color should change to that color. You can also change the current color without being in Read mode by clicking on a color on the color bar. Once the current color is the color you want, click on W to change to Write mode. In this mode every pixel in the edit area you point at and click on will change to the current color.

The point of the Read mode is that often you want to change a pixel to blend in with neighboring pixels. Suppose, for example, that there is an isolated black pixel inside a colored area. Click on R to go into Read mode. Then click on any pixel near the black imperfection to change the current colors to the background color surrounding the black pixel. Click on W to change back to Write mode, and then click on the black pixel. The formerly black pixel should now be blended into the background. Note that you don't have to use the Read mode at all if you set the current color from the color bar at the bottom.

Select Done to keep the changes or Cancel to abandon the changes. The Fat Bits editor is one of the few contexts in Improces that cannot be exited using the right mouse button; the only way to leave the editor is by clicking on Done or Cancel.

Copy

Copy and paste parts of image.

Icon: **Cpy**

Procedure: The Copy facility is very similar to the Cut and Paste of the Clip menu. The differences are that Copy is much faster, but does not have the Overlay and Average options, and can only be used to cut and paste within an image. Despite those limitations Copy is one of the really fun features of Improces, as you'll see momentarily.

Click on Cpy to invoke the Copy function. Define the area you want to copy by clicking on the upper-left corner of the area. Then, as you move the mouse, a rectangle will appear with one corner fixed where you clicked and

Figure 5-35 The Copy function

the other corner movable. Align the rectangle over the area to be copied and click the left mouse button. Now the fun starts. The mouse cursor is now a copy of the area you selected. As you move the mouse, this clipped image moves. Every time you click the left mouse button the image is pasted to that spot. It is very hard to resist the temptation of pasting pieces of the image all over the screen. When you are done pasting, click the right mouse button. You can then copy another area or click the right mouse button again to return to the menu.

Try loading TIME.GIF and using Copy to replicate the little clock face. If your use of Copy is as unrestrained as the author's, you will end up with something that looks like Figure 5-35.

If you choose a piece of image that is smaller then 32,000 bytes, the image will be erased and redrawn as the mouse is moved, as described above. If the piece of image is over 32,000 bytes, a rectangle will show where the image will be placed. 32,000 bytes is about half of a 320x200 screen. If the Copy Paintbrush switch is on, the copied piece must be less than 32,000 bytes.

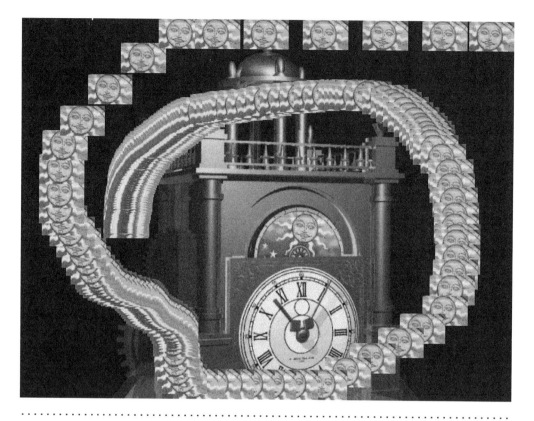

Figure 5-36 Result of Copy with Copy Paintbrush turned on

Copy Paintbrush Switch

Turns Cpy into a paintbrush.

Icon: **Prb**

Procedure: Click on Prb to turn the Copy Paintbrush toggle switch on and off. When this switch is on, the Copy function lets you define a piece of your image to use like a paintbrush. Follow the instructions for Copy above. Instead of just copying the piece of image once when the left mouse button is pressed, the piece will be copied wherever the mouse is moved, like a paintbrush. The result of using this option is shown in Figure 5-36. Note that in some places the clock face images are separated. Those are places where the mouse was moved more rapidly.

Eraser

Erase image.

Icon: **Small unfilled rectangle**

Procedure: Click on the Eraser icon. Move the eraser to where you want to erase, and press the left mouse button. The eraser keeps erasing until you press the right mouse button. Press the right mouse button again to return to the menu, or press the left mouse button to start erasing again.

Floodfill
Fill a shape.

Icon: **Fld Fll**

Procedure: Flood Fill colors all pixels in an uncolored area starting with a seed pixel until a colored boundary is reached.

To access the Flood Fill feature, click on Fld Fll. You will then be presented with the Flood Information control panel shown in Figure 5-37.

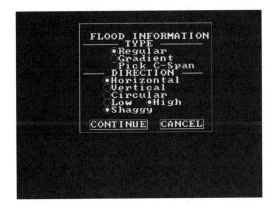

Figure 5-37 Flood Information control panel

The Flood Fill options are type and direction. The Type options are:

- Regular: Uses the current color and does a solid fill using the current color.

- Gradient: This type uses fill colors that smoothly change, depending on the current palette and colors selected with C-Span and the Direction setting, below.

- C-Span: This isn't really another type. C-Span allows you to set the endpoints of the colors that the gradient type uses. Figure 5-38 shows the color bar you use for selecting these two colors. At the top is a color-filled bar that shows the palette. The two selected colors are shown as vertical white lines in the color bar. They are initially set at the two extreme ends of the palette, 0 and 255. Under the color bar are two boxes with arrows at the ends. Holding down the left mouse button while the mouse cursor is pointing at these arrows moves the selected colors.

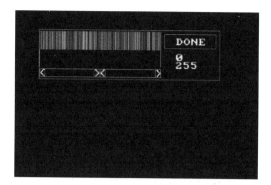

Figure 5-38 Color bar

Alternatively, you can click on either box to pick up one of the selected colors, and click the left mouse button to put it down. A pair of numbers next to the Done box let you see exactly what the selected endpoints are. When satisfied, click on Done.

The Direction options determine in what direction the colors change using the gradient fill:

- Horizontal: Colors are cycled horizontally, starting and ending colors use the Low/High and C-Span settings.

- Vertical: Colors are cycled vertically, starting and ending colors use the Low/High and C-C-Span settings.

- Circular: Colors start at the point the mouse is clicked and are cycled out in a circular fashion. This look creates a very attractive pattern.

- Low and High: Low and high are used to control which end of the palette starts when using the gradient flood.

- Shaggy: With a gradient flood, Shaggy produces a fuzzy look to the fill by randomly intermixing the neighboring colors. It is a very nice effect.

Once you are satisfied with the settings, click on Continue. Pick a seed point anywhere on the screen and click the left mouse button. All areas within a bordered area will be filled in the specified mode, either flood or gradient. While the area is being flooded, you may click the right mouse button to stop the flood. After the area is flooded, click on a new area to flood or click the right mouse button to return to the Icon Tool menu. Floodfill does not use the current fill pattern, rather it does a solid fill every time.

Curve
Draw a curved line.
   Icon: **small wavy line**

Procedure: To draw a curved line, click on the Curve icon. Then click on the locations you want for the starting and ending points of the curve. As you move the mouse, the curve will bend. Think of the line as a rubber band connecting the starting and ending points, and the mouse connected to the middle. When the curve is as you wish, click the left mouse button, or click the right mouse button to cancel. If no math chip is present on your machine, the curve is drawn in straight-line segments until it is finished, then it is plotted in its entirety. The curve uses the current color.

....

Scale

Copy and rescale a piece of an image.

Menu Access: Tool→Scale

Description: Scale operates very much like the Cpy tool in the Paint Icon menu. It allows you to copy a piece of an image and paste it elsewhere on an image. The big difference is that you can alter the size and aspect ratio of the copy.

To apply this function, click on Scale in the Tool menu. Define the source area with the mouse by clicking on the upper-left corner of the area to copy. A rectangle will appear as you move the mouse, with one corner fixed to the point where you clicked and the diagonal corner attached to the moving mouse cursor. Frame the rectangle around the source area and click the left mouse. Similarly, frame the area where you wish to paste the result. The target area can be larger or smaller than the original, and can have different proportions. Note that if the proportions are different, the cut image will be stretched appropriately to fit, altering the aspect ratio. Figure 5-39 shows several examples of the use of this function showing the possibility of expanding, shrinking, and stretching the image.

The scale operation can take some time. The larger the copied area is, the slower it will be. A disk swapfile will be used regardless of the presence of EMS or XMS memory, but only if the destination area is larger than 320x200 pixels.

When to Use: Use Scale to cut and paste when you wish to alter the size of the duplicate.

Limitations: Scale only works within an image. If you want to cut and paste between images, use the Clip functions.

See Also: Clip→Cut
Clip→Paste
Tool→Paint→Cpy

Figure 5-39 Result of the Scale function

Zoom x 2

Make a double-sized copy of a piece of an image.

Menu Access: Tool→Zoom x 2

Description: The Zoom x 2 function makes a double-sized copy of a selected area of the screen and copies it to the upper-left corner of the screen. When you click on Zoom x 2, a rectangular frame will appear on the screen. Frame the rectangle around the source area and click the left mouse button. A double-sized copy will appear. Click the right mouse button to restore the image, or the left mouse button to keep the expanded image. Click the right mouse button to return to the menu.

When to Use: Use Zoom x 2 when you want to exactly double the size of a piece of an image, preserving its aspect ratio (proportions). Otherwise use Scale, which is much more flexible.

Limitations: Zoom x 2 does not allow you to select where the target image will go. It always appears in the upper-left corner of the screen. It only works within an image. If you want to cut and paste between images, use the Clip functions.

See Also: Clip→Cut
Clip→Paste
Tools→Paint→Cpy
Tools→Scale

....

Line Measure

Measure the distance between points on the screen.
Menu Access:
Tool→Line Mes

Description: To measure an area on the screen, define a line to measure by clicking the left mouse button at the beginning and the end. The length of the line will be displayed. The default unit of measure is a pixel. This can be changed by using Calibrate (see below).

When to Use: Use Line Measure to find distances on digitized maps or engineering drawings.

See Also: Tools→Calibrate

....

Calibrate

Set the units used by Line Measure.

Menu Access: Tool→Calibrate

Description: Calibrate allows you to set the units of measure used by the Line Measure feature. To calibrate, define a line that you want to be 1 unit long by clicking the left mouse button at the beginning and the end.

When to Use: Use Calibrate to make the units of measure convenient when using Line Measure with digitized maps or engineering drawings.

See Also: Tools→Line Measure

....

Twirls

Mirror, flip, spin, and rotate image pieces.

Menu Access: Tools→Twirl

Description: The Twirl command allows you define a region of an image and make a copy transformed by various linear transformations. After clicking on Twirl, you will be presented with a submenu containing Mirror, Spin, Flip, and Rotate. Click on the type of Twirl you would like to try. All of these work in the same way. First define the source area with the mouse by clicking on the upper-left corner of the area to copy. A rectangle appears as you move the mouse, with one corner fixed to the point where you clicked, and the diagonal corner attached to the moving mouse cursor. Frame the rectangle around the source area and click the left mouse button. At this point you may be prompted for an option. After the option is selected, the transformed image will appear. The copy appears in different locations depending on the type of Twirl chosen.

Mirror

This Twirl option reflects the selected area about one of its sides. Define a rectangular area that you want to mirror, then choose the direction you want to mirror the area to from the pop-up menu. The directions are up, right, down, and left. Since the mirroring is done relative to the sides of the original, the original is not covered by the copy. For example, if you select the Up option, it is as though the selected piece was attached to the image with a hinge along its top side, and it was flipped over using the hinge. Figure 5-40 show the results of applying the four variations of Mirror to the clock in TIME.GIF.

Spin

This option replaces the selected image area with its left-right mirror image. The result is the same as Mirror→Left or Mirror→Right, except that the copy replaces the original instead of appearing at its side.

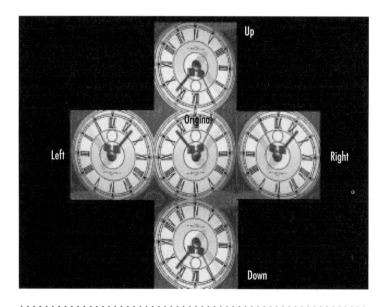

Figure 5-40 Result of the four Mirror options

Flip

This option turns the image upside down. The result is the same as Mirror→Up and Mirror→Down, except that the copy replaces the original instead of appearing above or below it.

Rotate

This option replaces an image with the result of rotating it 90 degrees to the left. No scaling is done. In some video modes, such as 320x200, pixels in the x (horizontal) direction are shorter than pixels in the y (vertical) direction. This means that if you choose what appears to be a square, it will be rectangular when rotated. This effect does not happen in modes with square pixels (where the ratio of the screen dimensions in pixels is the same as the screen aspect ratio of 4:3). The 640x480, 800X600, and 1024x768 modes all have square pixels.

When to Use: There is no special reason to use these options other than the sheer fun of cutting up and montaging together images!

See Also: Tool→Paint→Cpy

....

Clip

Tools→Scale

....

Terrain

Create a fractal landscape.

Menu Access: Tools→Terrain

Description: This option creates a random wire-frame fractal landscape partially submerged by an ocean. First define the area for the terrain with the mouse by clicking on the upper-left corner of the desired area. A rectangle appears as you move the mouse, with one corner fixed to the point where you clicked and the diagonal corner attached to the moving mouse cursor. Frame the rectangle around the desired area and click the left mouse. Then use the color bar to pick the colors to use when drawing the terrain. The low color is for the water and the high color is for the land. Figure 5-41 shows the color bar you use for selecting these two colors. At the top is a color-filled bar that shows the palette. The two selected colors are shown as vertical white lines in the color bar. They are initially set at the two extreme ends of the palette, 0 and 255. Under the color bar are two boxes with arrows at the ends. Holding down the left mouse button while the mouse cursor is pointing at these arrows moves the selected colors. Alternatively, you can click on either box to pick up one of the selected colors, and click the left

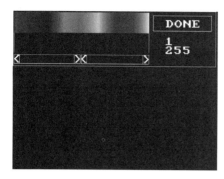

Figure 5-41 Color bar for selecting terrain colors

mouse button to put it down. A pair of numbers next to the Done box let you see exactly what the selected endpoints are. When satisfied, click on Done.

When to Use: Terrain is a great starting point for drawing landscapes.

Limitations: Terrain doesn't look very good in video modes under 640x400, and should be drawn in areas that are at least that large.

See Also: See the Fractint program for a similar but more extensive facility.

Plasma

Create a plasma image.

Menu Access: Tools→Plasma

Description: This option creates a random pattern of oozing colors. The name "plasma" comes from the effect these images give when the colors are cycled. First define the area for the plasma with the mouse by clicking on the upper-left corner of the desired area. A rectangle appears as you move the mouse, with one corner fixed to the point where you clicked and the diagonal corner attached to the moving mouse cursor. Frame the rectangle around the desired area and click the left mouse. Then use the color bar to pick the colors to use when drawing the terrain. Figure 5-41 shows the color bar you use for selecting these two colors. At the top is a color-filled bar that shows the palette. The two selected colors are shown as vertical white lines in the color bar. They are initially set at the two extreme ends of the palette, 0 and 255. Under the color bar are two boxes with arrows at the ends. Holding down the left mouse button while the mouse cursor is pointing at these arrows moves the selected colors. Alternatively you can click on either box to pick up one of the selected colors, and click the left mouse button to put it down. A pair of numbers next to the Done box let you see exactly what the selected endpoints are. When you are satisfied, click on Done. Improces will then ask you to select a graininess factor. Higher numbers give grainier results. Click on the desired number, and the plasma image will appear.

See Also: See the Fractint program for a similar facility. (The Improces author credits Fractint as his source for the Plasma feature.)

······················

Siner

Create a "bouncing stick" image.

Menu Access: Tools→Siner

Description: The Siner option creates a fun animation of a wandering line segment that works a lot like screen savers you may have seen. It works by computing the ends of a line segment using two sine functions, hence the name. As the moving segment moves around your screen, it leaves a ghost image of where it has been, building up a fascinating pattern. The Siner function in Improces has a big advantage over a screen saver, because the pattern it creates can be edited and incorporated into your images! But even if you dont want to save the image, it is a lot of fun to watch. Figure 5-42 shows what the result looks like.

The Color Menu

The Color item in the Main menu gives you access to powerful tools for manipulating the colors and color palettes used in Improces. Improces is inherently an editor of color-mapped images. (For a discussion of color-mapped

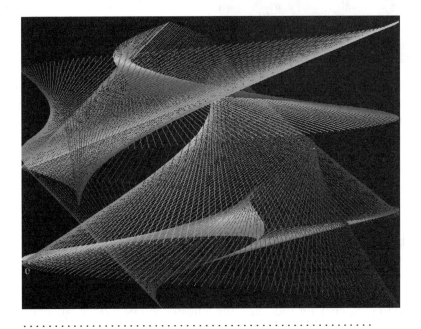

···

Figure 5-42 A Siner image

images, see Chapter 4.) Color-mapped images are based on color palettes, and Improces gives you a great deal of control over those colors.

....

Set Color

Set palette colors.

Menu Access: Colors→Set Colors

Description: When you invoke the Set Color menu item, a powerful palette-manipulating tool appears on the screen, as shown in Figure 5-43. This is your gateway to the 262,144 colors of the VGA palette. On the left are the 256 current colors in the current palette arranged in a rectangular array. Underneath the palette array is a large rectangle showing the current color. On the right is the adjuster for the current color, along with the values of the red, green, and blue attributes of the current color.

....

Figure 5-43 Set Color palette-manipulation tool

You can edit the palette one color at a time. Think of the palette as the 256 boxes in the palette array. The palette-editing tool allows you to change what color is assigned to each of those 256 boxes. To alter a particular color in the palette, click on that cell in the palette array. This will make that palette color the current color. It is important to understand that it is not the color itself that you have selected, but a particular position in the color palette corresponding to a box in the grid. The number of the palette entry you are editing shows in the lower-right corner of the palette grid. The idea is to alter the color assigned to that particular palette entry. When you change a color associated with that entry, the color of every pixel in the image that uses that color number will change.

You can also click on any pixel in the underlying image that is not covered by the palette tool. If the color adjuster is covering a color in the image you want to pick, click on Hide, and the adjuster will be hidden, allowing you to pick a color by clicking on it with the left mouse button. Click the right mouse button to bring back the hidden adjuster.

Once you have the made the palette entry you want to edit current, you can click on the top or bottom boxes under R, G, and B to change the color value of that entry. You can see the effect of the change in the underlying image. When one palette entry is acceptable, you can select another in the same way. When you are done, click on the Done box to keep the changes you made, or click on the Cancel box to reset the palette to where it was before you made any changes.

The Blender

Another option on the color adjuster is called the Blender. Using the Blender, you can make a smooth transition between two colors in your palette. To use the Blender, click on the Blend button. This will bring up the color bar. Use the color bar to choose the colors you want to blend between, and press Done or the right mouse button to cancel blending.

Cycle Keys

You can also cycle the palette while using the palette adjuster. This is useful if you want to blend around the top of the palette. The < and > buttons will move the palette one color in either direction, while the << and >> buttons will put the palette into motion until a mouse button is hit or the keyboard is hit. There are keyboard commands for cycling as well, the ⊙ and ⊙ keys are the equivalent of the single cycle buttons and ⊆ and ⊇ are the same as the continuous cycle buttons.

When to Use: Use Set Color to adjust the colors in your image to suit your creative imagination. Many of the effects in Improces are heavily dependent on the nature of the palette. You will generally get the best results if you use color palettes that use continuous gradations of color.

See Also: Color→Block

....

Block

Change all palette colors uniformly.

Menu Access: Color→Block

Description: The Block command increases or decreases the overall red, green, or blue in all the colors of the palette. It invokes a tool with the same interface as the Set Color function and works the same way, except that the changes take place across the entire palette.

When to Use: Use Block to correct overall color cast in your image.

See Also: Color→Set Colors

....

Cycle

Cycle palette colors.

Menu Access: Color→Cycle

Description: Color cycling rapidly rotates the colors in the palette, giving the effect of animation with some images. You can cycle any selected range of the 256 colors to create quite interesting effects. First you use the color bar to pick the colors that you want to cycle between. Figure 5-44 shows the color bar you use for selecting these two colors. At the top is a color-filled bar that shows the palette. The two selected colors are shown as vertical white lines in the color bar. They are initially set at the two extreme ends of the palette, 0 and 255. Under the color bar are two boxes with arrows at the ends. Holding down the left mouse button while the mouse cursor is pointing at these arrows moves the selected colors. Alternatively, you can click on either box to pick up one of the selected colors, and click the left mouse button to put it down. A pair of numbers next to the Done box let you see exactly what the selected endpoints are. When satisfied, click on Done, which will close the color bar and initiate color cycling.

Click on Done with the left mouse button, or click the right mouse button to abandon color cycling. While the colors are cycling, the left and right arrow keys control the direction of the cycle, while the up and down arrows define the speed of the cycle. The right mouse button stops the color cycle and returns you to the menu. When you save a file, whether it be PCX or GIF, the color-cycle settings are saved in a file with the same name as the file, only with a .CCL extension. When a file is loaded, if the correct .CCL file is in the same directory as the image file, the color cycle information from the .CCL file will be loaded and used.

When to Use: Use Color Cycling whenever your body and mind are exhausted and you want to stare mindlessly at beautiful swirls of colors writhing on the screen!

See Also: Color→Set Colors

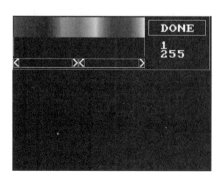

....

Figure 5-44 The color bar

Re-Align

Move unused colors to palette end.

Menu Access: Color→Re-Align

Description: Use this function to identify and locate colors that are not being used in the current screen image. After selecting this function, the program will perform a quick histogram of the image and report how many colors are being used and give you the option of remapping the unused colors to the bottom of the palette. If you select Yes, the unused palette entries will be remapped to the bottom of the palette and the current screen image will be adjusted so that pixels correspond the proper values. After the unused colors are at the bottom of the palette, it will be easy to identify them and modify their values without disturbing the on-screen image.

When to Use: Use Re-align when you want to combine images with different palettes, and identify which colors are not being used.

See Also: Color→Reduce

Reduce

Reduce the number of colors in an image.

Menu Access: Color→Reduce

Description: The Reduce function builds a shorter palette of a specified length that best fits the colors of an image. There is a submenu with the options Make 16, Make 32, Make 64, and Make 128.

This Function lets you specify a reduction level between 1 and 32. The reduction level is a threshold used to determine which colors will be consolidated into one color in the reduced palette. The reduction level is used like this: Each of the individual colors R, G, and B values are compared to all the other colors. If the R, G, and B values of the color are within the reduction level, the colors will be considered the same and will be set to the same values. After you select a reduction level and click on Done, the process will begin; and after it is over, you will be asked if you want to accept the changes you made. Used in conjunction with the Re-Align function, you can free up colors to draw with and then group them together on the palette.

Make 8/16/32/64/128

These options use a different method of reducing images. They will set the palette to the specified number of colors (that is, 16/32/64/128) by splitting the palette into the specified number of equal segments and then averaging each segment. Improces will ask if you want to accept the changes you made. If you select Yes, the palette and the image will be remapped so that the colors that are in use will be at the bottom of the palette.

When to Use: Use Reduce when you want to free up colors so you can combine images with different palettes.

See Also: Colors→Reduce

....

Palette

Select, save, and restore palettes.

Menu Access: Colors→Palette

Description: The Palette menu item brings up a submenu of palette-manipulation functions. These allow palettes to be converted to grayscale, converted to half-tone, loaded from disk or from internal storage, and saved to disk. These submenu functions are described below.

Col2Grey
The Col2Grey function converts a color palette to the Greyscale that is required for the enhance functions to work properly on colored images.

HalfTone
Halftones the image on the screen. A halftone is a black-and-white (two-color) pattern that simulates shades of gray at the expense of resolution. It is useful for converting images to a printable form.

Default/Ice/Heat/Green/Sun/Greyscale
Improces has six pre-saved palettes built in. Selecting one of these replaces the current palette.

Save
The save option lets you save and restore palettes to the MAP Format used by Fractint and Piclab or the Improes PAL Format.

1. Save→Save Pal: Saves the current palette to a file. Prompts for file name and saves the palette in the current directory. Uses the Improces PAL palette file format.

2. Save→Save Map: Saves the current palette to a file. Prompts for file name and saves the palette in the current directory. Uses the popular MAP file format, which is also used with Fractint, Piclab, and many other programs.

3. Open→Open Pal: Loads a palette from a file. Uses the Improces PAL palette file format. Uses the file picker.

4. Open→Open Map: Loads a palette from a file. Uses the popular MAP palette file format. Uses the file picker.

When to Use: The Greyscale conversion function should be used on color images before use with the Image-Processing functions for best results.

A good fast way to explore color is to load preexisting palettes. Many of the functions of Improces (such as the gradient fill under the Paint menu) require continuous palettes for best results. All of the built-in palettes have this characteristic.

See Also: File→Open
File→Save

The Enhance Menu

Improces is the image editor of the Image Lab suite of tools, and Piclab is the image-processing application. However, Improces does possess some considerable image processing capabilities in the Enhance section. These are not as versatile as the comparable functions in Piclab, because Piclab deals with true-color images. (These image types are discussed in the Chapter 4.) Even without true-color capabilities, Improces has powerful image-processing capabilities that should not be overlooked. For many desktop publishing purposes, grayscale images are used, and Improces handles grayscale images very well. For color images, the functions of the Enhance section are intended for images using the Ice, Heat, Green, Sun, or Greyscale palettes. The program will not stop you from using an Enhance function on an image with other palettes, but the results will be meaningless and random. To convert a color palette to one of the above, use the Col2Grey option in the Color-Palette menu. To do image processing on a color image with a different palette than one of these, use Piclab.

Work Area

Set image-process work area.

Menu Access: Enhance→Work Area

Description: All processes in the enhance menu work on a specified rectangular work area only. The default is the whole image. To redefine the current area, move the cursor to a spot you want to be one corner and click the left mouse button. A rectangle will appear with one corner fixed to the spot where you clicked, and the diagonal corner movable with the mouse. Resize the work area until it is the size you want, and click the left mouse button. Click the right mouse button to cancel the resizing. When you are done, click the right mouse button to return to the menu.

When to Use: Use Work Area to apply image processes to selected parts of the image. For example, you might want to sharpen a small fuzzy area of an image.

Limitations: The only way to see the current work area is to apply and undo a process. The Lpcian transform can be used for this purpose, since it is fairly easy to see the effects. Then you can reject the changes and the image will revert to its state before the Lpcian.

....

Area Histo(gram)

Analyze distribution of colors in the work area.

Menu Access: Enhance→Area Histo

Description: A histogram takes a measurement of the pixels in the work area. The histogram displays this measurement in values called *bins*. There are 256 bins, each corresponding to each of the 256 possible color values. Bin 0 is displayed to the left, and bin 255 (256 bins, 0 through 255) to the right and all bins in between are represented. The Max bin is displayed at the bottom. To see the value of a specific bin, click on its line or the color on the bottom with the left mouse button. Figure 5-45 shows a histogram after clicking on a bin to see its status. In the figure, cl=187 indicates color number 187 with a count of values vl=335. To save the histogram to disk, press the Ⓢ key and enter the file name to save it as, or enter Prn to send the information to the default printer. Click the right mouse button to restore the image.

....

Point Histo(gram)

Report color value and pixel coordinates of a pixel.

Menu Access: Enhance→Point Histo

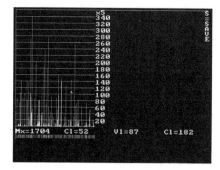

....

Figure 5-45 Histogram with bin status

Description: Click on the desired point with the left mouse button. Displays the coordinate, Color Value, and red, green, and blue attributes of the color. Click on OK to return to the menu.

....

Adjust Clip

Set clipping values for Contrast Stretch

Menu Access: Enhance→Adjust Clip

Description: Adjust Clip allows the clipping values used in the Contrast Stretch to be set.

See Also: Enhance→Contrast Stretch

....

Contrast Stretch

Increase contrast.

Menu Access: Enhance→Contrast Stretch

Description: Uses the clip value to cut the stretch off at the first low bin with a value equal to or greater than the Low clip and the first high bin with a value equal to or greater than the High clip.

See Also: Enhance→Set Clip

....

Contrast Vstretch

Increase contrast.

Menu Access: Enhance→Contrast Vstretch

Description: Uses the Clip values as the Low and High bins at which to cut off the stretch.

See Also: Enhance→Set Clip

....

Filters

Assorted image filters.

Menu Access: Enhance→Filters

Description: The Improces filters are area processes that adjust the color of a pixel according to algorithms that take account of the colors of neighboring pixels. The Filters menu item has a submenu that you can use to select the various filters. Each of these filters take an average of the eight surrounding pixels plus the pixel itself. The average is weighted using factors for each of the nine points. The filter is specified by the 3x3 matrix of weight factors.

Work Area

Same as above. See Enhance→Work Area.

Sharpen

Effect is to enhance boundaries.

Uses:		
-1	-1	-1
-1	9	-1
-1	-1	-1

Laplacian

Effect is to enhance boundaries.

Uses:		
-1	-1	-1
-1	8	-1
-1	-1	-1

Horiz (Horizontal)

Effect is to smear horizontally.

Uses:		
-1	-1	-1
0	0	0
1	1	1

Vertic (Vertical)

Effect is to smear horizontally.

Uses:		
-1	0	1
-1	0	1
-1	0	1

Average 3x3

Passes a 3x3 matrix over the work area and replaces the center pixel with the average value of the matrix. Has an unsharpening effect. This filter is useful to cut spot noise in an image.

Median 3x3

Passes a 3x3 matrix over the work area and replaces the center pixel with the median value of the matrix. Has an unsharpening effect. This filter is useful to cut spot noise in an image.

Custom

Allows you to specify a custom kernal to convolute the image.

Boost

Lets you select a boost value that is applied to the Sharpen, Laplacian, Horizontal, Vertical, and Custom filters.

Effects

Assorted special effects.

Menu Access: Enhance→Filters

Description: The functions in the Effects menu work on the whole screen, not just the Enhance work area. The Effects functions were intended to work on grayscale images only. The results will be meaningless and random for color images, although they might be interesting. The result of an Effect is to alter the appearance of the whole image.

For each of the effects, there is a description of how the image is altered. Some of them are difficult to describe, and really need to be seen to be understood.

Relief

Makes the image look like it was molded in sand.

Reverse

Reverse the color values. Turns a grayscale image into its negative.

Solarize

Has a similar effect as solarizing a monochrome print by exposing it to light halfway through development. The effect is half negative, half positive.

Melt

Slowly melts the image, somewhat like viewing the image through a pane of glass with dripping water. Click the right mouse button when you get tired of watching this!

Bentley

This effect treats the colors as a third coordinate and applies a 3D transformation. The result is a kind of mountain range. Try making a full-screen Plasma cloud with the default palette and then running the Bentley for an interesting effect.

Oil

Slow. Transforms a grayscale image into an oil painting. Does not affect the last three columns and the last three rows of pixels.

Replicate

Make multiple smaller copies.

Menu Access: Enhance→Rplicate

Description: Replicate tiles the screen with smaller copies of the whole image. A submenu gives you the choice of two or four images.

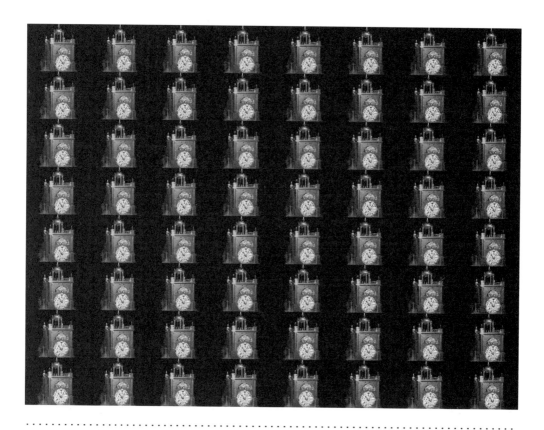

Figure 5-46 A screen tiled with clocks using Replicate

When to Use: Use this repeatedly to make wallpaper-like effects of repeated patterns.

Limitations: The X2 replication does not adjust for aspect ratio, so the images get skinnier and skinnier as you replicate. Since X4 cuts both the horizontal and vertical dimensions, aspect ratio is preserved.

Example: Figure 5-46 shows the result of several 4X replications on the clock tower image.

See Also: Tool→Scale

The Mode Menu

Menu Access: Mode

Description: The Mode menu lets you change video modes. This is also an effective clear-screen command. The highest mode shown in the menu can be set in the File→Set Preferences menu. You should be careful to study the documentation for your system and determine what video modes it supports.

Improces supports VGA adapters using the Ahead, ATI, Chips & Tech, Everex, Paradise, Trident, Tseng (both ET3000 and ET4000 chip sets) and Video7, as well as any card supporting the new VESA standard. Which modes are supported depend both on the chip set your adapter uses and how much memory it has. Table 5-4 shows how much video memory is required for different video modes.

When to Use: Set the video mode when you want to change image resolution or clear the screen.

Limitations: Improces only supports the video modes shown in Table 5-4. A VGA or Super VGA is required.

Video Mode	Video Memory Required
320x200 256 colors	64K
640x400 256 colors	256K
640x480 256 colors	512K
800x600 256 colors	512K
1024x768 256 colors	1024K

Table 5-4 Memory requirements of video modes

6

CHAPTER 6

FRACTINT

MOUNTAINS, PLANETS, AND WILD FRACTALS

magine a future computer historian delivering a learned dissertation entitled "The History of Computer-Generated Graphics Technology in the Late 20th Century." Our imaginary historian might well divide the "early graphics era" into two parts: Before Fractals and After Fractals. In the Before Fractals era, computers excelled at making spheres, cubes, circles, and lines. Computer-generated images had a mechanical feel to them, a kind of cartoonish quality stemming from the use of geometric shapes. But in the After Fractal era (starting in the early 1980s), a whole new dimension was added to the possibilities for computer images. This new dimension goes beyond simple shapes, and includes rich textures, irregular surfaces, realistic clouds, rugged mountains, and even lifelike plants and trees. This difference has to do with both roughness and detail. A fractal is an object that has detail and structure at all scales, no matter how closely you look at it. The natural world is full of examples of objects with fractal characteristics; indeed, it is difficult to find natural objects that do not have fractal characteristics. The ability of computers to create fractals is one of the keys to the ability of computers to simulate natural scenes.

Simulating the natural world is not the only use for fractals in the field of computer-generated images. For while it is true that natural objects almost invariably have fractal characteristics, it is not true that all fractals are natural looking. The world of fractals includes a kaleidoscope of impossibly textured patterns and shapes with unending variety. These images are a visual feast for those fascinated by patterns and colors, and a wonderful asset for the imaginative artist who uses computers.

The best part about fractals is that anyone with a computer can explore them. This chapter is about a program for doing just that on your very own PC. The program is Fractint, the PC fractal-generating program.

This chapter is different from the other chapters in this book that deal with the computer programs included on the companion disk. The Fractint program is not included with this book because it comes with another book, *The Waite Group's Fractal Creations*, by Tim Wegner and Mark Peterson. *Fractal Creations* contains an essay on fractals, a Fractint tutorial, the Fractint command reference, a reference to all the Fractint fractal types, a colorful poster, and 3-D glasses. Because *Fractal Creations* already covers the tutorial and reference material that is included in this book for the other Image Lab software, this chapter has a different focus. Here you will find a discussion of the role of fractals in computer art, how to use the image-processing functions of Fractint, and recipes for making outstanding images with Fractint that you can use with the other Image Lab software. In short, "How to use Fractint" written for the image-processing artist!

With Fractint you can:

- Generate images using any of over 70 fractal types, each of which has countless variations.

- Make 3-D transformations of images, using color as a third dimension.

- Wrap your images onto spheres, making "planets" out of your images.

- Combine images into montages, and allow certain parts of images to be transparent allowing the background image to show through.

- Make clouds and landscapes.

- Edit image palettes to change colors.

- Display images with color cycling for dazzling animation effects.

WHERE TO GET FRACTINT

Getting Fractint with a Book

The best way to get Fractint is with one of the books: *Fractal Creations* (DOS version) or *Fractals for Windows* (Windows version). Fractint is a full-featured program, and the books provide a helpful key to unlocking its secrets. If you can't find these books at your local book store, you can use the coupon in the back of this book to order your copy direct from the publisher.

Getting Fractint On-line

The current versions of both the DOS and Windows versions of Fractint are always available on CompuServe in the Computer Art forum (GO COMART). You will find them in LIB 15 with the names FRAINT.EXE (DOS version) and WINFRA.ZIP (Windows version.) If you are not a member of CompuServe, you can join using the CompuServe introductory kit. The *Fractal Creations* and *Fractals for Windows* books are recommended for use with the Freeware versions of Fractint as well as the versions bundled with the books.

Fractint is a program written by a group of programmers known as the Stone Soup Group, so named because the sources are publicly available and everyone is invited to contribute to "the soup." Stone Soup has an electronic home in the Computer Art (GO COMART) forum on CompuServe. If you have questions or ideas about Fractals or Fractint, you are invited to join the lively on-line discussion.

A Word about Fractint Versions

All the examples in this book have been written for Fractint for DOS version 15.1. This is the version that comes with the first edition of the book *Fractal Creations*. The examples will also work with any later version of Fractint, either the DOS or Windows version. If you are using a Windows version, the interface will be be slightly different than described here, but you should have no difficulty duplicating the examples. You can type in all the parameters for the examples by hand, or use the listing files as explained later in this chapter.

If you have version 16 or later, the instructions in this chapter will work fine, but you may find it more convenient to load the examples from the parameter file IMAGLAB.PAR. From the main menu use the ⎛&⎞ key, select the file IMAGLAB.PAR, then select the example you wish to run by name using the cursor keys.

UP AND RUNNING

Stone Soup programs share a file for setting the various defaults of all the different programs. Both Piclab and Fractint use this file. Fractint requires SSTOOLS.INI to be in a directory listed in the Path statement in your AUTOEXEC.BAT. You can place Fractint command-line options in the SSTOOLS.INI file.

A typical SSTOOLS.INI file might be placed in a directory called C:\IMLAB listed in the Path and also containing the Piclab and Fractint files, and look like this:

```
[fractint]
sound=off
warn=yes

[piclab]
tempdir=c:\temp
helpfile=c:\imlab\piclab\pl.hlp
display=svga2
```

You can see that the Fractint section is set off with [fractint], which is followed by several options. In this case the sound=off option turns off the various whistles that Fractint uses to inform you of conditions such as the completion of a fractal. Warn=yes prompts you when a file is about to be overwritten when you are saving an image.

Fractint and several other Image Lab programs (Improces, Piclab, and Image Alchemy) can read and write palette files with the .MAP extension. You will want to put these in one place so that the various programs can share them. The examples of this chapter assume that the .MAP files and .FRM files and all the Fractint example listings are in the current directory (such as C:\IMLAB\FRACTINT.) If they are in a different directory, you can change the examples accordingly.

In order to run Fractint, you should have plenty of free memory, although it will run on a 512K machine. Fractint will use extended or expanded memory if you have it for some functions. A math coprocessor is a definite plus. Those familiar with Fractint may be surprised at this; Fractint is famous for being fast without a coprocessor due to the use of fixed-point mathematics. However, if you zoom deeply into a fractal, you will run out of the precision possible with the faster fixed point math, and Fractint will automatically switch to floating point math. If you do not have a math coprocessor, calculations will slow down as much as ten to fifteen times. Fractint supports the special hardware matrix multiply feature of the IIT math coprocessors for use with 3D. To take advantage of an IIT coprocessor chip, add the line

```
FPU=IIT
```

to your SSTOOLS.INI file.

Start fractint by typing:

```
C:>FRACTINT (ENTER)
```

You should see the opening screen, which looks like Figure 6-1. (The screen shown belongs to the *Fractal Creations* book version; the Freeware version looks similar.) The opening screen lists the four main authors of Fractint and has a scrolling list of contributors who have added to the "pot" of Stone Soup.

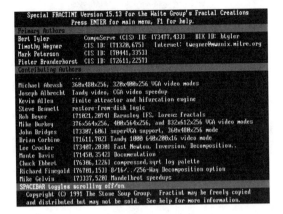

Figure 6-1 The Fractint scrolling credits screen

> **Warning!** If you get the message "Overlay not found," or if Fractint reports that its help file cannot be found (Freeware version), check your computer for viruses. Fractint does not tolerate viruses that append data to the program. This is a good thing — it makes Fractint a kind of primitive virus detector!

QUICK START

Once you have Fractint running and you can see the scrolling credits screen, press (ENTER) and you will see the Main menu. You can access Help using the (F1) key. All the other function keys are assigned to different video modes. To see what the video modes are, press (DEL) and you can scroll up and down a list of modes. Pressing (ENTER) will select the highlighted mode and initiate a fractal calculation. You can also directly select a video mode and start a calculation by pressing a function key. Try (F3) for the 320x200 256-color VGA mode or (F2) for the 640x350 16-color EGA mode. You will see the famous Mandelbrot set on the screen, which looks like Figure 6-2.

The one obligatory Fractint feature to try is color cycling. When any fractal is showing on the screen, press (+) to enter color cycling. The colors will wildly cycle through the palette, creating the effect of animation. Cycling can be stopped by pressing (ESC).

A bit later in the chapter, you will discover how to make some incredible images. Meanwhile, head off on your own and explore, or read on to learn about fractals.

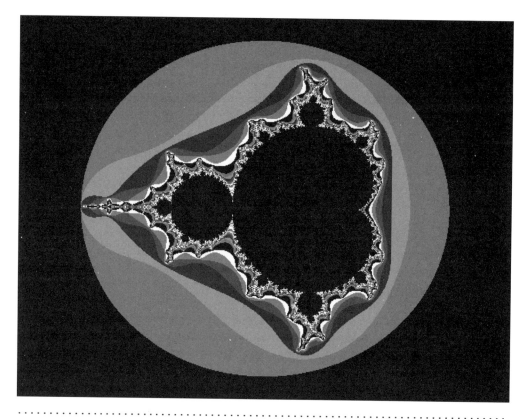

Figure 6-2 The Mandelbrot fractal

FRACTALS AND COMPUTER IMAGES

In this section you will learn about fractals and why they are important for image processing and computer simulation.

What Is a Fractal?

A fractal is an object that has detail at all scales. This means that no matter how close you look, you can see structure in a fractal. The structure of a magnified piece of a fractal may look similar to the whole fractal, in which case we say the fractal is self-similar. But the magnified piece may also look very different; what is important is that the texture or structure does not disappear when you look closely.

Classical geometric shapes such as cubes or spheres are not fractals. A perfect cube has six faces, and each of these faces has four edges. All the edges are the same length, and connected edges are at right angles to each other. That information tells you just about everything there is to know about cubes. The faces of a perfect cube are completely featureless.

Compare a classical cube to a mountain. Seen from a distance, a mountain has a jagged appearance. As you get closer, smaller features of the mountain come into view, but it is still characterized by a rough appearance. Finally, when you are right on the mountainside, you can see that the rough jaggedness of the mountain extends right down to the scale of your hands as you climb up a rock face gripping irregular outcroppings. If you happened to be carrying a magnifying glass or a microscope, you would be able to verify that the fractal nature of the mountain continues to the smallest observable scales, although its appearance might be dramatically changed.

Painting with Geometry

As soon as computers had graphics output capabilities, drawing with computers became a possibility. The first methods of computer drawing were based on classical geometry. When the Apple Macintosh computer first came out, it came bundled with two programs called MacDraw and MacPaint. Both of these programs worked by using drawing tools based on classical geometry. The paint program that comes with this book, Improces, has some of those same drawing tools. With MacDraw you could make squares, rectangles, circles, ovals, and lines. You could fill them in with various patterns and colors, move them, arrange them, and build complex images. The possibilities for creative drawing with theses programs are very exciting. But only a very skilled artist can use them to make natural scenes. The computer can help you draw perfect squares or circles, but if you want to draw a tree with a classical draw or paint program, the work is painstaking. You have to draw freehand, and build textures a pixel at a time.

In the same vein, the software industry provided architects and engineers with new tools for creating designs. These tools are called CAD programs, short for Computer Aided Design. These programs are really high-end drawing programs, some with extensive 3-D abilities. An architect might use a CAD program to draw a picture of a finished building. The shapes of classical geometry are ideal for this use; after all, most buildings are made of shapes from classical geometry. You have probably seen an architect's drawings made with CAD software. The lines of the building are crisp, clean, and exact, but the trees, grass, and clouds look cartoonish and stylized. What is missing is fractals!

Mandelbrot and Fractal Geometry

Throughout the 1950s and 1960s, the mathematician Benoit Mandelbrot studied the anomalous corners of many disciplines, gradually building up a picture of a phenomenon that transcended the boundaries between different academic fields. He studied the variations of commodity prices, noise in telephone transmission lines, the fluctuations in the level of the Nile river floods, and problems with measuring the length of irregular coastlines. Mandelbrot appended this statement to his own entry in *Who's Who:* "Science would be ruined if (like sports) it were to put competition above everything else, and if it were to clarify the rules of competition by withdrawing into narrowly defined specialities. The rare scholars who are nomads-by-choice are essential to the intellectual welfare of the settled disciplines." He was — and still is — an intellectual nomad-by-choice who is only beginning to gain grudging acceptance from the "settled disciplines."

In 1975, as Mandelbrot was preparing to publish his first major book, he decided a special name was needed to cover the common element in all these phenomena he had studied. He came upon the Latin word *fractus,* which means "to break." Because of the similarity to the English words fracture and fraction, the name fractal seemed just right.

If you want to learn more about Benoit Mandelbrot and the other pioneers of fractal theory, a good starting point is the popular book *Chaos* by James Gleick (Viking, 1987).

Snowflakes and the Magic of Iteration

What is missing from the architect's precise and regular drawing of his building is irregularity, texture, and bumpiness. The key to fractal irregularity turns out to be iteration. Iteration means the process of repeating something over and over. Consider, for example, the famous Koch snowflake, named after the Swedish mathematician Helge von Koch, who first described it in 1904.

Surely everyone who has grown up in the temperate zone has at one time or another contemplated snowflakes. Your author remembers lazy days in Minnesota when the snow drifted down like dandelion fluffs and covered his parka. Young eyes — eyes still decades away from needing bifocals — focused closely on those tiny fluffs and saw the repeated sixfold symmetry with wonder. The thought that no two of these fragile beauties were the same contained a hint of the not-yet-understood infinite. One would like to think that the Koch snowflake was invented out of a memory of such a youthful experience.

You can build a Koch snowflake with a pencil, a vivid imagination, or (as we'll see shortly) with Fractint and a computer. Start with an equilateral triangle. Divide each side into three parts. Remove the middle part, and add two joined segments to replace the removed segment, forming a triangular projection coming out of the originally straight edge. Then keep repeating this process for each edge systematically. The result is shown in Figure 6-3. At first the change is dramatic, but after a few iterations the basic snowflake is formed, and it doesn't appear to change any further. Appearances are deceptive, as we'll see shortly!

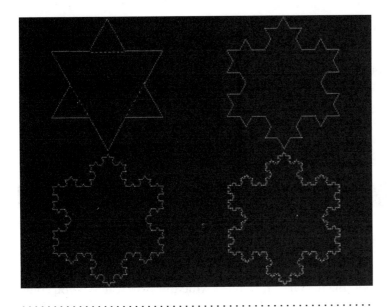

Figure 6-3 The Koch snowflake

One of the wonderful aspects of fractal mathematics is how it stretches our intuition. There is something about the infinite that we can contemplate but never quite fully grasp. The process of generating the Koch snowflake raises the question of the infinite. The subsequent iterations of the process used to build the Koch snowflake appear to be getting closer and closer to a final result. What is the resulting shape, and what are its characteristics? Mathematics tells us that there is indeed a definite curve that is the limiting result of iterating the snowflake process infinitely many times. Let's ask something really simple about the resulting "infinitely iterated" snowflake. What is its perimeter?

Suppose that the initial triangle has sides of length 1. Then the original triangle has a perimeter of 3. Look at Figure 6-3 and try to guess the distance around of the final snowflake. It looks somewhat larger than the original triangle. Maybe 4 or 5? Let's see.

The process of moving from step to step in building the snowflake always starts with a side, breaks it into three pieces, and replaces the original three pieces with four pieces. Thus each step increases the perimeter by $\frac{4}{3}$. Table 6-1 shows the perimeter of the first few iterations of the snowflake building process.

It is not too hard to see that the perimeter gets bigger and bigger without limit, and the "final" Koch snowflake will have an infinite perimeter. In mathematical terminology, the sequence $s(n)=3*(\frac{4}{3})^n$ diverges to plus infinity.

What is going on here? The answer is that even though the "Koch process" of adding triangles makes no visible difference after a few iterations, in fact

Iteration	Perimeter	
Original	$3 \times 1 =$	3.00
2nd	$3 \times (\frac{4}{3}) =$	4.00
3rd	$3 \times (\frac{4}{3}) \times (\frac{4}{3}) =$	5.33
4th	$3 \times (\frac{4}{3}) \times (\frac{4}{3}) \times (\frac{4}{3}) =$	7.11
5th	$3 \times (\frac{4}{3}) \times (\frac{4}{3}) \times (\frac{4}{3}) \times (\frac{4}{3}) =$	9.48
6th	$3 \times (\frac{4}{3}) \times (\frac{4}{3}) \times (\frac{4}{3}) \times (\frac{4}{3}) \times (\frac{4}{3}) =$	12.64
7th	$3 \times (\frac{4}{3}) \times (\frac{4}{3}) \times (\frac{4}{3}) \times (\frac{4}{3}) \times (\frac{4}{3}) \times (\frac{4}{3}) =$	16.86

Table 6-1 Lengths of Koch snowflakes of various iterations

microscopic corners of smaller and smaller size are being added, which keep on increasing the perimeter and the constant rate of $\frac{4}{3}$ or 1.333 for each iteration. The result is a true fractal — it displays structure at all scales. If you could look at a perfect Koch triangle with an electron microscope, each piece of it would be similar to — even identical to, in this case — the whole snowflake viewed at a much lower magnification. Figure 6-4 shows a self-similar piece of the Koch snowflake.

The Koch snowflake may look artificial, but its fractal properties make it very similar to such things as meandering rivers and craggy mountains. Other fractals have a much more natural appearance; you'll be introduced to some in a moment. The Koch snowflake shows that fractals and iteration go hand in hand. Iteration — repeating a process over and over — is what computers do really well. Computers and fractals were made for each other.

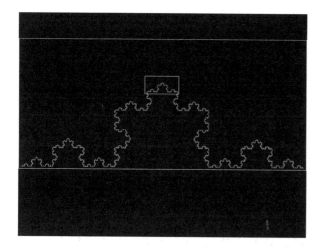

Figure 6-4 The self-similarity of the Koch snowflake

Clouds

So far we have established that fractals can be generated by iterative methods. It is not obvious at first blush that clouds are fractals at all, but it turns out that they are, and that clouds can be generated by an iterative process. After you learn how clouds are made, you will see that mountains are thrown into the bargain for free!

The algorithm described here is the one used to generate the *plasma* fractal type in Fractint. The tutorial a bit later on in the chapter will show you how to create this fractal with your computer. (The Improces program can also make plasma images.)

Let's assume that our computer is in a 256-color graphics mode, and that the current palette has colors that vary continuously from shade to shade. This means that if two color numbers are close together, then their colors are similar shades of color.

Start with a black graphics screen, colored completely with color 0, which is usually black. In each corner of the screen, write a pixel with a random color. Next calculate the color of pixels in between the four corner pixels. The algorithm is as follows. Pick a new random color. This color is averaged with the two corner colors of the pixels the new pixel is between. Here is the trick: In averaging the colors, the weight given to the new random color is proportional to the distance from the center pixel to the corner pixels. At the beginning, this distance is relatively far, so the color of the first center pixel is mostly random, and less determined by the average of the previous colors.

Now that the four in-between pixels have a color, the center pixel is colored according to the average of the four midpoint pixels.

The screen is now subdivided into a grid by the colored points. Starting with the upper-left box, the same process is repeated. The difference is that now the points are closer together, so that when the midpoint colors are calculated, the random part of the color affects the result less, and the existing colors affect the result more. This process is iteratively continued, subdividing the screen with a finer and finer grid until all the pixels are colored.

The result of this process looks very much like a cloud, as you can see in Figure 6-5. The calculation has been interrupted before the whole screen has been covered. The key to this algorithm is the random component of the coloring of pixels, and the averaging scheme that forces points close to each other to have colors of similar hues. This algorithm is very close to terrain-building algorithms such as the midpoint displacement method.

Mountains

Clouds and mountains go together. We know that clouds and mountains are good elements to use in creating beautiful scenes, as proven by the great Ansel

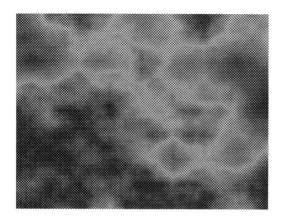

Figure 6-5 A fractal cloud

Adams photograph of the Tetons, a glorious view of spectacular peaks and billowy clouds. But from the perspective of fractals, the relationship between clouds and mountains is much closer than that. They are in fact the same mathematical reality, viewed in two different ways.

All that is needed to turn a cloud into a mountain is to treat the color value of each point in the cloud image as a height, and then plot the resulting surface. Figure 6-6 shows how this works. Another way to put this is that a cloud is a color-coded contour map of a mountain. Clouds look so soft and fluffy that it is hard to imagine a cloud as a picture of a rough and craggy mountain. The softness is a deception perpetuated by the coloring scheme. The colors

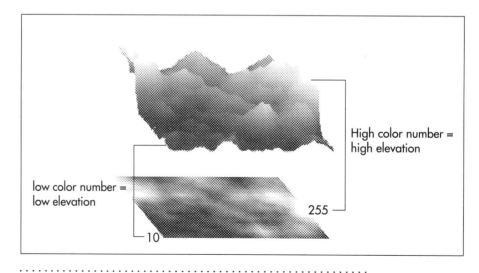

Figure 6-6 Turning a cloud into a mountain

ooze between gradations of shading as the mountain elevation changes. You can see the true fractal nature of the clouds next time you witness a sunset with backlit clouds. Sometimes the rays of the setting sun cause a shimmering edge to appear along the eclipsing cloud. Next time you see such a sunset, take note. That cloud outline does not appear fluffy at all, but looks as jagged as a lighting bolt, showing the cloud as a fractal mathematician sees it — an irregular, textured, fractal.

Mt. Mandelbrot

Clouds are not the only route to rugged landscapes. A fascinating thing about fractals is how many different approaches result in fractals. The one common denominator is the repeated iteration of a process.

The Mandelbrot set (shown in Figure 6-7) is the most famous fractal of all, and for good reason. The image of the Mandelbrot set is richly detailed, yet it comes from a formula of deceptive simplicity. Pictures of eerie beauty can be made using the Mandelbrot set. A picture of this set can be made with a few lines of computer code. Software like Fractint, which generates graphical pictures of the Mandelbrot set, allows you to zoom in and view tiny pieces of the set. Using such software is like parachuting into a strange landscape. As your

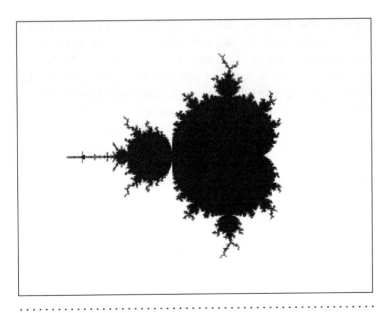

Figure 6-7 The Mandelbrot set

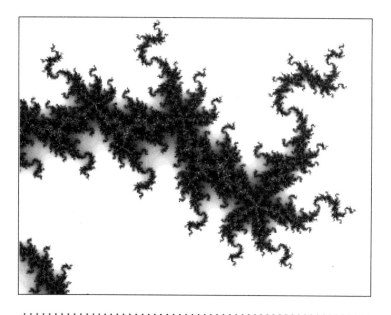

Figure 6-8 *Image Lab* Memorial Mandelbrot Patch

parachute sails lower and lower, the landscape before you expands, and you see more and more detail, until you land and can see clumps of rock. With a few minutes and a computer, you can "land" on a little patch of the Mandelbrot set knowing that the odds against anyone else having seen that spot are so astronomical as to make it a certainty. In this case the word astronomical is no exaggeration: You can view such a tiny fraction of the whole Mandelbrot set on your computer screen, yet at the same scale the whole set would fill the orbit of Jupiter! Figure 6-8 shows a unique, never-before discovered piece of the Mandelbrot set. The author is filing a claim to this piece of the Mandelbrot fractal in honor of this book, which is to be forever known as the *"Image Lab* Memorial Mandelbrot Patch." As an *Image Lab* reader, you have permission to visit it whenever you want; the coordinates are listed in Table 6-2. They correspond to the values of the Fractint corners= parameter, which will be discussed in the tutorial later in this chapter.

For a full discussion of how the Mandelbrot set is generated, you can read just about any book on fractals, including our own *Fractal Creations*. To draw the Mandelbrot set, a computer has to assign pairs of numbers to each pixel on the computer screen. Each of these pairs is called a complex number. Complex numbers have their own rules of arithmetic, and can be added, subtracted, multiplied, and divided much like familiar real numbers. For each pixel on the screen, the computer has to do the following:

. . . .

(Legal notice: this Mandelbrot patch is hereby declared to be the sole property of the readers of *The Waite Group's Image Lab*.)

x1 = -0.91714083600628540

x2 = -0.91714083288683970

y1 = +0.26074354191968460

y2 = +0.26074354423635120

Table 6-2 Coordinates of *Image Lab* Memorial Mandelbrot Patch

1. Set the variable c to the complex number corresponding to the pixel we want to color.

2. Set the variable z to 0.

3. Set the iteration counter n to 0.

4. Calculate z as $z^2 + c$

5. Is the size of z > 2? If yes, color the pixel color n , and goto step 1 for another pixel.

6. Increment the iteration counter n to n+1.

7. Goto step 4.

That is all there is to it. The crux of the algorithm is the step "calculate z as $z^2 + c$" that replaces the variable z with the sum of a number and the square of z. That is about as simple as a formula gets. The real secret may be line 7 of the pseudocode, which says innocently "Goto step 4." That is where the iteration happens. The appearance of a fractal has as much to do with the chaos generated by wild iteration as they do the formula that is iterated.

The image of the Mandelbrot set can be converted to a 3-D image in the same way as the cloud can be converted to a mountain. The colors are treated as heights of a surface, and then the computer can generate views of this surface from different angles. Along the way several other tricks are performed. The Mandelbrot calculation can be modified to give smoothly varying colors instead of the striped appearance of Figure 6-2. An imaginary light source can illuminate the landscape to provide shadings much like real-life shadows. The result of all these operations is shown in Figure 6-9.

The Future of Fractals in Graphics

This section has touched briefly on what fractals are and a couple of ways to make realistic looking landscapes. This represents only the tiniest glimpse of the impact fractals are having on the computer graphics world. At the begin-

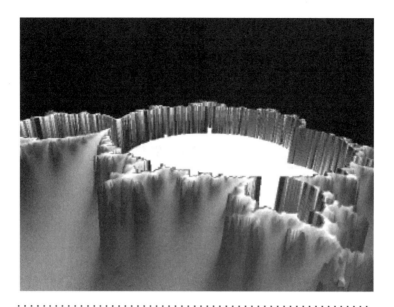

Figure 6-9 Mt. Mandelbrot

ning of this chapter, you were asked to imagine a future historian who divided graphics history into the Before Fractals and After Fractals eras. The After Fractals era is well under way, and the revolution of software it has brought is as close to you as your Image Lab companion disk. But you can expect much more in just a few years. The Improces program already has plasma clouds and fractal landscapes built in. The Persistence of Vision Ray Tracer can make photo-realistic scenes of illuminated fractal surfaces. And of course Fractint itself can make a universe of fractal patterns, landscapes, and planets.

Fractal tools are already becoming a stock part of paint, draw, and CAD programs. The architect's CAD program will have the capability to make realistic trees, grass, clouds, stonework, bricks, and paint textures. Fractals emancipate computer graphics from the continuous, the smooth, and the regular, providing a zestful variety of earthy textures to images.

A FRACTINT TUTORIAL

In this section we will look at how to create and modify images using Fractint. All the examples will include complete step-by-step instructions. Fractint has more features than can be covered in this short tutorial. For more information you should study the Fractint documentation or use the on-line help. If you would like a complete tutorial, command reference, and discussion of all the fractal types, you are referred to the book *Fractal Creations*.

Note: This tutorial assumes that you have Fractint version 15.1 or later, either the *Fractal Creations* version or a Freeware version. You can tell what version you have by looking at the top line of any menu screen. If you are using a version later than 15, some details of the video mode keys and screens will be slightly different than shown here, but all of the examples will work.

Finding Your Way Around Fractint

When you start Fractint, you will see the scrolling credits screen, which shows some of the people who have contributed code and features. Fractint has received contributions of code from all over the world, including Australia, Germany, Canada, and the United States. Pressing (ENTER) will get you to the Main menu. Figure 6-10 shows the Main menu.

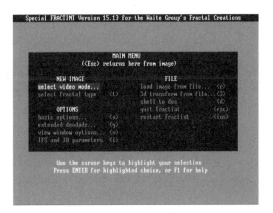

Figure 6-10 The Fractint Main menu

Fractint has several different ways to access its functions. From most screens you can directly type in single-letter commands. For example, the keystroke (T) will take you to the Fractal Type screen and allow you to select from the 70 different built-in fractal types. You can accomplish the same thing by using the cursor to highlight the menu item "select fractal type < + >" and then pressing (ENTER). The Main menu tells you what the keystroke is that corresponds to that menu item. Many commands can also be entered at the Fractint startup command line. If you knew at the time you started Fractint that you wanted to use the Newton fractal type, you could start Fractint with:

`C:> FRACTINT TYPE=NEWTON` (ENTER)

When you first start Fractint but haven't yet generated or restored an image, the Main menu is divided into three sections: New Image, Options, and File.

The New Image commands let you select a video mode and a fractal type. (Video modes will be discussed a bit later in this section.) The list of fractal types in Fractint gives you access to a large number of different methods by which fractals can be generated. Some of the fractal types are based on very specific algorithms that are of historical significance (such as the Mandelbrot set), or were either adapted from other sources or discovered by the authors in the course of Fractint's evolution (such as the Unity fractal type). Other fractal types are really whole universes of fractals in and of themselves, such as the formula, ifs, ifs3D, and lsystem types. These provide access to whole classes of fractal types by reading files containing parameters appropriate for their various fractal engines. For example, the fractal type *formula* lets you define almost any generalization of the Mandelbrot and Julia sets that you can imagine, using a simple language that lets you build formulas using addition, subtraction, multiplication, division, exponentiation, and functions like sine and cosine.

When you start Fractint, the fractal type is set to the default, which is the Mandelbrot set. If Fractint is able to detect what exact video hardware your PC has, a suggested video mode will be highlighted in the list of video modes when you invoke the Select Video Mode function. However, there is no default for the video mode; you must choose a mode in order to generate an image. But before you go ahead and choose a mode, let's discuss the other menu headings.

The Options menu items give you access to a number of alternatives, settings, and special effects. You won't need these right away, except possibly the View Window option. The View Window capability allows you to specify a very small image that can be calculated very rapidly. This capability is wonderful for getting a quick idea of what a fractal looks like.

The File menu category includes the ability to restore to the screen previously calculated images that were saved as GIF files. There are two ways to restore files: either as they were originally calculated, or by doing a 3-D transformation on the file. There are also handy commands to enter DOS without exiting Fractint (you return by typing "exit"), quitting Fractint altogether (ESC), and restarting Fractint (INS).

After you have generated an image, several sections of the Main menu will have a few more items, and there is an additional Colors section.

Selecting a Video Mode

Choose "select video mode" from the Main menu, and press (ENTER). (Pressing the (DEL) key has the same effect.) You are presented with a list of video modes, with a choice highlighted, which looks like Figure 6-11. This list shows all the various drivers available in Fractint for a variety of video hardware, along with credits to people who first verified that the modes worked on their machine. The list includes not only standard IBM-compatible modes such as the

640x350 EGA 16-color mode, but some unusual *tweaked* modes that can squeeze extra resolution out of a plain VGA. For example, the mode labeled "SF1" has a resolution of 360 pixels wide and 480 pixels high, with 256 possible colors. This mode results from directly programming the VGA registers, and should work on any VGA register-compatible with the IBM VGA.

Fractint can automatically detect most graphics hardware. If you have some variety of Super VGA graphics board, your best bet is to use one of the Super VGA/VESA Autodetetct modes. For almost all fractal and Image Lab purposes, the more colors the better, so that if you have a VGA, you should use a 256-color mode. The (F3) 320x200 pixel 256-color mode is great for exploring, because its lower resolution means that the image calculates quickly. After you have an image you really like, you may want to recalculate it at a higher resolution, such as 640x480 or even 1024x768.

. . . .
Figure 6-11 The Fractint video
mode list

For right now, however, the main concern is to find a good video mode for getting started. If you have a CGA, EGA, or VGA adapter, Fractint will have detected your adapter and chosen a mode for you, which you will see highlighted.

The "F3" means that pressing function key (F3) will directly select that video mode. Each video driver has a key combination associated with it, and pressing that key combination selects the video mode. Fractint has room for up to 100 different video modes, each with a different key combination. Here are some examples to show how the key-naming scheme works:

F2	The	function	key	F2	
SF2	Press	(SHIFT)	and	(F2)	together
CF2	Press	(CTRL)	and	(F2)	together
AF2	Press	(ALT)	and	(F2)	together
Alt−1	Press	(ALT)	and	(F1)	together
Ctl−1	Press	(CTRL)	and	(F1)	together

Once selected, a video mode will remain current until you select another or change it. Table 6-3 shows some good initial choices of video modes for different video hardware.

Graphics Adapter	Function Key	Pixels Across	Pixels Down	Colors
CGA	(F5)	320	200	4
EGA	(F2)	640	350	16
VGA	(F3)	320	200	256
Hercules	(ALT)-(G)	720	348	2

Table 6-3 Suggested initial video modes

Generating a Fractal

Go ahead and select a video mode. Fractint's highlighted choice should be a reasonable choice for your graphics hardware. Just press (ENTER) to select it, or use the arrow keys to select another mode first. The action of selecting a video mode begins the generation of a fractal image. The default image is type mandel, so you should now see a fractal being calculated on your screen. This is the famous Mandelbrot set, which we talked about a little earlier in the chapter. Your screen should look like Figure 6-12.

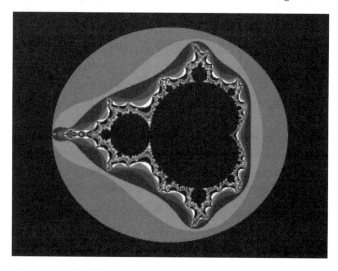

Figure 6-12 The Mandelbrot set

If you didn't get Fractint to display the Mandelbrot, the most likely cause was the selection of a video mode not supported by your hardware. While this can be disconcerting, it does no harm. Even if your screen is black, you can press (ESC) to get back to the Main menu. Then try again, this time selecting a different video mode. On a VGA (F3) should always work.

Once you get things working, try experimenting with other modes. This will give you a feel for how the resolution affects the speed. If you have a VGA and started off with (F3), try the higher-resolution modes. Not all VGA boards support all resolutions. The amount of graphics memory on your board is the main limiting factor. Table 6-4 shows how much video memory is required on your graphics adapter for different video modes.

Video Mode	Video Memory Required
320x200 256 colors	64K
640x400 256 colors	256K
640x480 256 colors	512K
800x600 256 colors	512K
1024x768 256 colors	1024K

Table 6-4 Memory Requirements of video modes

To allow quick evaluation, Fractint plots its images, such as the Mandelbrot, using multiple passes. The first pass rapidly plots the image at a coarser resolution, and the subsequent pass adds missing pixels to make a finer image. This way you don't have to wait for the image to be completed before continuing your explorations. You can generally tell what the fractal will look like after pass one. As an added bonus, Fractint uses this multiple-pass approach to guess areas that have solid colors, greatly speeding up the calculation.

Zooming In

Fractals are full of interesting details that unfold as you expand them. The Zoom function of Fractint lets you verify this fact for yourself. Pressing the (PGUP) key creates a Zoom box around the outer edge of the screen. Continuing to press (PGUP) makes the Zoom box smaller. The Zoom box can be moved around the screen using the arrow keys. The Zoom box can also be controlled with the mouse. Clicking the left mouse button brings up the Zoom box; holding the left button down while moving the mouse away from you shrinks the Zoom box; and simply moving the mouse with no buttons pressed moves the Zoom box. The idea is to locate some interesting detail in the fractals and place the Zoom box around it. Then pressing (ENTER) (or double-clicking the left mouse button) will cause the entire screen to be filled with the piece of the image that was in the Zoom box, so the Zoom box acts as a magnifier. The (PGDN) key is used to make the Zoom box larger. Repeatedly pressing (PGDN) will make the Zoom box disappear. To do the same thing with the mouse, hold the left button down and pull the mouse toward you. The movement of the Zoom box with the cursor keys can be speeded up on some machines by holding down the (CTRL) key while pressing the cursor keys. You can even Zoom out by making a small Zoom box and pressing (CTRL)-(ENTER). The effect of this is to Zoom out so that the whole image is shrunk to the size of the Zoom box. The equivalent mouse command is to double-click the right mouse button.

Try zooming in on the spike on the left side of the Mandelbrot image. See if you can find some "baby Mandelbrot" sets hiding there. It should be easy — their numbers are infinite!

Color Cycling

Fractint can rapidly alter displayed colors of an image, giving an effect of animation. This is accomplished by rotating the colors through the color palette so the mapping of numbers to colors changes.

Most fractal images have more information in them than the mind can comprehend. By assigning colors differently, different details become visible in the same image. Playing with the colors is at least half the fun of Fractint. Alas, this feature only works if your video hardware supports at least 16 colors (EGA), and works best in the VGA and Super VGA 256-color modes. If you have a CGA or Hercules monochrome graphics adapter, skip on to the next section.

To cycle the colors, press (+). Showtime! The colors of your fractal will now start wildly gyrating!

The (−) key reverses the direction of the color rotation. To freeze the color scheme, press (BACKSPACE). The outside border of the screen will now be white to remind you that Fractint is still in the color-cycling mode even though the colors aren't moving.

When you first enter the color-cycling mode, Fractint causes the existing colors to be rotated. The original color scheme will return periodically (every 256 colors if you have VGA, every 16 colors if you have EGA). Pressing any of the function keys (except (F1), which is always Help) causes Fractint to randomly create new colors, so that the color schemes do not repeat — at least not any time soon. Indeed, the number of color schemes obtained by pressing the function keys is astronomical! The lower function keys ((F2) through (F7)) cause the colors to change abruptly. The higher function keys ((F8), (F9), (F10)) cause the colors to change more smoothly and continuously between more widely spaced random colors. Pressing (ENTER) while the colors are cycling causes the color scheme to be completely and randomly altered.

There are two ways to control the speed of color cycling in Fractint. The first way is to use the (↑) and (↓) keys while colors are cycling. This feature was originally put in to control flicker on machines with slower graphics adapters. On these machines slowing down the cycling with (↓) cleans up the flicker. But if you have one of the new breed of faster computers, you may find the color cycling is just too fast for enjoyment, and use (↓) to slow it down. The other way to change the color cycling speed is to press any of the number keys, (1) through (9). These keys cause colors to be skipped, effectively increasing the rotation speed. The higher-numbered keys cause colors to rotate faster. Suppose, for example, you have a very striped fractal, and you wish to see more smoothly changing colors, so you press (F10). The new colors are being added to the end of the 256-color palette, and it takes a little time to flush out the old colors. To speed things up, press (9) until you see the smoother color changes have taken effect, then press (1) to slow things down again.

The easiest way to understand color cycling is to play with the keys. Press (+) to start color cycling. Then successively press (F2), (F3), and so on, going slowly enough to see the effect. In 256-color modes, it takes a little time to rotate all the old colors out of the palette and to see the effect. Assuming your fractal type is still set for the Mandelbrot, at first the image you are color cycling will have a strongly striped appearance. As you use the higher-numbered function keys, the colors of the stripes will start to blend, and your attention will be drawn more to the lake outline than to the stripes. When you see the image the way you want it, press (BACKSPACE) or (SPACE) to freeze it, and (ESC) to exit the color-cycling mode and return to the regular display mode.

Saving a File

The command to save a fractal image to a file is (S). You must be viewing your fractal, and not be in the color-cycling mode. Press (S) to save. You will see two multicolored stripes moving down the right and left sides of the screen like a bar as the saving progresses. Fractint saves images as GIF files, so when done, a window appears on the screen with the message "File saved as fract001.gif." The number 001 will increment as you save more images. These files take up a lot of space, so watch out for your disk filling up with too many images! Even with the built-in compression that the GIF format provides, a typical 640x480 256-color image can be 100 KB or more.

The Expanded Main Menu

Press (ESC) to return to the Main menu. You will see that he Main menu is no longer the same. Since you have created a fractal image, there are more func-

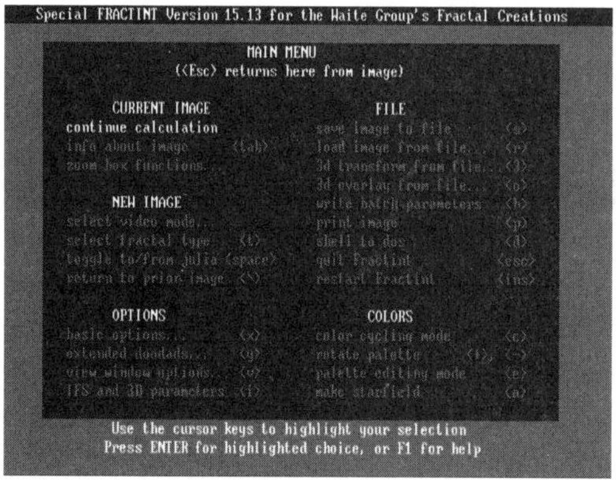

Figure 6-13 Expanded Main menu

tions Fractint can perform, so the menu is expanded. Figure 6-13 shows the expanded Main menu.

Here is a word of explanation about the additional items in the Main menu.

Current Image

Fractint can move back and forth nondestructively between menu and information screens and graphics screens. The menu item "continue calculation" returns you to the graphics screen, and if the calculation was interrupted when you returned to the Main menu, it will be resumed where you left off. The "info about image" selection gives you a screen of status information about the current image. This is particularly useful to find out if an image has been completed. The (TAB) key allows access to this status screen directly from an image. The remaining item, "Zoom box functions," takes you to the Help screen describing keystrokes for manipulating the Zoom box.

> Hint: You should try generating images with the higher-resolution video modes such as 800x600x256, or 1024x768x256 (if your video board supports those modes), and go back and forth between the image and the information screen using (TAB). If your graphics image is corrupted, you should place the line
>
> `textsafe=save`
>
> in your SSTOOLS.INI file to clear up the problem.

New Image

There are two new items here. The first allows the recalculation of the previous image. Fractint keeps track of the last few images you made, and the (\) key allows you to go back and recalculates them. If you began with the Mandelbrot and zoomed in several times, pressing ⬭ several times will get you back to the full Mandelbrot image. Do this now.

The second new item is the (SPACE) command, which makes use of the relationship between Mandelbrot and Julia fractals. The Mandelbrot fractal can be thought of as a catalog of Julia fractals. Each point of the Mandelbrot corresponds to the Julia fractal with parameters equal to the coordinates of that point. The (SPACE) key automates that relationship and makes it easy to go back and forth. Once you have the Mandelbrot back on the screen, make a small Zoom box by pressing the (PGUP) key several times or by holding down the left mouse button and moving the mouse away from you. Using the cursor keys or the mouse, move the Zoom box over a point right on the Mandelbrot "coastline," and press the (SPACE) key. Fractint will generate the Julia set corresponding to the point that was at the center of the Zoom box when you pressed (SPACE). Pressing (SPACE) again will return you to the Mandelbrot. The appearance of the Julia set can be predicted form the position of the point on the Mandelbrot set used to generate it. If the selected point is in the "lake," the corresponding Julia set will have a lake. If the point is "on land," the Julia will not have a single connected lake. Some of the most interesting Julia sets are created with parameter values that are very near the Mandelbrot shoreline.

There are many types in Fractint that have this Mandelbrot-Julia relationship. The (SPACE) toggle works with any of them. Table 6-5 shows all the these Mandelbrot-Julia pairs.

"Mandelbrot" Variant	"Julia" Variant
barnsleym1	barnsleyj1
barnsleym2	barnsleyj2
barnsleym3	barnsleyj3
cmplxmarksmand	cmplxmarksjul
manfn+exp	julfn+exp
manfn+zsqrd	julfn+zsqrd
mandel	julia
mandel4	julia4
manzpower	julzpower
manzzpwr	julzzpwr
mandelfn	lambdafn
mandellambda	lambda
magnet1m	magnet1j
magnet2m	magnet2j
manowar	manowarj
marksmandel	marksjulia

Table 6-5 Mandelbrot-Julia pairs in Fractint

Options

This part of the Main menu is the same as before you generated an image. It allows setting parameters that affect how images are calculated.

File

This menu covers different ways of getting information into and out of Fractint. The Save Image command (Ⓢ key) creates a file in CompuServe's GIF format. These images can be viewed on a variety of different machines, using any software that can decode the GIF89a format, and read back into Fractint with the Load Image From File function. When a Fractint GIF file is read back in, all system settings are returned to the values that created the image. Another way to save all the Fractint settings is to use the Write Batch Parameters (Ⓑ) command, which saves these settings in the file named FRABATCH.BAT in the form of command-line options. You can modify the FRABATCH.BAT file with a text editor and read the settings back in a form that can be modified with a text editor.

Colors

This menu item covers the controls for color cycling that we have already discussed. You will only see this if you are in a graphics video mode that allows color cycling, such as EGA or VGA 16 or 256-color modes.

A 3-D Mandelbrot Set

Next, we are going to perform some 3-D transformations of the Mandelbrot fractal. For the mathematically curious, the result will be a 3-D plot of the escape times of the Mandelbrot formula.

From the Main menu, select "restart fractint" or press the (INS) key, which accomplishes the same thing. This command reinitializes settings to their default values, with the same result as exiting and restarting Fractint.

Press the (X) key, and set "Inside Color" to "maxiter." To do this, use the (↓) key to move the highlight down to "Inside Color" and type in the word "maxiter."

The inside color is the palette number of the color used to color the "lake" areas of fractals, where the orbit never escapes and the maximum iterations limit is reached. This inside color value defaults to 2, which is the color blue in the standard IBM color palette on both EGA and VGA adapters. Setting the inside color to maxiter has the effect of setting the inside color to the maximum iteration value. Normally the choice of inside color is purely aesthetic, but not for what we are about to do. For interpreting fractals for 3-D purposes,

Fractint treats the color as a number. The color is interpreted as the height above the plane. Setting the inside color to maxiter has the effect of making the "lake" float at the top of the 3-D surface. This makes mathematical sense because the resulting image is a graph of the iteration count of the escape-time calculation. Of course, "making mathematical sense" is not necessary when creating fractals. You can do what you want, and if the result looks good, you are right! The important point is that setting the inside color affects the height of the "lake" when you are doing a 3-D transformation.

When you are done with the (X) command screen, press (ENTER) to accept the values and return. If you have a VGA, press (F3) to generate a Mandelbrot in the 320x200 256-color mode. If you don't have a VGA or other adapter with a 320x200x256 mode, then use the (ALT)-(M) Disk/RAM Video 320, 200, 256 mode. This mode is buried way down the list. You can either cursor down to it, highlight it, and press (ENTER) , or just press (ALT) and (M) together to select it. (The Disk/RAM video isn't really video at all. Rather, it is a way of creating images using your disk, or, if you have enough, your extended or expanded memory.)

When the image is complete , save the image by pressing the (S) key. Make a mental note of the file name that was reported at the top of the screen.

Return to the Main menu with (ESC). Select "3-D transform from file" under the File menu. (You could also have pressed (3).) You will now be presented with a list of files. Move the highlight to the file you just created with the save operation, and press (ENTER). Next you will see a list of video modes. The video mode you used to generate the Mandelbrot should be highlighted. If you have a VGA, you can use the same (F3) mode. Press (ENTER) to select it.

Fractint is now going to lead you through some screens that allow setting all manner of parameters and effects for 3-D. The default values almost always make sense — you do not have to understand what they all mean. You can use the on-line help for a synopsis of what all these options do.

The first screen is entitled 3-D Mode Selection. Here is where you can turn on stereo and make red/blue 3-D images, or use the sphere mode to create a fractal planet. Press (ENTER) to accept all the values. The next screen is entitled Select 3-D Fill Type. Here is where you will find the Fractint light source options, that let you illuminate your fractal and create shadows. The "just draw the points" option will be highlighted, which is just fine for now, so press (ENTER) . The next screen, entitled Planar 3-D Parameters, presents options for various three-dimensional rotations and scale factors. You can view your fractal from different angles, spin it in space, stretch it, and shrink it, and move the viewer's perspective right into the middle of it. When making fractal landscapes, you can control the roughness of mountain ranges, and the height of floods in the valleys. The default values are all OK, so press (ENTER) to accept them. After this tutorial you can come back and experiment.

You have now launched the 3-D transformation, which takes a few minutes. You will see the blue background of the Mandelbrot appear just as you saw it on the screen a few moments before, but laid at an angle like a piece of paper on a desk. As the image develops, you will see that the colored stripes of the Mandelbrot are raised, like the steps of a Mexican pyramid. Floating above everything is the dark blue Mandelbrot lake, mysteriously supported by a column of sparkling points. You should now understand why we set the inside parameter to maxiter. If we had left the default inside=2, the "lake" would have been at the same level as the blue background, instead of floating mysteriously above it. Figure 6-14 shows what the 3-D Mandelbrot looks like.

Let's try a few variations. For each variation, start with the ③ command. Fractint will remember your previous settings, and you can move from screen to screen by pressing (ENTER), pausing only to make the indicated changes. If you overshoot a screen, you can back up with (ESC). The one setting that will not be remembered is the video mode, if you used a different video mode for the 3-D transformation than you did for the original fractal. If that is the case for you, when you get to the video mode screen just reselect the video mode you would like to use. If you have a VGA and used (F3) to generate the original image, you will not have this minor complication, because in your case the

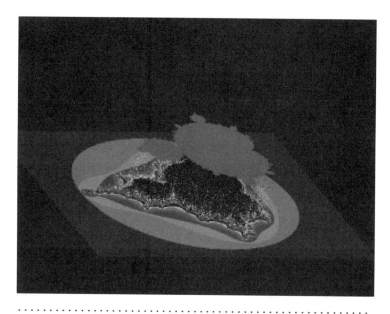

Figure 6-14 Mandelbrot lake floating in space

Figure 6-15 Mandelbrot cliffs in perspective

video list will come up with the (F3) mode highlighted. You can accept it by pressing (ENTER), just as you do for the other screens that do not require changes.

The first variation makes solid cliffs. Start with the (3) command, and move through the screens with (ENTER). When you come to the Select 3-D Fill Type screen, select "Surface Fill (colors interpolated)", but otherwise leave the settings unchanged, pressing (ENTER) until the image regenerates. This option definitely slows things up, so take another break! This time the floating Mandelbrot will become the top of a mountain with precipitous cliffs.

The second variation adds a perspective viewpoint. Start with (3), and move through the screens with (ENTER). When you come to the Planar 3-D Parameters screen, look for "Perspective distance [1–999, 0 for no persp]" about half-way down. Type in 150. Smaller numbers provide the more extreme perspective of a closer viewpoint, while higher numbers create a flatter perspective, such as photographers obtain through a telephoto lense. Press (ENTER) to regenerate the image. As a side-effect, the image edges will look a little bit rougher. But you are now in the scene, with closer features expanded! Figure 6-15 shows the Mandelbrot cliffs in perspective.

The third variation depresses the Mandelbrot floating island and makes it a lake at the bottom of a canyon. Start with (3), and move through the screens with (ENTER). When you come to the Planar 3-D Parameters screen, look for

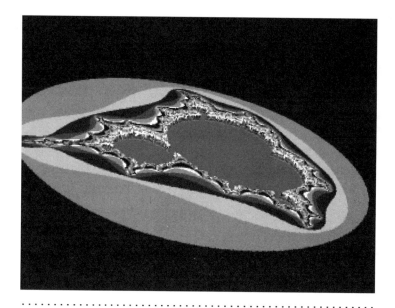

Figure 6-16 Mandelbrot canyon

"Surface Roughness scaling factor in pct," which should have the default value of 30. We want you to depress the mountaintop and make it a lake, so change the surface roughness value to -5. That's right, the new value is negative 5, which means that the z coordinate will be scaled by negative 5 percent — depressing the mountaintop below the surrounding plain. Press (ENTER) to re-generate the image. Figure 6-16 shows the result.

Snowflakes

Until now, this tutorial has been restricted to the Mandelbrot fractal type, ex-cept for a brief interlude with the Julia types. The Mandelbrot type by itself is enough for many hours of fascinating fractal explorations, especially given the options of zooming, color cycling, and 3-D transformations. But now it is time to venture still further, and explore some new territory. Since the discussion of fractals earlier in this chapter used the Koch snowflake as an example, we'll deal with the fractal type lsystems, which is where the snowflakes are hiding.

The term L-systems is short for Lindenmayer systems, so named for Aristid Lindenmayer, who developed the L-systems idea as a way of modeling plants. The book *The Algorithmic Beauty of Plants,* by Prezemyslaw Prusinkiewicz and Aristid Lindenmayer (Springer Verlag, 1990), gives a concise treatment of the theory, along with many beautiful images. L-systems are a logical system for generating strings of symbols, which when interpreted as graphics commands, result in drawings. Every L-system image is defined in terms of axioms, which are starting strings of symbols, and production rules, which determine how the strings can be used to generate other strings. The idea is to start with the axioms, and then apply the production rules to create new strings. The process is repeated for a number of iterations, which is called the order of the L-system. In the Fractint implementation, the axioms and production rules are stored in a file called FRACTINT.L. The particular setup that generates the Koch snowflake is:

```
Koch1 {
  Angle 6
  Axiom F--F--F
  F=F+F--F+F
}
```

To start with, no meaning is assigned to the strings. There is one axiom, which is the string of characters F--F--F. The meaning of the production rule F=F+F--F+F is that everywhere you see F in a string, you should replace it with F+F--F+F. Thus after one application of the production rule, the resulting string is:

```
F+F--F+F--F+F--F+F--F+F--F+F
```

To see this a little more clearly, let's put parentheses in to show where the production rule was applied:.

```
(F+F--F+F)--(F+F--F+F)--(F+F--F+F)
```

You can see that each substring surrounded by parentheses is the result of applying the production rule.

Now for the fun part. After generating a string by applying the production rules some number of times, the resulting string is used to draw a picture. The meaning of the symbols is as follows. Think of yourself as a drawing computer holding a pen. If you see an "F", you draw a line forward one unit. If you see a "+", the drawing direction turns left, or counterclockwise, by a predetermined angle. If you see a "-", the drawing direction turns right, or clockwise. The angle used for the turns is defined by the "angle 6" statement. The angle parameter is interpreted as the fraction of the whole circle to turn, so 6 means 360/6 or 60^0.

With those definitions, the axiom F--F--F means "forward, right 60^0, right 60^0, forward right 60^0, right 60^0, forward." With a little thought, you can see that those instructions define a triangle.

Now look at the production rule. The string F+F--F+F means "Forward, left 60^0, forward, right 60^0, right 60^0, forward, left 60^0, forward." This is exactly the sequence of commands needed to draw the modified triangle side that results in the Koch snowflake.

Here is how to generate the Koch snowflake in Fractint.

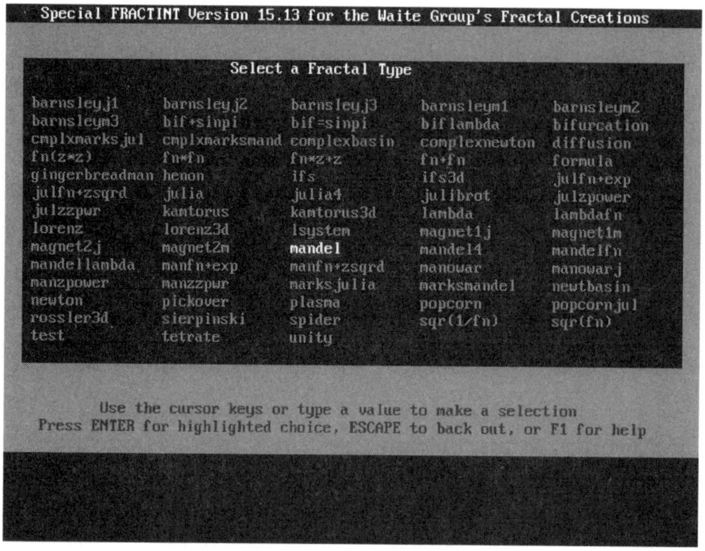

```
Special FRACTINT Version 15.13 for the Waite Group's Fractal Creations

                        Select a Fractal Type
  barnsleyj1      barnsleyj2      barnsleyj3      barnsleym1      barnsleym2
  barnsleym3      bif+simpi       bif=simpi       biflambda       bifurcation
  cmplxmarksjul   cmplxmarksmand  complexbasin    complexnewton   diffusion
  fn(z*z)         fn*fn           fn*z+z          fn+fn           formula
  gingerbreadman  henon           ifs             ifs3d           julfn+exp
  julfn+zsqrd     julia           julia4          julibrot        julzpower
  julzzpwr        kamtorus        kamtorus3d      lambda          lambdafn
  lorenz          lorenz3d        lsystem         magnet1j        magnet1m
  magnet2j        magnet2m        mandel          mandel4         mandelfn
  mandellambda    manfn+exp       manfn+zsqrd     manowar         manowarj
  manzpower       manzzpwr        marksjulia      marksmandel     newtbasin
  newton          pickover        plasma          popcorn         popcornjul
  rossler3d       sierpinski      spider          sqr(1/fn)       sqr(fn)
  test            tetrate         unity

            Use the cursor keys or type a value to make a selection
       Press ENTER for highlighted choice, ESCAPE to back out, or F1 for help
```

Figure 6-17 The Fractal Type screen

After starting Fractint, press Ⓣ to get to the Fractal Type screen, which is shown in Figure 6-17. Select fractal type lsystem by using the cursor to move the cursor to lsystem, or by using Fractint's speed key feature and typing in the letters "lsy". Then press (ENTER). You will then see a list of files that end in .l in the current directory. (If you are not in the directory where the file FRACTINT.L resides, you can navigate to that directory by selecting ".." to move up a directory, or by selecting a subdirectory name to move down a directory.) Move the highlight to the file name FRACTINT.L with the arrow keys and press (ENTER). You will now see the names of the different L-systems stored in the file. Select the L-system "koch1." Once again, you can use the arrow keys to move the highlight, or you can type the first few letters of "koch1" and use the speed key feature. Press (ENTER). Now you will be asked to fill in the order, which is how many times the production rule will be iteratively applied. Always start with low orders and increase slowly. The time it takes to calculate an L-systems fractal increases dramatically with the order, so unless you like to sit a long time watching the little spinning line that indicates the L-system calculation is working, start with a low number. In this case, start with order 0. This means that the production rule is not applied at all, so what you are seeing is a plot of the axiom by itself. If you have already selected a video mode, the L-system will plot now. If you haven't selected a video mode, you will find yourself back at the main screen with the "select video mode" menu item highlighted. In that case, press (ENTER), and select the highest video mode that your graphics hardware supports, 1024x768 if possible. As expected, the result is an equilateral triangle. Now press (T) to return to the Fractal Type screen, and repeatedly press (ENTER) to cycle through all the options again, accepting the previous value, until you come to the screen asking for the order. Try the value "1" this time. By incrementing the order each time, you can duplicate the sequence of snowflake images shown a few pages back in Figure 6-3. Keep increasing the order. After you reach order 5 or 6, you will see no visible change. At this point the L-systems iteration results in new bends in the shape that are so small that they are too fine to display with the pixels on your screen, so no change is visible.

The file FRACTINT.L contains many interesting L-system files. Some of these make interesting patterns that you can use in your graphics images. You can even try to write your own L-systems formulas, placing them in a new L-systems file with a name like MYLSYS.L. You will find, for example, that the axiom in KOCH1 is very noncritical. You can replace it with most any shape you wish.

Clouds and Mountains

The plasma fractal type allows the creation of both cloud and mountain range images. You will see before your eyes that the claim made earlier — that clouds and mountains are very closely related — is true.

The plasma type makes a random pattern of smoothly changing colors that look like clouds. This type works best with a 256-color mode. If you have an EGA, you can follow along, but the results will be different.

Press the (INS) key to reinitialize Fractint. Then select a video mode. The (F3) mode is a good choice for VGA, (F9) for EGA. You can choose a video mode by selecting "select video mode" from the menu, or you can press (F3) or (F9) directly. After you have selected a video mode (and pressed (ENTER) if you selected the mode from the mode list), press (T) to display the Fractal Type screen. Use the arrow keys to select the Plasma Fractal.

As soon as you pressed (ENTER) to accept your parameters choice, the plasma calculation will have begun. What you are seeing on the screen is a fascinating algorithm that recursively subdivides the screen, randomly choosing colors as it goes. No two plasma images are quite the same, because of the random element in the calculation. When the image is complete, start color cycling with the (+) command. You can see why this type is called "plasma." The screen colors ooze and writhe in graceful undulations of ethereal plasma waves. Be sure to try the function keys while color cycling. The lower-numbered function keys ((F2) through (F7)) are for paisley pattern fans, the higher ones ((F8), (F9), (F10)) yield more graceful patterns.

To create a mountain, you first have to save a plasma image. If you are still in the color-cycling mode (as visually indicated by either moving colors or a white screen boundary), then you should exit to the display mode by pressing (ESC). Press (S) to save the plasma screen, once again making a note of the file name reported on the screen.

We can turn a cloud into a mountain by doing a 3-D transformation on the colors of the cloud. A cloud image can be considered a color-coded contour map of a mountain, where areas of equal color are the same height. By performing a 3-D transformation, we are transforming the contour map back into the mountain it represents.

Press the (3) key to invoke the 3-D function, and select the just-saved file from the file list. At the video mode selection screen, select the same video mode used to generate the plasma in the first place ((F3) for VGA, (F9) for EGA). Accept the default values of the "3D Mode Selection" by pressing (ENTER). At the Select 3-D Fill Type screen, select "surface fill (colors interpolated)" and press (ENTER). This will bring you to the Planar 3-D Parameters screen. If you have an EGA and are reading in a 16-color plasma file, set Surface Roughness to 500. VGA users reading in a 256-color plasma file can leave the default value of 30 unchanged. Press (ENTER), and watch a mountain emerge before your eyes.

Varying some of the parameters will give you an idea of the control you have when making 3-D images. You can flood the valleys and make the mountain emerge from water. Repeat all the instructions for making a mountain from a saved plasma cloud in the previous paragraph, until you reach the Planar 3-D Parameters screen. Then set the "water color (minimum color value)" item to 47. This will cause all color values less than 47 to be mapped to a flat lake surface. After the mountain landscape has been created, enter the color-cycling mode by pressing (C). You will be in color-cycling mode, but the colors will not be moving. Then press (L) (for "load map"). This color-cycling command allows you to load various color maps. There is a special map called TOPO.MAP that has color values tailored to plasma mountains, complete with water, rocks, greenery, and snow. Select TOPO.MAP from the file list. If it is not in the list, type in the drive letter and directory where you put the Fractint files. For example, type:

`c:\IMLAB\fractint\` (ENTER)

Then the Map File screen will be refreshed and you should see TOPO.MAP. Select it, and press (ENTER). Exit color-cycling mode by pressing (ESC). You should then see a plasma mountain with more realistic landscape coloring. Figure 6-18 shows an example.

Another variation is to use the sphere 3-D function to make a plasma planet. Repeat the plasma mountain instructions above, beginning with the

Figure 6-18 A "plasma" mountain rising from a lake

③ command, selecting the same plasma file, and using the (F3) video mode. At the 3-D Mode Selection screen, cursor down to the "Spherical Projection" item, type "yes", and press (ENTER). Continue to press (ENTER), accepting all the defaults for the next screens. The plasma image will be projected onto the surface of a sphere, making a plasma planet. You can project any GIF image onto a sphere in this way, whether or not it originated in Fractint. We'll be using this technique quite a bit in later examples.

FRACTAL RECIPES

If the tutorial above got your feet wet in fractal-making fun, this section invites you to dive in. Here is a collection of fractal recipes from various gifted fractal artists. Fractint makes it very easy to make images of dizzying beauty and fascination. At first it is difficult to imagine that images could be more spectacular. Experienced fractal artists learn to recognize the "easy" fractals, and develop an appreciation for truly outstanding efforts. The recipes in this section are the kinds of examples that a fractal aficionado loves.

Before we start, there are a few conventions that need to be made clear so you can follow the recipes. Virtually every Fractint setting that you can set by using the menus can also be set from that command line. Unfortunately your computer only allows you 128 characters when you type in a command, and some fractal settings have so many options that the command-line invocation of all the options exceeds 128 bytes. Fractint provides an alternative method: it can read commands from a file. The recipes will be given to you in a form such that the Fractint settings can be read in from a file. To take a simple example, suppose you wanted to calculate the type Newton fractal with maximum iterations set to 1000. You could set the maximum iterations with the (x) menu, and set type Newton with the (T) menu. You could also type in the command line

```
C:>FRACTINT TYPE=NEWTON MAXITER=1000 (ENTER)
```

However, suppose you created a file with your text editor called MYNEWTON that contained the lines:

```
TYPE=NEWTON
MAXITER=1000
```

Then you could achieve the same results with

```
C:>FRACTINT @MYNEWTON (ENTER)
```

The little @ character is really important; it tells Fractint that what follows is a file with commands. All the recipes below will be in the form of commands that you can type in a file. This is a good idea anyway, because by typing the commands in a file, you have a record of what you have done and can systematically modify your experiments to achieve different results.

You can automate the generation of fractals with indirect files by adding the line batch=yes to the file. Adding batch=yes causes the Fractint to generate your fractal with no interactive prompts, and to save the resulting image when the fractal calculation is finished.

Mt. Rock

The book *Fractal Creations* comes with a spectacular poster that features a surrealistic image called Mt. Rock, showing a craggy landscape in psychedelic colors under a fractal planet. The authors have been asked many times how that image was made, and now you'll get a chance to see for yourself.

Fair warning: This is an advanced topic; duplicating Mt. Rock takes a number of steps that use a lot of different Fractint features. You will need to create the mountain, create the planet, and then combine them. We'll touch on what the various Fractint settings do so that you have an idea of what Fractint is doing without explaining them in depth.

Make a Continuous Potential File

In the previous examples, a Mandelbrot fractal was converted to 3-D. With the usual method of rendering the Mandelbrot method called "escape time coloring" the image is divided into many stripes. When converted to 3-D, these stripes become little horizontal terraces. However, the Mandelbrot algorithm can be modified using a method called *continuous potential*. This method works by assuming that the Mandelbrot *lake* (the solid area in the middle, which is actually the Mandelbrot set itself) has an electrical charge, and the electrostatic potential field surrounding this charged area is plotted. The importance of this approach has nothing to do with potential or electrostatic charges; all you need to understand is that the continuous potential method results in continuously changing colors rather than stripes. Continuous potential images often make excellent landscapes when converted to 3-D.

To access the continuous potential parameters, use the ⒴ menu. There are three parameters. The Max Color menu item is the color index assigned to the highest point. This is usually set to 255 if you are using a 256-color video mode. The Slope menu item affects how rapidly the colors change. If this value is too high, you will run out of colors and the "bottom" will be a solid color. If it is too low, the whole range of colors will not show in the image. The best value varies with circumstances — you will have to experiment with values from 200 and up. The Bailout is the value used to test whether an iterated orbit value has escaped. The normal value is 4, but continuous potential works much better with a larger value like 200 to 1000. Notice that such large values require the use of floating point math, so you should have the setting FLOAT=YES in your command files. The last potential parameter is a flag for 16-bit values. This is only necessary if you are intending to convert your continuous potential image to 3D, as we are in this example. With this option turned on, Fractint creates double-width GIF files that hold the fractional part of the color value, which when interpreted for 3-D purposes is the third dimension. Having this extra precision gives much smoother results with the light source option. But we're getting ahead of ourselves. Look in \IMLAB\EXAMPLES for the files needed to duplicate these fractals.

The input file to create the continuous potential image for Mt. Rock is as follows:

```
type=mandel
corners=-0.397243/0.136537/-1.17733/-0.778195
float=yes
maxiter=255
inside=213
potential=255/1100/1000/16bit
video=SF5
savename=mtrock.pot
```

Listing 6-1 Mt. Rock continuous potential image

To generate this image, either type the listing into a file or use the file LIST6-1 on the companion disk. To run the commands in the file, type:

`C:>FRACTINT @LIST6-1` (ENTER)

You can run the command file in batch mode and automatically save the image when done by adding the line batch=yes to the command line. In this case you would type:

`C:>FRACTINT @LIST6-1 BATCH=YES` (ENTER)

The batch form is useful if you want to generate several fractals when you are away from the computer. It causes Fractint to automatically save the image when done. You can also add the batch=yes line to the indirect file. The advantage of typing batch=yes on the command line rather than in the indirect file is that you have the option of using the batch mode or not without having to change the indirect file.

The result of running the Fractint indirect file LIST6-1 is shown in Figure 6-19. The image is saved in the double-wide GIF file called MTROCK.POT. A couple of observations are in order. Notice that the maximum iterations is set at 255, but the inside color is 213. We want to make a canyon out of the Mandelbrot

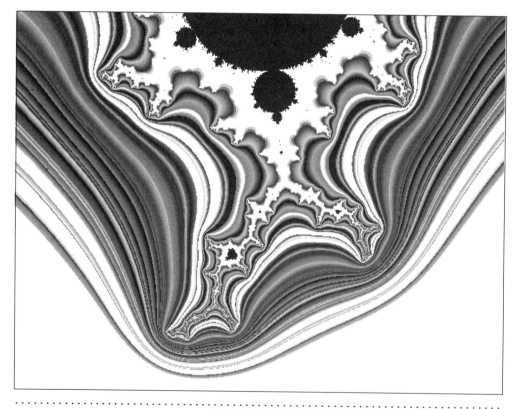

Figure 6-19 Continuous potential image

set with a lake lower than the canyon walls. The inside value, which is the number assigned to values which have orbits that reach the maximum iterations limit of 255 without escaping, is set less than 255. Notice also that this listing has the video mode set for SF5, which is the 640x480x256 color mode. You can use another mode, but make sure it has 256 colors. After generating the image, save the result by pressing Ⓢ. (Generating this image will take a long time if you do not have a math coprocessor.)

Because the IBM default color palette is very dark in the higher end of the palette, the lake area is hard to see. You need to rotate the colors to see the result. The colors are not important at this point, because they are really 3-D elevations. The color *number* is what we care about, not the color itself, and the numbers don't change when we color cycle.

Do a 3-D Transform Using a Light Source

The next step is to convert the file we just made to a 3-D file with a 3-D transformation. The commands to do this are shown in Listing 6-2. Type them in a file called LIST6-2 or use the LIST6-2 file from your book disk. Running this indirect file creates the image MTROCK3D.GIF.

. . . .

```
3d=yes
filename=mtrock.pot
filltype=6
rotation=65/5/0
scalexyz=100/100
roughness=200
waterline=0
perspective=0
xyshift=0/0
lightsource=0/-1/1
xyadjust=0/-80
ambient=0
savename=mtrock3d.gif
map=altern.map
```

Listing 6-2 Mt. Rock 3-D transformation

This listing contains a lot of the magic of Fractint's 3-D capability. The file name MTROCK.POT is the file generated by Listing 6-1. Make sure that the file name is correct. Filltype=6 turns on a lighting option that shades the image according to the angle with a light vector which is specified in the lightsource= parameter. The color map ALTERN.MAP is a grayscale map included with Fractint, and is designed for use with the lightsource mode. The roughness parameter affects the steepness of the slopes. The correct setting of this parameter varies with the video mode. The value of 200 creates a terrain similar to the Mt. Rock poster when the resolution is 640x480. The roughness parameter should be adjusted proportionally to the image resolution when you change modes. For example, if you want to use the (F3) 320×200×256-color mode with the original continuous potential image, then the roughness should be 100. On the other hand, if you aspire to duplicate the *Fractals Creation* poster result, you will need to use a 2048x1756 disk video mode, in which case the roughness value should be set to 200*(2048/640) or 640.

To generate Mt. Rock, type:

`C:>FRACTINT @LIST6-2` (ENTER)

Use the same 256-color video mode that you used to make the POT file. At all the other prompts, just type (ENTER). The result, a 3-D transformed grayscale version of Mt. Rock, is shown in Figure 6-20.

Figure 6-20 The grayscale Mt.Rock

Create a Newtbasin Fractal

To accomplish properly adding a planet to the Mt. Rock image requires Piclab. This is because Fractint does not have any mechanism for reconciling the different palettes of the landscape and the planet. However, an approximation of the *Fractal Creations* poster image can be made using only Fractint.

The first step is to make a Newton image. Listing 6-3 shows the parameters. Type these parameters into a file called LIST6-3. Running this indirect file creates the image NEWT.GIF.

```
type=newtbasin
corners=0.983693/2.25798/-2.9956/-2.03989
params=3/0/0/0
type=newtbasin
savename=newt
```

Listing 6-3 Parameters for the Mt. Rock Newton

Figure 6-21 The Newton fractal

To generate the Newton fractal, type:

`C:>FRACTINT @LIST6-3` (ENTER)

Use a 640x480 video mode such as (SHIFT) (F5) or (F4). Newtbasin does not need a lot of colors; it uses as many colors as the polynomial order, in this case 3. The resulting image NEWT.GIF is shown in Figure 6-21.

Overlay the Newtbasin Planet

Fractint contains a mechanism to overlay images on top of each other. It works exactly like the (3) command for doing 3-D transformations, except that the screen is not cleared. The Newton image will be converted to a planet and overlayed on top of the landscape image in one operation. Use the (R) command to load in the file MTROCK3D.GIF you made above. Then type (O) to access the overlay mode and Fractint will display a list of files. Select the file NEWT.GIF that you just created and press (ENTER). At the 3-D Mode Selection screen, type in "yes" for the sphere option, and (leaving the other settings unchanged) press (ENTER). At the Select 3-D Fill Type screen, select "just draw the dots" and press (ENTER). The next screen prompts you for a MAP file. For now just press (ENTER). The next screen is called Sphere 3-D Parameters. These affect the size and position of the overlayed planet image. Set the Radius scale factor to 40, the Roughness factor to 0, the Image non-perspective x shift to -30, and the Image non-perspective y shift to 30. These settings map the Newtbasin fractal onto a

Figure 6-22 The Mt. Rock image after overlaying the planet

sphere, which is overlaid onto the Mt. Rock image in the upper- left corner. Press (ENTER) when done. You should now see the Newtbasin planet appearing on top of Mt. Rock. The result is shown in Figure 6-22.

Editing the Colors

When the image is done, the planet colors should look like the original Newton, but the Mt. Rock colors probably look pretty bad. To make it look like the poster, you need to load a color map file called CHROMA.MAP. To load this file while viewing the image, press (C) to enter the color-cycling mode without actually cycling the colors. Then press (L) for "load a map file." Select the file CHROMA.MAP. If you don't see this file on the list, you can either navigate the directory tree to the directory where the file is stored (it should be with your Fractint files) or you can directly type in the directory name by typing (for example):

`C:\IMLAB\FRACTINT` (ENTER)

After you have loaded CHROMA.MAP, press (ESC) to get out of color-cycling mode. (A white border around your screen is the visual indicator of the color cycling mode.) Now the Mt.Rock image should be vibrant with color, but the planet has become almost invisible. There are difficulties combining images that use different color palettes, since the color numbers in the original planet and mountain images represent colors in two different color palettes, and only one color palette can be used at a time. The Newton planet only uses three colors, so we will change those colors. Where those same color numbers are used in Mt. Rock, those colors will change also, but Mt. Rock looks so psyche-delic with the CHROMA.MAP palette that it won't noticeably affect the mountain colors.

While viewing the Mt. Rock-with-planet image, press ⓔ to invoke the palette editor. The Fractint palette-editor is a powerful facility for manipulating color palettes. You will see a dotted line outline of the palette editor tool on the screen. You should move it with the cursor keys or mouse so that it is not covering the planet, and then press (ENTER). The palette editor tool has a grid that shows all 256 colors. The Newtbasin planet uses colors 1, 2, and 3. There is a small cross hair that you can move with the cursor keys or with the mouse. Move it to the second little color patch·in the palette editor color grid in the top row. Since the color numbers start with 0, the second patch is color 1. Figure 6-23 shows where this is. Press Ⓡ. This allows you to type in the red component of color 1. Type "7", and the patch should turn bright red. Move the cross hair to the second patch with the arrow keys (color 2). Press ⓑ to edit the blue component of color 2. Enter the number 7, and the patch for color 2 should now be bright blue. Then move the cross hair to the fourth patch (color 3). Press ⓖ and then 7. Now the planet should have bright colors, at the expense of three of the colors of Mt. Rock having also changed.

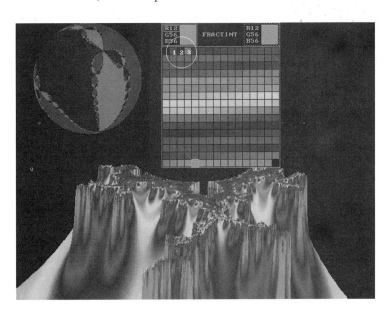

Figure 6-23 Editing colors 1, 2, and 3 with the palette editor

Press (ESC) to end the color editor and save the image by pressing (S). What you have now is a pretty good approximation of the *Fractal Creations* poster image. You'll learn how to do an even better job in Chapter 9, where we will make a more realistic planet using the Persistence of Vision Ray Tracer.

Fractal Origami

The title of this section tells you that we are headed toward fractals that look like colorful Japanese origami paper foldings. First, however, several topics need to be discussed.

The Fractint Formula Parser

One of the features that makes Fractint's enjoyment inexhaustible is writing your own fractal formulas. Formulas we have supplied are stored with the .FRM extension. There are two formula files on the companion disk. The file FRACTINT.FRM contains the standard examples distributed with Fractint. The file IMAGELAB.FRM contains examples used in the book. The way you access the Fractint formula type from the Main menu is to access the Fractal Type screen by pressing (T), and then select type formula. Next you will see a list of all the files with the .FRM extension in your current directory. Select the file IMAGELAB.FRM. If you don't see that file in the list, you can navigate through your disk's directory tree by selecting ".." to go up a directory level, or by selecting a subdirectory name to go down. You can also type in the full pathname to directly change directories.

Once you have opened a formula file, you will see a list of fractals formulas that are defined in the file. You can select any one of them and run them with various options as if they were normal fractal types built in to Fractint. Here is where the fun starts for a true fractal adventurer. You can edit the formula files with any text editor and invent whole new fractals!

Inside the file IMAGELAB.FRM, you will find the following formula:

```
Zexpe (XAXIS) = {
    z = Pixel:
    z = z ^ 2.71828182845905 + pixel,
    |z| <= 100
}
```

To fully understand what this formula is doing, you have to know a little bit about complex numbers. Don't worry if you haven't studied much mathematics; the truth is you can play with these formulas even if you don't know exactly what they are doing! The best approach is to use your text editor and make small changes in the examples and see what happens.

Let's go through this file and see what each line means. The first line of the formula assigns the name that you see after you open the formula file. After the name you can optionally specify the symmetry of the fractal to save time. In this case the fractal has XAXIS symmetry, which means that the bottom of the fractal is the mirror reflection of the top half with respect to the x axis. If XAXIS symmetry is specified, Fractint makes use of this to do half as much work by only calculating the top half of a fractal. (If you have zoomed into a region that is completely contained in the top half or the bottom half, then specifying symmetry doesn't have any advantage.) You can add a symmetry statement whether or not the fractal really has symmetry. If you do, Fractint will dutifully calculate only the top half and just copy that to the bottom half; the only problem with doing that is that you won't see the real fractal if the fractal doesn't really have the mathematical symmetry you specify.

You might wonder how to determine what the real symmetry of a formula is. If you are a world-famous mathematician, you can probably figure out the symmetry from what you know about the properties of the functions making up the formula. A more practical approach, especially for those of us who are *not* world-famous mathematicians, is to calculate a sample of the fractal and just look at it to see if it seems to have visual symmetry. If the part above the x axis looks like the reflection of the part below the x axis, go ahead and add the symmetry identifier after the name. If the result looks the same with and without the symmetry= line, then for all practical purposes the fractal is symmetrical, and you might as well enjoy the speed benefits of specifying the symmetry. Just be a little cautious — some formulas look symmetrical but aren't really. In the case of the Zexpe fractal, not only does it look symmetrical, but it really is symmetrical because of the nature of the power function z^e. Table 6-6 shows the kinds of symmetry that Fractint can exploit. (You can also force the use of symmetry with the "symmetry=" command-line option.)

. . . .

Symmetry Name	Effect
NONE	No symmetry assumed
XAXIS	Below the x axis is a reflection of above x axis
YAXIS	Left of y axis is a reflection of the right
XYAXIS	Combination of x axis and y axis symmetry
ORIGIN	Upper left is a reflection of lower right
PI	Fractal repeats every 180 degrees along the x axis

Table 6-6 Symmetry options

Following the optional symmetry specification is an equal sign and a curly bracket. The matching curly brackets contain the formula itself. The formula is divided into three parts. The first part is executed once per screen pixel. The second part is the formula that is iterated to calculate the fractal, and the third part is the criterion for continuing the iteration. The first section continues up until a colon character ":" is found. There is no division between the iteration section and the bailout criterion section; the last statement is assumed to be the bailout criterion.

In the Zexpe example, the once-per-pixel calculation is

```
z = Pixel:
```

This line creates a variable z and gives it the value of Pixel, which is a predefined variable that has the value of the complex number assigned to the current pixel on the screen. (In Fractint fractal calculations, a region of the complex plane is assigned to the visible area of the screen. When you zoom in, you are changing the assigned region to a smaller one.) Typically the variable Pixel takes on values like (1.2, –.0333) with the x and y components less than 2.0 and greater than –2.0.

The iterated formula for Zexpe is

```
z = z ^ 2.71828182845905 + pixel,
```

The little "hat" symbol, ^, is called a caret and means raise to the power of. For each iteration, the variable z is given the value of z raised to the power of 2.71828182845905 plus the current value of Pixel. The number 2.71828182845905 is an approximation of the famous number e known to students of calculus. This is *almost* the formula for the Mandelbrot set. If the number 2.71828182845905 is changed to 2 in the iteration line of the formula, then the result would indeed be the Mandelbrot set. (You can verify this for yourself. The file IMAGELAB.FRM contains another formula Zexp_mandel which is identical to Zexpe except for this small change.)

The last section of a formula is the criterion for bailing out of the iteration of the formula. The line

```
|z| <= 100
```

means that the iteration of the formula will continue until the size of the variable z exceeds 10.

The notation |z| doesn't quite mean what a math student might expect. The Fractint definition of |z| is |z| = (real part of z)^2 + (imaginary part of z)^2, whereas the usual mathematical definition of |z| is the square root of ((real part of z)^2 + (imaginary part of z)^2.) This is what separates mathematicians from programmers; a mathematician would take the square root and compare the result with 10, but a programmer can't bear to waste all that computer time on an unnecessary square root, so the square root is not taken and the result is compared with 100! The result is the same except that the programmer's method is faster.

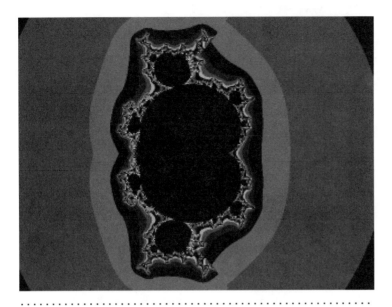

Figure 6-24 The Zexpe fractal with default corners values

Generating the Zexpe Fractal

With these preliminaries out of the way, run the Zexpe formula. To do this from the main Fractint menu, press ⓣ, select fractal type formula, select the .FRM file IMAGELAB.FRM, and select the formula fractal Zexpe. If you haven't already done so, select a video mode. Pressing ⒡③ for the 320x200 mode is fine if you have a VGA. The result is shown in Figure 6-24.

Because this fractal uses transcendental functions like sine, cosine, and the exponential, it is very, very slow on a computer with no math coprocessor. The results with a math coprocessor are much better. Fractal enthusiasts who are sticklers for accuracy often set float=yes and passes=1. But with these settings, even on a reasonably fast computer such as a 33-MHz 386, some of these fractals can take somewhere between 2 and 12 hours at 640x480 pixels. Our examples use the default faster integer math (no float=yes statement) and solid guessing (passes=guess), which gives much faster results. However, for the really deep zooms, Fractint will automatically turn the use of the floating point back on. These *are* advanced examples; consider yourself warned that some of them take hours to run! There is an up side to this. In a few years, when 1000-MHz wrist-top computers have become commonplace and these fractals will take a second or two to generate, you can tell your children that you can remember back when you generated fractal images that took hours!

The Zexpe fractal shown in Figure 6-24 is indeed different from the Mandelbrot set. But let's face it, on the surface it looks like a zillion other fractals, more or less, right? It turns out that the Zexpe fractal is full of incredible surprises. It is like a vein of gold hidden in a mountain, waiting for an intrepid prospector to discover it. There are many variations of the Mandelbrot set that allow you to create different images, but the Zexpe formula is more than a variation; it is fundamentally different.

The Fractint enthusiast who brought the Zexpe formula to the author's attention is Lee Skinner, who is also responsible for the fractals on the front and back covers of *Fractal Creations* as well as many others he has made. Lee has two words of advice for fractal exploration. One bit of advice is not to judge a fractal by its appearance using the normal default corner values, but to zoom in to find out what the fractal is really like. Many fractals that look superficially the same turn out to be completely different when you look more closely. The other suggestion is to spend effort applying colors to the fractal, because different coloring schemes bring different features to your attention. A change of color palette can make the difference between a nondescript image and a masterpiece.

Lee kept his computer running continuously for several months doing nothing but generating fractals using the Zexpe formula. You are going to be the beneficiary of his research, because in this section you will be treated to some of his best artistry.

A Closer Look at Zexpe

Listing 6-4 shows the Fractint parameters needed to generate a very revealing example using the Zexpe formula. The fractal is saved with the name ZEXPE37.GIF because this image is number 37 of the several hundred images that Lee made. These parameters are stored in a file called LIST6-4 on your Image Lab disk.

. . . .

```
type=formula
formulafile=imagelab.frm
formulaname=Zexpe
corners=-0.110702/-0.108244/+1.047780/+1.049624
maxiter=1023
inside=0
logmap=yes
map=zexpe37.map
savename=zexpe37.gif
```

Listing 6-4 The Zexpe37 parameters

The formulafile and formulaname parameters show you how to access a particular named parser formula stored in a formula file. The corners define

Figure 6-25 Zoom into the Zexpe fractal

the region of the complex plane assigned to the screen. In this case the region is quite small, representing a magnification of over 1000 compared with the default corners values. The logmap=yes option turns on a stretched iterations-to-colors mapping that allows colors to vary smoothly deep into the fractal. The map=zexpe37.map loads the color palette that Lee created for this particular fractal.

To run this fractal, type:

```
C:>FRACTINT @LIST6-4 (ENTER)
```

and select a video mode. The result is shown in Figure 6-25.

Anyone who has spent much time exploring the Mandelbrot set will notice that this image has some unusual features that you will never see in a Mandelbrot image. The usual escape-time rendering of the Mandelbrot set consists of a series of color bands that surround the Mandelbrot lake. The outer bands have a smooth shape, and the bands closer to the lake become increasingly convoluted. Mathematicians have proved that each of these bands is topologically the same, which means that each band is essentially the same shape, but some are stretched to form complex boundaries more than others. All the bands are continuous and unbroken. A glance at the Zexpe37 image reveals that the Zexpe fractal contains many discontinuous patches of colors. For example, look at the folded spiral in the lower-right corner. The end of the spiral butts up against a boundary of another series of colors. The Zexpe fractal has many discontinuities, and they are distributed in a fractal fashion throughout the image. Close study of the image reveals that the spiral structure just pointed out has literally an infinite number of copies of all sizes throughout the image.

Discontinuities from Another World

Where do these discontinuities come from? The difference between this fractal and the Mandelbrot is particularly striking because the formulas are so similar; the only difference is that the number 2 in the Mandelbrot formula is changed to the number 2.71828182845905 in the Zexpe formula. An explanation for this is given in the box for the mathematically curious.

The Source of the Zexpe Discontinuities

The function z^y is equal to $e^{\ln(z)*y}$. The logarithm function $\ln(z)$ has multiple values when considered over the complex plane. In order to define a valid function $\ln(z)$, one of the multiple values must be picked. No matter what choice is made, the graph of the function $\ln(z)$ must have a discontinuous seam somewhere. This discontinuous behavior carries over to the function z^y which is used in the Zexpe fractal. The chaotic dynamics of iterating the formula propagate this discontinuity at all scales throughout the resulting fractal. In the case of the Mandelbrot set, y has the value 2, so the iterated formula involves z^2, which is just $z*z$, giving a very well-behaved function that is continuous for all values of z. Similarly, the result is also continuous for y=3, 4, 5, ... To summarize: The Zexpe fractal has discontinuous patches because the function z^y used to generate it is discontinuous if y is not an integer.

The collection of images that Lee Skinner made using the Zexpe formula show a wide variety of mixtures of discontinuous patches and Mandelbrot-style fractal appearance. The next few examples will illustrate this.

Origami at Last

Since this section is entitled Fractal Origami, it is about time we produced some! The spiral structure just pointed out in Figure 6-25 looks for all the world like it was made from cut and folded paper. You can zoom on one of those spirals and see for yourself, or you can try another example from Lee's Zexpe series, shown in Listing 6-5.

```
type=formula
formulafile=imagelab.frm
formulaname=Zexpe
corners=-0.110685960/-0.110218773/+1.036601476/+1.036951867
maxiter=1023
inside=0
logmap=yes
map=zexpe51.map
savename=zexpe51.gif
```

Listing 6-5 Zexpe51

To run this fractal, type:

`C:>FRACTINT @LIST6-5` (ENTER)

The result is shown in Figure 6-26.

Figure 6-26 Zexpe origami

This image shows fractal origami at its best. The spiral looks very much like the result of some expert folding of colored tissue paper, but the smooth lines of the paper have strange fractal splotches, like some sort of fractal fungus.

Fractal Bubbles

Other regions of the Zexpe fractal show still different kinds of structure. Listing 6-6 shows how to generate an image that has a Mandelbrot-like fractal spiral set off by bubbles.

```
type=formula
formulafile=imagelab.frm
formulaname=Zexpe
corners=-0.12300766/-0.12295530/+1.119712816/+1.11975208
maxiter=1023
inside=0
logmap=yes
map=zexpe68
savename=zexpe68
```

Listing 6-6 Zexpe68

To generate this fractal, type:

`C:>FRACTINT @LIST6-6 ` (ENTER)

Figure 6-27 shows the result. This image illustrates the importance of the color palette. With the default palette IBM, this image is very drab. With Lee's colors, the bubbles are pastel colors, and the fractal spirals are vivid oranges and reds.

Zooming into the Zexpe Microcosm

Fractint is a kind of mathematical microscope of considerable power. The magnification of this microscope is defined in terms of a standard patch of the

Figure 6-27 Zexpe68 — spirals and bubbles

complex plane with *x* extending from -1.3333 to 1.3333 and *y* extending from -1 to 1. This standard patch represents a magnification of 1. The vertical height of this patch is 1-(-1) or 2. The magnification of a zoomed fractal image is defined as 2 divided by the height of the zoomed image. For example, if you zoomed in a short way, and the *y* values of the image ranged from -.25 to .25, the height of the image would be .25-(-.25) or .5 and the magnification would be 2/.5 or 4. You can see the magnification of your zoomed images by using the (TAB) key; it is listed after the label "mag." The Zexpe37 has a magnification of 1084, Zexpe51 a magnification of 5707, and Zexpe68 a magnification of 50,932. You might think that a magnification of 50,932 is extreme, and indeed it is. Imagine a piece of graph paper with 50,000 horizontal lines and 50,000 vertical lines. There are over 2 *billion* tiny squares on that piece of graph paper, and that is how many different tiny zoomed images of the Zexpe fractal there are at a magnification of 50,000. Put on your scuba gear, we're going to dive *much* deeper than that!

In the next few subsections, youll see some examples of the endless variety of the Zexpe fractals, some at magnifications that defy imagination.

A Fractal Spiral

The next example is five-armed spiral at magnification 717,724. Listing 6-7 shows the parameters.

```
type=formula
formulafile=imagelab.frm
formulaname=Zexpe
corners=+0.241345057/+0.241348775/+0.723341846/+0.723344634
maxiter=1023
inside=0
logmap=yes
map=zexpe86.map
savename=zexpe86
```

Listing 6-7 Zexpe86

To generate this fractal, type:

```
C:>FRACTINT @LIST6-7 (ENTER)
```

The result is shown in Figure 6-28.

Deep Sea Vegetables

Lurking in the depths at magnification 2,720,986 are two green-headed vegetables of some unknown species. Listing 6-8 shows the parameters.

Figure 6-28 Zexpe86 — a
fractal spiral

```
type=formula
formulafile=imagelab.frm
formulaname=Zexpe
corners=-0.079567553/-0.079566573/+1.030303823/+1.030304558
maxiter=1023
inside=0
logmap=yes
map=zexpe89.map
savename=zexpe89
```

Listing 6-8 Zexpe89

To generate this fractal, type:

`C:>`**FRACTINT @LIST6-8** (ENTER)

The result is shown in Figure 6-29.

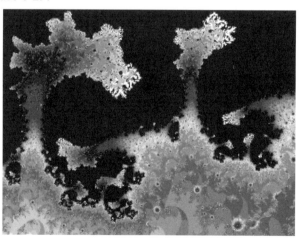

Figure 6-29 Zexpe89 — deep-
sea vegetables

Hodge Podge

A popular misconception about fractals is that they are self-similar. A self-similar object is one whose parts are an exact miniature of the whole object. Self-similar objects are often fractals, but the converse is not true. If the Zexpe fractal were self-similar, then at extreme magnifications the images would look the same as they do at moderate magnifications. As you zoom deeper and deeper, the structures appear to get more complex and varied. The next example was calculated at a magnification of 34,345,522,939, or over 34 *billion*! The image is full of a variety of shapes, and shows spiral structures as well as the fractured character of the Zexpe fractal. The name is no longer Zexpe but Zexpf; this is really Lee's Zexpe fractal number 118, but he ran out of digits!

```
type=formula
formulafile=imagelab.frm
formulaname=Zexpe
corners=+0.2410953951092/+0.2410953951868/+0.7231363249835/+0.7231363250418
maxiter=2047
inside=0
logmap=yes
bailout=100
map=zexpf18.map
savename=zexpf18
```

Listing 6-9 Zexpf18

To generate this fractal, type:

`C:>FRACTINT @LIST6-9` (ENTER)

The result is shown in Figure 6-30.

Figure 6-30 Zexpf18 —
hodge-podge

Arrowhead Army

At a magnification of 23,301,330, we find some arrowhead shapes marching in step in overlapping spiral formations. At this depth the discontinuous fractures we observed at low magnifications have been multiplied considerably. The parameters are shown in Listing 6-10.

....

```
type=formula
formulafile=imagelab.frm
formulaname=Zexpe
corners=-0.18644095784707830/-0.18644084340433410/+1.09669371058906800/
+1.09669379642107600
maxiter=1023
inside=0
logmap=512
map=zexpf88.map
savename=zexpf88
```

Listing 6-10 Zexpf88

To generate this fractal, type:

`C:>FRACTINT @LIST6-10` (ENTER)

The result is shown in Figure 6-31.

....

Figure 6-31 Zexpf88 — arrowhead army

282

Eightfold Flower

Hiding in the depths at a magnification of 113 billion is a colorful flower with eightfold symmetry. The parameters are shown in Listing 6-11.

. . . .

```
type=formula
formulafile=imagelab.frm
formulaname=Zexpe
corners=-0.29699124297020730/-0.29699124294683150/+1.13367366288545900/
+1.13367366290300900
maxiter=2047
inside=0
logmap=1024
map=zexph44.map
savename=zexph44
```

Listing 6-11 Zexph44

To generate this fractal, type:

`C:>FRACTINT @LIST6-11` (ENTER)

The result is shown in Figure 6-32.

Flightless Birds

At a magnification of a little over 1 trillion, our journey into the depths of the Zexpe fractal reaches an end. Fractint is capable of still greater magnifications,

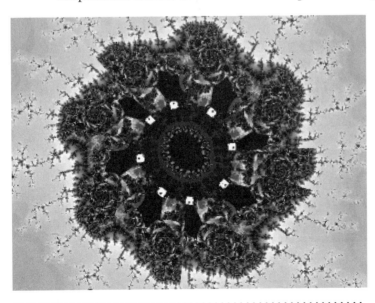

. . . .

Figure 6-32 Zexph44 — Eightfold flower

and can go as deep as about 10 trillion. This limit is due to the limitations of the 64-bit double-precision numbers Fractint uses for its calculations. There is no bottom to the fractal ocean, and there is no absolute limit to how far into that ocean a computer can potentially explore. But for now you'll have to be content with a magnification a little over 1 trillion!

At these great depths we find a hillside with two flightless birds going for a stroll. The parameters are shown in Listing 6-12.

```
type=formula
formulafile=imagelab.frm
formulaname=Zexpe
corners=+0.24109539477607830/+0.24109539477865000/+0.72313632518128400/
+0.72313632518319850
maxiter=2047
inside=0
logmap=yes
bailout=100
map=zexpf33.map
savename=zexpf33
```

Listing 6-12   Zexpf33

To generate this fractal, type:

`C:>FRACTINT @LIST6-12` (ENTER)

The result is shown in Figure 6-33.

Figure 6-33 Zexpf33 —
flightless birds

Fractal Centipede

On our way back up to the surface, at the magnification of a "mere" 436,688, we pass a fractal centipede. The parameters are shown in Listing 6-13.

. . . .

```
type=formula
formulafile=imagelab.frm
formulaname=Zexpe
corners=-0.053216261/-0.053210155/+0.854182445/+0.854187025
maxiter=1023
inside=0
logmap=768
map=zexpg08.map
savename=zexpg08
```

Listing 6-13 Zexpg08

To generate this fractal, type:

`C:>FRACTINT @LIST6-13` (ENTER)

The result is shown in Figure 6-34.

. . . .

Figure 6-34 Zexpg08—fractal
centipede

This ends our exploration of the Zexpe fractal. We'll finish off this chapter
with several examples using other fractal types.

Pseudo 3-D

Earlier we discussed the continuous potential option in connection with the
Mt. Rock example. Continuous potential makes smoothly varying colors that,
under the right conditions, generate images that have an eerie 3-D appearance. In the IMAGELAB.FRM file you will find the formulas shown below.

```
{ Use the following for version 15.14 or later }
MarksMandelPwr_tan {
   z = pixel, c = z ^ (z - 1):
   z = c * sin(z)/cos(z) + pixel,
   |z| <= 4
}

{ Use the following for version 15.13 or earlier }
```

```
MarksMandelPwr_tan_old {
  z = pixel, c = z ^ (z - 1):
  z = c * sin(z)/conj(cos(z)) + pixel,
  |z| <= 4
}
```

Two different versions are shown because in Fractint versions prior to 15.14, the cos() function returns the complex conjugate of the correct value. For these earlier versions, the composite function conj(cos()) returns the same value as the corrected cos().

The file LIST6-14 contains the parameters needed to make an image with a great pseudo 3-D effect. Listing 6-14 shows the parameters. If your version of Fractint is 15.13 or earlier, be sure to change the formula name to MarksMandelPwer_tan_old.

. . . .

```
type=formula
formulafile=imagelab.frm
formulaname=marksmandelpwr_tan
corners=-0.949173/0.822114/-0.664232/0.664232
maxiter=1024
inside=maxiter
logmap=yes
potential=256/511/0
map=injector.map
savename=injector.gif
```

Listing 6-14 Bubbles with MarksMandelPwr

To generate this fractal, type:

`C:>FRACTINT @LIST6-14` (ENTER)

You can see the result if Figure 6-35. The image looks more like the kind of result you would expect from POV-Ray rather than Fractint.

Daisies

Fractint images need not be difficult to create to be beautiful and fun. Here is a simple example that looks like some pretty daises, and can be generated in a few seconds. Listing 6-15 shows the parameters needed for the daisy image.

. . . .

```
type=magnet1m
corners=2.02284/2.36895/0.880899/1.14048
maxiter=10000
inside=maxiter
biomorph=0
map=daisy.map
savename=daisy.gif
```

Listing 6-15 Daisies

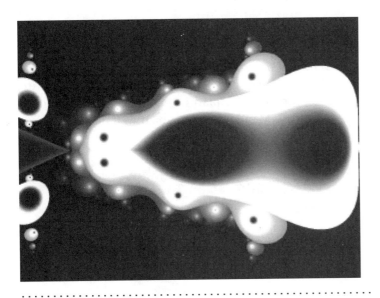

Figure 6-35 Pseudo 3-D with continuous potential

These parameters are in the file on your Image Lab disk called LIST6-15. To generate the image, type:

```
C:>FRACTINT @LIST6-15 (ENTER)
```

Figure 6-36 shows the result.

Figure 6-36 Daisies

287

Dune Aliens

There is a certain fascination about mysterious and inaccessible places, whether they be in the depths of the oceans, the far interior of the earth, or the unimaginable reaches of space. Late-night TV has as standard fare of monster movies about creatures that inhabit these places. To end this chapter, we take you on a journey deep into the Mandelbrot set, down to a depth of over 3 million linear magnification. And we do indeed find — aliens! And not just aliens, but aliens charging up at us over the sand dunes!

After preparing yourself appropriately for such a dangerous undertaking, consider the parameters in Listing 6-16.

```
type=mandel
corners=+0.25005091699/+0.25005167552/+0.00000034914/+0.00000091785
maxiter=2000
map=dune.map
savename=dune
```

Listing 6-16 Dune Aliens

These parameters are in the file on your Image Lab disk called LIST6-16. To generate the image, type:

`C:>FRACTINT @LIST6-16 (ENTER)`

Figure 6-37 shows the result.

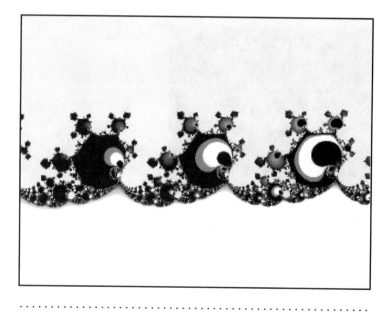

Figure 6-37 Dune aliens

7

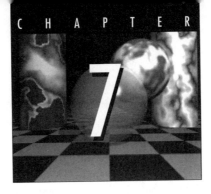

CHAPTER 7

PERSISTENCE OF VISION-RAY TRACER

POV-Ray requires a 386 PC with at least
2MB RAM and a math co-processor

THE WORLD OF RAY TRACING

A Window into a World of Shapes and Shadows

What makes a scene look real? Look up from this book and study your surroundings for a moment and think in terms of everything being made of simple shapes, like cubes, cylinders, spheres, and cones. For you to see at all there must be light, and some objects for the light to illuminate. The objects are located within three-dimensional space. The scene before you is created by the interplay of light on the objects in your field of vision. Each of these objects has a visual texture that affects how it looks in the light: objects may be shiny or dull, plain or patterned, or even glowing. Light reflects off objects, casts shadows, and fills the room with a background glow. The interplay of these elements — light, objects, texture, and their positions in space — creates your visual world and gives you a sense of the reality of your surroundings.

Now imagine you are watching a late-night science-fiction movie. In this movie there is another reality, a netherworld of abstractions, populated by shadowy alien shapes invisible to the normal senses. The movie's heroes stumble on a device with strange lenses. They look through this device, and to their amazement the objects of this alien world suddenly become real, just as sharp and clear as the objects in your room are to you. They are amazed, full of fear, and stunned with fascination.

But there is an even bigger surprise. The netherworld exists; in fact, some pieces of it are found on this book's companion disk. The alien viewing device is the Persistence of Vision ray tracing software described in this chapter. This is no science fiction scenario at all, but a possibility you can experience right now, with your own PC. The world you can view is one that is made up of rays of light bouncing off abstract objects in a text file. Called a *ray tracer,* this program accesses a mathematical world built out of spheres, cubes, planes, and cylinders, glowing lights, and a multitude of textures. In this 3-D world, you will find mountains, lakes, clocks, trains, panthers, clouds, sunsets, dangerous skies, and slimy snails. Because the objects exist only as abstract representations, without a ray tracer you can't see this world. The ray tracer brings the scenes to life, literally turning on the lights and following every individual light beam as it bounces its way from object to object on its way to an imaginary eye. (The ray tracer actually tracks the light backwards from the eye to the light, but you have to allow the author some poetic license!)

The Persistence of Vision-Ray Tracer

The Persistence of Vision-Ray Tracer (POV-Ray) is a remarkable software program that *renders* abstract descriptions of scenes into compelling and realistic images. It is an artistic tool that uses computer models of those basic elements of a scene that were described above — light, objects, and textures in space. Until recently, only a lucky few with access to expensive scientific workstations could experience the pleasures of creating images with ray tracers. Almost overnight, the state-of-the-art of ordinary PCs has reached a level of performance where ray-tracing software is practical for anyone who can afford the new 386 technology.

POV-Ray was created by a group of volunteers who call themselves the Persistence of Vision Group, or POV Group for short. The term persistence of vision refers to the physiological effect of an image appearing visible even after the light forming the image no longer enters the eye. The POV Group is a friendly, intelligent group of artists and programmers that is open to anyone who would like to participate. The POV Group's headquarters is CompuServe's COMART forum (GO COMART). The COMART forum is dedicated to promoting computer art including ray tracing, fractals, and computer animation, and is frequented by artists, programmers, and curious beginners. The COMART forum is also the home of Fractint, the fractal-generation program discussed in Chapter 6 and also in the author's book *Fractal Creations.* POV-Ray and

Fractint work very well together, and this close synergy is not entirely accidental; quite a number of programmers have contributed to both programs.

POV-Ray began as the ray-tracing program DKBTrace by David Buck and Aaron Collins. David and Aaron provided their program as the starting point for POV-Ray, which has since gained many enhancements while continuing the strong tradition of its predecessor. One of the particular strengths of DKB and POV-Ray is that the source code can be compiled and run on many kinds of computers (it's very portable), so that you will find these programs on Amigas, Ataris, and all manner of UNIX computers.

In this chapter you will learn to use POV-Ray to create and render three-dimensional images that look incredibly realistic, but only exist inside of your computer as binary numbers. However, rest assured, you don't need to be a programmer or a mathematician to do this. Just follow along with the examples and you'll be ray tracing with POV-Ray in no time, using it as your personal window into the netherworld of shadows, shapes, and textures.

LEGAL STATUS

POV-Ray is proof that some of the best things in life are free. POV-Ray is copyrighted software with some limitations on how it can be distributed. It is legally Freeware with some basic restrictions. For the exact details, see the POVLEGAL.DOC in the POVRAY archive on your companion disk. Here are the main points.

The Persistence of Vision-Ray Tracer may be freely distributed. However, the authors retain the copyright to the program but authorize free distribution by BBSs, networks, magnetic media, and so on. The distributor may charge no more than five dollars ($5) U.S. for this software. The software may not be renamed, nor can it be given away as an incentive to buy other software.

GETTING POV-RAY UP AND RUNNING

Directories and Installation

The installation instructions for the POV-Ray software may be found in Chapter 1. This chapter assumes that the POV-Ray executables are in the directory \IMLAB\POVRAY; that the POV Include files with the extension .INC are in the directory \IMLAB\POVRAY\INCLUDE; and that the example data files are in the directory \IMLAB\EXAMPLES. All the examples assume that you are using drive C. If these assumptions are not correct, you will need to make adjustments in the examples to reflect your actual configuration.

Hardware Requirements

POV-Ray comes in two flavors; a regular conventional-memory version and an 80386/80486 protected-mode version. These programs have different hardware requirements. The regular version runs under almost all hardware and software configurations, and is sufficient for all the examples in this chapter. The 80386 protected-mode version only runs on an 80386 (or better) with at least 2 MB extended memory and is required to run many of the examples in Chapter 9. The protected-mode version is included with this book. You can find the conventional-memory version in LIB 16 of CompuServe's COMART Forum.

The Conventional-Memory Version

You must use the regular POV-Ray if you have an 80286 or lower machine. The advantage of the regular version is that it runs on just about any class of PC, and is not sensitive to your computer's configuration. However, the regular POV-Ray is limited to the use of conventional memory, which cannot exceed 640K. This means that you will be able to render smaller POV-Ray data files, but not the larger ones. You can do amazing things with a conventional-memory ray tracer, but if you possibly can, use the protected-mode version to free yourself from the 640K memory limitation.

The conventional-memory version of POV POV.EXE requires the following hardware:

1. An 8088, 8086, 80286, or better CPU.

2. An 8087, 80287, or 80387 or compatible math coprocessor is not strictly a requirement, but is highly desirable. Ray tracing uses floating point math intensively, and a math coprocessor can speed up floating point math ten times or more.

3. At least 640K of conventional memory installed.

The Protected-Mode POV

The protected-mode version of POV-Ray will let you use your extended memory to allow you to trace complex data files. The hardware and software requirements are much more stringent than for the regular version. The protected-mode version of POV-Ray requires the following:

1. An 80386SX, 80386DX, 80486SX, 80486 or better CPU. You cannot use an 8088, 8086, 8186, or 80286 PC.

2. At least 2 MB of extended memory. Some users have reported that more than this was required. At least 4 MB is highly recommended.

3. You cannot be running under any other protected-mode software such as Microsoft Windows, with some exceptions. The safest thing to do is add a REM to any lines in your CONFIG.SYS file that load protected-mode memory manager programs as 386Max, QEMM, and the 386EMM.SYS that comes with Windows. If there is any conflict, POVRAY will report it when it runs. If you get a message at startup about an incompatible protected-mode program in operation, you should reboot your machine immediately. Then look for software in your CONFIG.SYS and AUTOEXEC.BAT files that might be causing the problem, precede those lines with a REM statement, and try again.

4. An 8087, 80287, or 80387 or compatible math coprocessor is a requirement for most versions.

Setting the POV-Ray Options

POV-Ray is a command-line-driven program. A number of options can be set on the command line when you start POV-Ray. These options can also be set using the POVRAYOPT environment variable, or by using a file called POVRAY.DEF in the current directory. The preferred method is to use the environment variable, because it will work from any directory. To use the environment variable, add the line:

```
SET POVRAYOPT=+Lc:\IMLAB\POVRAY\INCLUDE +d1 -v0 +p +x +ft -a -q9 -w160 -h200
```

to your AUTOEXEC.BAT. You should also edit your AUTOEXEC.BAT so that the Path statement lists the directory where the POV-Ray executables reside. The suggested directory is \IMLAB\POVRAY. These changes to your AUTOEXEC.BAT will take effect after you reboot. Table 7-1 shows what each of these options mean.

These instructions assume that the Include files SHAPES.INC, TEXTURES.INC, COLORS.INC have been copied to the directory C:\IMLAB\POVRAY\INCLUDE. They also assume that your hardware supports the VGA 320x200 256-color video mode. (If your display adapter is not a VGA, change the +d1 option to -d. This will turn off POV-Ray's attempt to display the image as it works, which is fine for now.)

After you have modified your AUTOEXEC.BAT so that the directory \IMLAB\POVRAY is in your Path and so that the environment variable POVRAYOPT has been set, reboot your computer. To verify that the Path and POVRAYOPT are correctly set, type:

```
C:>SET  (ENTER)
```

+lc:\IMLAB\POVRAY\INCLUDE	Directory where POV-Ray searches for the include files
+d1	Display the image while tracing, using VGA 320x200 256-mode
-v0	Verbose off, doesn't show line numbers during trace
+p	Prompt before exiting to let you look at the picture
+x	Allow exiting with a key hit before the trace is finished
+ft	Output format is Targa
-a	Don't antialias, which smooths out jagged edges but takes longer
-q9	Quality level –9 is highest quality
-w160	Width of image in pixels (half of 320)
-h100	Height of image in pixels (half of 200)

Table 7-1 POV-Ray options

You will see all your environment variables on your screen with their values, and you can make sure they are correct. If they are, you are ready to try POV-Ray. If you start POV-Ray without specifying an input file, a usage screen will display. Just type:

C:> **POVRAY** (ENTER)

You should see a screen that looks like Figure 7-1.

```
Usage:
    povray [+/-] Option1 [+/-] Option2 ...

Options:
    t   = CASE SENSITIVE y = yes(old style) n=no o=opt(default)
    dxy = display in format x, using palette option y
    vx  = verbose in format x
    p   = prompt exit
    x   = enable early exit by key hit
    fx  = write output file in format x
          ft - Uncompressed Targa-24  fd - DKB/QRT Dump  fr - 3 Raw Files
    a   = perform antialiasing
    c   = continue aborted trace
    qx  = image quality 0=rough, 9=full
    lxxx = library path prefix
    wxxx = width of the screen
    hxxx = height of the screen
    sxxx = start at line number xxx
    exxx = end at line number xxx
    bxxx,= Use xxx kilobytes for output file buffer space
    ifilename = input file name
    ofilename = output file name

C:\IMLAB\POV>
```

Figure 7-1 The POV usage screen

Figure 7-2 Sphere rendered
from the data file
KWIKSTRT.DAT

Next, change directories to the \IMLAB\EXAMPLES directory and run the
data file KWIKSTRT.POV. To do this, type:

```
C:>CD \IMLAB\POVRAY\EXAMPLES ENTER
C:>POVRAY -iKWIKSTRT.POV ENTER
```

If all is well, you should see a small colored sphere appear on your screen. It should
look like Figure 7-2. You saw the red ball displayed line by line as it was being traced in
POV-Ray. Now to see what appears as a somewhat crude representation of the ball,
one lacking in fine shading, lets view the Targa file with **CompuShow**. Type:

```
C:>CSHOW *.TGA ENTER
```

Select the file DATA.TGA with the mouse or arrow keys. Then select a 256-color
video mode. **CompuShow** will display the red sphere, but with the smooth
shades of red broken into several wide bands. This does not mean there is anything wrong with the image, its just that a 256-color video mode is not capable of
accurately displaying 24 bit Targa true color images. (If your graphics adapter has
a Sierra DAC chip, you can directly view .TGA files with good quality by using
CompuShow's hicolor driver.) A bit later in this chapter you'll see how to use
either Piclab or Alchemy to convert the .TGA file to a GIF and make it look much
better when viewed with **CompuShow** using a VGA 256-color video mode.

Congratulations, you've just rendered your first POV file! Now that you've
had success you're ready to be a real ray tracer.

POV-RAY QUICK TOUR

This section will explain the basics of what goes into a POV-Ray input data file,
and how to render an input file. You will learn how to run any of the example
input files that come on your companion disk. The tutorial later in this chapter
will give you much more detailed information.

The Ray-Tracing World

Ray tracing lets you see objects that are defined in the ray-tracing language. In order to understand these objects, you must understand the three-dimensional coordinate system of POV-Ray. It is pretty simple, really.

A Basic POV-Ray Data File

Three fundamental parts of any POV-Ray data file must be present in order to create an image. These parts are the camera viewpoint, the definition of an object, and the definition of a source of light.

You can think of the camera as the location of an observer in a three-dimensional world, along with instructions for pointing the camera. The defined object is the subject of your photograph. The light source is a shining object that illuminates the defined object so that it can be seen. These three basic components are illustrated in Listing 7-1, which shows the contents of the file KWIKSTRT.POV we just rendered.

. . . .

```
// The Waite Group's Image Lab
// KWIKSTRT.POV
// Really basic quick start file.
//

/* Where you are, and which way you are looking */
camera
{
   location <0.0  0.0  -150.0>
   direction <0.0 0.0  1.0>
   up  <0.0  1.0  0.0>
   right <1.33333 0.0 0.0>
}

// A red sphere of radius 50 centered at the origin.
object
{
   sphere{ <0 0 0>  50.0 }
   texture
   {
      color red 1.0
   }
}

// A white light source
object
{
   light_source
   {
      <0.0  1000.0  -1000.0>
      color red 1.0 green 1.0 blue 1.0 // This is white light
   }
}
```

Listing 7-1 A basic POV-Ray data file

This POV-Ray data file represents just about the most basic ray-tracing data file possible. This data file causes POV-Ray to create a red sphere illuminated by a white light. The first few lines of the data file begin with double slashes. The "//" characters are one of two methods for writing comments in a POV-Ray data file. Everything after an occurrence of "//" on the same line is ignored. You can have a whole line be a comment, as in the lines

```
// Persistence of Vision Raytracer
// Really basic quick start file.
```

or you can use a comment at the end of the line, as in

```
color red 1.0 green 1.0 blue 1.0 // This is white light
```

The other comment method is the use of "/*" to start a comment and "*/" to end it. Both of these methods have been borrowed from the C and C++ programming languages. Use of "//" is the most convenient because no ending comment notation is needed.

You can see that parts of the data file are partitioned into sections or *blocks* using the curly braces "{" and "}". With the exception of comments that cause POV-Ray to ignore everything to the end of the line, carriage returns in a POV-Ray data file are not significant. Thus the single line

```
sphere{ <0 0 0> 10.0 }
```

has exactly the same meaning as the three lines

```
sphere{
   <0 0 0> 10.0
}
```

or

```
sphere
{
   <0 0 0> 10.0
}
```

You can see that the lines of the KWIKSTRT.POV file have been carefully indented to help show off the block structure. This indentation is for the benefit of human readers of the data file, not the computer readers such as the POV-Ray software. Since blocks can occur inside blocks, the structure of *nested* blocks can get quite complicated. Careful indentation of the lines of the file make it much easier to read and understand. The facility for comments is also useful to jog your memory about different features of a data file.

The Camera

After the initial comments at the top of the data file is the camera block. The word camera is a reserved word in the POV-Ray language that alerts the ray-tracing software to the fact that a block is beginning that will define the point of view of an observer looking at the scene. The various items inside the block

299

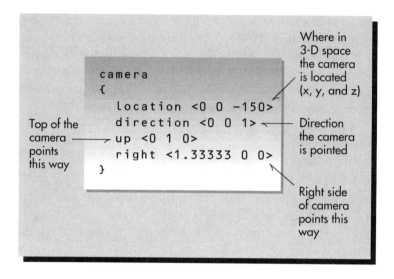

Figure 7-3 The Camera block

tell where the camera is, where it is aimed, and how it is oriented. Figure 7-3 shows the Camera section of KWIKSTRT.POV with annotations showing what each line does.

Location

The first line inside the Camera block is the line

```
location <0.0 0.0 -150.0>
```

Whenever you see three numbers bracketed off with < and >, you are dealing with a position or a direction in a three-dimensional coordinate system. The x axis is horizontal with positive numbers on the right. The y axis is vertical, with positive numbers on the top side. The z axis is also horizontal, and at right angles to the screen. The Location vector (a *vector* is an ordered triple of numbers) is the position of our imaginary camera. The camera is located 150 units behind the x-y plane. Because the x and y components of the location are both 0, the location is right on the z axis. The size of a unit of measurement is arbitrary, since you can scale the objects to any number of units you wish.

Understand that terms like "horizontal" and "vertical" assume conventions concerning the orientation of the camera relative to the coordinate axes. The camera can be held upside down, on its side, or can be tilted at any crazy angle in a POV-Ray data file just as in real life. In order to maintain your bearings in 3-D space, you should establish some conventions for your data files. A convention that makes good sense in POV-Ray is to place the objects in the

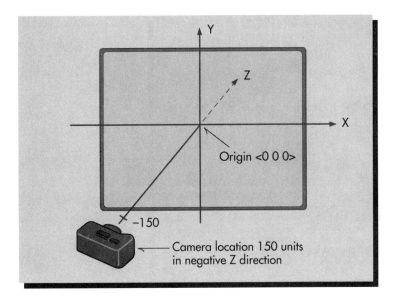

Figure 7-4 The camera location in KWIKSTRT.POV

scene at or near the origin <0 0 0>. Then place the camera on the negative z axis, and visualize the z axis as perpendicular to your computer screen, with the negative z axis coming out of the screen toward you and the positive z axis extending into your screen. Figure 7-4 shows a coordinate system attached to a computer screen in this way, with the camera location <0 0 -150> marked. All of the data files in this chapter will follow the basic scheme shown in the figure.

Viewing Pyramid

Anyone who has ever taken a picture of a large group in a small room is acutely aware that a camera has a particular field of view, and sometimes the field of view is too narrow to get everyone in the picture. Since a photograph is rectangular, the field of view may be represented as a horizontal pyramid, with the apex of the pyramid located at the camera's position. The pyramid spreads in front of the camera, representing how wide the field of view is at different distances. Figure 7-5 shows this imaginary camera superimposed on a coordinate system with the viewing pyramid. You can see that the camera and the apex of the pyramid are located at position <0 0 -150>. Using the camera parameters in the KWIKSTRT.POV file, a camera distance of 150 units covers an area approximately 154 units wide and 120 units high.

The next line of the Camera block is the *direction*. This vector points in the direction the camera is facing. The size of the numbers indicate the zoom fac-

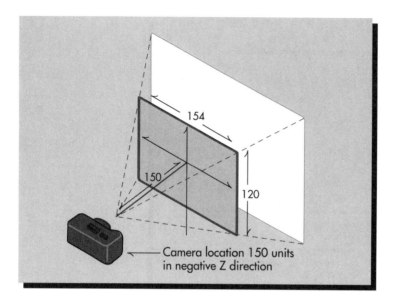

154

150

120

Camera location 150 units
in negative Z direction

Figure 7-5 The camera field of view pyramid

tor of the camera. A Direction vector of <0 0 1> is a "normal" lens directed along the z axis. The viewing pyramid shown in Figure 7-5 assumes a Direction vector of length 1 (the length of a vector is the square root of $x^2+y^2+z^2$). A Direction vector of <0 0 2> is a "2X telephoto" lens with a narrower field of view, and a more sharply pointed pyramid.

Up and Right

The *Up* vector is the direction the top of the camera points, and the *Right* vector is the direction the right side of the camera points. Imagine that the camera has two little arrows glued to it, one coming out of the top of the Camera, and one coming out the right side, as you view the Camera from the back. The Up and Right vectors tell you which way these arrows will try to point. Imagine that the direction vector is coming out of the camera lens, and that the camera is fixed to it but can still be rotated using the direction vector as an axis as shown in Figure 7-6. POV-Ray will rotate the camera to the position that brings arrows coming out of the top and side of the camera as close as possible to the Up and Right directions.

The Right vector serves a second purpose; it adjusts the aspect ratio of the image. If the Right vector were <1 0 0>, the sphere in the KWIKSTRT.POV example would have been deformed into an oval egg shape. The value 1.33333 adjusts for the 4:3 screen that is a standard in the PC industry. With this value spheres will look round and not oval.

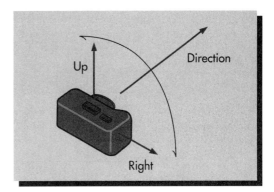

Figure 7-6 The Up and Right vectors

What to Change

You will want to experiment with the Direction and Location statements in your Camera block. A powerful feature of POV-Ray (and all ray tracers) is that once you have defined a scene, you can view it from any angle, whether above, below, right, left, near, or far. Keep in mind that if you change *location*, you may also have to change *direction* to compensate and keep your objects in view. (See the discussion of Look_At in the tutorial section later in this chapter for an easier way to keep your objects visible.) You can also adjust the size of *direction* to control the zoom factor of your camera. To prevent confusion, most experts use standard values of direction and location while they are building their scenes so that they can most easily visualize the coordinate system. Once the scene has been created, the camera can be moved around by changing these vectors.

The Up and Right vectors are generally never changed. While there is no harm in experimenting, you will quickly see that POV-Ray provides so many degrees of freedom that you do not need to adjust every parameter and will want to keep some elements constant. Every data file in this book uses the same Up and Right vectors.

The Object Definition

A POV-Ray data file can have hundreds or even thousands of objects. An object is a visible shape in a ray tracing. Like the camera, an object is defined in a block set off by curly braces. The Object block has two parts, a shape and a texture. Figure 7-7 shows the parts that make up an Object definition.

There are a number of shapes (called primitives) built into the POV-Ray language, and many more that can be defined from those. A sphere is one of the primitives; it is specified by a vector giving its center and a number indicating its radius. The sphere in the example has radius 50 and is centered on the origin, and is defined by the single line

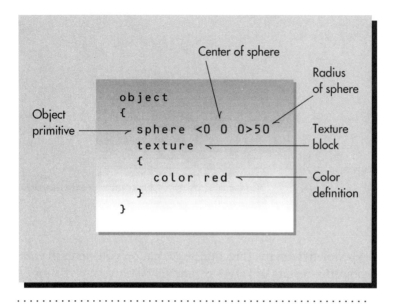

Figure 7-7 The Object definition block

```
sphere{ <0 0 0> 50.0 }
```
Figure 7-8 shows the defined sphere superimposed on the coordinate system.

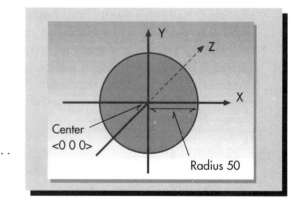

Figure 7-8 The sphere primitive

Just below the Sphere block is another block introduced with the keyword Texture. The Texture block looks like this:

```
texture
  {
    color red 1.0
  }
}
```

A texture defines the surface characteristics of an object. In this case the texture consists only of the color red. Colors are defined in terms of the primary colors red, green, and blue. The numbers following the color name indicate the brightness of that color component. Color brightness is represented as a number from 0 (totally dark) to 1.0 (bright).

The Light Source

The last block in the example is a light source. A light source is another kind of object, so the keyword Light_Source appears inside an Object block.

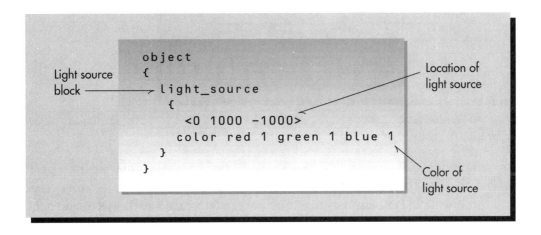

Figure 7-9 Definition of a light source

Figure 7-9 identifies each part of the Light Source definition. A light source consists of a position in space and a color. The position of the light in this example is

```
<0.0 1000.0 -1000.0>
```

In POV-Ray a light does not get weaker with distance as it does in real life. A light source thousands of units away from the objects illuminates them the same amount as a much closer light source. The important aspect of the position of the light is the direction from the light to the object. In this case the position has a large y component and a large z component. This places the light behind the camera high in the sky. Figure 7-10 shows the light position.

You can place as many light sources as you wish throughout your scene. They are generally not in the field of view, but are placed so that they illuminate the objects in the scene. In the example, the light is pure white because all three primary color components have a brightness value of 1.0.

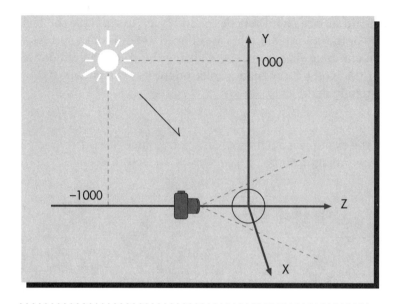

Figure 7-10 Position of the Light_Source in KWIKSTRT.POV

This concludes the brief discussion of POV-Ray data files in this Quick Start. The KWIKSTRT.POV example is very simple, but still has the three components all POV-Ray data files must have: a camera, defined objects, and light sources. You will find more information in the tutorial later in this chapter. Now we'll move on to some of the mechanics of tuning the operation of POV-Ray on your PC.

Rendering the Data File

If you have set up the Povrayopt environment variable and placed the \IMLAB\POVRAY directory in your path, you can render the file by typing:

```
C:>CD \IMLAB\POVRAY\EXAMPLES (ENTER)
C:>POVRAY -iKWIKSTRT.POV -oKWIKSTRT.TGA (ENTER)
```

This command line reads the POV input file KWIKSTRT.POV and creates a Targa output file called KWIKSTRT.TGA. You should see the image of a sphere appear on your screen.

There are a number of other options you can specify on the command line when you invoke POV-Ray to override its default actions. You might want to use a different video mode than the VGA 320x200 that was set earlier using the +d switch. You can specify the name of the output file with the -o option. Finally, you might want to render the image using a higher resolution using the -h and -w options.

Video Support

POV-Ray does not need any hardware graphics capabilities at all. If you use the -d option, the graphics output will be turned off, and a Targa output file will be produced without an image showing on your screen. This may sound silly, but many people have upgraded their computer, and have an older computer sitting around unused. Why not put your old computer to work ray tracing? If it has an old monochrome graphics adapter, no problem. Just use the -d switch. You can then view the resulting Targa file on your fancy new 486 with Super VGA.

It is a good idea to monitor the progress of the image on your screen in order to have a visual indication that everything is working. If you have a VGA or Super VGA without true-color capabilities, then the video output of POV-Ray will only be an approximation of the final image. When the image is done, you can process the Targa output file using Piclab to convert the image to a form such as GIF that looks good on your VGA. But if you have a graphics board with a Sierra DAC chip, such as the STB Powergraph Ergo with a Sierra DAC replacing the regular DAC, you will be treated to a very accurate view of the image while it is being created.

Table 7-2 shows the different variations of the +d switch that create graphics suitable for different hardware.

Don't be concerned if your graphics adapter is not listed in Table 7-2. Most of the adapters on the market use one of the chip sets listed, and POV-Ray may be able to automatically detect which chip set is present. The plain +d option invokes POV-Ray's autodetect feature. If the +d option does not work for you, most likely POV-Ray is unable to detect your adapter. In this case look at your graphics board's documentation to try to determine what chip set it uses, and then use the option for that chip set. You can also tell the chip set by opening your computer and looking at the chips on the graphics board. For example, the Orchid Prodesigner uses the Tseng 3000 chip set. The Tseng chip will be marked "TSENG ET3000". In Table 7-2 this chip set is listed as 3, so an owner of this board would use +d3.

At the bottom of Table 7-2 are the palette options. Ray tracing produces true-color output, with a red, green, and blue value for any point. Most VGA boards do not have true-color capabilities, but do have modes with a 256-color palette. The palette options provide different ways to approximate the true-color output on your screen. Remember that there is much better color information stored in the output file than you can see on the screen with one of these palette options; the screen display's purpose is just to give you an idea of what the image looks like.

The first palette option, which is the default, converts the internal HSV (Hue Saturation Value) color to red, green, and blue and picks the closest color

. . . .

+dxy enables display adapter type x, with palette option y.

Display Adapter Types:

0 - (default) Autodetect display adapter from types below:
1 - Basic, Plain Vanilla VGA 320x200
2 - MVGA (Mode 13X) Tweaked VGA 360x480 (if > 320x200)
3 - Tseng Labs 3000 SVGA 640x350, 640x480, 800x600
4 - Tseng Labs 4000 SVGA 640x350, 640x400, 640x480, 800x600, 1024x768
5 - AT&T VDC600 SVGA 640x400
6 - Oak Technologies OTI-067 SVGA 640x480
7 - Video 7 SVGA, VRAM FastRAM 640x480
8 - Video 7 Vega VGA, Cirrus Chip (uses Mode 1 or 2 above)
9 - Paradise SVGA 640x480
A - Ahead Systems Version A SVGA 640x480
B - Ahead Systems Version B SVGA 640x480
C - Chips And Technologies SVGA 640x480
D - ATI VGA Wonder 640x480
E - Everex SVGA 640x480
F - Trident SVGA 640x480
G - VESA Standard SVGA 640x400, 640x480, 800x600, 1024x768, 1280x1024
H - N reserved, unassigned (S)VGA adapter types
O - TIGA/Hercules Graphics Workstation 16-bit
P - TIGA/Hercules Graphics Workstation 24-bit
Q - Z reserved, unassigned True-Color adapter types

Palette Options:

0 - (default) HSV->RGB method
3 - 3-3-2 RGB method
G - Grey Scale (optimized 64-shade palette for IBM PC's)
H - Sierra High Color pallete DAC

Table 7-2 POV-Ray IBM PC display options

in the color palette. This is fine for most purposes. Since this option is the default, you do not need to specify it.

If you have a Sierra DAC chip in your graphics board, you can see the image in true-color and the screen display will look very much like the true-color image stored in the Targa output file. If you have a Sierra chip, use the "H" parameter with the "+d" option. For example, suppose you have an STB Powergraph Ergo VGA equipped with the Sierra DAC chip. That particular STB board uses the Tseng 4000 chip, so the POV-Ray video option to use with this board is +d4H.

Once you find the best video option for your hardware configuration, you should edit your AUTOEXEC.BAT file so that the correct video option is set in the POVRAYOPT environment variable. (The POVRAYOPT variable was discussed in the section Getting POV-Ray Up and Running earlier in this chapter.) For example, if you have the STB/Sierra combination just mentioned, you should have a line in your AUTOEXEC.BAT that looks like:

```
SET POVRAYOPT=+lc:\IMLAB\POVRAY +d4H -v0 +p +x +ft -a -q9 -w80 -h60
```

You can also use the video option on the command line when you start POV-Ray; any command-line options supersede those set in the POVRAYOPT environment variable. Notice that the image dimensions have been changed in this example to keep the aspect ratio correct. The +d4H option will use a video mode with a 4:3 screen dimension ratio such as 640x480. The 80 pixels wide by 60 pixels high dimensions specified in the above example have the 4:3 ratio. Small dimensions are used because you will want to quickly generate examples while you are experimenting.

Converting the Output File

The Targa output file created by POV-Ray contains more colors than can be simultaneously displayed on your Super VGA, unless you have one of the newer boards that supports 16-bit true-color or better. POV-Ray can display the image as it is being generated using VGA 256-color modes, but the resulting image only approximates the 24-bit true-color image stored in the Targa file. POV-Ray does not attempt to color reduce the image from true color to 256 colors in an optimum way; the purpose of displaying the image is to give you visual feedback that the operation of POV-Ray is proceeding correctly.

A true-color image can be accurately displayed using 256 colors if those colors are well chosen. The programs Piclab, Image Alchemy, and Improces on your Image Lab companion disk can all do color reduction. For example, to use Piclab to convert KWIKSTRT.TGA to a GIF file, type:

```
C:>PL (ENTER)
PL>TLOAD KWIKSTRT (ENTER)
PL>MAKEPAL (ENTER)
PL>MAP (ENTER)
PL>GSAVE KWIKSTRT (ENTER)
```

This sequence of commands assumes that your AUTOEXEC.BAT Path statement has been arranged so that Piclab has been set up and can be run from any directory. See the Piclab chapter for instructions if you have not yet set up the Piclab software.

You can also color reduce images using the Image Alchemy program on your companion disk. Because they use different algorithms for color reduction, for some images Alchemy may work better, for others Piclab gives better results. Try converting your ray-traced Targa images with both Alchemy and Piclab to get an idea how well the two programs work, then standardize on one or the other for most of your images. (Piclab has had problems color reducing images of ray-traced spheres. See the READ.ME file on the companion disk to determine if this problem had been resolved by press time.)

Assuming Alchemy is in a directory in your Path, to color reduce the KWIKSTRT.TGA image using Image Alchemy, type:

`C:>ALCHEMY KWIKSTRT.TGA -g` (ENTER)

Image Alchemy is able to detect that the input file is a Targa. The -g option tells Alchemy to create a GIF file. Alchemy will use the same file name and add the .GIF extension.

Automating POV-Ray with a Batch File

You can automate your running of POV-Ray by invoking it indirectly with a batch file. You will find a batch file for this purpose on the companion disk. The file is called POV.BAT. The contents of the file are shown in Listing 7-2.

. . . .

```
C:\IMLAB\POVRAY\POVRAY +LC:\IMLAB\POVRAY\INCLUDE -i%1.POV -o%1.TGA -p %2 %3 %4 %5
%6 %7 %8
if errorlevel 0 goto ok
goto done
:ok
pause
REM Uncomment the next line to use Piclab for color reduction
REM PL C:\IMLAB\PICLAB\CNVTGA %1
REM Uncomment the next line to use Alchemy for color reduction
REM ALCHEMY %1.TGA -g -o
:done
```

Listing 7-2 The POV.BAT file

The POV.BAT file saves typing by letting you enter just the input and output file name once. It will also invoke Piclab automatically to color reduce the resulting output file for you. The batch file variable %1 is replaced by a command-line parameter that you give the POV.BAT file when you invoke it. This parameter is the name of the input file without the .POV extension. An output file with the same name as the input file will be generated, only with the .TGA extension. You can also type in other parameters at the line to do such things as override the default image size. This batch file assumes that:

1. The POVRAY.EXE file is in the C:\IMLAB\POVRAY directory.

2. The POVRAY Include files are in the C:\PIMLAB\POVRAY\INCLUDE directory.

3. The Piclab color reduction program is C:\IMLAB\PICLAB\CNVTGA.

If any of these assumptions is not correct, edit the batch file accordingly by correcting the directory names where these files reside. You can also add the options you put in the POVRAYOPT environment variable to the batch file if you wish.

To use the batch file to render KWIKSTRT.POV, type:

`C:>POV KWIKSTRT` (ENTER)

You can add up to seven other space-separated options on the command line. These options will take precedence over options set in the POVRAYOPT environment variable. If you would like to render KWIKSTRT.POV at 640x480 resolution, for example, you would type:

`C:>POV KWIKSTRT -w640 -h480` (ENTER)

Resolution vs. Rendering Time

Be aware of the fact that the larger the image, the longer it takes for POV-Ray to generate the image. Ray tracing is not a hobby for the impatient! The examples so far have been set up for images of modest dimensions so that tracing can go relatively fast. Tracing time is proportional to the number of pixels. Therefore, if you double both the horizontal and the vertical resolution, the number of pixels and the time to render will by multiplied by 4. Table 7-3 shows factors indicating the relative rendering time for a number of resolutions, using a factor of 1 for the recommended 80x60 resolution for experimenting.

width	height		times slower
+w80	+h60	=	1
+w160	+h120	=	4
+w320	+h200	=	15
+w640	+h480	=	64
+w800	+h600	=	100
+w1024	+h768	=	164

Table 7-3 Rendering time factors for different image resolutions

For example, an image that takes 1 minute to render at the 80x60 postage stamp size will take 164 minutes at 1024x768. You can see why the tiny resolutions are handy!

This ends the Quick Tour. You will see a lot of data files with the .POV extension in the \IMLAB\EXAMPLES directory on the companion disk. You can render any of these files the same way as you ran KWIKSTRT.POV. Later in this chapter, a tutorial will take you step by step through a whole series of these examples. You will also find some advanced ray-tracing examples in Chapter 9.

HOW RAY TRACING WORKS

A ray tracer is a computer program that creates realistic images of objects that are defined using an abstract input language. The power of a ray tracer is that it uses the computer's ability to mathematically simulate rays of light to produce realistic reflections and shading in generated scenes.

Ray Tracing: Left-brained or Right-brained?

Before launching into an explanation of ray tracing, let's address the question of just who this subject of ray tracing is for. Much has been made in recent years about the difference between "left-brained" and "right-brained" activities. The left brain is said to be more adept at rational analysis and the right brain good for integrative and intuitive thinking. This is a useful distinction, and valuable insights can be gained using it. However, it is important not to impose these categories too heavily where they may not fit. Ray tracing has from its beginning labored under the mystique that it was a left-brained activity for highly mathematical and analytical people. While there is a basis for this mystique, it can be an unnecessary barrier for those who do not consider themselves to be mathematical or technical.

Ray tracing had its genesis in the world of graphics programmers and graduate-level computer science departments. A great debt is owed to the extraordinarily talented individuals who wrote the first public domain ray tracers, and are still working to improve them. Writing a ray tracer requires an extensive knowledge of programming as well as a deep understanding of certain elements of mathematics and physics. As a result of these origins, until recently the use of ray tracing was an activity limited to academia, out of reach of ordinary people. An additional factor limiting ray tracing to the academic and scientific communities is that until recently, only high-priced graphics workstations or even mainframe computers could handle the intensive computational requirements of a ray tracer.

Today there are a number of high-quality ray-tracing programs that run on a variety of computer hardware, including the POV-Ray program that comes with this book. Personal computers now have formidable processing capabilities. As a result, ray tracing is available to everyone.

You don't need to be the proverbial rocket scientist to use and enjoy a ray tracer. Some of the most impressive images in this book were made by designers and artists with a limited background in programming and mathematics. Yes, it takes a little discipline to use the POV-Ray input format. Yes, you do need to be able to plan and think using three-dimensional coordinate systems. And yes, a "for the rest of us" point-and-click interface for ray tracers has yet to be devised. But anyone with enough interest to read this book undoubtedly has more than enough ability to handle the "left-brained" side of ray tracing. If you are excited by the prospect of visualizing scenes and bringing them to life on your computer screen, then POV-Ray is for you, even if you never saw the inside of a college math or programming classroom. Ray tracing is where the left and right brains meet; dive in and enjoy the stimulation of exercising your whole mind!

An Analogy with Photography

A ray tracer is an artistic tool. The analogy between ray tracing and photography is useful for understanding what ray tracing is all about, so let's discuss photography for a few moments.

Prior to the invention of photography, a great amount of artistic talent was required to create realistic paintings. Photography allows anyone to make a realistic picture. When photography first appeared, many people thought of it as a technical marvel but not as an art form. After all, anyone can take a picture by aiming a camera and pressing a button, so where is the art? Even today photography has not achieved the same status enjoyed by painting. But millions of photographers have snapped photos at Yosemite National Park in California, and only very rarely does one of these photos capture the mystery and essence of that place in a way approaching the classic photographs of Ansel Adams. The art world has finally granted respectability to photography, and museums are now devoted to exhibitions of photographs by extraordinary photographers.

A photograph is created by aiming a camera at a scene. Light from the sun and the sky illuminate the scene. Rays of light travel from the light source, reflect off the objects in the scene, and are focused by the camera lens on the film. The objects in the scene modify the reflected light. The surfaces of the objects have color and texture. Some are shiny, and some dull. Some objects are transparent and allow light to shine through. A good photographer becomes very conscious of light and how the interplay of direct light, indirect light, and shadow affect the picture.

Photography's strength is that it allows the photographer to create realistic scenes. But this is also its weakness; photography needs a scene to photograph! (Granted there is the specialized area of effects achievable in the darkroom without a physical scene.) Ansel Adams was a gifted photographer, but he needed Yosemite to make his famous photographs. In this respect painting and photography are different. A painter need only see the scene in his or her imagination.

The basic elements between photography and ray tracing are the same. There is a "camera" placed at a particular location in space. The camera is aimed at "objects." There are "sources of light" that illuminate the object, and the image is created by the reflections and refractions of light on the objects. Objects have "textures" that modify the light which illuminates them.

There is, however, one huge difference between photography and ray tracing. In ray tracing the light, the objects, and the camera are not physical, but mathematical. All three exist in the intangible world of computer simulation. To create a ray-traced scene, you tell your computer where the light source is, the shape, texture, and position of the objects in the scene, and where the camera is using the input language of the ray tracer. The computer then laboriously traces single rays of light between the camera and the light source one at a time and builds the image from the perspective of the camera. In this one respect, ray tracing is more like painting than photography. The ray-tracing artist needs only imagination to create a scene. A ray-tracing artist can create a Yosemite Falls on some alien planet under the gaze of unearthly moons, surrounded by mountains covered with trees unlike any seen in California. Or the artist can imagine a slimy snail made up of basic shapes and textures.

Unless you happen to be a very skilled painter, you can take photographs that achieve effects that would be very difficult for you to achieve through painting. Now, you can easily create ray-traced images that are beyond your ability to create with paint. In one of the first tutorial examples, you will create an image of three colored spheres and their reflections on the rippled surface of a pond. Imagine trying to paint such a scene. Later in the book you will learn how to make images of thousands of spheres of all sizes, shapes, and textures, some polished and reflecting the others with the distortion of a curved mirror.

As with photography, even though certain realistic effects are easy to achieve using ray tracing, it takes great talent and skill to make outstanding images. But lest you be too awestruck by the skill of the artists who created those images, remember that you can enjoy taking photographs without necessarily having the skill of an Ansel Adams. In the same way, you can derive a tremendous amount of enjoyment creating and modifying ray-traced scenes. Who knows? Among the readers of this book may be an artist whose work will some day grace the walls of an exhibition devoted to ray tracing. Whether or not that is your destiny, you are in for a lot of fun.

The Inner Workings of a Ray Tracer

From what has been said so far, you might think that a ray tracer works by mathematically following rays from the light to the objects and finally to the camera. There are in fact computer programs that do this sort of simulation. They are called *radiosity* programs. Radiosity methods are very powerful, but also require a lot of computation. The reason is that the vast majority of light rays leaving the light source never reach the imaginary camera. Radiosity methods create a view-independent model of all the light in a scene, whether it reaches a particular viewpoint or not. Ray tracing cuts down the amount of calculation by tracing rays backwards, starting from the Camera. Ray tracing does just the computation needed to create a view from one and only one perspective.

Figure 7-11 shows how a ray tracer works. Think of the camera as though it were a pinhole camera. A pinhole camera is a box with a piece of film on one end and a small hole instead of a lens. (Serious photographs can be made with a pinhole camera, which has a very small effective lens aperture and an enormous depth of field.) For each point on the "film," which is really your computer screen, the computer calculates a straight-line ray of light from that point through the pinhole heading out toward the scene. Some rays never strike an object, in which case no light would hit that particular point on the film. (Some ray-tracing artists enclose their scenes within a large sphere so that there is always an illuminated background.) If the backwards ray does intersect

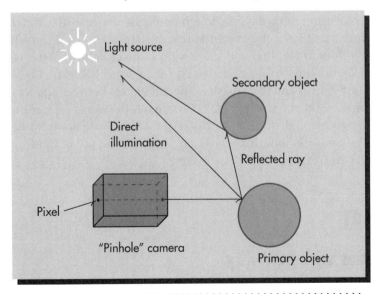

Figure 7-11 Tracing light rays backwards from camera to object

an object, then the program checks the path from the point of intersection to each light source in the scene. The result of this check tells whether the surface is illuminated, and if so by which light sources. If the surface is illuminated, the angle to the light source and the texture characteristics are used to figure out the color characteristics of that spot on the object. If the object reflects or refracts light, then the ray tracer calculates the continued direction of the reflected or refracted light ray and continues to trace the ray. Figure 7-11 shows a reflected light ray continuing toward another sphere. This process is continued until there are no more reflecting or refracting surfaces hit, or a limiting ray length is achieved. Eventually a single pixel on your screen is given a certain color value based on all the interactions between the rays emanating from that pixel and the objects and light sources in the scene. If objects in the scene reflect the light from the light sources directly to that pixel, it will be given a light color. On the other hand, if objects block all the paths of possible light rays from the pixel to the light source, the pixel is shrouded in shadows and will be given a dark color.

The ray tracer repeats these complex calculations for every pixel in your image. When you create an image to display on your Super VGA screen at 640x480, POV-Ray has to do all those calculations for 307,200 pixels! Ray tracing even simple scenes at high resolutions requires calculating millions of rays. That is why ray tracing can take so long. The results can be spectacular, and well worth the wait.

Scenes rendered using POV-Ray, although impressively realistic, differ from reality in important respects. The intensity of light does not diminish with distance as it does in real life, and there is no indirect lighting. That is, Objects are not illuminated by light reflected off of other Objects. Light Sources are all point sources and have no size. The differences between the way the physics of world works and the way POV-Ray models the world are significant enough that you would think creating very realistic images would be difficult. Yet POV-Ray works amazingly well, and with careful use of lighting and textures, you can create eerily lifelike images.

A POV TUTORIAL

Creating Scenes with POV-Ray

In this section you will learn how to create scene descriptions for POV-Ray. It is assumed that you have already installed POV-Ray according to the instructions earlier in this chapter. If not, see the Getting Started and Quick Tour sections, above. You should be able to run POV-Ray from any directory on your hard disk. This tutorial will make use of a number of ready-to-run examples that are on the companion disk. These examples should be copied to a directory on your hard disk such as C:\IMLAB\EXAMPLES.

The First Example Scene

The first scene in this tutorial is very simple, consisting of one red ball lit by one light. You can type the following listing into your text editor, or use the file EXAMPLE1.POV on your companion disk.

. . . .

```
// Persistence of Vision Ray Tracer 1.00
// The Waite Group's Image Lab
// EXAMPLE1.POV
// Red Ball.

// Camera
camera{
  translate <0  0  0>
  direction <0 0 1>
  up <0 1 0>
  right <1.33333 0 0>
  look_at <0 0 3>
}
// Red ball
object {
  sphere{ <0 0 3> 1 }
  texture{
    color red 1
  }
}
// Light
object {
  light_source {
    <2 4 -3>
    color red 1 green 1 blue 1
  }
}
```

Listing 7-3 EXAMPLE1.POV.

You can invoke POV-Ray with all its options from the command line, but most of these options can be set in the environment variable POVRAYOPT using the line:

```
SET POVRAYOPT=+lc:\IMLAB\POVRAY +d -v0 +p +x +ft -a -q9 -w80 -h60
```

in your AUTOEXEC.BAT. You can also put these options in a file called POVRAY.DEF. The contents of this file would look like

```
+d -v0 +p +x +ft -a -q9 -w80 -h60
```

You can put the DEF file in the current directory, or in the directory where all the Include files have been put. In both of these examples, the video mode is the +d option, which means that POV-Ray will try to autodetect your video hardware and set the mode accordingly. If this doesn't work for you, see the discussion about setting the video mode in the POV Quick Tour section, and in particular Table 7-2.

If you have set the POVRAYOPT environment variable or have a POVRAY.DEF file with the main POV options, then all you have to specify on the POV command line are the input and output file names, and any parameters that you want to set different from the defaults. To render EXAMPLE1.POV, type:

```
C:>POVRAY -iEXAMPLE1.POV -oEXAMPLE1.TGA (ENTER)
```

To save having to enter both file names and remembering the i and o options, you can use the POV.BAT file to invoke POV-Ray. This file uses batch parameter variables to use the same file name for both the input and output files. The simplest form of this file would contain the line

```
POVRAY -i%1.POV -o%1.TGA %2 %3 %4 %5 %6 %7 %8 %9
```

Then if you type

```
C:>POV EXAMPLE1 (ENTER)
```

the parameter "EXAMPLE1" would replace %1 and accomplish exactly the same thing as the command line suggested above. The variables %2, %3, and so forth allow you to add more options to overrride the defaults. It is a good idea to use a more complete POV.BAT file such as the one suggested in the Quick Tour.

The file POV.BAT tells POV-Ray where to look for the Include files (we'll get to those later), and also carries out the color reduction that converts from Targa true-color to 256-color GIF files. The Piclab line in the batch file is commented out with REM. If you would rather use Piclab than Image Alchemy to create a GIF file, delete the REM in the Piclab line and insert REM at the beginning of the Alchemy line.

For the rest of this chapter, we will assume that you are using the POV.BAT file to invoke POV-Ray. Now go ahead and render the file EXAMPLE1.GIF by typing:

```
C:>POV EXAMPLE1 (ENTER)
```

A small white box will appear on your screen, and an approximation of the image will appear within the box. The white box will completely disappear when the image is done, and the POV.BAT file will invoke one of the color reduction programs to convert the Targa output file to a GIF. When all processing is complete, you should find both the file EXAMPLE1.TGA produced by

POV-Ray and the file EXAMPLE1.GIF converted from the Targa file by Alchemy or Piclab.

You can view EXAMPLE1.GIF using CompuShow. Type:

`C:>CSHOW EXAMPLE1.GIF` (ENTER)

and press (SPACE) to view the image. EXAMPLE1.GIF should look something like Figure 7-12.

The result is a red sphere shaded naturally according to the angle with the light.

Let's go through the EXAMPLE1.POV file and see what every line does. You will see that there is a pattern to many of the statements. You will find that you can copy and modify parts of previous images to create new ones.

Figure 7-12 The image created with EXAMPLE1.POV

The Camera

The first section of the EXAMPLE1.POV input data file is labeled "//Camera". The "//" causes everything else on a line to be ignored, and allows you to enter comments and annotations.

```
// Camera
camera{
  translate <0  0  0>
  direction <0 0 1>
  up <0 1 0>
  right <1.33333 0 0>
  look_at <0 0 3>
}
```

The Camera block, like every other POV block, is set off with the curly brackets { and }. The first line of the block is

```
translate <0  0  0>
```

This means to move the camera (or whatever else is appropriate for the context where translate appears) in the *x, y,* and *z* directions by the quantities specified inside the < > brackets from its current position. In this case, the numbers are 0, so this statement actually doesn't do anything, although it is a handy placeholder for a command that will generally be present. The current position of the camera before applying the translation was the origin <0 0 0>. All cameras, objects, and shapes in POV-Ray start out at the origin.

You may have noticed that the KWIKSTRT.POV file used the Location keyword rather than Translate in the Camera block. There really isn't any practical difference between the lines

```
translate <1  2  3>
```

and

```
location <1  2  3>
```

The first statement using Translate means that starting from the current position, go 1 unit in the *x* direction, 2 units in the *y* direction, and 3 units in the *z* direction. Since the starting point is <0 0 0>, the result is to move to the position <1 2 3>. The second statement using Location specifies the position <1 2 3> in 3-D space absolutely without any regard to a previous position. The results in either case are identical. However, if the lines occur twice, then the results differ. The lines

```
translate <1  2  3>
translate <1  2  3>
```

translate the position twice, ending up at position <2 4 6>. By way of contrast,

```
location <1  2  3>
location <1  2  3>
```

merely asserts twice that the position is <1 2 3>, so following these statements the specified position is still <1 2 3>.

The next line in the Camera block is

```
direction <0 0 1>
```

The quantity <0 0 1> is a vector indicating the direction the camera is pointed. The magnitude of the vector determines the field of view of camera, much like a zoom lens. Larger values give a narrower field view. It is a little tricky to know just where a camera is pointing by giving a direction vector. A somewhat more intuitive approach is to specify a point where the camera is aimed. This is accomplished by

```
look_at <0 0 3>
```

To understand the difference between Direction and Look_At, consider what happens if the camera is moved to a new location. Figure 7-13 shows two cameras at two locations pointing in Direction <0 0 1>. Both cameras are pointed in a direction parallel to the z axis. The camera at location <0 0 0> is "looking at" the point <0 0 3> (and all the other points on the positive z axis.) But the camera located at <1 0 0> is not aimed at <0 0 3>, but since the camera has been shifted one unit along the x axis, it is now "looking at" <1 0 3>.

When you use the statement

```
look_at <0 0 3>
```

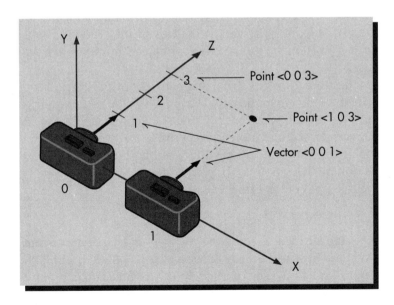

Figure 7-13 Direction <0 0 1>

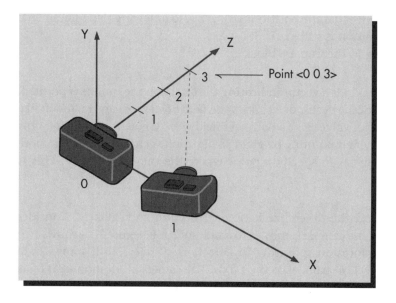

Figure 7-14 Look_At <0 0 3>

then the camera adjusts so that even if it has moved it is still aimed at the point <0 0 3>. The same two cameras are shown in Figure 7-14, only this time the camera located at <1 0 0> has twisted so that it is still "looking at" the point <0 0 3>. The advantage of using Look_At is that you are saved the trouble of calculating a new Direction vector to keep your objects in view when you move the camera.

A reasonable question to ask is, what happens if both Direction and Look_At are specified, but are inconsistent? That is, what if a camera pointed at the Look_At point is not aimed according to the Direction vector? The answer is that the Direction vector is ignored except for its size, which still determines the zoom factor. The camera actually faces the Look_At point, no matter what direction the Direction vector points.

The remaining two lines of the camera are:

```
up <0 1 0>
right <1.33333 0 0>
```

These two lines are standard and need not be changed under normal circumstances. The Up vector tells where the top of the camera is pointed, and Right indicates where an arrow coming out of the right side of the camera is pointing, and also adjusts the horizontal magnification. The number 1.33333 is correct for virtually all PC monitors that have a 4:3 aspect ratio (ratio of width to height).

The Object

The next block defines the object in the scene, which in this case is a red sphere.

```
// Red ball
object {
  sphere{ <0 0 3> 1 }
  texture{
    color red 1
    phong 1
  }
}
```

The Object block contains two sub-blocks defining the shape and texture of the object. The Sphere block includes the center location and size of the radius of the circle. The Texture block can contain many different surface qualities. A number of these will be introduced later in the tutorial. This example just sets the color to red and adds some shine to the sphere. The number following the Red keyword tells the brightness of the color. The number 1 means full brightness. The line "phong 1" adds a little pizazz to the sphere. The Phong highlight is named for Phong Bui-Tuong, who developed an illumination model with a variable specular reflection component, which is a fancy way of describing a shiny highlight. You can modify the number to get different degrees of shiny reflection.

The Light Source

The final element making up a scene is a light source, which is a special kind of object. A light source has a position and a color. This example has white light, since each of the three primary colors have brightness value 1. The brightness values are shown as integers in this example, but they can be any number between 0 and 1.

```
// Light
object {
  light_source {
    <2 4 -3>
    color red 1 green 1 blue 1
  }
}
```

The position of the light source has a big effect on the appearance of the final rendered scene, because it determines what parts of objects will be lit and what will be in shadows. Beginning photographers are advised to make sure that the sun is behind the camera, and the same advice holds true for ray tracing. But don't let this rule of thumb limit you — sometimes backlighting (placing the object between the camera and the light source) makes very interesting images.

Adding a Floor

A POV-Ray scene is certainly not limited to a single object. There are a number of basic shapes built in to POV-Ray, and still more that can be constructed from the basic shapes. The first variation we'll try is to add a floor. Listing 7-4 below shows the same example with a new object added, a green plane under our red sphere.

```
// Persistence of Vision-Ray Tracer 1.00
// The Waite Group's Image Lab
// EXAMPLE2.POV
// Red Ball with floor.

// Camera
camera{
  translate <0  0  0>
  direction <0 0 1>
  up <0 1 0>
  right <1.33333 0 0>
  look_at <0 0 3>
}
// Floor
object{
  plane{ <0 1 0> -1 }
   texture {
     color green 1
     }
}
// Red ball
object {
  sphere{ <0 0 3> 1 }
   texture{
    color red 1
    phong 1
  }
}
// Light
object {
  light_source {
    <2 4 -3>
    color red 1 green 1 blue 1
  }
}
```

Listing 7-4 EXAMPLE2.POV.

The Plane definition looks exactly like the Sphere definition, but the numbers have a different meaning. A plane is defined by a vector at right angles to the plane. This vector is called a *surface normal*. It is followed by a number that indicates the distance between the plane and the origin. Figure 7-15 shows

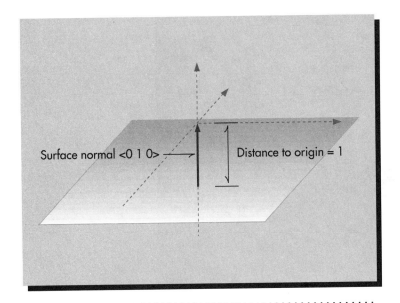

Surface normal <0 1 0>

Distance to origin = 1

Figure 7-15 The definition of a plane

how this works. Because the plane surface normally is in the *y* axis direction, the plane is parallel to the *x-y* plane, and one unit below it.

Render the file EXAMPLE2.POV by typing:

`C:>POV EXAMPLE2` (ENTER)

Take a look at the completed file EXAMPLE2.GIF using CompuShow. It should look like Figure 7-16. The floor makes this scene more realistic. Notice the shadow of the ball on the plane and the way the light falls off in the distance. This scene has depth, accurate shadows and highlights, all generated from that simple data file.

Altering the Camera Position

Once you have created a scene in POV-Ray, with very little effort you can view the same scene from different angles and perspectives. In order to do this, you need to become comfortable with 3-D coordinate systems so that you can accurately locate the camera in your scene.

In the first two examples, the camera location for the scene was placed at the origin. Let's move the camera location up higher so we can look down at the ball. To do this the line in the Camera block that says translate <0 0 0> is changed to translate <0 10 0>. This just moves the camera up 10 units in the *y* direction. This change is greatly simplified by the fact that the Camera block uses the Look_At keyword. In order to keep the sphere in view from the new viewpoint, the camera has to point in a downward direction. Because the

325

Figure 7-16 The rendering of EXAMPLE2.POV

Look_At position is the center of the sphere, no matter where the camera is placed, it will still be aimed at the sphere. Without the Look_At statement, you would have to recalculate the Direction vector to keep the camera pointed.

The file with the modified viewpoint is EXAMPLE3.POV. To render it, type in:

`C:>POV EXAMPLE3` ENTER

The result is shown in Figure 7-17. The sphere is smaller because the camera location is farther away from the sphere, and the perspective is clearly from a much higher position. The shadow of the sphere on the plane makes it easier to judge the relative positions of the sphere and the camera location.

Try changing the position of the camera and sphere to different positions using the same methods as above, saving the file as a different name, rendering the new scene and viewing the results to get a feel for what the numbers mean. It is possible to position the camera so nothing can be seen, move the objects so that they can't be seen, or to set a light source so everything is in shadow. If that happens, just load the original file again and try some different numbers, making smaller changes from the examples.

Adding More Spheres

You can add as many spheres as you want to your data file. The position of objects within a data file makes no difference. POV-Ray assembles all the objects and light sources in your scene before it renders the scene. Listing 7-5

Figure 7-17 EXAMPLE3 — Red sphere viewed from a high camera location

shows the contents of EXAMPLE4.POV, which contains the definitions of five different spheres.

```
// Persistence of Vision-Ray Tracer 1.00
// The Waite Group's Image Lab
// EXAMPLE4.POV
// Five spheres and a floor

// Camera
camera{
  translate <0 0 -1>
  direction <0 0 1>
  up <0 1 0>
  right <1.33333 0 0>
  look_at <0 0 3>
}

// Floor
object{
  plane{ <0 1 0> -1 }
   texture {
     color green 1
     }
}
```

Listing 7-5 EXAMPLE4.POV *(continued on next page)*

327

. . . .

```
// Yellow ball behind the red one
object {
  sphere{<1 1 4> 1}
  texture{
    color red 1 green 1
    phong 1
  }
}

// Red ball
object {
  sphere{<0 0 3> 1}
  texture{
    color red 1
    phong 1
  }
}
// Light
object {
  light_source {
    <2 4 -3>
    color red 1 green 1 blue 1
  }
}
// Blue ball
object {
  sphere{ <-2 1 4> 1 }
  texture{
    color blue 1
    phong 1
  }
}
// Little ball
object {
  sphere{ <0 -0.8 1.5> 0.2 }
  texture{
    color red 0.5 green 0.2 blue 0.7
    phong 1
  }
}
// Sinking ball
object {
  sphere{ <1 -1 2> 0.6 }
  texture{
    color red 0.7 green 0.5 blue 0.1
    phong 1
  }
}
```

Listing 7-5 EXAMPLE4.POV *(continued)*

Figure 7-18 EXAMPLE4.POV — five colored spheres

Since there is a little more detail in this scene, it is a good idea to make the image a little larger. You can type different image dimensions in at the command line whether or not you are using the POV.BAT file to do the rendering. The POV.BAT file can handle up to nine different command-line parameters using the batch file variables %1 through %9, counting the name of the file, which must be the first parameter. If you have been doing the examples up until now as tiny 80x60 images, as suggested in the text, keep in mind that doubling the dimensions to 160x120 will increase the rendering time 4 times. On a 33-MHz 386 machine, EXAMPLE3.POV can be rendered in about 36 seconds at 160x120 pixels. To do this, type:

```
C:>POV EXAMPLE4 -w160 -h120 (ENTER)
```

The result is shown in Figure 7-18.

First let's study the Camera block in Listing 7-5. The position of the viewer is determined by the line

```
translate <0 0 -1>
```

which places the viewer directly behind the *x-y* plane and one unit away. A useful approach to placing your camera locations and objects is to keep the camera location on the negative *z* side of the *x-y* plane and the objects themselves near the origin. If you do this, you can then visualize the coordinate system with the horizontal *x* axis and a vertical *y* axis both in the center of your computer screen, and the *z* axis perpendicular to the screen with the negative side coming out of the screen toward you, the viewer, and the positive side extending behind the screen. The line

```
look_at <0 0 3>
```

means that the Camera is still directly facing the familiar red sphere, which is still at the same location centered at <0 0 3>. The other lines in the Camera block are standard and the same as before.

Just behind the red sphere are two new spheres, one yellow, and one blue. Both are the same size as the red sphere, but look smaller because they are farther from the camera. The yellow ball is defined by the Object definition

```
// Yellow ball behind the red one
object {
  sphere{<1 1 4> 1}
  texture{
    color red 1 green 1
    phong 1
  }
}
```

Its center is <1 1 4>, which places it 1 unit to the right, 1 unit up, and 1 unit farther back from the camera location than the red ball, which is at <0 0 3>. The z coordinate of 4 places it farther away from the camera location because the camera location is on the negative side of the x-y plane with z coordinate -1. The z position of -1 is 4 units away from the center of the red sphere and 5 units away from the yellow sphere. Notice that the Texture block of the yellow sphere contains a red and green component. The red and green primary colors mix to form yellow.

A little purple ball is defined in this data file. Its color is defined using varying amounts of all three primary colors.

```
// Little ball
object {
  sphere{ <0 -0.8 1.5> 0.2 }
  texture{
    color red 0.5 green 0.2 blue 0.7
    phong 1
  }
}
```

The purple ball appears to be resting on the floor plane. You can check to see if it really is, and gain an understanding of how the coordinates work in the process. The line defining the position of the floor is

```
plane{ <0 1 0> -1 }
```

As we mentioned earlier, the vector part of a Plane definition points in a direction at right angles to the plane it defines. The vector <0 1 0> points straight up in the y direction, so the floor, as expected, is perpendicular to the y axis and hence parallel to the x-y plane. This is in keeping with the convention of visualizing the *y* axis as vertical. The number -1 means that the plane is located a distance -1 from the origin, which in this case means -1 in the *y* direction. The center of the small purple sphere is the point <0 -0.8 1.5>, which has a *y* component of -.8. The radius of the sphere is 0.2 unit, so that the sphere extends 0.2 below the center. Everything works out, because that means that the very bottom of the sphere has a *y* coordinate of -0.8 minus 0.2, or -1, which causes it to just touch the floor plane. There is one additional sphere in the image, defined by the line

```
sphere{ <1 -1 2> 0.6 }
```

This sphere is clearly intersecting the floor, because the *y* coordinate of the center of the sphere is -1. This sphere is exactly cut in two by the plane. Since the plane is opaque, you cannot see the lower half of the sphere.

Changing Textures

So far, you have learned how to place objects in the scene, change the camera, and alter the color of the objects. You can do a lot more to modify the appearance of the objects in your scenes. The next example shows some things that you can do with textures. Render the file EXAMPLE5.POV, which is shown in Listing 7-6. If should look like Figure 7-19.

Figure 7-19 Using textures in EXAMPLE5.POV

. . . .

```
// Persistence of Vision-Ray Tracer 1.00
// The Waite Group's Image Lab
// EXAMPLE5.POV
// Texture experiment

// Camera
camera{
  translate <0 0 -1>
  direction <0 0 1>
  up <0 1 0>
  right <1.33333 0 0>
  look_at <0 0 3>
}
// Floor
object{
  plane{ <0 1 0> -1 }
   texture {
     checker
     color green 1
      color blue 1
    }
}
// Agate ball
object {
  sphere{<1 1 4> 1}
  texture{
    agate
    phong 1
  }
}

//  ball
object {
  sphere{<0 0 3> 1}
  texture{
    color red 1 green 1 blue 1 alpha 0.7
    phong 1
  }
}
// Light
object {
  light_source {
    <2 4 -3>
    color red 1 green 1 blue 1
  }
}
```

Listing 7-6 EXAMPLE5.POV.

This file has several of the spheres from the previous example, but they look very different. The Texture blocks are what made the difference. The Texture block contains the information used to calculate how the surface of an object looks. Color or color pattern, roughness, transparency, and reflectance can all be described in the Texture block.

First of all, the plane has been turned into a checkerboard with the Texture block

```
texture {
  checker
  color green 1
   color blue 1
 }
```

POV-Ray supports named textures. Quite a few have been built in, and the inventive programmers are adding new ones by the minute. The checker texture turns the surface of the object into a checkerboard using the two colors that follow the Checker keyword.

Second, one of the spheres has been given the agate texture, using the lines

```
texture{
  agate
  phong 1
}
```

In this case there are no color parameters; the brown and white agate colors are built into the Texture.

Finally, the last sphere has been turned into a semitransparent glass ball with the texture

```
texture{
  color red 1 green 1 blue 1 alpha 0.7
  phong 1
}
```

The magic is done with the words "alpha 0.7" at the end of the Color statement. You can get more zip from textures by using alpha properties of color. Every color you define in POV-Ray is a combination of red, green, blue, and alpha. The red, green, and blue we have already discussed. The alpha determines how transparent that color is. A color with an alpha of 1.0 is totally transparent. A color with an alpha of 0.0 is totally opaque. Alpha 0 is the default if you do not specify an alpha value.

Using the Include Files

The philosophy of POV-Ray is to give you a modest number of built-in shapes, colors, and textures, and the means to multiply these basic shapes, colors, and textures so you can render any object imaginable. Three files are provided with POV-Ray that give you a big head start in defining the shapes, textures, and colors for your scenes. These three files are SHAPES.INC, COLORS.INC, and TEXTURES.INC. You can access Include files in your data file by adding the lines

```
#include "shapes.inc"
#include "colors.inc"
#include "textures.inc"
```

to the top of your data file. POV-Ray treats the included files exactly as though the lines in the files are inserted in the text. The idea of using Includes is to store in one place declarations or fragments of data files that you want to use in different scenes.

The COLORS.INC File

Exactly three primary colors are built in to POV-Ray: red, green, and blue. Each of these colors is available in an unlimited number of shades and any other color can be created by combining these three. The problem is that when you see a color definition like

```
color red 0.647059 green 0.164706 blue 0.164706,
```

it is not immediately clear just what color that is without a lot of hands-on use of POV. But the word "brown" immediately communicates a color.

POV-Ray provides the facility for you to add your own keywords to the POV-Ray language. A keyword in a ray-tracing language is a word that has a built-in meaning. For example, while "brown" is not a built-in keyword, you can add it by using the declaration mechanism. The statement that defines the color brown is

```
#declare Brown = color red 0.647059 green 0.164706
      blue 0.164706
```

Each of these numbers specifies the brightness of one of the primary color components on a scale of 0 (completely dark) to 1 (fully saturated bright color.) This declaration means that the keyword Brown specifies the color obtained by mixing a 64.7% brightness of red, 16.5% brightness of green, and a 16.5% brightness of blue together.

Once a term is declared, you can use the declared term in any context where the terms used to define it would be meaningful. Thus the Texture statement

```
texture{
  color red 0.647059 green 0.164706 blue 0.164706
}
```

can be replaced with the much more understandable

```
texture{
  color brown
}
```

334

The file COLORS.INC contains many colors, ranging from the familiar black and magenta to colors with suggestive names like Orchid or CornflowerBlue. (Identifiers in POV-Ray are case sensitive, so if you want to use the color Orchid, you have to capitalize the first letter of the color name.) The best part about this is that you can name your own favorite colors and add them to your own Include file. Table 7-4 shows a few of the colors provided in the COLORS.INC file. (POV will accept either the international English spelling "colour" or the US "color.")

#declare Aquamarine	=	color red 0.439216	green 0.858824	blue 0.576471
#declare BlueViolet	=	color red 0.62352	green 0.372549	blue 0.623529
#declare Brown	=	color red 0.647059	green 0.164706	blue 0.164706
#declare CadetBlue	=	color red 0.372549	green 0.623529	blue 0.623529
#declare CornflowerBlue	=	color red 0.258824	green 0.258824	blue 0.435294
#declare Dark green	=	color red 0.184314	green 0.309804	blue 0.184314
#declare DarkOlivegreen	=	color red 0.309804	green 0.309804	blue 0.184314
#declare Firebrick	=	color red 0.556863	green 0.137255	blue 0.137255
#declare Gold	=	color red 0.8	green 0.498039	blue 0.196078
#declare IndianRed	=	color red 0.309804	green 0.184314	blue 0.184314
#declare Khaki	=	color red 0.623529	green 0.623529	blue 0.372549
#declare LightBlue	=	color red 0.74902	green 0.847059	blue 0.847059
#declare Maroon	=	color red 0.556863	green 0.137255	blue 0.419608
#declare NavyBlue	=	color red 0.137255	green 0.137255	blue 0.556863
#declare Orange	=	color red 0.8	green 0.196078	blue 0.196078
#declare Palegreen	=	color red 0.560784	green 0.737255	blue 0.560784
#declare Pink	=	color red 0.737255	green 0.560784	blue 0.560784
#declare Salmon	=	color red 0.435294	green 0.258824	blue 0.258824
#declare Tan	=	color red 0.858824	green 0.576471	blue 0.439216
#declare Violet	=	color red 0.309804	green 0.184314	blue 0.309804
#declare Wheat	=	color red 0.847059	green 0.847059	blue 0.74902
#declare Yellowgreen	=	color red 0.6	green 0.8	blue 0.196078

Table 7-4 A COLORS.INC sampler

The TEXTURES.INC File

The predefined textures in TEXTURES.INC can save a lot of time and effort when creating scenes. Just include the name of the predefined texture in the Texture block of the Object definition and the object is covered with that texture. You can use a predefined texture name in a Texture block and add additional texture attributes to further alter the texture appearance.

The texture feature of POV-Ray is powerful because it consists of many surface attributes that apply to a whole surface. In addition, you can use procedural textures that generate different patterns by invoking different texture-generating computer routines. Using textures is easy. You don't have to understand how they are generated to use them; you just use their names in Texture blocks.

The TEXTURES.INC file contains the declarations of many textures that you can use in your scenes. They have names like White Marble, Sapphire Agate, Rippling Water, Stained Wood, and Shiny Mirror.

Texture definitions use the same declaration mechanism that was used for the colors. Here is an example.

```
// Brown wood - looks stained
// Nice color map by Tom Price
#declare Tom_Wood = texture {
   wood
   turbulence 0.31
   color_map {
     [0.0 0.8  color red 0.7 green 0.3 blue 0.0
               color red 0.7 green 0.3 blue 0.0]
     [0.8 1.01 color red 0.5 green 0.2 blue 0.0
               color red 0.4 green 0.1 blue 0.0]
   }
}
```

Every declaration is of the form

```
#declare name = type definition
```

Here "name" is whatever the new keyword is that you are creating with the declaration. "Type" specifies what kind of thing you are declaring. So far you have seen two types, color and texture. "Definition" is replaced by whatever descriptions are needed to define what you are declaring. The definition can use built-in POV-Ray keywords, or keywords you created with previous declarations. This really is a pretty powerful facility!

In the example above, the name of the declared texture is Tom_Wood. If you wanted to use this declaration in a scene you would use the name Tom_Wood in the Texture blocks where you wanted this effect. The definition of Tom_Wood in the declaration is a Texture block.

Let's look at the Tom_Wood Texture block. (Browsing through the .INC files is a good way to learn how things are accomplished in POV-Ray.) Tom_Wood is a variation of a built-in texture called "wood." This illustrates how you can build new textures by modifying other textures. Any texture attributes added to the Texture block after the name of the texture modify the result. In the case of Tom_Wood, there are two changes. The first is the line

```
turbulence 0.31
```

Textures in real life can have random variations. This turbulence distorts the texture so it doesn't look quite so perfect, and makes it more interesting. The number after the Turbulence keyword gives the degree of turbulence. A turbulence value of .1 to .3 is usually best; 0.0 has no effect.

The other attribute modifying the regular wood texture is a *color map*. A color map is a very powerful mechanism for producing textures. A color map divides a texture into strips. The boundaries between the strips are assigned numbers between 0 and 1. Each line of the color map has two numbers and two colors. The two numbers and two colors represent the position and color of the two boundaries of the strip. In between the boundaries, the colors smoothly change between the two colors.

The SHAPES.INC File

Finally, if you thought from the examples so far that you were going to have to make all your tracings with spheres, the SHAPES.INC Include file gives you access to a large variety of different shapes.

Throughout this discussion you have read encouraging little notes that you really don't have to understand the inner workings of the Include files to use them. This applies quadruple to the SHAPES.INC file! The reason is that POV-Ray uses a powerfully general shape primitive called a *quadric*. Just this once, we'll give the mathematical definition of a quadric for the curious, but remember, you don't have to understand the definition to use quadrics!

Quadrics

Quadric surfaces can produce shapes like spheres, cones, cylinders, paraboloids (dish shapes), and hyperboloids (saddle or hourglass shapes). Fortunately the work of defining these common shapes has already been done for you in the SHAPES.INC file.

The syntax for defining a quadric shape is:

```
quadric {
    <a b c>
    <d e f>
    <g h i>
    j
}
```

This defines a surface in three dimensions that satisfies the following equation:

$$A\,y^2 + B\,y^2 + C\,z^2 + D\,xy + E\,xz + F\,yz + G\,x + H\,y + I\,z + J = 0$$

Different values of the constants A,B,C, ... J will give different shapes. So, if you take any three-dimensional points and use its *x, y,* and *z* coordinates in the lefthand expression of the above equation, the result will be 0 if the point is on the surface of the object. The result will be negative if the point is inside the object and positive if the point is outside the object. Here are some examples:

```
X² + Y² + Z² − 1 = 0    Sphere
X² + Y² − 1 = 0         Cylinder along the Z axis
X² + Y² − Z² = 0        Cone along the Z axis
```

The SHAPES.INC uses the #declare mechanism of POV-Ray to define common shapes using the quadric primitive. If you want to learn how it is done, you can look at SHAPES.INC and see how the quadric coefficients are given values to make that particular shape.

Here is an example. A shape called a Cylinder_Y is an infinitely long cylinder with the *y* axis running through it; in other words, a vertical column. The entry for this shape in SHAPES.INC is

```
#declare Cylinder_Y = quadric {
        <1.0 0.0 1.0>
        <0.0 0.0 0.0>
        <0.0 0.0 0.0>
        −1.0
}
```

This declaration follows the same pattern of the earlier declarations. The name is given to what is declared, then the type, then the actual definition.

An Include File Example

The next example adds two cylinders to the EXAMPLE5.POV file you rendered earlier, and uses some textures and colors from the Include files. Listing 7-7 shows the data file, and Figure 7-20 shows what the rendered file looks like.

. . . .

```
// Persistence of Vision-Ray Tracer 1.00
// The Waite Group's Image Lab
// EXAMPLE6.POV
// Cylinders and spheres

#include "shapes.inc"
#include "colors.inc"
#include "textures.inc"

// Camera
camera{
  translate <0 0 −1>
  direction <0 0 1>
  up <0 1 0>
  right <1.33333 0 0>
  look_at <0 0 3>
}
```

Listing 7-7 Using the Include files — EXAMPLE6.POV *(continued on the next page)*

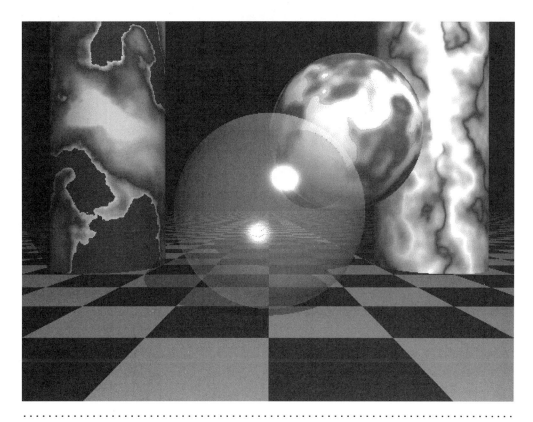

Figure 7-20 EXAMPLE6.POV — cylinders

```
object {
  quadric {
   Cylinder_Y
   translate <-3 0 6>
  }
  texture {
   Blood_Sky
  }
}
object {
  quadric {
   Cylinder_Y
   translate <3 0 6>
  }
  texture {
   White_Marble
   phong 1
  }
}
```

Listing 7-7 Using the Include files — EXAMPLE6.POV *(continued on the next page)*

339

```
// Floor
object{
  plane{ <0 1 0> -1 }
   texture {
     checker
     color green 1
      color blue 1
     }
}
// Agate ball
object {
  sphere{<1 1 4> 1}
  texture{
    agate
    phong 1
  }
}

// Transparent ball
object {
  sphere{<0 0 3> 1}
  texture{
    color red 1 green 1 blue 1 alpha 0.7
    phong 1
  }
}
// Light
object {
  light_source {
    <2 4 -3>
    color red 1 green 1 blue 1
  }
}
```

Listing 7-7 Using the Include files — EXAMPLE6.POV *(continued from the previous page)*

There are two new objects in this file, both cylinders. The first cylinder is created with the lines

```
object {
  quadric {
  Cylinder_Y
  translate <-3 0 6>
  }
  texture {
   Blood_Sky
  }
}
```

Whenever you use a declaration in POV-Ray, you have to introduce the declared keyword with a word that indicates the type of what was declared. In this case the cylinder is a quadric, so the Quadric keyword is used. Inside the Quadric block you will find the declared name Cylinder_Y.

All the shapes in the POV-Ray standard Include file have a default position and size. They are always centered on the origin and extend one unit from the origin in whatever direction is appropriate for the particular shape. The Cylinder_Y shape extends infinitely far in both directions along the y axis, and has radius 1. The statement line

```
translate <-3 0 6>
```

moves the cylinder from this default position to 3 units to the left (the negative x direction) and 6 units in the positive z direction (away from the camera location.) The y component of the translation is 0, because there is no point in moving an infinitely long cylinder along its length! However, once a texture is applied to the cylinder, you might indeed want to move the cylinder up or down depending on exactly how you want the textured pattern to appear on the cylinder surface.

The other block within the Object definition is a Texture block, which contains the rather ominous-sounding texture name Blood_Sky. The texture Bood_Sky is a reddish background with a patchwork of yellow clouds and is declared in TEXTURES.INC. Once again, since Blood_Sky is a texture, it can only be introduced by the Texture keyword, and appear in a Texture block.

The file EXAMPLE6.POV contains one other cylinder, which is very similar to the first. It is translated to the right rather than the left and it illustrates a different texture.

You can try out the different textures by changing the texture names in either the cylinders or the spheres in this image. Some you might want to try are Mirror, which is a reflecting polished surface, Gold_Texture, or White_Marble. You might also try different shapes by replacing Cylinder_Y with Cone_Y.

Transformations

You can make spheres of any size in POV-Ray, but all the objects declared in SHAPES.INC are one fixed size. We have already seen how the Translate command can move camera locations and shapes to different positions. As you might guess, several other kinds of transformations are possible in POV. You can translate (move), scale (expand or shrink), or rotate objects. Let's take these one at a time.

Translation

Translation moves an object or camera location relative to its current position. The three numbers used in the Translate command form a vector (a quantity with a size and direction) rather than a fixed position. The line

```
translate <1  2  -3>
```

means to move from the current position 1 unit to the right in the *x* direction, two units up in the *y* direction, and 3 units in the negative *z* direction (usually off the screen). Since the Translate command is relative, not absolute, you can have more than one Translate command. The effects are cumulative. Remember that the default starting point for most objects is the origin, or <0 0 0>. If an object's initial position is <0 0 0> and you apply Translate < 1 2 -3>, then it ends up at location <1 2 -3>. Starting at the origin is the only case where there isn't much different between relative and absolute position.

If you want to track the position of an object, just add the translation values. See if you can figure out where the center of the following sphere is:

```
object {
  sphere{<0 0 3> 1}
  translate <1 2 -2>
   color red 1 green 1 blue 1 alpha 0.7
   phong 1
 }
}
```

The sphere starts out with the center located at <0 0 3>. After the Translate <1 2 -2> the position of the center is figured by adding the components of the Translate vector to the corresponding components of the original location. The new center is <0+1 0+2 3-2> or <1 2 1>. In this particular case we could have placed the sphere at that position to begin with using

```
sphere{<1 2 1> 1}
```

but there are many other cases where the Translate capability is indispensable. In particular, translations are essential in order to make scaling and rotations work correctly, as we'll see shortly.

Scaling

Scaling allows you to expand or shrink objects. This expanding or shrinking is done by multiplying the positions of points by the *x*, *y*, and *z* scaling factors. Therefore

```
scale <1  1  1>
```

has no effect, because multiplying any number by one does not change the number. Applying

```
scale <2  2  2>
```

doubles the size of an object. You can also scale some objects differently in each dimension to alter their proportions. For example, if you added the line

```
scale <1  1  2>
```

to the cylinders used in EXAMPLE6.POV, they would change and have an ellipsoidal cross-section instead of a circular cross-section, because the *z* dimension is doubled while the *x* and *y* dimensions are not. Note that spheres can only be uniformly scaled; you cannot turn a sphere into an ellipsoid. If you want to do that, you must use the quadric Sphere (note the capital "S") defined in SHAPES.INC instead. Regular spheres are very easy to use and render much faster than Spheres, so you should use them when you need a real sphere. If you want an egg-shaped figure, use a Sphere and apply nonuniform scaling.

A Scaling Side-Effect

Applying scale factors has a side-effect when done with objects that are not centered at the origin. If you scale by a factor of 2, all the components of every point in the object are multiplied by 2. If the object is not centered on the origin, not only will the object double in size, but it will move to a position twice as far from the origin. The cure for this is to scale objects while they are still centered on the origin, or if they are not, translate them to a centered position first before applying the scale factors. Then you can translate the object to its final position after scaling. Now you can see why the beginning positions of objects defined in SHAPES.INC are centered at the origin.

Applying Scaling to Textures

You can use scale factors with textures too. Many textures have patterns to them, and look quite different when magnified or shrunk. You can add a scale factor inside a Texture block. The exact order and location of a Scale statement determines what it affects. Figure 7-21 shows four cylinders with the Checker texture applied. The first cylinder on the left does not use a scale factor with either the cylinder or the Checker texture. The Checker texture renders at its natural size.

```
// Checkered cylinder - no scale applied
object {
  quadric {
    Cylinder_Y
    translate <-3 0 6>
    texture {
      checker color green 1 color blue 1
    }
  }
}
```

The second cylinder has the line

```
scale <.25 .25 .25>
```

added inside the Texture block. This applies a scale factor of 0.25 to the texture, making the squares smaller, but not affecting the size of the cylinder.

```
// Checkered cylinder - scale applied to texture
object {
  quadric {
    Cylinder_Y
    translate <0 0 6>
    texture {
      checker color green 1 color blue 1
      scale <.25 .25 .25>
    }
  }
}
```

The third cylinder has the scale command after the Cylinder_Y keyword but before the Texture block. In this case the cylinder is scaled, but not the texture. The result is a skinny cylinder with a checkerboard pattern made up of large squares.

```
// Checkered cylinder - scale applied to cylinder before texture
object {
  quadric {
    Cylinder_Y
    scale <.25 .25 .25>
    translate <2 0 6>
    texture {
      checker color green 1 color blue 1
    }
  }
}
```

The fourth cylinder definition has the Scale command after both the Cylinder_Y keyword and the Texture block, so it applies to both. The result is a skinny cylinder with a checkerboard pattern made up of small squares.

```
// Checkered cylinder - scale applied to cylinder after texture
object {
  quadric {
    Cylinder_Y
    texture {
      checker color green 1 color blue 1
    }
    scale <.25 .25 .25>
    translate <3 0 6>
  }
}
```

Figure 7-21 EXAMPLE7 — applying scaling to a texture vs. applying to the object

In case you want to experiment with this, a complete data file that renders the four cylinders is found in the file EXAMPLE7.POV. The results are shown in Figure 7-21.

Rotating

The last kind of transformation is *rotation*. Like the other two transformations, a rotation has three associated numbers. These numbers represent angles for rotating the object about each of the x, y, and z axes in units of degrees.

Like scaling, rotation also has a side effect if the object being rotated is not centered on the origin. Suppose an object is being rotated around the x axis, but is located a long way from it. The rotation is accomplished as if there were a rod connecting the object with the x axis. Therefore a rotation of 90 degrees swings the object a quarter of the way around a large circle whose radius is the distance to the x axis. Figure 7-22 illustrates this effect. The side effect is that the object ends up being moved a large distance. Occasionally this is the effect you want, but usually it isn't. The cure is simple: Apply rotations to objects that are centered on the origin. Since all the predefined objects in SHAPES.INC are already centered, simply apply rotations first.

A second complication of rotation is that the order of rotation about the axes definitely affects the results. The best approach is to rotate about one axis at a time and make sure you can visualize the results.

345

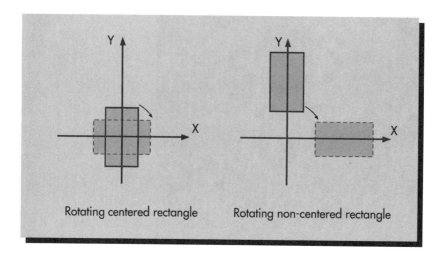

Figure 7-22 The side effect of rotating objects far from the origin

Finally, in order to master rotation you have to know what a positive angle is. For each axis, there is one direction of rotation about that axis that is positive, and one negative. To visualize the correct directions, imagine you are grasping an axis with your left hand with your thumb pointed in the positive direction. Your fingers will wrap around the axis in the positive rotation direction around that axis. This is shown in Figure 7-23.

In order to demonstrate rotations, we'll use a cube, because it is a lot easier to spot the rotation of a cube than a sphere! The file EXAMPLE8.POV is shown in Listing 7-8.

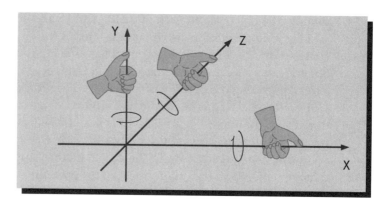

Figure 7-23 The lefthanded coordinate system rotation directions

```
// Persistence of Vision-Ray Tracer 1.00
// The Waite Group's Image Lab
// EXAMPLE8.POV
// Rotating cubes

#include "shapes.inc"
#include "colors.inc"
#include "textures.inc"

// Camera
camera{
  translate <0 0 -100>
  direction <0 0 25>
  up <0 1 0>
  right <1.33333 0 0>
  look_at <0 0 3>
}
// Cube
object {
  intersection { Cube }
  texture {
    checker color green 1 color blue 1
    scale <.15 .15 .15>
  }
  rotate <0 0 0>
  translate <-2 1 3>
}

// Cube
object {
  intersection { Cube }
   texture {
     checker color green 1 color blue 1
     scale <.15 .15 .15>
    }
  rotate <-25 0 0>
  translate <0 0 3>
}

// Cube
object {
  intersection { Cube }
   texture {
     checker color green 1 color blue 1
     scale <.15 .15 .15>
    }
  rotate <-25 25 0>
  translate <2 -1 3>
}
```

Listing 7-8 Rotating cubes—EXAMPLE8.POV *(continued on the next page)*

```
. . . . . . . . . . . . . . . . . . . . . . . . . . . . . . . . . . . . . . . . . . . . . . . . . . . . . . . . . . . . . . .
// Light
object {
  light_source {
    <2 4 -3>
    color red 1 green 1 blue 1
  }
}
```

Listing 7-8 Rotating cubes—EXAMPLE8.POV *(continued)*

This image can use a little higher resolution when rendering so that you can see the details better. To render at 160×120 using the POV.BAT file, type:

`C:>POV EXAMPLE8 -w160 -h120 `(ENTER)

This example shows three small checkered cubes in different positions. From a very close distance, the three cubes would appear to be rotated differently from each other just from the affects of a close perspective. Therefore the camera location has been changed, to the very far distance of 100 units away. At this distance the three cubes would have become tiny dots, so the direction vector was multiplied by 25 to compensate. As was mentioned in earlier discussions of the camera, the Direction vector can be used as a zoom lens. A Direction vector value of <0 0 25> is like a 25-power telephoto lens. This high magnification gives the scene a flat perspective so that the rotation angles of

Figure 7-24 EXAMPLE8.POV — rotated cubes

348

the cubes can be more clearly seen. For the same reason a smart photographer uses a medium telephoto lens for a close-up portrait. A normal or wide-angle lens exaggerates the size of the subject's nose because the nose is closer to the camera than the rest of the face.

Constructive Solid Geometry (CSG)

The cube shape is declared in SHAPES.INC as the intersection of six planes. POV-Ray supports a method of combining objects called constructive solid geometry, or CSG for short. CSG in POV-Ray has three operations for combining objects: intersection, union, and difference. With CSG every object has an inside and an outside. The *intersection* of two objects consists of all the points that are inside *both* objects. The *union* of two objects is the joint object formed from all the points inside *either* of the two objects — in other words, the overlap between the two objects. The *difference* between two objects is the inside of the first with the inside of the second cut out. This is the same as the intersection of the inside of the first and the outside of the second. (For some wonderful examples of the use of these CSG operations, see the mantel clock example in Chapter 9.) A cube is the intersection of six planes. You might not think of a plane as having an inside and an outside, but planes in POV-Ray do. By definition, the surface normal of the plane points towards the outside of the plane. If you look inside SHAPES.INC, you can find the definition of a cube in terms of an intersection of planes. The definition is:

```
#declare Cube = intersection {
  plane {< 0.0  0.0 -1.0> 0.5 }
  plane {< 0.0  0.0  1.0> 0.5 }
  plane {< 0.0-1.0  0.0> 0.5 }
  plane {< 0.0  1.0  0.0> 0.5 }
  plane {<-1.0  0.0  0.0> 0.5 }
  plane {< 1.0  0.0  0.0> 0.5 }
```

Since the Cube declaration is of the intersection type, when you use the cube shape you have to use the Intersection keyword. Otherwise you can treat it in the same way you treat other shapes.

This data file illustrates a number of topics we have discussed in the tutorial so far. Three cubes are defined, and each one is translated to a different location. The Checker texture that was used for the floor in earlier examples is used here as a pattern to decorate the cubes. The textures for the cubes are scaled smaller to make a finer checkerboard appearance. This is accomplished by placing a

```
scale <.15 .15 .15>
```

statement within the Texture blocks of the cubes.

Texture and Rotation — A Useful Subtlety

Each cube is rotated before being translated to its final position. This is to avoid the side effect mentioned earlier of moving noncentered objects when they are rotated. The rotation and translation statements have been placed after the Texture block that applies the Checker texture. This is a subtlety, but one well worth understanding. The application of a patterned texture like checker to the surface of an object is dependent on the orientation of the cube. What we want in this example is to see identical cubes rotated by different amounts. If the translation and rotation were applied rather than the texture, the pattern on the different cubes would be different because the cubes would have different orientations at the time the texture was applied. By applying the textures first, the textures are applied when all three of the cubes are resting in their default position centered on the origin. Then the applied texture is rotated and translated along with the cube. This approach makes all three cubes identical except for their position in space.

The first cube has a rotation of <0 0 0>, which is no rotation at all. Exactly one face of this cube is visible, since it is being viewed head on. This is why the "telephoto lens" camera was used; the usual camera location of the previous examples would have placed the camera only 4 units away, and the angle to the camera would have made the cube appear rotated. You can see this by altering the Translate and Direction of EXAMPLE8.POV to

```
translate <0 0 -1>
direction <0 0 .8>
```

The first cube will no longer be head on, but you will be able to see some of its right side.

The second cube has a rotation of <-25 0 0>. This is a good time to test the lefthanded rule. Imagine grasping the *x* axis with your left hand, with your thumb pointed to the right, in the positive *x* direction. The curl of your fingers shows what direction a positive rotation would be. You can see in your mind's eye that a positive angle would tip the front of the cube up. Since we wanted to tip it down, a negative angle was used, and we'll see the top of this cube.

The third cube has a rotation of <-25 25 0>. Now try the lefthand rule again. This time visualize grasping the vertical *y* axis with your left hand, with your thumb pointed up, in the positive *y* direction. You can see that the positive rotation is clockwise as you look down on the *y* axis. This direction moves the front face of the cube to the left. The top is tilted down like the previous cube.

You can refer back to Figure 7-23 to verify these rotation directions in your mind. Note that when three non-0 rotations are specified, the rotation about the *x* axis is done first, followed by rotation about the *y* axis and rotation about the *z* axis. Thus the line:

```
rotation < 1 2 3>
```

has the same effect as the three lines

```
rotation < 1 0 0>
rotation < 0 2 0>
rotation < 0 0 3>
```

Composites — Transforming Groups

Suppose you have built a shape made of many pieces. You may want to move this shape as though it were one object. This is particularly convenient, because you can apply a single Translate, Scale, or Rotate command that will apply to the whole shape. POV-Ray provides a way to do this by forming a composite of the objects.

To form a composite, just make a new block with the Composite keyword. Then at the bottom of the block you can add some transformation commands to apply to the composite or union as a unit.

As an example, let's take the three cubes in the EXAMPLE8.POV example and form a composite, then rotate the whole group by 90 degrees around the z axis. To achieve the same end result without grouping the three cubes together would take some thought and a little more complication. Listing 7-9 shows the data file EXAMPLE9.POV. The result of rendering this file is shown in Figure 7-25.

```
// Persistence of Vision-Ray Tracer 1.00
// The Waite Group's Image Lab
// EXAMPLE9.POV
// Composite of three cubes

#include "shapes.inc"
#include "colors.inc"
#include "textures.inc"

// Camera
camera{
  translate <0 0 -100>
  direction <0 0 20>
  up <0 1 0>
  right <1.33333 0 0>
  look_at <0 0 3>
}
composite {
  // Cube
  object {
    intersection { Cube }
    texture {
      checker color green 1 color blue 1
      scale <.15 .15 .15>
    }
```

Listing 7-9 EXAMPLE9.POV *(continued on the next page)*

```
. . . . . . . . . . . . . . . . . . . . . . . . . . . . . . . . . . . . . . . . . . . . . . . . . . . . . . . . . . . . . . . . . . . . . . . . . . . . . .
    rotate <0 0 0>
    translate <-2 1 3>
    }

    // Cube
    object {
      intersection { Cube }
       texture {
         checker color green 1 color blue 1
         scale <.15 .15 .15>
        }
      rotate <-25 0 0>
      translate <0 0 3>
    }

    // Cube
    object {
      intersection { Cube }
       texture {
         checker color green 1 color blue 1
         scale <.15 .15 .15>
        }
      rotate <-25 25 0>
      translate <2 -1 3>
    }
    translate <0 0 -3>
    rotate <0 0 90>
    translate <0 0 3>

    bounded_by { sphere {< 0 0 3 > 4 }}

}
// Light
object {
  light_source {
    <2 4 -3>
    color red 1 green 1 blue 1
  }
}
```

Listing 7-9 EXAMPLE9.POV

This data file is pretty straightforward, but a few observations are in order. As you can see, the three cube objects are just grouped together in a block that looks like

```
composite {
  object {  }
  object {  }
  object {  }
  translate <>
```

· ·

Figure 7-25 EXAMPLE9 — result of rotating composite object 90 degrees

```
rotate <>
translate <>
bounded_by { }
}
```

The middle cube is between the other two cubes, so it was elected to be the center of the rotation. The command

```
translate <0 0 -3>
```

provides the exact translation needed to move the middle cube so that it is centered on the origin. Then the 90-degree rotation about the z axis is performed. Finally, the reverse translation is performed, returning the middle cube to its original location. But now the other two cubes have orbited around the middle cube 90 degrees.

At the bottom of the Composite block is a Bounded_By block. No matter how much you love ray tracing, you'll have to admit that it can be very slow. If you think like a ray tracer, you will see the value of the Bounded_By block. Suppose a complex scene contains several composite objects, each composed of many objects. Each composite object may optionally contain a Bounded_By block. The idea is that you, the ray-tracing artist, guarantee that all the objects in the composite are within whatever shape is in the Bounded_By block. Many rays miss a composite object entirely, but the ray tracer normally has to test for the intersection of the ray with every single object within the composite. If there is a Bounded_By block, the ray tracer can test for intersection of a ray with the Bounded_By shape. If they don't intersect, then the ray tracer does not need to test all the objects within the composite. This can result in a huge increase in efficiency. In this particular case, it does not show any speed increase; but if this composite were embedded within a larger scene or included more objects, it would make a difference.

Extra Touches

To end this tutorial, you will learn about a few extra touches to make your scenes more interesting. Let's look at some scenes with water. Water is a tricky thing to paint realistically, but is the kind of thing ray tracers are good at. Listing 7-10 shows a POV data file that generates three colored spheres reflected in a pond. When you render this file, it should look like Figure 7-26.

The objects in this example are spheres with simple textures consisting of coloring with a single primary color and Phong highlighting. What makes this scene different is the water.

Figure 7-26 EXAMPL10.POV — three spheres reflected in a pond

```
// Persistence of Vision-Ray Tracer 1.00
// The Waite Group's Image Lab
// EXAMPL10.POV
// Three spheres reflected in a pond

#include "shapes.inc"
#include "colors.inc"
#include "textures.inc"

camera{
  location <0.0  20.0  -125.0>
  direction <0.0 0.0  2.0>
  up  <0.0  1.0  0.0>
  right <1.33333 0.0 0.0>
  look_at <0.0 10.0 10.0>
}

object {
  sphere{ <-20.0  10.0  5.0>  10.0 }
  texture {
   color red 1.0
   phong 1.0
   }
}
object {
  sphere{ <20.0  10.0  5.0>  10.0 }
  texture {
   color green 1.0
   phong 1.0
   }
}
object {
  sphere{ <0.0  25.0  20.0>  10.0 }
  texture {
   color Yellow
   phong 1.0
   }
}

object {
  plane { <0 1 0> 0 }
  texture{
   color blue 1.0
   ripples 0.7
   reflection 0.8
   diffuse 0.2
   scale <10 10 10>
   }
}
```

Listing 7-10 EXAMPL10.POV *(continued on the next page)*

355

. . . .

```
object{
  light_source {
   <100.0  140.0  -130.0>
   color red 0.6 green 0.6 blue 0.6
  }
 }
object{
  light_source {
   <-100.0  40.0  -130.0>
    color red 0.6 green 0.6 blue 0.6
   }
}
```

Listing 7-10 EXAMPL10.POV

The water is a just a plane similar to the plane that was used in earlier examples, but the texture attached to this plane is very different. Let's look at that texture line by line.

```
texture{
 color blue 1.0
 ripples 0.7
 reflection 0.8
 diffuse 0.2
 scale <10 10 10>
 }
```

The first line is not at all surprising for water—the color blue! The second line is something new,

```
ripples 0.7
```

Ripples are an example of a surface perturbation texture, which doesn't change the color but does change the angle of the surface. The number following the Ripples keyword affects the depth of the ripples.

The next line is

```
reflection 0.8
```

Reflection does exactly what you expect — it causes the surface to reflect images like a mirror. This is what causes the colored spheres to appear as broken reflections in the waves. The number indicates the degree of reflection. A value of 1 reflects all light; 0, the default, does not have any mirror effect at all.

Following reflection is

```
diffuse 0.2
```

Diffuse light is light coming from a light source that is scattered in all directions. An object lit only by diffuse light looks like a rubber ball with a spotlight shining on it. The value can range from 0.0 to 1.0. By default, there is mostly diffuse lighting, a value of 0.7. In this example the diffuse characteristic is less than usual because the idea is to make the water highly reflective.

Figure 7-27 EXAMPL11.POV — alternate textures for the three spheres

The last line in the Texture block is

```
scale <10 10 10>
```

which makes the waves larger. This is a good example of the use of scale to modify the appearance of a texture as opposed to scaling an object.

A variation of this image is shown in Figure 7-27 and is in the file EXAMPL11.POV on your disk. The only difference is that some interesting textures have been applied to the spheres. They are:

```
texture {
Blood_Marble
phong 1.0
scale <4 4 4>
}

texture {
Gold_Texture
phong 1.0
scale <4 4 4>
}

texture {
Brown_Agate
phong 1.0
scale <4 4 4>
}
```

You're on Your Own Now!

The POV-Ray tutorial is now officially ended, but your enjoyment may only be beginning. From here there are several ways you can continue your journey with ray tracing. You can experiment on your own, and see where your own creativity and POV-Ray's capabilities will take you, using the POVRAY.DOC file that comes with the POV-Ray package to find out about the other features of the program. Then, when you are ready, you can look at the examples in Chapter 9. There you will find some truly world-class examples created by gifted artists. You will also find some descriptions of handy utility programs that allow you do make some amazing images. Enjoy!

8

IMAGE ALCHEMY

SMART FILE CONVERSION

The Curse of the Graphics Tower of Babel

In the story of the Tower of Babel, humanity began building a high tower in an act of self-aggrandizing pride. The tower offended the divine power, who punished humanity for their arrogance by destroying the tower and condemning humankind to be split into small groups, each with its own language unintelligible to the others. A look at the current state of graphics file formats makes a convincing case that the Tower of Babel curse is still in force, but in the computer graphics world and not in the ancient Near East. Every vendor seems to have created a new graphics file format incompatible with every other. There is no universal file format understood by every graphics application.

Image Alchemy is a powerful file conversion program that allows you to move bitmapped files between different applications — something akin to giving the Babelites dictionaries so that they could at least translate each other's dialects! This chapter will show you how to use Alchemy for this purpose. Alchemy also has other features for controlling the color and size of the images. Since these duplicate functions available in other programs in the Image Lab suite, those features are not discussed here. You can learn more about the program and all its features by reading the file ALCHEMY.DOC in the self-extracting archive MANUAL.EXE.

Two Types of Graphics Formats

Graphics file formats can be divided into two types. The first type consists of bitmapped graphics files containing color information about each individual pixel in a rectangular array. The other type is made up of formats that contain descriptions of various objects. This second format is inherently more complex because there is no limit to the kinds of objects that can be defined and included in a format. Roughly speaking, this distinction is the same one that divides paint programs, which place individual pixels on the screen, from draw programs, which manipulate shapes that keep their identity. It is not surprising that the task of converting between various bitmapped formats is a simpler job than converting between object-oriented formats. Still, the task of converting one pixel-based image to another is harder than it seems at first glance. Some formats are inconsistently implemented in different applications, and the conversion software can never be sure exactly which variation will be encountered. For example, one format may store color information in a look-up table, while another might include it with each pixel. Another difficulty is that different formats contain different amounts of color information, and it is not obvious how a file containing more information can best be converted to a format containing less. Still another complication is that many formats contain as part of their specification, compression algorithms, requiring the conversion software to decompress and recompress images.

Given all the difficulties and the multitude of graphics formats, you'll find Image Alchemy a welcome addition to the Image Lab suite of tools. Alchemy can read and convert just about any bitmapped image format to any other. Currently Alchemy supports over 30 different formats, and new formats are always being added. The authors of Image Alchemy have as a goal the ability to read and write every bitmapped graphic file format in the world! Image Alchemy can also make changes in an image. For example, Image Alchemy can resize an image, change the number of colors in an image, change an image from color to black-and-white, and change the color space an image uses. Finally, Image Alchemy performs JPEG compression. This is a new standard for image compression that, as we shall see, can achieve much higher compression ratios than conventional compression techniques.

SHAREWARE INFORMATION

The version of Image Alchemy included with this book is an unregistered Shareware version that is limited to 640x480 resolution. The program authors encourage you to freely copy and distribute the Shareware version of Image Alchemy, provided that you distribute the complete package.

If you use Image Alchemy beyond a two-week trial period, you must register the program using the accompanying order form. For the registration fee, you will receive the current, retail version of Image Alchemy without the 640x480 image size restriction and a typeset and printed manual (complete with a table of contents and an index). You will be notified of significant upgrades to Image Alchemy, you will be placed on a mailing list to receive information about future products from Handmade Software, and you will be entitled to phone and email support.

For ordering information see the order form in the file ORDER.FRM.

GETTING ALCHEMY UP AND RUNNING

Image Alchemy is very easy to install. All you need to do is copy the ALCHEMY.EXE file to a directory list in your Path or accessible via a batch file. You can place all your Alchemy files in the directory C:\IMLAB\ALCHEMY and invoke Image Alchemy using a batch file placed in C:\IMLAB. The contents of the batch file is

```
C:\IMLAB\ALCHEMY\ALCHEMY %1 %2 %3 %4 %5 %6 %7 %8 %9
```

Make sure C:\IMLAB is in your Path directory list if you are using this approach. You can also simply copy ALCHEMY.EXE to a directory listed in your Path.

Required Hardware

At a minimum you must have the following hardware and software to run Image Alchemy:

- An MS-DOS computer equipped with an 80286 or better.

- At least 380K of free memory (more is better).

- A hard drive with at least as much free space as four times the size of the image being converted (that is a 640x480 image will require approximately 1.2 MB of free space).

- A supported SVGA or 8514/A board, if you wish to view images. Supported SVGA boards include those with the Paradise, Everex, Trident, Video 7, and the Tseng Labs chip sets. Supported 8514/A boards include IBM and those with the Western Digital chip set. (Note: Image Alchemy does not require graphics capabilities in order to convert files. You only need graphics capabilities if you want to view images using Alchemy. You can also use Piclab or CompuShow to view files.)

Setting the Tmp Variable

Image Alchemy will use the environment variable Tmp, if set, to tell it where to put temporary files. You can specify the Tmp directory by placing a line like

`SET TMP=C:\TMP`

in your AUTOEXEC.BAT file. If you have enough memory to make a big enough RAM drive, you can improve performance by placing the Tmp directory on the RAM drive. Be aware that Alchemy needs up to four times as much space on that drive as the size of the image, so a 640x480 image requires about 1.2 MB.

ALCHEMY QUICK TOUR

Image Alchemy is a command-line-driven program. This means that you can give Alchemy instructions for what to do at the time you start Alchemy. Since Alchemy automatically identifies file formats of files, all that is necessary to convert a file is to give Image Alchemy the name of the file you wish to convert and to specify the output format.

There are basically two uses for Image Alchemy within the Image Lab tool suite. The first is to convert a foreign file format to a format usable by the Image Lab tools. The second is to convert a finished image to a foreign format required by some other software.

When converting a foreign file format for use with the Image Lab tools, you should convert to GIF. If the file you wish to convert has more than 256 colors, Alchemy will perform color reduction for you. If you prefer to perform the color reduction using Piclab or to preserve the larger number of colors, you can convert the file to a 24-bit Targa file. The -g option causes Alchemy to create a GIF format file, and the -a creates a Targa file. For example, to convert a file called FOREIGN to a GIF file, you would type:

`C:>ALCHEMY FOREIGN -g` (ENTER)

Alchemy would then create a GIF file with the name FOREIGN.GIF.

To make a Targa 24-bit file, type:

`C:>ALCHEMY FOREIGN -a -24` (ENTER)

The -a specifies Targa, and the -24 specifies 24-bit.

Conversely, to convert an Image Lab file to a foreign format, just invoke Alchemy with the file as a parameter and add the option that specifies the foreign format. For example, to convert TIME.GIF to the TIFF format, type:

`C:>ALCHEMY TIME.GIF -t` (ENTER)

This will create the file TIME.TIF.

GRAPHICS FILE FORMATS

Image Alchemy can read and write 30 different graphics file formats that are used on many different software and hardware platforms. A few of the most important formats for PC users are discussed here.

Encapsulated PostScript (EPS)

EPS files are a subset of the PostScript language developed by Adobe Systems, Inc. They may be used by some word processors without requiring that the importing software be able to interpret the file. You can convert an image to EPS when you want to include the image using a word processor that supports imbedding EPS, such as Aldus PageMaker or Microsoft Word for Windows. You can also use this file format for printing; just send the EPS file to your PostScript printer using:

`C:>PRINT EXAMPLE.EPS PRN` (ENTER)

This is an excellent method of printing images if you have a PostScript printer. The reason is that most of the images that you are dealing with in this book have 256 or more colors. Most printers are basically two-color devices. They can print a black dot or a white dot. The PostScript language contains the ability to specify shades of gray using patterns of dots. If you print your images by converting to EPS and sending the EPS file to a PostScript printer, the colors in your image will be rendered as shades of gray. On a 300-dots-per-inch laser printer, the result should look very good.

GIF Files

GIF files were originally developed by CompuServe as a machine-independent image format for viewing on-line images. Even though GIF was intended for on-line viewing, it rapidly gained widespread acceptance as a file format. GIF files are the most popular way of storing 8-bit scanned or digitized images. In addition the compression ratio achieved by GIF files is usually better than any other 8-bit format in common use. GIF uses the same LZW (Lempel-Ziv-Welch) compression method used in popular archiving utilities like Zip, Arc, or Lharc. The GIF format comes in two flavors; GIF87a and GIF89a. The latter allows the storage of nongraphics information such as comments and even fractal information within an image. All of the Image Lab programs support GIF; it is the format of choice unless true-color is required. The CompuShow program supports all of the new GIF89a features.

IFF/ILBM

IFF (Interchange File Format) files are used by Amiga computers for storing a number of types of data, including images, text, and music; ILBM (InterLeaved

BitMap) is a type of IFF file used to store images. Use this graphics format to share your images with Amiga users. It also is used by some paint programs such as Electronic Arts Deluxe Paint.

JPEG

JPEG is a new type of image file format utilizing compression designed by the Joint Photographic Experts Group (JPEG) that uses a *lossy* compression technique to achieve high compression ratios. Compression programs like PKZIP must use reversible compression algorithms; if even one bit of your favorite executable program has changed after you decompress the program, it may not run. Graphics images do not necessarily require this kind of accuracy. Greater compression can be achieved if a small amount of information may be thrown away. JPEG makes use of the fact that not all of the information encoded in an image is necessary for human perception of the image. The ability to discard certain image information allows files to be compressed to a smaller size with little apparent image degradation. Ordinary methods achieve 2X or 3X compression; JPEG can compress 20X or more for some images. Since JPEG compression was designed for use with continuous tone (grayscale) images, poor results can be expected when compressing line drawings.

Macintosh PICT/PICT2

PICT files were created by Apple Computer as a common format for Macintosh applications to use. Use the PICT format when you want to convert files to and from Macintosh computers. Virtually every Macintosh application can use PICT files. There are a lot of variations of this format, including some that handle drawing objects. Alchemy cannot handle them all.

PCPAINT/Pictor Page Format

The Pictor format was designed so that an image could be loaded into an IBM graphics adapter very quickly; it does this by arranging its format to nearly duplicate the organization of the graphics adapter memory. It is used by the programs Pictor and GRASP from Paul Mace Software and PCPaint the forerunner of Pictor. This makes the format very hardware dependent, but also very useful for fast animation. Table 8-1 shows the different variations of this format.

. . . .

Type	Mode
0	320x200x4 CGA
1	320x200x16 PCjr/Tandy
2	640x200x2 CGA
3	640x200x16 EGA
4	640x350x2 EGA
5	640x350x4 EGA
6	640x350x16 EGA
7	720x348x2 Hercules
8	640x350x16 VGA
10	640x400x2 AT&T/Toshiba
11	320x200x256 VGA/MCGA
12	640x480x16 VGA
14	640x480x2 VGA/MCGA
15	800x600x2 EGA/VGA
16	800x600x16 EGA/VGA
17	640x400x256 SVGA
18	640x480x256 SVGA
19	800x600x256 SVGA
20	1024x768x2 SVGA
21	1024x768x16 SVGA
22	360x480x256 VGA
23	1024x768x256 SVGA

Table 8-1 Pictor image formats

PCX

PCX files are used extensively by many PC graphics applications. Originally created by ZSoft for use by their paint packages, PCX files can be read and written by almost all PC-based paint and desktop publishing software. PCX files suffer if not compressed very well, and are often written out incorrectly. Use the PCX format to interoperate with many paint programs such as the PC Paintbrush program supplied with Windows.

Tagged Interchange File Format (TIFF)

TIFF is designed to be a universal raster image format; it is very popular with desktop publishing packages. Use it for transferring your images to programs like PageMaker on either the PC or the Macintosh. Be aware that the TIFF format has a very rich specification, and so is almost always implemented as a subset of the true specification. Always test the ability of your software to read and write TIFF files in advance of any time-critical deadlines. The subsets of TIFF supported by two applications might be incompatible.

TIFF is not actually a single "format," but a loosely connected set of alternative specifications for storing images in files. TIFF files span the entire spectrum of bitmapped images from monochrome to 24-bit color.

Targa

Targa files were created to support the line of Targa graphics cards from Truevision, Inc. The Targa format is popular with scanners and high-end paint packages, and is useful for transferring 24-bit files. Targa files are generally not well compressed. Piclab, CompuShow, and Improces can all deal with Targa files.

Windows Bitmap (BMP)

Windows BMP files are used by Microsoft Windows. You can make your own Windows wallpaper by converting your images to BMP. BMP files come in compressed and uncompressed flavors. The compression uses RLE (run length encoding). Several of the programs which read and write the RLE variant of BMP files do not do so correctly; writing RLE files is not recommended unless you have the application and can test the results. The Windows Paint Brush program (PBRUSH.EXE) can read and write BMP files.

WordPerfect Graphic Files

WordPerfect files are images that can be imported into WordPerfect and various other word processors and desktop publishing programs. Use this file format to place your image creations in WordPerfect documents.

IMAGE ALCHEMY TUTORIAL

The simplest thing to do with Image Alchemy is convert one kind of file to another. The syntax for converting files is as follows (items shown with [ ] are optional):

```
C:>ALCHEMY INPUTFILENAME [OUTPUTFILENAME] [OUTPUTPATHNAME] -OPTION [-OPTION] (ENTER)
```

If you don't specify the output file name, then the input file name will be used with only the extension changed to match the output file type. Here are some examples of different things you can do with Alchemy. Since Alchemy is very good at detecting the format of the input file, and since there is a good default for naming the output file, using Alchemy is very simple. Most conversions can be accomplished with two parameters: the input file name and an option designating the output format. In a few cases a second option may be needed to specify variations on the conversion process.

Convert a GIF File to a 24-Bit Targa File

To convert a GIF file called IMAGE.GIF to a Targa file called IMAGE.TGA, type:

C:>ALCHEMY IMAGE.GIF -a -24 (ENTER)

This example creates a 24-bit Targa file. If you want a Targa file with fewer colors (lower color resolution), the -24 can be changed to -15 or -8. There are also several options for different kinds of Targa files. Replacing the -a with -a 1 causes the Targa file to be compressed with run-length encoding (RLE), which is a form of compression. RLE works by compressing strings of identical items by specifying what the item is and how many. For example, "xxxxxxxxxxxxyyyyyyyyy" can be represented as "12x9y." This is not as good a form of compression as the LZW compression used in the zip format, so that if space is an issue, you can just store your Targa files in a zip archive using Phil Katz's PKZIP or another archiving program.

Convert a Targa File to a GIF File

You can use Image Alchemy to color reduce your Targa files created by the POV program to GIF files. For example, one of the Targa files created in the POV tutorial is the 24-bit true-color file EXAMPLE1.TGA. Suppose you want to convert this file to 256 colors and save it as a GIF file so you can view it better on your VGA hardware (Piclab can also do this, as we'll see). To convert this file to a GIF file, type in:

C:>ALCHEMY SCENE01.TGA -g (ENTER)

In this example, since the original file is a 24-bit true-color file, color reduction will take place. This means that Alchemy will analyze the Targa file, compute the best 256-color palette, and map the colors to that palette. This is the same color reduction accomplished in Piclab with the commands:

PL>TLOAD SCENE01.TGA (ENTER)
PL>MAKEPAL (ENTER)
PL>MAP (ENTER)
PL>GSAVE OUTPUT.GIF (ENTER)

Color reduction is a tricky process, and there is no one algorithm for accomplishing it that is equally satisfactory for all images. Piclab generally does a good job, but if the results using Piclab are not satisfactory, try Alchemy and compare. Even though a GIF file has only 256 colors (very few compared to the 16,777,216 possible colors in the Targa file), the result of this color reduction usually looks very good, because those 256 colors are selected from a much larger number of possible colors based on Alchemy's analysis of the image.

This example is a lot more general than it looks. The command line

`C:>ALCHEMY ANYFILE -g` (ENTER)

creates a GIF file from just about any kind of file that Alchemy can read. The type of input file is automatically detected by Image Alchemy; the -g signifies that the output file is a GIF. In this example the output file would be named ANYFILE.GIF.

Converting to and from JPEG Format

The JPEG format is particularly interesting because it uses a nonreversible compression method. This means that some information is lost in the compression process, so that when the image is decompressed, it is not identical to the original. The LZW compression used in the GIF format, on the other hand, is completely deterministic and reversible, so that when a decoder decompresses the image for display, every pixel has the correct color. You might think that it is undesirable to lose information, but what would be fatal when compressing executable programs may make good sense when compressing images. The Zip and Arc utilities are often used to compress programs and data format, and you can imagine the problems that would be caused if the compression methods used by these utilities were not 100 percent reversible. A small error of even 1 bit can turn your favorite utility program into a computer-freezing monster. But a mountain scene with lazy clouds in a blue sky can undergo subtle alterations that are virtually unnoticeable; it all depends on just how the image is simplified. Remove a single white pixel and replace it with an off-white one in a cloud — who will notice?

A compressed JPEG image is included with your Alchemy package on the companion disk. You will find it in the directory where you install Alchemy — if you followed the installation suggestions it will be in \IMLAB\ALCHEMY with the name SAMPLE.JPG. To convert this image to GIF, type:

`C:>ALCHEMY SAMPLE.JPG -g` (ENTER)

Now compare the size of the original and the GIF version using the DOS command, as shown below.

```
C:>DIR SAMPLE.*  (ENTER)
SAMPLE    JPG    64929 11-11-91   1:50a
SAMPLE    GIF   253089 12-23-91  12:01p
```

As you can see, the JPEG file is a quarter the size of the GIF file! Of course what you can't see is how much the original image was degraded by being converted to JPEG. An interesting experiment is to start with a GIF or Targa file, convert to JPEG, then convert back and compare. A good file to try is the T38.GIF in the \IMLAB\EXAMPLES directory. Type:

`C:>ALCHEMY T38.GIF T38a.JPG -jh` (ENTER)
`C:>ALCHEMY T38a.JPG T38a.GIF -g` (ENTER)

The first command creates the file T38.JPG, and the second command converts T38.JPG to T38A.GIF. The "h" in the -jh switch allows slightly better compression. You can also follow the -jh switch with a number that determines the quality. The default value is 38; a value of 100 would cause virtually no quality loss but would not compress nearly as well.

Use CompuShow to view both T38.GIF and T38A.GIF. In this particular case the quality of the result is quite good, and the T38A.GIF image does not look noticeably worse under casual inspection.

Now try the same experiment twice more using lower quality levels. Type:

```
C:>ALCHEMY T38.GIF T38b.JPG -jh8  (ENTER)
C:>ALCHEMY T38b.JPG T38b.GIF -g  (ENTER)
C:>ALCHEMY T38.GIF T38c.JPG -jh1  (ENTER)
C:>ALCHEMY T38c.JPG T38c.GIF -g  (ENTER)
```

If you have plenty of free disk space (at least several MB), you will find it very enlightening to also convert the same T38.GIF image to an uncompressed 24-bit Targa file for comparison. Type:

```
C:>ALCHEMY T38.GIF -a -24  (ENTER)
```

Now for the fun result of our experiment. How big are all these files? To find out, use the DOS DIR command. You can pipe the output to the DOS SORT command to sort the results by size. Type:

```
C:>DIR T38*.* | SORT /+13  (ENTER)
```

```
T38C    JPG     3781  3-07-92   9:22p
T38B    JPG    15828  3-07-92   9:21p
T38A    JPG    41546  3-07-92   9:20p
T38C    GIF    62058  3-07-92   9:34p
T38B    GIF   217230  3-07-92   9:33p
T38A    GIF   221000  3-07-92   9:32p
T38     GIF   221190 11-03-91  11:30p
T38     TGA   924059  3-07-92   9:23p
```

Incredible! The smallest JPEG file is 1/300th the size of the 24-bit Targa version of the same 640x480 image! However, that small JPEG file has a seriously degraded image. Figure 8-1 shows four versions of the T38 image. The first is the original image, and the next three show the JPEG versions using a quality factor of 32, 8, and 1. The JPEG T38 with quality factor 32 is visually indistinguishable from the original except under very close scrutiny. If you look very closely at the NASA logos on the airplanes, you will see a slight fuzziness. The JPEG image with quality factor 8 is obviously degraded, but the image still looks good at a casual glance. The final image with quality factor 1 has completely broken up into a tile pattern. (In the spirit of this book, let's say that this effect is a "feature" not a "defect!")

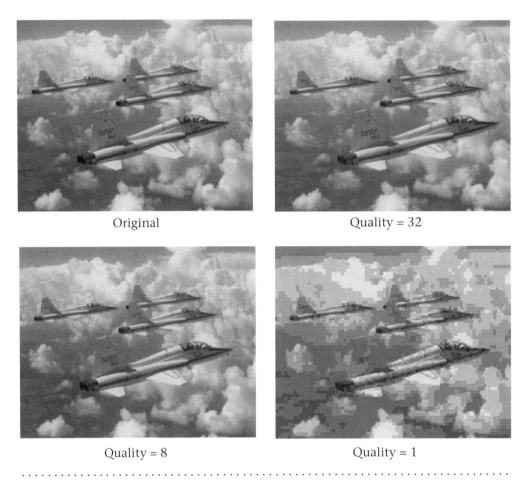

Original   Quality = 32

Quality = 8   Quality = 1

Figure 8-1 Effect of the quality factor in JPEG conversions

The real insight from this experiment comes not from the comparison between the 1 MB Targa and the tiny but degraded 4 KB JPEG image, but rather from the comparison between the original 221 KB GIF the nearly identical-looking 62 KB JPEG file. The JPEG compression results in a file a third the size of the original GIF.

Certain kinds of files do not work well with JPEG, in particular line art and dithered images that are the result of color reduction. You have to use careful judgment when using JPEG to save storage space. Use it for noncritical images with continuous tones like the file T38.GIF. You should keep your very best artwork in original file format in order to preserve the greatest amount of information. But JPEG can be a great space saver for storing images or trying to get images to fit on a floppy disk. Always check to make sure the image is not degraded unacceptably and that the result is really smaller. Some highly complex fractal images are actually smaller in GIF format that in JPEG format.

Sort an Image Palette for Improces

Improces is basically a grayscale paint program. Many of its functions can be used with color images also, but only if the image has a special palette that has darker colors with lower color numbers and brighter colors with higher color numbers. Unfortunately most color files do not have such a palette. Here is where Alchemy can come to the rescue. (Newer versions of Improces, including the version that comes with this book, contain an option that gives you another way to sort the color palette.)

You can use the T38.GIF image again for this exercise. The T38.GIF image was created by scanning a photograph and then color reducing the image to 256 colors using Piclab. The palette is not very suitable for Improces. To see this, start Improces and load T38. The image should look quite good using a 256-color mode. Click on COLOR and PALETTE, and select any of the built-in Improces palettes such as SUN. The result is terrible! The reason is that the various colors in T38.GIF are randomly distributed throughout the range of color numbers. When viewed using a palette with continuously varying colors ranging from dark to light as the color number goes from 0 to 255, the results appear random. Now convert T38.GIF to the 24-bit Targa T38.TGA with:

`C:>ALCHEMY T38.GIF -a -24` (ENTER)

Now type:

`C:>ALCHEMY T38.TGA TMP.GIF -g -z4` (ENTER)

The Alchemy -z option causes the palette to be sorted before remapping when Alchemy does color reduction. -z2 sorts from white to black, and -z4 sorts from black to white. This creates the file TMP.GIF with a sorted palette.

The color numbers used in a color-mapped image have no significance at all by themselves. They are just used to look up colors in the palette. For example, suppose the 4th palette entry has red, green, blue values of 22, 43, and 34. Every pixel in the image that is supposed to be color red=22, green=43, and blue=34 will have color number 4. If the palette was changed so that color 22, 43, 34 is now the sixth palette entry, and all the pixels that were color number 4 are changed to color number 6, the image would look the same. Sorting the palette rearranges the palette in order of brightness, and then changes the color numbers in the image so that they still point to the same colors. The result is no change in the image.

Try loading this into Improces and changing the palette to SUN or one of the other built-in palettes and compare the results with what you saw a moment ago. The result should now look quite reasonable. Many of the Improces image-processing features will now work with the file TMP.GIF.

Note that Alchemy options can generally be placed anywhere on the command line. Since some options have parameters, there is ambiguity if the options come first. If the example above is rearranged to:

`C:>ALCHEMY -z 4 T38.TGA TMP.GIF -g` (ENTER)

with a space between the "z" and "4", then Alchemy cannot tell if the "4" is a parameter of the z options (as it is meant to be) or a file name. The moral of the story is to put the options at the end.

Convert an Image Lab File to Another Format

The Image Lab tools use primarily the GIF and Targa formats. After you have made some beautiful and intriguing images, you are bound to have an occasion to need them converted to another format. Perhaps you have a friend with an Amiga who wants IFF format, or perhaps you would like to create some Windows wallpaper, and so need a BMP file. In all these cases the procedure is exactly the same as the conversions just described, except the option switch is different. Table 8-2 shows the switches for a variety of formats. Note that the - (dash) character is used to indicate a switch, but that some of the switch options themselves use a dash; hence some of these options have a double dash (--).

. . . .

Format	Switch
ADEX	--A
Autologic	--a
Binary Information Files (BIF)	--B
Encapsulated PostScript (EPS)	-e
Erdas LAN/GIS	--e
Freedom of the Press	--f
GEM VDI Image File	--g
GIF	-g
HP Printer Command Language (PCL)	-P
HP Raster Transfer Language (RTL)	--r
HSI JPEG	--j
HSI Palette	-l
HSI Raw	-r
IFF/ILBM	-i

Table 8-2 File conversion switches

. . . .

Format	Switch
JPEG/JFIF	-j
Jovian VI	--J
Macintosh PICT/PICT2	-m
MTV Ray Tracer	--M
PCPAINT/Pictor Page Format	-A
PCX	-p
Portable BitMap (PBM)	-k
Q0	--q
QDV	--D
QRT	--T
Scodl	--s
Silicon Graphics Image	-n
Stork	-K
Sun Raster	-s
Tagged Interchange File Format (TIFF)	-t
Targa	-a
Utah Raster Toolkit (RLE)	--u
Vivid	--I
Windows Bitmap (BMP)	-w
WordPerfect Graphic File	-W
XBM	--b
XWD	--w

Table 8-2 File conversion switches *(continued)*

ALCHEMY REFERENCE

Image Alchemy includes a reference manual in the file ALCHEMY.DOC. You can also access a summary of the same information from the on-line help using the -h switch. Typing

`C:>ALCHEMY -h` (ENTER)

brings up the main Help screen. By adding a digit from 1 to 6 after the h switch, six other help screens can be viewed. Figure 8-2 shows the main Help screen.

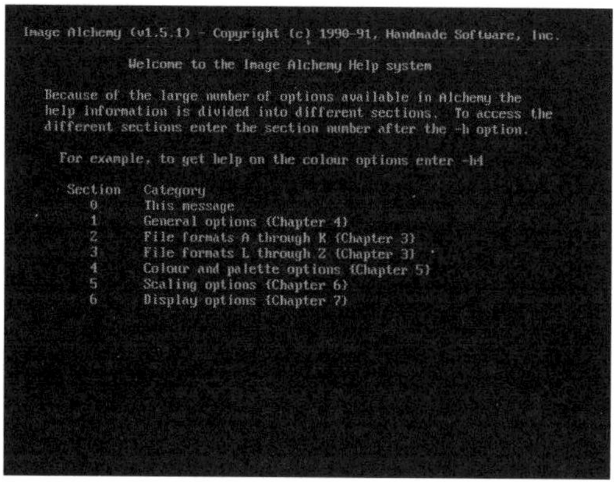

Figure 8-2 The main Help screen

For your convenience, details of selected file formats are included here. For the complete Alchemy options, see ALCHEMY.DOC.

Encapsulated PostScript (EPS)

Syntax   -e previewtype

Description: There is one parameter, previewtype. The possible values are:
0: None
1: Device-independent
2: TIFF
The default is device-independent.

When to Use: Use EPS for printing on a PostScript printer or for inclusion in desktop publishing files.

Limitations: Alchemy can only write, not read, EPS images.

Example: Convert the file INPUT.GIF to a color EPS file called INPUT.EPS, which will not require level 2 PostScript (but will require CMYK extensions),with no preview:

`C:>ALCHEMY INPUT.GIF -e0 -24` (ENTER)

Convert the file INPUT.GIF to a grayscale EPS file called GRAY.EPS, with a device-independent preview:

`C:>ALCHEMY INPUT.GIF GRAY.EPS  -e -b` (ENTER)

....
GIF

Syntax -g version

Description: There is one parameter, the GIF version. The possible values are:
    0: GIF87A
    1: GIF89A
    The default is GIF87A.

Limitations: When reading GIF89A files only the first image in the file is read. Any text, overlays, pauses, palette changes, and so on are ignored.

Example: Convert the image TEST.PCX to a GIF87A image.

`C:>ALCHEMY TEST.PCX -g` (ENTER)

....
IFF/ILBM

Syntax -i

Description: IFF and ILBM are the image formats used by Amiga computers. There are no parameters. The file extensions used are .LBM, .IFF, and .ILBM

Example: Convert the file INPUT.PCX to an IFF/ILBM file called OUTPUT.IBM with 32 colors:

`C:>ALCHEMY INPUT.PCX OUTPUT.LBM -i -C32` (ENTER)

....
JPEG/JFIF

Syntax -j[coding] quality

Description: JPEG is the Joint Photographic Experts Group format. The parameters are coding and quality. The coding parameter, if present, is h, which causes optimum Huffman coding to be used for better compression. The quality parameter is a number from 1 through 100 (larger is higher quality). The default quality is 32. The file extension is .JPG.

Limitations: Alchemy cannot read noninterleaved JPEG files. JPEG files are always lossy, which means that the compressed image is not identical to the original image. At high-quality factors (32 and above), this loss is generally so slight as to be barely noticeable. There is no quality factor that is guaranteed to be lossless.

Example: Convert the file T38.GIF to a JPEG file called T38.JPG, using a high-quality setting:

```
C:>ALCHEMY T38.GIF -j70    (ENTER)
```

....

Macintosh PICT/PICT2

Syntax   -m

Description: PICT and PICT2 are common Macintosh image formats. The extension is .PIC.

Example: Convert the fileT38.GIF to a Mac PICT file called T38.PIC.

```
C:>ALCHEMY T38.GIF -m  (ENTER)
```

....

PCPAINT/Pictor

Syntax   -A type

Description: This is the format used by the Pictor and PCPaint programs. The parameter "type" can have the foillowing values:

       0: 320x200x4 CGA*
       1: 320x200x16 PCjr/Tandy*
       2: 640x200x2 CGA*
       3: 640x200x16 EGA
       4: 640x350x2 EGA
       5: 640x350x4 EGA
       6: 640x350x16 EGA
       7: 720x348x2 Hercules*
       8: 640x350x16 VGA
       9: 320x200x16 EGA
      10: 640x400x2 AT&T/Toshiba*
      11: 320x200x256 VGA/MCGA
      12: 640x480x16 VGA
      13: 720x348x16 Hercules InColor*
      14: 640x480x2 VGA/MCGA
      15: 800x600x2 EGA/VGA
      16: 800x600x16 EGA/VGA
      17: 640x400x256 SVGA
      18: 640x480x256 SVGA
      19: 800x600x256 SVGA

20: 1024x768x2 SVGA
21: 1024x768x16 SVGA
22: 360x480x256 VGA
23: 1024x768x256 SVGA
The default is 640x480x256 SVGA.
*These modes are not yet supported.
The extension is .PIC.

Limitations: Only the EGA and VGA modes are supported at this time. Text modes are not supported.

Example: Convert the file T38.GIF to a Pictor file called T38.PIC, for 800x600x256 SVGA mode:

`C:>T38.PCX ALCHEMY -A19` (ENTER)

....

PCX

Syntax -p type

Description: PCX is the Zsoft corporation's paint program format. The parameter type can have the values:

0: Standard PCX
1: DCX

The default is standard PCX. The extension is .PCX.

Example: Convert the GIF file T38.GIF to a PCX file:

`C:>ALCHEMY T38.GIF -p` (ENTER)

....

Tagged Interchange File Format (TIFF)

Syntax -t compressionType

Description: The parameter compression type takes the values:

0: None
1: LZW
2: PackBits
3: Group III Fax
4: Group IV Fax
5: CCITT RLE

The default is LZW Compression.
The file extension is .TIF

Example: Convert the file T38.GIF to an uncompressed grayscale TIFF file called OUTPUT.TIF:

```
C:>ALCHEMY T38.GIF OUTPUT.TIF -t0 -b (ENTER)
```

Targa

Syntax   -a outputtype

Description: The Targa format is the Truevision company's format designed for use with their line of video boards. The parameter outputtype takes as values:

    0: Uncompressed
    1: Run length coded
   10: Uncompressed, no footer
   11: Run-length coded, no footer
The default is 0 (uncompressed).
The file extension is .TGA.
Targa files come in 8-, 16-, and 24-bit flavors. Use with the -8, -16, and -24 options.

Example: Convert the file T38.GIF to an uncompressed 24-bit Targa file:

```
C:>ALCHEMY T38.GIF -a -24  (ENTER)
```

Windows Bitmap (BMP)

Syntax   -w compressiontype

Description: This file type is used by Microsoft Windows. The parameter compression Type can have as values:

    0: None
    1: RLE
The default is none.
The file extension is .BMP.

Example: Convert the image T38.GIF to a 16-color Windows BMP file to be used as wallpaper:

```
C:>ALCHEMY T38.GIF -w (ENTER)
```

....
WordPerfect Graphic File

Syntax   -W

Description: This format is used by the WordPerfect word processor. The extension is .WPG.

Example: Convert the image, T38.GIF, to a black-and-white WPG file:

```
C:>ALCHEMY T38.GIF -b -c2 -W (ENTER)
```

9

GRAPHICS PORTFOLIO

T his chapter will guide you through the steps needed to create world-class graphics images on your PC. These images were created by talented experts who know how to get the most out of the Image Lab software. You can learn their secrets by following these examples, and you'll find more than enough ideas here to launch out and create your own graphics portfolio!

MT. MANDEL — RAY TRACING FRACTALS

About the Image

One of the classic books on fractals is *The Beauty of Fractals* by H.O. Peitgen and P. H. Richter. On the cover is a beautiful mountainous landscape in gray, with a Mandelbrot-set-shaped lake in front of a dramatic red sky, with a mysterious blue fractal moon setting behind the mountain. This book was a source of inspiration for the authors of the famous Fractint Freeware program described in Chapter 6 of this book. Many of Fractint's features were developed just to duplicate some of the fractals in *The Beauty of Fractals*. Therefore we hope that Peitgen and Richter will take it as the sincerest kind of flattery that we here attempt to reverse-engineer their artistry.

The Mt. Mandel image, complete with moon, can be made using only the Fractint program, in much the same style as the Mt. Rock image discussed in Chapter 6. Fractint can generate the fractal underying the mountainous surface, render it in 3-D with the terrain shaded with light from an imaginary sun, and even create the fractal moon. However, the Persistence of Vision Ray Tracer can provide the same rendering effects with some additional subtle touches, including the ominous red sky.

The Mt. Mandel terrain is made from a small piece of the Mandelbrot set. One of the interesting things about the Mandelbrot set is that it contains infinite miniature images of itself. These miniatures are connected by infinitesimal strands that radiate from the cardioid-like projections of the Mandelbrot shape. When the Mandelbrot set is rendered with a method known as the *continuous potential algorithm* (see pages 262–65), the numbers generated vary smoothly and the 3-D terrain is created by treating these numbers as elevations. The hair-like connections between the minitaure Mandelbrot midgits become razor-sharp ridges on the mountain. In this particular rendering, the actual Mandelbrot set has an elevation of 1 unit, compared to the peaks, which have elevation 255 units, so it appears as a canyon. Those snaking ridges actually contain a thin crevasse that is an extension of the canyon!

The fractal planet is a Julia set projected onto a sphere with POV using a *bump map*. A bump map interprets the values of the original fractal as elevations and gives the planet an elevated surface with a texture. You could use just about any fractal for the planet surface; you might try experimenting with using your own. The Mt. Mandel image is shown in Figure 9-1 is grayscale.

Image Credits

The main credit for this image belongs to Dietmar Saupe, who generated the original on the cover of the *The Beauty of Fractals*. The remaining credits read like a who's who of the Stone Soup Group. Mark Peterson was the first to reverse-engineer Dietmar's image. Yours humbly added the 3-D and continuous potential features that duplicate the image in Fractint. Douglas Muir incorporated the height field feature that allows POV-Ray to read Fractint continuous potential files, and finally Dan Farmer wrote the POV-Ray data file. The result of these people's labors is not only a beautiful image, but some quite general capabilities of the Fractint and POV software. The beauty of the original image directly inspired most of these efforts.

Image Lab Tools and Files Needed

To make this image you will need the following Image Lab tools. All except Fractint are provided on the disk accompanying this book:

Figure 9-1 Mt. Mandel

1. Fractint, version 15 or later

2. Persistence of Vision Ray Tracer, version 1.0 or later, protected-mode version

3. Piclab or Image Alchemy

You need the protected-mode version of POV-Ray because this ray tracing uses the image-mapping capabilities of POV-Ray, which requires more memory than the conventional-memory version of POV-Ray can provide. This means that you need a 386 or better machine, and at least 2 MB of free extended memory.

You will need the parameter files MTMAND and MTMANDJ for Fractint, and the file MYMAND.POV for Persistence of Vision. You will find all these files in the \IMLAB\EXAMPLES directory on your companion disk after you install the archive file EXAMPLES.EXE according to the instructions in Chapter 1. The two files for Fractint are very short and therefore optional, since it is easy to type in the information from the listings. The POV-Ray data file is longer.

The MTMAND.POV file needs three standard POV-Ray include files, SHAPES.INC, COLORS.INC, and TEXTURES.INC. These need to be accessible in the current directory, or via the +l option of POV that specifies a library directory.

The amount of free disk space needed depends on the final resolution of the image. If you use 640x480, the Targa file produced by POV will be almost 1 MB; at 360x480 it will be about half that. You should have several megabytes free before generating the image. A math coprocessor installed on your PC will dramatically reduce the time needed to create this image. On a 33-MHz 386 machine with a math coprocessor, generating the 640x480 Fractint continuous potential file takes a little over three minutes, and the POV rendering at 640x480 takes about half an hour.

How to Create the Image

The steps for creating the Mt. Mandel image are as follows:

1. Make the Mandelbrot continuous potential image using Fractint. This step produces a file called MTMAND.POT, and takes about 4 minutes on a 33-MHz 386 to generate at 640x480 resolution using a math coprocessor.

2. Make the Julia image for the planet using Fractint. This produces the file MTMANDJ.GIF, which should only take a minute or two.

3. Render the data file MTMAND.POV using the POV-Ray. This step requires the two files created in steps 1 and 2, and produces a Targa file called MTMAND.TGA. This is a 24-bit true-color file. You can view it directly with CompuShow, although the quality will not be good unless your PC has true-color capabilities.

4. Convert the true-color file MTMAND.TGA to the GIF file MTMAND.GIF using Alchemy or Piclab. You can view this image in its full glory using VGA graphics and CompuShow.

Step 1. Create the Continuous Potential Fractal

The Fractint parameters for creating the continuous potential file are contained in the file MTMAND. Listing 9-1 shows the contents of the file MTMAND.

. . . .

```
; Continuous Potential: Used for MTMAND.POT Height field.
type=mandel
corners=-0.1992/-0.1099914/1.0000046/1.06707
float=yes
maxiter=1500
potential=255/2200/1000/16bit
savename=mtmand
```

Listing 9-1 Fractint commands for MTMAND.POT

The easiest way to enter these parameters is to use Fractint's indirect file capability. When you are in the directory containing MTMAND, type:

`C:>FRACTINT @MTMAND` (ENTER)

Fractint will start with all the parameters set. You only need to press a function key corresponding to the video mode you want to use. Remember, the higher the resolution, the longer this will take. Use (SHIFT)-(F1) for the 360x480 mode, or (SHIFT)-(F5) for the 640x480 mode if you have a Super VGA and plenty of disk space.

Refer to Listing 9-1. The first two lines specify that the fractal type is the classic Mandelbrot (type mandel), and give the region in the complex number plane (the corners values). The floating point flag is set to Yes, because Fractint's fast integer math limits the iteration bailout value to 128, and continuous potential works better with a higher bailout. The maximum iterations is set for 1500. There are three continuous potential parameters. The first sets the highest value calculated, which is 255. Points with this value will be at the top of the mountain. The second parameter, which is 2200, affects the slope of the mountain. The value of 2200 causes this particular fractal to generate all the values between 255 and 0. If the slope were any higher, areas within the corners of the rectangle would "bottom out" at 0; if any lower, the entire range of numbers between 255 and 0 would not be covered. The third parameter is 1000. This is the bailout value used in the Mandelbrot calculation. This is why floating point math is used for this fractal; integer math is limited to a bailout of 128. The last parameter is a flag. The 16BIT flag causes Fractint to save the fractional part of the potential value. The resulting file is a double-wide GIF with a *.POT extension. ("POT" stands for "potential.") This file is twice as large because it contains extra information about the fractional part of the potential values, creating smoother slopes.

After you have pressed the appropriate keys to select a video mode, the fractal will calculate. When done, press (S) to save it. A message will come on the screen with the name of the file. The name should be MTMAND.POT. If you already have a file with that name, Fractint may use another name, depending on how you have configured the program. In that case make a note of the actual name.

Step 2. Create the Planet Fractal

The parameters for the Julia fractal to be used for the Mt. Mand planet are shown in Listing 9-2.

```
;Julia set for MtMand planet
type=julia
corners=-1.568/1.568/-1.176/1.176
params=-0.1545957/1.0335373
float=yes
maxiter=256
savename=mtmandj
```

Listing 9-2 The Mt. Mand planet Julia fractal

This fractal also uses continuous potential, but without the 16BIT flag, so a regular GIF file is created. To run this file, type:

`C:>FRACTINT @MTMANDJ` (ENTER)

You should definitely use the 360x480 mode for this fractal, so press (SHIFT)-(F1). Since the planet is relatively small, there is no need to use a higher resolution. Remember to save the result with (S). The file name should be MTMANDJ.GIF.

Step 3. Render the Mt. Mand Image with POV

In order to render the file MTMAND.POV, you will need to use the protected-mode version of POV included with this book. This means you may need to disable any other extended memory managers that your system is using. You can disable any 386 memory managers by placing a REM in front of the appropriate Device= command in your CONFIG.SYS file. Also, make sure that some of your extended memory is available, and that it is not all used up by a disk cache or RAM disk. If POV-Ray does not have enough memory, it will terminate and report this to you.

Listing 9-3 shows the POV-Ray input file for creating Mt. Mand.

```
// Persistence of Vision Ray Tracer
// MTMAND.POV By Dan Farmer
#include "shapes.inc"
#include "colors.inc"
#include "textures.inc"
#declare PlanetColor = color red 0.65 green 0.65 blue 1.00

// The following constants simply make it easier to swap images of different
//scales. Change ScaleX and ScaleZ if you generated the MTMAND.POT file at
// a resolution different from 360 x 480 which Dan used.

#declare ScaleX = 0.5625    // 360/(pot image width)
#declare ScaleZ = 1.0       // 480/(pot image height)
```

Listing 9-3 MTMAND. POV data file *(continued on the next page)*

. . . .

```
camera {
   location <-150.0 300.0  -650.0>
   direction <0.0  0.0  4.0> // "Telephoto" lens, "compresses" distance
   up <0.0  1.0  0.0>        // The distance also seems to smooth the h-field
   right <1.333333 0.0 0.0>
   look_at <-40.0 150.0  0.0>
}


// Define a couple of colors for the light sources.
#declare MainLight = color red 0.8 green 0.8 blue 0.8
#declare FillLight = color red 0.23 green 0.23 blue 0.25
// Light source (main)
object { light_source { <-400.0  300.0  -60.0> color MainLight } }
// Light source ( shadow filler )
object { light_source { <-50.0  300.0  -60.0> color FillLight } }


object {
   height_field {
      // 16 bit continuous potential Fractint fractal,
      // floating point activated to allow a large bailout value
      // Fractint parameters are:
      //    type=mandel
      //    corners=-0.1992/-0.1099914/1.0000046/1.06707
      //    float=yes
      //    maxiter=1500
      //    potential=255/2200/1000/16bit
      //    savename=mtmand
      pot "mtmand.pot"
      scale <640 256 480>
      water_level 0.0
   }

   texture {
      0.025    // dither  - not used often, but this image needs it.
      color White
      ambient 0.02      // Very dark shadows
      diffuse 0.8       // Whiten the whites
      phong 0.75        // Fairly shiny
      phong_size 100.0   // with tight highlights
      specular 1.0
      roughness 0.005
   }
   scale <ScaleX 0.5 ScaleZ> // Reduce the height, scale to 360 x 480
   translate <-180 0.0 -240> // Center the image by half of ScaleX and ScaleZ
   color Brown
}
```

Listing 9-3 MTMAND. POV data file *(continued on the next page)*

```
. . . . . . . . . . . . . . . . . . . . . . . . . . . . . . . . . . . . . . . . . . . . . . . . . . . . . . . . . . . . . . . . . . . . . . . . . .
// Sky sphere
object {
   sphere { <0.0  0.0  0.0> 1200.0 }
   color SummerSky
   texture {
      gradient <0 1 0> // Fade from yellow to orange to red to black
      color_map {
         [0.00 0.10 color Yellow color Orange] // Yellow at horizon
         [0.10 0.15 color Orange color Red]    // Fade to orange to red
         [0.15 0.27 color Red   color Black ]  // then to dark red
         [0.27 1.01 color Black  color Black ] // to Black at zenith
      }
      scale <1000 1000 1000>     // Big enough to surround the universe
      translate <0.0 -240.0 0.0> // This ajusts for the viewer position
      ambient 1.0                // Keep objects from casting shadows
      diffuse 0.0                // All light comes from ambient sources
   }
}


object {   // Planet
   sphere { <-95.0  50.0  600.0> 35.0 }
   texture {
      color PlanetColor
      bump_map { // Bump texture with corresponding julia image
               //    type=julia
               //    corners=-1.568/1.568/-1.176/1.176
               //    params=-0.1545957/1.0335373
               //    float=yes
               //    maxiter=256
         <1.0 -1.0 0.0> gif  "mtmandj.gif"
         bump_size 15.0
         interpolate 4.0 // Smooth the image
      }
      // mapped image is 1x1x1, with lower left corner at 0,0,0
      translate <-0.5 -0.5 0.0>     // Center the image at origin
      scale <35.0 35.0 35.0>
      rotate <0.0 00.0 95.0>        // Tweak the positioning a littl
      specular 0.35              // Fairly "dull" surface
      roughness 0.5              // spread the highlight
      ambient 0.0                // Dark shadows
      diffuse 0.75
   }
}

// end of file
```

Listing 9-3 MTMAND. POV data file *(continued)*

There are several things to check in this file. First of all, there are two file names mentioned in MTMAND.POV, MTMAND.POT and MTMANDJ.GIF. These two names must match the names of the Fractint files produced in steps 1 and 2. Second, look for the lines

```
#declare ScaleX = 0.5625    // 360/(pot image width)
#declare ScaleZ = 1.0       // 480/(pot image height)
```

The values of ScaleX and ScaleY depend on the resolution of the MTMAND.POT file that you created. The values in the MTMAND.POV file assume a resolution of 640x480. The resolution referred to is the image resolution of the fractal saved in the POT file. (This is the resolution corresponding to the function key you hit in Fractint. It is not the actual width of the POT file considered as a GIF — a 640x480 POT file is actually in 1280x480 GIF format.) If your MTMAND.POT file is 360x480, then you should change the value of ScaleX to 1.0. You can calculate the values for other modes using ScaleX=360/(MTMAND.POT image width) and ScaleZ=480/(MTMAND.POT image height).

Once you have the scale factors and file names right, you are ready to go. Since ray tracing is quite slow, it is a good idea to make low-resolution test runs to make sure everything is working OK. If you have a POV.BAT file set up to make running POV-Ray easy, then just type:

```
C:>POVPRO MTMAND -w80 -h60 ENTER
```

If you haven't set up a batch file, you can learn how to do it in Chapter 7. Your POV.BAT file could look something like:

```
\IMLAB\POVRAY\POVRAY -i%1.POV -o%1.TGA -p %2 %3 %4 %5 %6 %7 %8
if errorlevel 0 goto ok
goto done
:ok
REM pause
REM Uncomment the next line to use Piclab for color reduction
REM PL C:\IMLAB\PICLAB\CNVTGA %1
REM Uncomment the next line to use Alchemy for color reduction
\IMLAB\ALCHEMY\ALCHEMY %1.TGA -g -o
:done
```

You can also type in the whole command line directly. The +d option causes an approximation of the image to show on the screen during calculation. You may need to edit this option to fit your equipment — see the POV chapter for details. The complete command line is:

```
C:>POVRAY +lc:\imlab\pov\include +d -iMTMAND.POV -oMTMAND.tga -w80 -h60 ENTER
```

The +l option specifies the directory where the *.INC files will be searched for in case they are not in the current directory. The -i and -o options are immediately followed by the names of the input and output files, respectively.

The -w and -h options give the width and height of the generated image. If you have problems, make sure you were using the protected-mode version of POV and that your system extended memory is set up correctly, the *.INC files are in the right place, and also check that the file names are correct in MTMAND.POV.

If all goes well, in a minute or two a miniature Mt. Mand image should be produced. If you are satisfied with the results, and you can afford to tie up your computer for a few hours (or days, if you don't have a math coporcessor!), you can change the resolution to 640x480 using the options -w640 -h480 in either of the alternative command lines above. After an hour or two or more, depending on the speed of your machine, the image will be done. The final image will be in the file MTMAND.TGA.

Step 4. Convert MtMAND.TGA to GIF

There are two good reasons for converting the Targa file with your ray-traced image to a GIF file. GIF files are much smaller, and GIF files are viewable on many more machines than Targas, including yours, unless you have special true-color graphics hardware. But keep in mind that the GIF file has less information than the original Targa. Given the amount of processing time a POV Targa output file represents, if an image is at all good you should archive the Targa file by compressing it with one of the popular archiving programs, such as Phil Katz's PKZIP and saving it on your hard disk or on a floppy disk.

To convert the MTMAND using Piclab, start Piclab by typing:

`C:>PL` (ENTER)

Enter the Piclab commands:

`PL>TLOAD MTMAND` (ENTER)
`PL>MAKEPAL` (ENTER)
`PL>MAP` (ENTER)
`PL>GSAVE MTMAND` (ENTER)
`PL>SHOW` (ENTER)

Then you can view your very own version of the incredible and famous Mt. Mandelbrot classic.

Discussion of the POV-Ray Data File

A close look at the POV-Ray input file MTMANDEL.POV is very enlightening. The file has five sections. The first defines the camera, and sets up the coordinates system used for the image. The other four sections each define an object in the final image. Let's go through it section by section (refer to Listing 9-3).

The coordinate system used for this ray tracing is shown in Figure 9-2. The origin of the x, y, z coordinate system is at the center of the planet.

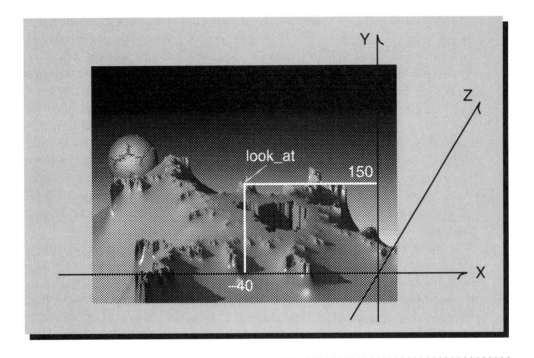

Figure 9-2 The Mt. Mand coordinate system

The first section of the file is the Camera block. The Location vector gives the position of the camera. The z coordinate has a large negative value, -650. That means that the camera is located a long way outside the computer screen, toward you, if you want to think of the coordinate system as attached to your screen. The positive z axis points away from you into your screen. The Direction vector of <0 0 4> means the camera is facing the screen. The real importance of this vector is its length. Making the Direction vector longer is like zooming a zoom lens toward the telephoto position. The Up and Right vectors determine the standard camera position (top of the camera going up, right side of the camera pointing along the x axis, as expected). The Look_At vector is the exact point in 3-space that the camera is aiming at, which is near the "Mandelbrot canyon." This replaces the camera direction set in the Direction vector, although the zoom factor (the length of the Direction vector) still applies.

Setting the camera is really not so hard if you realize that some of these settings can be left alone. There is usually no reason to change Up and Right —

usually when you take a picture, the camera is horizontal and pointing forward. You only need to set Location and Look_At, and even those can start out with standard values which you change after you have things working.

Following the camera, several objects are defined. The after the light source is the key to the Mt. Mandel image. It is called a Height_Field, and its action is very similar to Fractint's 3-D function. It reads in an image, in this case the file MTMAND.POT, and interprets the image values as heights. A fractal surface is created in the x-z plane using these height values to create a lattice of little triangles. The original width and height of the fractal are laid out along the x and z axes, respectively. The next part of the Object definition is a Texture, which defines the properties of the fractal surface created by the Height_Field. It is a white color. The Phong and Specular keywords create little highlights that make the landscape more realistic.

The next object is a giant sphere that surrounds the whole mountain and is used as a sky. Using a sphere this way gives a gently curving appearance to the sky. Another Texture section defines the characteristics of the sky. A Color_Map creates the shades of color going from black to red to yellow that you see in the final image. Notice that the sky is defined as a sphere of radius 1200 centered on the origin (<0 0 0>). At the end of the definition, a Translate keyword moves the sky color. Because this Translate keyword is in the Texture block, and not in the Object block proper, it doesn't move the giant sphere but rather it slides the color pattern arround the sphere. You can move the graduated black-to-red coloring of the sky up and down by modifying the Translate parameters. For example, if you changed

```
translate <0.0 -240.0 0.0>  // This ajusts for the viewer position
```

to

```
translate <0.0 -300.0 0.0>  // This ajusts for the viewer position
```

this would have the effect of moving the color pattern down 60 units. The values used in the Translate command were determined by experiment in an attempt to match the resulting image with the *Beauty of Fractals* cover.

The next object is very simple — it specifies the position of the source of light, thereby determining where the shadows will be. A position and color are given.

The last object is the planet. This object uses the POV bump_map. A bump_map wraps a GIF file around an object (in this case a sphere), but instead of coloring the object, the bump_map perturbs the surface according to the colors in the original image. This is very much like doing a Fractint 3-D transform onto a sphere with the roughness factor non-0. The bumpmap keyword appears inside a Texture block along with other keywords that affect the surface characteristics. The nature of the fractal image used here is not critical; try your own image instead of MTMANDJ.GIF.

That is all there is too it. Four elements: the land, the moon, the sky, and the sun, are all defined as POV objects.

Variations

There are a lot of ways you can modify MTMAND.POV to create your own images.

1. You can use different fractal files. The Height_Field image does not have to be a Fractint POT image. You can use a regular GIF file; just change the keyword POT to GIF. Keep in mind that the colors of the image are used as heights, not colors. A digitized photo of your spouse or friend may not produce a flattering result! It is also possible to wrap an image around an object, but that is not what Height_Field and Bump_Map do.

2. You can alter the viewpoint to see Mt. Mand from different angles. If you alter location, just keep in mind that your position has to remain within the sky sphere. If the viewpoint goes outside, you won't see anything. "Outside" the sky is black; the light source is inside the giant sphere.

3. You can adjust the colors of the various objects. A particularly fun and enlightening object to try to change is the sky sphere. Try changing the values of the Color_Map. If you want to try different colors, look inside the file COLORS.INC for other possibilities.

SUDS — RAY TRACING OSCULATING SPHERES

About the Image

Everybody has contemplated soapsuds at one time or another, whether while taking a bubble bath as a child, blowing bubbles with a little bottle of bubble suds, or doing something as mundane as washing the dishes. Most likely your mind was on either the simple pleasures of life or on getting through an onerous but necessary chore, but maybe there was one time when the suds themselves caught your attention. Suds are made up of little bubbles of all sizes. The larger bubbles are visible to the eye, and in between the larger bubbles are legions of smaller and smaller bubbles that merge into a frothy white, with the identity of individual bubbles lost to the keenest vision.

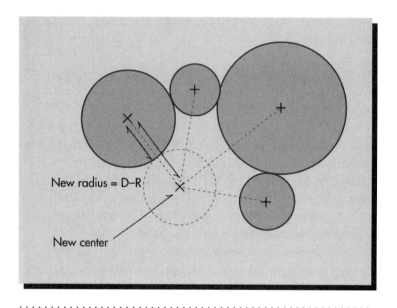

Figure 9-3 The SUDS algorithm

For many an artist or technonerd, suds have inspired a way to make interesting patterns out of spheres. The idea is to generate an image of many spheres of all sizes that are just touching each other. The technical term for this is *osculating spheres*. The word "osculating" literally means "kissing." You may never have heard the word "osculating" used in its primary meaning, but in the technical world it is commonly used to refer to objects that are just touching. For example, when NASA's space shuttle must rendezvous with a satellite, this is accomplished by calculating an "osculating orbit" for the shuttle — an orbit that just touches the orbit of the errant satellite.

The algorithm for creating an image of osculating spheres is very simple. Imagine that we are building a list of spheres to be constructed within a region of space. To start out the list, a point is selected at random to be the center of the sphere, and similarly a radius is randomly chosen. (A sphere is specified by its center and radius.) Using some random method, more prospective centers of spheres are selected. Each one is checked to see if it is inside any of the spheres already on our list. If it is inside a sphere, the point is ignored. If it is not inside any sphere, all the spheres on the list are checked to see how far the new point is from the edge of each sphere. This is easy — the distance from the new point to the center of the sphere is calculated, and then the radius of the sphere is subtracted. Figure 9-3 illustrates this. As the list of spheres is

Figure 9-4 A ray tracing made using the SUDS program

checked, the minimum distance from any of the spheres to the point is recorded. For each sphere, if its distance to the point is less than the current minimum distance, then the minimum value is revised to be that distance. When the entire list of spheres is gone through, the minimum distance is used as the radius for the new sphere, which is then added to the list. The new sphere osculates with at least one other sphere; its radius is equal to the distance from the center to the closest sphere, so it just touches that sphere.

A program on the companion disk provided with this book generates osculating spheres. The program creates a list of spheres and their positions that the POV-Ray can understand. The result is a bunch of beautiful ray-traced suds, as shown in Figure 9-4. There are a lot of options to this simple program, allowing you to create many different kinds of suds. You can have more or fewer spheres, you can vary the algorithm that randomly selects new points, you can change the minimum and maximum sizes of the spheres, and choose whether they will be all in a plane or distributed in three dimensions. This is fun stuff!

You will find that after you get involved with ray tracing, your perception of the world will change. You will notice shapes and textures, the interplay of light and shadow, the way objects are in relation to each other. You may even volunteer to do the dishes in the sink instead of using the dishwasher, just to enjoy your new-found awareness of suds. Then again, maybe not!

Image Credits

The images in this section were made using the program POV Suds, which is a heavily modified version of the program written by Sam Hobbs and published in *C User's Journal* (September 1991). The basic algorithm is from Clifford Pickover's book *Computers, Pattern, Chaos, and Beauty* (St. Martin's Press, 1990). The program has been adapted by Dan Farmer to create ray-tracing output, and was further modified by the author of this book to work in three dimensions. The images used in this section were generated by John Hammerton, Dan Farmer, and the author.

Image Lab Tools and Files Needed

You will need the POVSUDS.EXE program, and the SUDS.POV POV-Ray data file in the \IMLAB\EXAMPLES directory on your companion disk. You will also need POV-Ray installed on your hard disk with the companion Include files. For small numbers of spheres, you can use the regular mode version of POV. However, you will probably want to go off the deep end with your suds generation and make images with many hundreds of spheres. The non-protected-mode POV will fail if the number of spheres in the image gets much above 50. With the protected-mode version included with this book, if you have a 386 machine and several megabytes of free extended memory, then you can increase the number of spheres in your image into the thousands.

You will need enough free space on your disk to allow for the large POV-Ray Targa files. Several free megabytes is a good idea. If you are only experimenting with small images, you can get by with a lot less.

Time Needed to Create Image

The length of time needed to render a SUDS image is dependent on the number of spheres used in the image. Using the default value of 200 spheres, the rendering time for a 640x480 image is about an hour and a half on a 33-MHz 386 machine with a math coprocessor. Of course the more spheres in your image, the longer the rendering time. If you make an image using several thousand spheres and render it at a resolution such as 1024x768 or higher, plan on taking a vacation while your computer is running!

Procedure

To create a suds image, run the POVSUDS.EXE program and create a file called SUDS.INC. This file is #included in your SUDS.POV file, which you then render with POV. Finally, you convert the file SUDS.TGA created by POV to SUDS.GIF for viewing on Super VGA graphics hardware.

Step 1. Create the SUDS.INC File

The POV SUDS program is a simple utility that generates a data file containing the definitions of the osculating spheres that you will render in POV. The program has a simple and unpretentious interface. It is not highly refined, but it does its job well.

Place the POVSUDS.EXE program in a directory included in your Path statement, or place it in the directory where you will be running POV-Ray. Invoke POVSUDS by typing:

C:>**POVSUDS SUDS.INC** (ENTER)

You can use another name instead of SUDS.INC. Whatever name you use, be aware that if an existing file has that name, it will be overwritten. The POVSUDS program requires an EGA or a VGA to work.

. . . .
Figure 9-5 POVSUDS Opening screen

After POVSUDS starts, you will see a screen in graphics that looks something like Figure 9-5. There are various settings with the current values shown that affect how the output will look. You will be prompted for possible changes to each of these in turn. Let's look at the options one by one. The first time through you can press (ENTER) and accept the defaults for each option.

1. **Ray tracer.** POVSUDS supports various versions of the POV-Ray. The default value selects POV 1.00, which is correct for the ray tracer included with this book, so there is no need to change this value.

2. **Type of bounds.** The suds spheres can be constrained to a region three different ways. The default works the way the POV SUDS program was originally written; the centers of the spheres, but not their surfaces, are constrained to a rectangular region. The outer parts of the spheres can be outside the constraining region.

The second option looks similar, but is slightly different; the complete sphere is forced inside the rectangular region for this case. It is like dumping the suds balls in a box. The third option is similar to the first, but in this case the constraining shape is a sphere.

3. **Region containing the spheres.** This is the region in three-dimensional space that is filled by the spheres. The x and y values are tied to the screen coordinates and are not set by the user. On a VGA the x values will be between 0 and 639 and the y values between 0 and 479. You will be prompted to provide a value for zmax. The default value is 0, which means that the z values for the sphere centers have the fixed value 0, and that the sphere centers are all on the x-y plane. To start with, use the default value. If you use another value for zmax, say 100, then the spheres will not have centers all in a plane and will fill a region of space. The shape of this space depends on the type bounds, it is either a rectangular solid, a sphere, or a sphere with the ends clipped.

4. **Number of textures.** If you want the balls to all have the same surfaces, leave this at 0. If you would like the spheres to have different appearances, set a number from 2 to 10. The texture names suds0, suds1, suds2, and so forth will be inserted in SUDS.INC. The actual textures assigned to these names are declared in SUDS.POV. The SUDS.POV that comes on your disk only defines 11 textures. You can use a much larger number than 11, but you will have to modify SUDS.POV with declarations for the additional textures beyond suds0 through suds10 that are already declared. The program continually runs through the sequence of the number of textures you have selected. For example, if you specify ten textures, then the first ten spheres generated by the program will be given the names suds0 through suds9, and the next ten will be given these same names again, and so forth. To start with, use the default of 0 textures, which will give all the spheres the same chrome texture. After you have everything working, you can come back and try different textures.

5. **Max spheres.** This determines how many spheres will be created. The default of 200 is good as a first try, unless you are unable to use a protected-mode version of POV. In that case try 50. If POV reports running out of memory, reduce the number. If you can run the protected-mode version of the compiler, later you can try numbers like 1000. The built-in (somewhat arbitrary) limit of the program is 2048.

6. **Min radius.** This determines the smallest sphere size. The default is 0.5. Use this value.

7. **Max radius divisor.** This determines the size of the largest sphere. The default of 5 is fine. The number is used to divide the screen height to get the maximum sphere size, so a larger number results in smaller spheres.

You can press (ENTER) at each prompt to use the default values. Notice that each prompt tells you the current value of that option; this is handy if you come back and change the settings. Figure 9-6 shows what the screen looks like after all the values have been filled in.

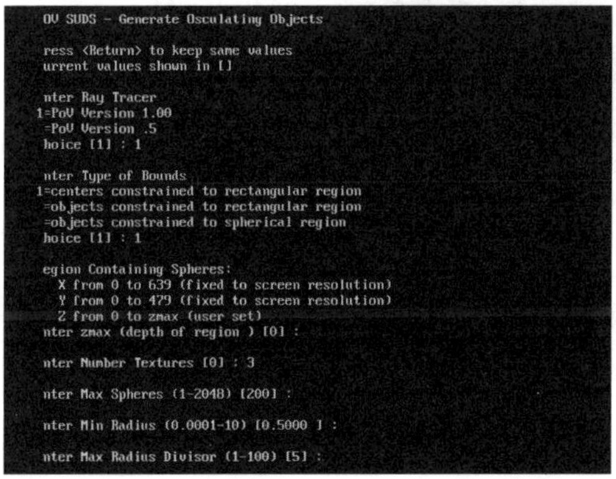

Figure 9-6 The POVSUDS
Parameter Input screen

After the last question is answered and you have pressed the final (ENTER), you will see osculating circles drawn on the screen. If you selected zmax=0, the circles will be osculating (just touching). If you set zmax > 0, the circles will overlap. They are really osculating in three dimensions, but the computer screen can only show the projections of the sphere outlines in two dimensions, so they appear to overlap.

Your screen should look something like Figure 9-7. In the lower- lefthand corner of the screen is the prompt:

<W>rite   <Q>uit   <A>gain.

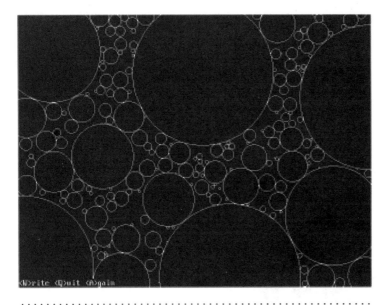

Figure 9-7 The POVSUDS Write/quit screen

If you want to write the SUDS.INC file, type:

(W) (ENTER)

which will write out the file and terminate the program.

If you would like to run the program again, press

(A) (ENTER)

and you will be taken back to the Opening screen. If you would like to exit the program without writing the file, press

(Q) (ENTER)

After pressing (W) and exiting the POV SUDS program, use a text editor to look at the SUDS.INC file. You should see lines that look something like:

```
#declare Suds = composite {
   object { SudsObject scale < 39  39  39> translate <373 320 163> }
   object { SudsObject scale < 63  63  63> translate <394  66 260> }
   object { SudsObject scale < 63  63  63> translate <518 227 308> }
   object { SudsObject scale < 63  63  63> translate <309 331 435> }
   object { SudsObject scale < 63  63  63> translate <397 393  24> }
   object { SudsObject scale < 63  63  63> translate <162 284 297> }
   object { SudsObject scale < 63  63  63> translate <267 177 384> }
                              .
                              .
                              .
   object { SudsObject scale <  9   9   9> translate <554 254  85> }
```

404

```
    object { SudsObject scale <  7   7   7> translate <476 373  23> }
    object { SudsObject scale < 18  18  18> translate <247 389 604> }
    translate < -321  -237  -310>
}

#declare Bounding_Box = intersection {
    box { <0 0 0> < 760 598 746 > }
    }

//Object Extents:  min x =   -59 min y =   -62 min z =   -63
//             max x =   701 max y =   536 max z =   683
//             max radius = 63
//             201 objects generated
```

The objects are declared to be SudsObjects. "SudsObject" is declared in the file SUDS.POV. This gives you great flexibilty. You could define SudsObject to be anything you want, and the results would be reasonable as long as the object fits inside a sphere of radius 1. Notice the statistics at the bottom of the SUDS.INC file. These will help you adjust the camera when you fine-tune your image. The max and min *x*, *y*, and *z* values tell you the region containing all the spheres. It is a little larger than the region described when you ran POV SUDS. This is because the region described in POV SUDS contains the centers of the spheres. Spheres with centers near the edge will go outside that region.

Step 2. Render the File SUDS.POV

Now that you have created the file SUDS.INC, you are ready to create the suds image. The POV-Ray data file required to render the suds image is called SUDS.POV. Look quickly through SUDS.POV. It contains the line:

```
#include "suds.inc"      // NOTE: Change this line accordingly
```

The name of the included file should match the name of the file you created using the POVSUDS.EXE program. If you want to use a different name, change it with your text editor.

If you have a POV.BAT file set up to run POV easily, type:

```
C:>POV SUDS -w80 -h60 (ENTER)
```

If you haven't set up a batch file, you can see Chapter 7 for details. Alternatively, you can type in the whole command line directly. Any options that are set in the POVRAYOPT environment variable do not need to be repeated. The +d option causes an approximation of the image to show on the screen during calculation. You may need to edit this option to fit your equipment, as explained in the POV-Ray chapter. The complete command line is:

```
C:>POVRAY +lc:\imlab\povray\include +d -iSUDS.POV -oSUDS.tga -w80 -h60 (ENTER)
```

The +l option specifies the directory where the *.INC files will be searched for in case they are not in the current directory. The -i and -o options are

Figure 9-8 A postage-stamp-sized POV suds image

immediately followed by the names of the input and output files, respectively. The -w and -h options give the width and height of the generated image. The values given make a small image that can be generated very quickly.

If all is well, you will see a little postage-stamp version of the suds image appear rapidly on your screen. Figure 9-8 shows a screen with a postage-stamp suds image. To render the image at full resolution, just add something like:

```
-w640 -h480
```

to the command lines with the resolution you want.

Step 3. Convert SUDS.TGA to GIF

To convert file SUDS.TGA to GIF, type:

```
C:>PL (ENTER)
PL>TLOAD SUDS (ENTER)
PL>MAKEPAL (ENTER)
PL>MAP (ENTER)
PL>GSAVE SUDS (ENTER)
PL>QUIT (ENTER)
```

Discussion of the POV Data File

Let's go through SUDS.POV together and see what is going on. Listing 9-4 shows the SUDS.POV POV data file.

```
// Persistence of Vision Ray Tracer
// This datafile is designed as a "root" datafile for the output
// generated by the program POVSUDS.EXE.  The name of the #include file
// containing the "suds" data must be changed to match your filename.
// For use with POV Ray 1.00

#include "colors.inc"
#include "shapes.inc"
#include "textures.inc"
```

Listing 9-4 The SUDS.POV data file (*continued on the next page*)

. . . .

```
#declare SudsObject = object {
// Note: you could substitute any of the following, or more:
//    intersection { Cube }
//    intersection { Z_Disk }
//    also, cone segments, hexagons, teapots, etc.
//    if you've got enough time.
    sphere { <0 0 0> 1 }
    texture {
      Chrome_Texture
    }

}


#declare suds0  = texture { Blue_Agate    }
#declare suds1  = texture { Brass_Texture }
#declare suds2  = texture { Blue_Sky      }
#declare suds3  = texture { Y_Gradient    }
#declare suds4  = texture { Gold_Texture  }
#declare suds5  = texture { Apocalypse    }
#declare suds6  = texture { Rusty_Iron    }
#declare suds7  = texture { Candy_Cane    }
#declare suds8  = texture { Water         }
#declare suds9  = texture { Tom_Wood      }
#declare suds10 = texture { Blood_Sky     }

#include "suds.inc"      // NOTE: Change this line accordingly

camera {
    location <0 0 -700>
    direction <0 0 1>
    up  <0 1 0>
    right <1.33333 0 0>
    look_at <0 0 0>
}


// I am using three light sources here, one, white and two, colored.
// You may wish to change these, even elimate the two colored ones
// completely, at least during the debugging phase.
object {  // BLUE light
  light_source { <50 65 -1500> colour RichBlue}
}

object {  // WHITE light
  light_source { <0 -100 -5000> colour White }
}

object {  // VIOLET RED light
  light_source { <-150 -165 -1500> colour VioletRed }
}

composite { Suds
  //  rotate <30 0 0> //  to place on x/z PLANE
}
```

Listing 9-4 The SUDS.POV data file (*continued*)

All the objects generated by the POVSUDS.EXE program use the Object Type name SudsObject, and therefore have the characteristics determined by the declaration of SudsObject in SUDS.POV. This means that you can change the SudsObject declaration and get very different results. Here's the part of the listing that contains the declaration of SudsObject.

```
#declare SudsObject = object {

// Note: you could substitute any of the following, or more:
//    intersection { Cube }
//    intersection { Z_Disk }
//    also, cone segments, hexagons, teapots, etc.
//    if you've got enough time.

    sphere { <0 0 0> 1 }
    texture {
        Chrome_Texture
    }
}
```

A SudsObject is declared to be a sphere of radius 1 centered on the Origin. It has the Chrome_Texture, which is a silvery metallic texture defined in TEXTURES.INC. The texture part of the declaration is only needed if you did not ask POVSUDS.EXE to add textures for you. If you did specify textures, they will be added on top of the textures listed in the declaration of SudsObject. POV allows layered textures. The last texture listed is on the top of the surface. If a texture is partially transparent, the textures underneath will show through. Each instance of a SubsObject in the file SUDS.INC scales the sphere to a different size and moves it in place. The comments within the SudsObject declaration suggest that the declaration can be changed by using other objects. You will see how to do this in the Variations subsection below.

Just below the SudsObject declaration you will find declarations of the textures suds0, suds1, and so forth. These look like:

```
#declare suds0  = texture { Blue_Agate   }
#declare suds1  = texture { Brass_Texture }
#declare suds2  = texture { Blue_Sky      }
#declare suds3  = texture { Y_Gradient    }
#declare suds4  = texture { Gold_Texture  }
#declare suds5  = texture { Apocalypse    }
#declare suds6  = texture { Rusty_Iron    }
#declare suds7  = texture { Candy_Cane    }
#declare suds8  = texture { Water         }
#declare suds9  = texture { Tom_Wood      }
#declare suds10 = texture { Blood_Sky     }
```

These declarations make use of ready-made textures that are found in the file TEXTURES.INC. Eleven are defined here. If you tell the POV Suds program to make more than eleven textures, you will have to add more declarations for suds11, suds12, and so forth. Since the textures are numbered starting with 0, remember to add 1 to the highest texture number you want to use when you tell POVSUDS how many textures to use. If you want to use suds0 through suds10, for example, you should specify the use of eleven textures. You can use up to 999 different textures if you have the patience to declare them all! If you have many more spheres than the number of textures you requested, then the list of textures is used over and over to cover all the spheres. You can easily add as many as you want. You can use more of the textures defined in TEXTURES.INC, or you can create your own. It is fun to make some of the textures very reflective so you can see the reflection of the other spheres in that sphere. The Mirror texture is an extreme case. It has no color of its own, but is a perfectly reflective globe. You can see by looking at the beautiful example by John Hammond that much fancier textures are possible.

Following the texture declarations is the all-important #include statement, which looks like:

```
#include "suds.inc"     // NOTE: Change this line accordingly
```

Notice that whatever names are used in SUDS.INC have to be declared before the file is included. POV-Ray reads the file SUDS.POV until it comes to the #include statement. Then it jumps to the included file and reads it just as if its contents were actually present in the original SUDS.POV file. When done, POV-Ray continues to read the additional lines in SUDS.POV below the #include statement.

Following the include is the Camera block, which looks like:

```
camera {
    location <0 0 -700>
    direction <0 0 1>
    up  <0 1 0>
    right <1.33333 0 0>
    look_at <0 0 0>
}
```

This a very standard Camera block. If you think of the x-y plane attached to your computer screen with the origin right in the middle, then the Camera is located 700 units directly in front of the screen, aiming right at the middle. Near the bottom of SUDS.INC is a Translate statement. The composite of all the SudsObjects is translated to a position centered at the origin. Hence the Look_At vector is <0 0 0>.

Near the bottom of the SUDS.POV file are the light sources. There are three. The main light source is at a conventional location with a large negative z component behind the Camera. The two colored ones are probably buried inside the suds spheres — sometimes you can see their light trying to peek through. They have been left in because of the spirit of SUDS.POV, which has a purpose of providing you with a starting point for your own creativity. Be brave — dive in and change things!

At the very end is the innocent-looking statement:

```
composite { Suds
    rotate <30 0 0>  //  to place on x/z PLANE
}
```

The suds spheres have been declared but not actually inserted in the scene prior to this point. The Composite {Suds} statement inserts the composite object made up of all the spheres into the scene. If you leave the Rotate command commented out, the camera will be aimed directly at the suds objects which are on the x-y plane. The Rotate statement shifts all the spheres so that they are viewed from an angle.

Variations

The SUDS.POV and SUDS.INC files are so basic that they are easy to understand. The better you understand a POV data file, the easier it becomes for you to make successful changes. The suggested modifications listed here hardly scratch the surface of your possibilities.

1. Use multiple textures. When you are asked for the number of textures, answer 11. That is the number of textures built in to SUDS.POV. If you feel confident that you can add more Texture declarations to SUDS.POV, then go ahead and try more than 11. The easy way to create more textures is just to copy the ones that are there now, and change the names of the textures to suds11, suds12, suds13, and so on. Then you can edit the actual texture itself. A really good way to learn is to study the textures in the file TEXTURES.INC, and see what different parameters create the different effects. For example, here is the definition of the Chrome_Texture:

```
// Good looking "metal" textures
// important:
// They require that colors.POV be included before textures.

#declare Chrome_Texture = texture {
    ambient 0.3
    diffuse 0.7
    reflection 0.15
    brilliance 8.0
    specular 0.8
    roughness 0.1
    color LightGray
}
```

You could change the name Chrome_Texture to your own name, place it at the top of SUDS.POV somwhere, and modify these various values and see what happens. It is a good idea to leave the textures defined in the standard TEXTURES.INC alone, so that you can duplicate accurately other people's work. You could even develop your own library of named Texture declarations and keep it in a file YOURNAME.INC.

2. Set zmax to a positive value. When running the program POV SUDS using zmax equal to 0, all the spheres have centers in a single plane. If you set zmax=100, then the region populated by the suds spheres will have a completely different appearance, because the suds will spread into three dimensions. It is best not to make zmax too large, because then as the number of spheres increase, many of them will be hidden by the spheres in front. A hidden sphere adds nothing to the image, but it increases the rendering time of the image. A value of 100 seems like a good value, but there are no hard and fast rules. Experiment!

3. Set the bounding shape to a sphere. This will make your suds spheres clump into a round mass. If you change the textures to bright colors, you could make a jar of jawbreakers.

4. Use shapes other than spheres. SUDS.INC was generated with spheres in mind. The spheres were assumed to have radius 1 and assumed to be centered on the origin before being scaled to their proper size and translated to their final position. Other shapes will work well if they have simililar properties. For example, in SHAPES.INC the shape Cube is defined. This Cube is half the size it should be in order to be somewhat the same as the circle. Therefore you could change the declaration of SudsObject to:

```
#declare SudsObject = object {

    intersection { Cube scale <1.414 1.414 1.414>}
    texture {
        Chrome_Texture
    }
}
```

A Cube needs the keyword intersection because it is defined as an intersection in SHAPES.INC. (It is the intersection of the "inside" of six planes, where one side of each plane is designated as the inside.) The reason for

```
scale <1.414 1.414 1.414>
```

is that the Cube declared in SHAPES.INC has a side 1 unit, so it has to be scaled by the square root of 2.0 in order to make the diagonals have distance 1 from the center, just like a sphere. This is the closest you can get to osculating cubes, at least with the simple POV SUDS program. You could also use

```
scale <2 2 2>
```

in which case the cubes might intersect somewhat.

You might also check the COMART forum of CompuServe and look in LIB 16, the ray-tracing library, for SUDS*.*. Improvements are being made to this nifty utility all the time.

MANTEL CLOCK — DESIGNING COMPLEX RAY TRACES

About the Image

Imagine a clock-maker building a mantel clock. The clock is made of many pieces. Each of these pieces is quite simple; many of them are basic geometric shapes cut out of sheets of metal. The artistry of building a clock lies in the painstaking assembly of these pieces step by step into subassemblies of the clock. Finally, the subassemblies are put together to form the finished clock.

This clock-maker does not make every clock component from raw materials, but orders from a catalog of standard parts. Supplies of standard gears, couplings, brass balls, legs, and screws are stored in a parts cabinet ready when needed.

You may be all thumbs, and have never been close to a lathe or a drill press in your life, but you can become a "virtual clock-maker" who creates beautiful and intricate machines that exist only within the netherworld of abstract mathematics. Fortunately there is a way to share your artistry with the world: You can use a ray-tracing program to photograph your creations and bring them to life! Figure 9-9 shows a beautiful clock that was built of "virtual pieces" step by step. Your method of building clocks will parallel that approach used by the imaginary clock-maker we just described. But instead of working with physical materials, you will work with abstract geometric shapes. This systematic method is not limited to building clocks; you can use it to build images of any complex object you can imagine.

If you aspired to be a real clock-maker, you would apprentice yourself to a skilled craftsperson and learn the trade. You would discover that the magic of building a clock comes down to a sequence of different steps, each of which is very simple. In order to learn to make virtual clocks, the strategy is the same. You need to find a master craftsman and become an apprentice. Fortunately one is available, and introductions are now in order.

Figure 9-9 A mantel clock

Image Credits

Mike Miller is a graphics artist who recently discovered ray tracing. He is the creator of many impressive and unique images, including the image TIME.GIF included on this book's companion disk. One of Mike's hobbies is building images of beauty and realism using the Persistence of Vision Ray Tracer included with this book. He is more than a gifted artist; he is an enthusiastic teacher as well. Mike has developed a methodical approach to building images of physical objects such as clocks. He firmly believes that creating such images is a learnable skill, and would like to prove that you too can create such intricate ray tracings. Mike is active in the Persistence of Vision section of the Computer Art (COMART) forum on CompuServe. There you can download his latest images, as well as the data files that created them.

Image Lab Tools and Files Needed

In order to generate the mantel clock image, you will need the protected-mode version of the POV Ray Tracer POVRAY.EXE. Since the ray tracer creates 24-bit Targa files, if you wish to end up with GIF files for viewing on a super VGA PC, you will need either Piclab or Image Alchemy to convert the Targa files to GIF. The POV-Ray data file for the mantel clock is contained in the file MANTEL.POV. This file requires two other GIF files that are used in the image. The file CFACE.GIF contains the clock face, and the file ST.GIF contains the fractal background. The clock face is provided on the disk; instructions for creating a fractal backdrop using Fractint are given, but you can use any image you wish. Just make sure the fractal is copied into your POVRAY directory and renamed to ST.GIF.

To run POV you will need the file POVRAY.EXE, accessible via the Path statement or through the use of a batch file. You will need the files SHAPES.INC, COLORS.INC, and TEXTURES.INC, installed in the directory \IMLAB\POVRAY\INCLUDE. If this is not set up, see the POV-Ray chapter for instructions. You will also need the file MANTEL.POV, which contains the POV data file for the mantel clock. This file should be in the \IMLAB\EXAMPLES directory.

Procedure

This section explains the steps needed to create the mantel clock image by rendering the POV data file MANTEL.POV on your computer. Mike went through a fascinating series of steps to create the data file. In the next section you will learn how it was done.

Step 1. Create the Background Fractal

You can use any fractal image or other scene for the backdrop using Fractint. Try the following:

```
C:>FRACTINT corners=-0.17515/-0.0859414/1.0/1.06707 savename=ST (ENTER)
```

The resolution you use depends on the final resolution you use for the mantel clock image. When POV-Ray uses this image, it will be scaled for you to the correct size. Therefore the only consideration in selecting a video mode for the fractal is the quality you wish to have for the fractal in the final image. For example, try pressing (F3), which will select the 320x200 256-color VGA mode. After the fractal has been generated, you may wish to cycle the colors using the <+> command to get better colors than the default IBM palette. You can stop cycling by pressing (C), and exit the cycling mode with (ESC). When the image is done, and you are sure you have left the color-cycling mode (a white border around the image tells you that Fractint is still in the color-cycling mode), press Ⓢ to save the image. The image will be saved in the file ST.GIF, unless a file by that name is already in the current directory. If Fractint reports it used another name, delete or rename the file ST.GIF to another name, and then rename the saved file to ST.GIF. Finally, quit Fractint, and then copy this file to the directory \IMLAB\EXAMPLES.

Step 2. Copy the Clock Face GIF

The clock face is in a GIF file with the name CFACE.GIF. This file is in the \IMLAB\EXAMPLES directory on your companion disk.

Step 3. Render the Mantel Clock with POV-Ray

The POV data file required to render the mantel clock is called MANTEL.POV. This file is also in the EXAMPES.EXE archive on the companion disk, and should be installed in the \IMLAB\EXAMPLES directory on your hard disk.

If you have a POV.BAT file set up to run POV-Ray easily, then you just type:

```
C:>POV MANTEL -w80 -h60 (ENTER)
```

If you haven't set up a batch file, you can see Chapter 7 for details. Alternatively, you can type in the whole command line directly. You may need to edit this option to fit your equipment as explained in the POV-Ray chapter. The complete command line is:

```
C:>POVRAY +lc:\imlab\povray\include +d -iMANTEL.POV -oMANTEL.tga -w80 -h60 (ENTER)
```

The +d option causes an approximation of the image to show on the screen during calculation. The +l option specifies the directory where the *.INC files will be searched for in case they are not in the current directory. The -i and -o options are immediately followed by the names of the input and output files, respectively. The -w and -h options give the width and height of the generated image. The values given make a small image that can be generated very quickly. If everything works OK, you can generate a higher-resolution image sometime when the computer is not needed for several hours. For example, to create a 640x480 image, replace the -w and -h options with

```
-w640 -h480
```

If you have problems, make sure you were using the protected-mode version of POV-Ray and that your system extended memory is set up correctly, the *.INC files are in the right place, and also check that the file names are correct in MANTEL.POV. Listing 9-5 shows the data file MANTEL.POV.

. . . .

```
//   POV Data - Mantel Clock          M.Miller 11/1/91
//   Modified for POV 1.00

#include "colors.inc"
#include "shapes.inc"
#include "textures.inc"

camera {
  location <0 60 -220>
  direction <0 0 1>
  up <0 1 0>
  right <1.333 0 0>
}

#declare DCone = //--CONE POINT DOWN /POINT at 000--
intersection {
  quadric { Cone_Y scale <1 1 1> }
  plane { <0 -1 0> 0 }
  plane { <0 1 0> 1  }
}

#declare UCone = //--CONE POINT UP /POINT at 000--
intersection {
  quadric { Cone_Y scale <1 1 1> }
  plane { <0 1 0> 0 }
  plane { <0 1 0> -1 inverse }
}

#declare GOLD = texture {  //--Bright Reflective Gold--
  0.02 ambient 0.3 diffuse 0.5
  color red 0.62 green 0.55 blue 0.0
  reflection 0.6 brilliance 8.0
  specular 0.5
}

#declare SILVER1 = texture { //--Bright REFLECTIVE SILVER--
    0.05 ambient 0.2 diffuse 0.5
    color red 0.6 green 0.6 blue 0.6
    reflection 0.6 brilliance 7.0
    specular 0.5
}

object { //--LIGHT Source1--
  light_source { <250 300 -500>  color White }
}

object { //--LIGHT Source2--
  light_source { <-100 200 -100> color White }
}
```

Listing 9-5 Mantel clock data file *(continued on the next page)*

. . . .

```
#declare A01 = object { //--CLOCK BASE--
  difference {
    union {
      quadric { Sphere scale <62 15 62> }
      quadric { Sphere scale <55 5 55> translate <0 10 0> }
      intersection { Y_Disk scale <50 3 50> translate <0 12 0> }
      intersection { Y_Disk scale <43 1 43> translate <0 15 0> }
    }
    plane { <0 1 0> 0 }
  }
  texture { GOLD }
}

#declare A02 = intersection { //--RING--
  Y_Disk scale <7 2 7> }

#declare A03_1 = intersection { //--Squash Disk to make rib--
  Y_Disk scale <1 56 4> }

#declare A03 = union {     //--Make Rib Column--
  intersection { A03_1 rotate <0   0 0> }
  intersection { A03_1 rotate <0  30 0> }
  intersection { A03_1 rotate <0  60 0> }
  intersection { A03_1 rotate <0  90 0> }
  intersection { A03_1 rotate <0 120 0> }
  intersection { A03_1 rotate <0 150 0> }
}

#declare A04 = union {   //--Colum Caps--
  intersection { Y_Disk scale <5 5 5> }
  quadric { Sphere scale <4 2 4> translate <0 5 0> }
  quadric { Sphere scale <1.5 1.5 1.5> translate <0 8 0> }
  quadric { Sphere scale <3 2 3> translate <0 10 0> }
}

#declare A06 = object {   //--Cross Support for Gear Box--
  union {
    intersection { Y_Disk scale <6 2 6> translate <27 -1 0> }
    intersection { Y_Disk scale <6 2 6> translate <-27 -1 0> }
    intersection { Cube scale <17 1 8.5> translate <0 0 10.5> }
    intersection { Cube scale <6 1 11.5> translate <0 0 11.5>
       rotate <0 45 0> translate <-27 0 0> }
    intersection { Cube scale <6 1 11.5> translate <0 0 11.5>
       rotate <0 -45 0> translate <27 0 0> }
  }
  texture { GOLD }
  bounded_by {
    intersection { Cube scale <35 2 14> translate <0 0 4> }
  }
}
```

Listing 9-5 Mantel clock data file (*continued on the next page*)

. . . .

```
#declare A07 = object { //--Bracket for Pivot Rod of Counter Balls--
   difference {
     union {
       intersection { Cube scale <17 8 0.5> }
       intersection { Cube scale <9 0.5 6.5> translate <0 -7.5 7> }
     }
     quadric { Cylinder_Z scale <8 8 8> translate <-17 -8 0> }
     quadric { Cylinder_Z scale <8 8 8> translate <17 -8 0> }
   }
   texture { GOLD }
   bounded_by {
     intersection { Cube scale <18 9 8> translate <0 0 6.5> }
   }
}


#declare ASS1 = object {  //--The Column Assembly--
   union {
     intersection { A02 }
     union { A03 translate <0 2 0> }
     intersection { A04 translate <0 56 0> }
   }
   texture { GOLD }
   bounded_by {
     intersection {
       Y_Disk scale <7.2 71 7.2> translate <0 -0.5 0>
     }
   }
}


#declare B01 = intersection {  //--Ball Brace--
   difference {
     union {
       intersection { Cube scale <1 10 0.6> translate <1 18 0> }
       intersection { Cube scale <5 3 0.6> translate <2 25 0> }
       intersection { Cube scale <6 1 0.6> translate <14 1 0> }
       intersection { Cube scale <5.8 1 0.6> rotate <0 0 -45>
         translate <4.5 4.5 0> }
     }
     quadric { Cylinder_Z scale <8 8 8> translate <10 22 0> }
   }
}

#declare B02 = union {  //--Brass Balls--
   quadric { Sphere scale <9 9 9> }
   quadric { Sphere scale <3 2 3> translate <0 12 0> }
   intersection { Y_Disk scale <3 2 3> translate <0 8 0> }
}
```

Listing 9-5 Mantel clock data file (*continued on the next page*)

. . . .

```
#declare B03 = object { //--Combined Ball & Support--
  union {
    intersection { B01 }
    union { B02 translate <13 11 0> }
  }
  texture { GOLD }
  bounded_by {
    intersection { Cube scale <14 15 9> translate <10 14 0> }
  }
}

#declare B04 = object {   //--Pivot Support for B03--
  union {
    intersection { DCone scale <3  4  3> }
    intersection { Y_Disk scale <3 20  3> translate <0  4 0> }
    intersection { Y_Disk scale <2 10  2> translate <0 24 0> }
    intersection { Y_Disk scale <7  2  7> translate <0 28 0> }
    intersection { Y_Disk scale <1 13  1> translate <0 35 0> }
    intersection { Y_Disk scale <11 1 11> translate <0 34 0> }
    intersection { Cube   scale <14 0.5 2> translate <0 7 0> }
    intersection { Cube   scale <2 0.5 14> translate <0 7 0> }
  }
  texture { GOLD }
  bounded_by {
    intersection { Y_Disk scale <12 50 12> translate <0 -1 0> }
  }
}

#declare ASS2 = composite {   //--Pivot Support w/balls--
  object { B04 }
  object { B03 translate <8 4 0> rotate <0 0 0> }
  object { B03 translate <8 4 0> rotate <0 90 0> }
  object { B03 translate <8 4 0> rotate <0 180 0> }
  object { B03 translate <8 4 0> rotate <0 270 0> }
  bounded_by {
    intersection {
      Y_Disk scale <32 50 32> translate <0 -1 0>
    }
  }
}

#declare C01 = intersection { Z_Disk scale <2 2 20> }
```

Listing 9-5 Mantel clock data file (*continued on the next page*)

. . . .

```
#declare CO2 = object {  //--GEAR BOX--
   union {
     intersection { Cube scale <17 26 1> }
     intersection { Cube scale <17 26 1> translate <0 0 17> }
     intersection { C01 translate <-14 -23 -1.5> }

     intersection { C01 translate <14 -23 -1.5> }
     intersection { C01 translate <-14 23 -1.5> }
     intersection { C01 translate <14 23 -1.5> }
   }
   texture { GOLD }
   bounded_by {
     intersection { Cube scale <18 27 11> translate <0 0 9> }
   }
}

#declare G01 = intersection {    //--TOOTH of GEAR--
Cube scale <1 0.5 0.5> translate <12 0 0> }

#declare G02 = intersection {   //--GEAR RING--
   difference {
     intersection { Z_Disk scale <12 12 1> }
     quadric { Cylinder_Z scale <10 10 10> }
   }
}

#declare G03 = union {    //--GEAR SPOKE--
   intersection { Cube scale <1.5 11 0.5> }
   intersection { Cube scale <11 1.5 0.5> }
}

#declare G04 = object {    //--ASSEMBLE THE GEAR PARTS--
   union {
     intersection { G02 translate <0 0 -0.5> }
     union { G03 }
     intersection { G01 rotate <0 0 0> }
     intersection { G01 rotate <0 0 10> }
     intersection { G01 rotate <0 0 20> }
     intersection { G01 rotate <0 0 30> }
     intersection { G01 rotate <0 0 40> }
     intersection { G01 rotate <0 0 50> }
     intersection { G01 rotate <0 0 60> }
     intersection { G01 rotate <0 0 70> }
     intersection { G01 rotate <0 0 80> }
     intersection { G01 rotate <0 0 90> }
     intersection { G01 rotate <0 0 100> }
     intersection { G01 rotate <0 0 110> }
     intersection { G01 rotate <0 0 120> }
     intersection { G01 rotate <0 0 130> }
```

Listing 9-5 Mantel clock data file (*continued on the next page*)

```
      intersection { G01 rotate <0 0 140> }
      intersection { G01 rotate <0 0 150> }
      intersection { G01 rotate <0 0 160> }
      intersection { G01 rotate <0 0 170> }
      intersection { G01 rotate <0 0 180> }
      intersection { G01 rotate <0 0 190> }
      intersection { G01 rotate <0 0 200> }
      intersection { G01 rotate <0 0 210> }
      intersection { G01 rotate <0 0 220> }
      intersection { G01 rotate <0 0 230> }
      intersection { G01 rotate <0 0 240> }
      intersection { G01 rotate <0 0 250> }
      intersection { G01 rotate <0 0 260> }
      intersection { G01 rotate <0 0 270> }
      intersection { G01 rotate <0 0 280> }
      intersection { G01 rotate <0 0 290> }
      intersection { G01 rotate <0 0 300> }
      intersection { G01 rotate <0 0 310> }
      intersection { G01 rotate <0 0 320> }
      intersection { G01 rotate <0 0 330> }
      intersection { G01 rotate <0 0 340> }
      intersection { G01 rotate <0 0 350> }
    }
  texture { GOLD }
  bounded_by {
    intersection { Z_Disk scale <14 14 2> translate <0 0 -1> }
  }
}

#declare D01 = object {   //--CROWN PLATE--
  difference {
    union {
      intersection { Cube scale <24 17 1> }
      intersection { Cube scale <4 21 1> }
    }
    quadric { Cylinder_Z scale <6 6 6> translate <-10 17 0> }
    quadric { Cylinder_Z scale <6 6 6> translate <10 17 0> }
  }
  texture { GOLD }
  bounded_by {
    intersection { Cube scale <25 22 2> translate <0 0 -1> }
  }
}
```

Listing 9-5 Mantel clock data file *(continued on the next page)*

. . . .

```
#declare D02 = object {  //--CROWN CAPS--
   union {
      intersection { UCone scale <2 14 2> translate <0 14 0> }
      quadric { Sphere scale <4 1 4> translate <0 3 0> }
      quadric { Sphere scale <0.7 1 0.7> translate <0 14 0> }
   }
   texture { GOLD }
   bounded_by {
      intersection {
         Y_Disk scale <4.5 16 4.5> translate <0 -0.5 0>
      }
   }
}


#declare ASS3 = composite { //GEAR BOX & CROWN ASSEMBLY
   object { C02 }
   object { D01 translate <0 23 2> }
   object { D02 translate <20 40 2> }
   object { D02 translate <0 44 2> }
   object { D02 translate <-20 40 2> }
   bounded_by {
      intersection { Cube scale <25 45 11> translate <0 15 8> }
   }
}


#declare F01 = object {    //--CLOCK FACE RIM --
quadric { Sphere scale <33 33 6> }
texture {  GOLD }
 }


#declare F02 = object {    //--CLOCK FACE--
   quadric { Sphere scale <30 30 4> }
   texture {
      image_map { <1.0 -1.0 0> gif "cface.gif" }
      scale <60 60 4> translate <-30 -30 -4>
      ambient 0.3  diffuse 0.6 reflection 0.1
   }
}
```

Listing 9-5 Mantel clock data file (*continued on the next page*)

. . . .

```
#declare CLOCK = composite { //--SOME ASSEMBLY REQUIRED--
  object { A01 }                          //base
  object { ASS1 translate     <27   16 -19> }   //r.column
  object { ASS1 translate     <-27  16 -19> }   //l.column
  object { A06 translate      <0    77 -19> }   //support
  object { A07 translate      <0    70 0.5> }   //pivot sup
  composite { ASS2 translate  <0    16  9> }    //balls
  composite { ASS3 translate  <0    104 -17> }  //crown/box
  object { G04 translate      <-18 120  -3> }   //t.gear
  object { G04 translate      <-22 100  -5> }   //b.gear
  object { F01 translate      <0   110 -21> }   //face rim
  object { F02 translate      <0   110 -24> }   //face
  bounded_by {
    intersection {
      Y_Disk scale <64 170 64> translate <0 -1 0>
    }
  }
}

//--PLACE CLOCK--
composite { CLOCK rotate <0 -30 0> }

//--FLOOR PLANE--
object {
  plane { <0 1 0> -3 }
  texture { color Black ambient 0.8 reflection 0.3 phong 0.5 }
}

//--BACK DROP--
object {
  intersection { Cube scale <1000 500 5> }
  texture {
    image_map { <1.0 -1.0 0> gif "st.gif" }
    scale <2000 2000 5> translate <-1000 -1000 -5>
    ambient 0.4 diffuse 0.0
  }
  rotate <0 0 0> translate <0 400 1200>
}
```

Listing 9-5 Mantel clock data file (*continued*)

Step 4. Convert MANTEL.TGA to GIF

To convert the MANTEL.TGA using Piclab, start Piclab by typing in

`C:>PL` (ENTER)

Enter the Piclab commands:

`PL>TLOAD MANTEL` (ENTER)
`PL>MAKEPAL` (ENTER)
`PL>MAP` (ENTER)
`PL>GSAVE MANTEL` (ENTER)
`PL>SHOW` (ENTER)

Discussion of the POV-Ray Data File

Just as remarkable as the quality of the mantel clock image is the process that the image artist went through to create it. Here is an outline of the steps that he went through. The methodical approach described here breaks the design process for the complex clock image into easily reproducible steps.

The Mantel Clock Design Process

1. A broken mantel clock was purchased from a local clock repair shop.

2. The clock was disassembled.

3. All the parts were measured with a clear ruler with graduations that matched the grid paper (10 units to the inch).

4. The measurements of each clock part were transposed to the 10-units-to-the-inch grid paper.

5. The POV language description was written for each piece as it was drafted.

6. The front view was drafted first, then the side and top views. At least two views are needed to fix the relative position of each object in three dimensions.

7. During this drafting process, decisions were made concerning which parts were to be combined into one object and which were to remain as separate objects. This depended on what parts needed to be freely movable, or whether a part needed its own texture. Even though all parts in this clock were metallic gold, reflection was decreased on some parts for final rendering enhancements. Touching up of surface characteristics of a part requires that it remain a separate object. The advantage of combining parts is that then they could be moved as a unit.

8. The grid paper was marked out with a fixed universe origin <0 0> and tick marks placed every 10 units. The clock was drafted from

the base up. The center origin of each part was marked as it was drafted into place. This gave a translation distance of each part from the fixed <0 0>.

9. Many of the complex assemblies were drafted on a separate grid sheet using the same scale. Then a light table was used to trace the complex assembly into the master drawing.

10. The blueprint drawing made it easy to determine the Bounded_By shape for all objects and composites. (A Bounded_By shape is a simple shape that completely contains an object. It is used by the ray tracer to speed up the calculation.)

11. Each element in the scene is a declared object or composite. The complete object is formed by translating all declared objects to their correct positions using one Composite statement. The approach of building declared objects allows using the objects in other scenes. The declared objects can be kept in a parts file that can be inserted into data files using the #include directive as Include files. One composite name can place the entire object using one translate statement.

Figure 9-10 shows ray-traced images of the various components, labeled to match Mike's drafting diagrams. You can match the part labels to its definition in MANTEL.POV using the same labels.

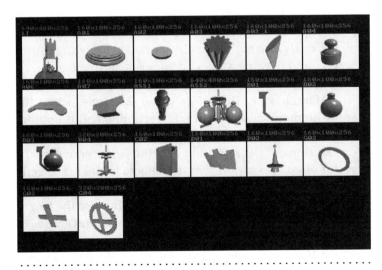

Figure 9-10 Mantel clock parts

The Data File

The mantel clock data file uses many POV-Ray features, more than can be fully documented in this chapter. For more information you can see the file POVRAY.DOC on the companion disk. We'll go through the data file section by section. It is well worth studying. A good method of learning is to modify parts of the data file and see what happens.

The Include Files

At the very top of the data file are the standard POV Include files. These define the colors, shapes, and textures that are available for use in your data files. Most POV data files have these Include statements near the top.

```
#include "colors.inc"
#include "shapes.inc"
#include "textures.inc"
```

The Camera

The lines in MANTEL.POV defining the camera are:

```
camera {
   location < 0 60 -220 >
   direction < 0 0 1 >
   up < 0 1 0 >
   right < 1.333 0 0 >
}
```

This particular Camera definition is made up of Location, Direction, Up, and Right vectors. Recall that a vector is made of three numbers, corresponding to coordinates for the x, y, and z axes. Remember that the x axis runs horizontally along the width of your computer screen, the y axis runs up and down vertically, and the z axis runs at right angles to the screen, with positive values behind the screen, and negative values on your side of the screen.

The Location vector gives the position of the imaginary camera that is taking the picture of the Mantel clock. The values <0 60 -220> mean that the camera is located at the origin in the left-right (x) direction, 60 units up from the origin in the y direction, and 220 units along the z axis on the negative side of the x-y plane. You can think of the z position as being where your eye is.

The Direction vector of <0 0 1> means that the camera is looking directly toward the x-y plane using the regular zoom setting. The length of the Direction vector determines the magnification of the image. In this case the length is 1.0. A value of 2.0 or 3.0 would be like using a telephoto lens, and a value of .5 is like a wide-angle lens.

The Up and Right values are standard, and you normally won't change these. The number 1.333 in the Right vector means that the proportions of your screen are in the ratio of 4 to 3, which is correct for almost all PC video modes.

Since there is no Look_At vector, the Direction vector determines which way the camera is pointing. In this case that direction is straight toward the *x-y* plane, pointing neither up nor down.

The Clock Textures

A bit farther down in the data file, two textures are defined. Every object defined in a POV data file can be given a texture that has various properties. The clock uses two: GOLD and SILVER1. A Texture statement can be directly placed in the definition of an Object. Because the mantel clock is made up of many parts, it is more efficient to use the POV #declare facility to attach the name GOLD to a particular texture. Then it can be used over and over just by adding the line

```
texture GOLD
```

to the definitions of different objects. The GOLD Texture definition has a color specified in terms of red, green, and blue components. It also contains a number of other attributes that affect how a surface with the GOLD texture will look. The listing below shows the declaration of the texture GOLD. Comments have been added explaining what each of the attributes do.

```
#declare GOLD = texture {  //--Bright Reflective Gold--
    0.02          // Adds slight random variations
    ambient 0.3   // light from all directions
    diffuse 0.5   // illumination by light sources is scattered
    colour        // definition of GOLD color
      red 0.62
      green 0.55
      blue 0.0
    reflection 0.6 // moderate mirror property
    brilliance 8.0 // metallic appearance
    specular 0.5   // reflective highlight
}
```

Light Sources

After the Texture declarations are the definitions for two objects that are light sources. They are both white. The sources are identical except for their position. Two light sources are used to prevent harsh shadows.

The definitions of the light sources begin with the keyword Object. This means that the light sources are defined and placed in the scene immediately. Most of the objects in the MANTEL.POV file are defined in #declare statements, which simply attaches a name to the object, but does not place it in the scene yet. For example,

```
#declare  snowman = object {
   three big snowballs, one on top of the other,
   with two pieces of coal in the top snowball for eyes.
}
```

defines what the "snowman" object is but doesn't place it in the scene. After this declaration, the line

```
object snowman {
   texture ...
   translate ...
}
```

actually places the snowman in the scene, and additionally adds a texture to it or translates it or otherwise modifies it. The two light sources are examples of direct Object definitions. This is the usual way Objects are added to scenes in most POV data files. The MANTEL.POV file uses a different approach; many #declares are used to attach part names to shape definitions because the final image is made up of many parts. The parts are assembled and placed in the scene at the very end.

The light source definitions are:

```
object { //--LIGHT Source1--
   light_source {
      < 250 300 -500 >  color White
   }
}

object { //--LIGHT Source2--
   light_source {
      < -100 200 -100 > color White
   }
}
```

The Clock Base

Following the light sources, the part labeled A01 is declared. This is an illustration of the approach used to build the clock that was just discussed. All the #declare statement does is attach a meaning to "A01"; at this point the part is not placed in the scene. The delaration that defines A01 is:

```
#declare A01 = object { //--CLOCK BASE--
   difference {
      union {
         quadric { Sphere scale < 62 15 62 >  }
         quadric { Sphere scale < 55 5 55 > translate < 0 10 0 >  }
         intersection { Y_Disk scale < 50 3 50 > translate < 0 12 0 >  }
         intersection { Y_Disk scale < 43 1 43 > translate < 0 15 0 >  }
      }
      plane { < 0 1 0 > 0  }
   }
   texture { GOLD  }
```

The POV language supports a method of defining objects called CSG, short for Constructive Solid Geometry. Using this approach, shapes can be built by combining shapes, or cutting shapes out of other shapes. The key idea in CSG is that every object has an inside and an outside. The clock base illustrates three of these operations: difference, union, and intersection. It also introduces the use of some of the predefined POV shapes:

- The union of several CSG objects is the new object consisting of all the points that are inside any one or more of the separate objects. In effect, union lumps objects together to maker larger objects.

- The intersection of several overlapping objects is a new object consisting of all the points that are inside of all the objects. In other words, the intersection consists of the points shared by all the objects.

- The difference of two objects is the first object with the inside of the second object cut out.

In order to read the definition of part A01, you have to read from the inside of the curly braces outward. Inside the definition of A01 is the keyword Union with two Spheres and two Y_Disks included inside the curly brackets.

A Sphere (capitalized) is a generalized sphere. The POV language allows you define spheres directly. When you want a plain sphere, the uncapitalized keyword sphere is the one to use. In this case we need a squashed sphere that has been scaled differently in the vertical direction. A regular sphere can only be scaled uniformly. The advantage of a Sphere is that you can warp its shape to your heart's content. The line

```
quadric { Sphere scale < 62 15 62 > }
```

defines a sphere that started out having a radius of 1 unit, centered at the origin. Then is was scaled 62 in the x dimension, only 15 in the y dimension, and 62 in the z dimension. This means that the sphere has been nicely squashed into a rounded disk that has a radius of 62 units in the x-z direction and a radius of 15 in the y direction. Now look at the clock base in Figure 9-10. At the bottom of the diagram you can see the base. The very bottom piece is our squashed ellipsoid. It has been sliced in two, but don't worry about that, we'll get to it in a minute.

There is a very straightforward correspondence between the data file definitions of these shapes and the blueprint. There are a lot of unfamiliar terms in the data file, like "quadric," but you really don't have to understand them all. All you need to know in this case is that a Sphere is a squashable sphere, and that you need the keyword Quadric when you use it.

Now that you have the first Sphere figured out, you can easily find the second one in the data file. It has a little smaller radius (55 instead of 62) in the *x-z* plane, and has been squashed more in the *y* direction.

There are two more pieces in the base object. These are Y_Disks. The Y_Disks consist of disks 1 unit high with radius 1. The lines in the A01 definition that use them are:

```
intersection { Y_Disk scale < 50 3 50 > translate < 0 12 0 > }
intersection { Y_Disk scale < 43 1 43 > translate < 0 15 0 > }
```

These have to be introduced with the keyword Intersection because they are declared as Intersections in SHAPES.INC. (A Y_Disk is the intersection of an infinitely long cylinder, the region above the bottom plane, and the region below the top plane — you can look this up yourself in SHAPES.INC.) The Y_Disks are scaled in the same way as the Spheres were. By now you are convinced — the first one has radius 50 and the second one radius 43. Now that you see the pattern, you can probably figure out exactly what the

```
translate < 0 12 0>
```

statement is doing; it moves the disk up 12 units.

Part number A01 is built from the union of these four objects, two squashed ellipsoids and two flat cylinders. The last step is to take the intersection of the combined object with:

```
plane { < 0 1 0 > 0 }
```

In this context a plane is not quite what you think. The positive side of a plane is considered to be the "inside" for CSG purposes. So when you take the intersection of an object with a plane, you take the part of the object that is on the positive side of the plane. (For the mathematically curious, the plane defined above is the plane perpendicular to the vector <0 1 0> which points vertically, 0 units from the origin. This makes it the *x-z* plane.)

You can now see why the bottom half of our first squashed Sphere got sheared off. It was below the *x-z* plane.

After all that work, look back to Figure 9-10 to see what part number A01 looks like. There they are real as life like a stack of pancakes–two rounded disks, the bottom one sawed in half, then glued to two smaller nested disks.

The Gear

There isn't space to cover how all the parts in MANTEL.POV are built, but from the clues presented so far, and the documentation in the POVRAY.DOC file, you can go through the file and look up explanations for each operation as you come to it. We'll cover one more part, because it is especially interesting. This is part number G04, the gear. It is a wonderful example of the power and flexibility of the POV language.

Part G04 is built from G01, G02, and G03. Look at the declaration of G01 below:

```
#declare G01 = intersection {    //--TOOTH of GEAR--
Cube scale < 1 0.5 0.5 > translate < 12 0 0 >  }
```

This part is simply a scaled cube that is used as a gear tooth. By now you should be able to read these declarations. Part G01 is defined as a rectangular solid (a stretched cube) that is 2 units long in the x direction and 1 unit wide in the y and z directions.

Part G02 is a ring formed by cutting a cylinder out of a Z_Disk. The ring is thin in the z direction.

```
#declare G02 = intersection {   //--GEAR RING--
   difference {
     intersection { Z_Disk scale < 12 12 1 >  }
     quadric { Cylinder_Z scale < 10 10 10 >  }
   }
}
```

Part G03 is the union of two flat bars formed by squashing two cubes in different dimensions, "welding" them together to form a crosspiece.

```
#declare G03 = union {    //--GEAR SPOKE--
   intersection { Cube scale < 1.5 11 0.5 >  }
   intersection { Cube scale < 11 1.5 0.5 >  }
}
```

Look at the picture of G04 in the blueprint and see how the ring and the crosspiece are put together. Find part G04 in both the side view and the front view. Notice that the part is very thin in the side view, and that the scale factor in the z dimension in the declaration of G03 above is 1 (you have to multiply both scale factors together — 2 x 0.5 = 1). This shows how both the front and side view are important for correctly scaling the pieces. The front view shows dimensions in the x and y directions, and the side view shows the dimensions in the y and z directions.

Now for the fun. Using the power and flexibility of the POV language, that one lone gear tooth will be propagated all along the circumference of the gear ring! Go back and study the definition of the gear tooth again and fix in your mind exactly where it is. The tooth started out as a cube with all sides 1, centered on the origin. It is stretched to 2 units long along the x axis. Then it is translated 12 units to the right along the x axis. This means that it extends from x coordinate 11 to x coordinate 13.

Here is the definition of G04. It is the union of G02, G03, and many copies of the tooth G01.

```
#declare G04 = object {    //--------ASSEMBLE THE GEAR PARTS --------
  union {
    intersection { G02 translate < 0 0 -0.5 > }
    union { G03 }
    intersection { G01 rotate < 0 0 0 > }
    intersection { G01 rotate < 0 0 10 > }
    intersection { G01 rotate < 0 0 20 > }
    intersection { G01 rotate < 0 0 30 > }
    intersection { G01 rotate < 0 0 40 > }
    intersection { G01 rotate < 0 0 50 > }
    intersection { G01 rotate < 0 0 60 > }
    intersection { G01 rotate < 0 0 70 > }
    intersection { G01 rotate < 0 0 80 > }
    intersection { G01 rotate < 0 0 90 > }
    intersection { G01 rotate < 0 0 100 > }
    intersection { G01 rotate < 0 0 110 > }
    intersection { G01 rotate < 0 0 120 > }
    intersection { G01 rotate < 0 0 130 > }
    intersection { G01 rotate < 0 0 140 > }
    intersection { G01 rotate < 0 0 150 > }
    intersection { G01 rotate < 0 0 160 > }
    intersection { G01 rotate < 0 0 170 > }
    intersection { G01 rotate < 0 0 180 > }
    intersection { G01 rotate < 0 0 190 > }
    intersection { G01 rotate < 0 0 200 > }
    intersection { G01 rotate < 0 0 210 > }
    intersection { G01 rotate < 0 0 220 > }
    intersection { G01 rotate < 0 0 230 > }
    intersection { G01 rotate < 0 0 240 > }
    intersection { G01 rotate < 0 0 250 > }
    intersection { G01 rotate < 0 0 260 > }
    intersection { G01 rotate < 0 0 270 > }
    intersection { G01 rotate < 0 0 280 > }
    intersection { G01 rotate < 0 0 290 > }
    intersection { G01 rotate < 0 0 300 > }
    intersection { G01 rotate < 0 0 310 > }
    intersection { G01 rotate < 0 0 320 > }
    intersection { G01 rotate < 0 0 330 > }
    intersection { G01 rotate < 0 0 340 > }
    intersection { G01 rotate < 0 0 350 > }
  }
  texture { GOLD }
  bounded_by {
    intersection { Z_Disk scale < 14 14 2 > translate < 0 0 -1 > }
  }
}
```

In the body of the definition of the gear G04 are many lines that look like

```
intersection { G01 rotate < 0 0 nn > }
```

where nn is a number of degrees counting by 10s. The keyword Intersection is needed because G01 is a Cube which is in turn the intersection of six planes. The expression

`rotate < 0 0 nn >`

means that the tooth declared as G01 is rotated nn degrees about the Z axis. Since the gear is centered on the origin, this rotation moves the tooth around the gear. The result of these 36 statements is the addition of 36 teeth to the gear.

At the bottom of the declaration of the gear G04 are two other statements worth noting. The first is the statement

`texture { GOLD }`

which applies the Gold texture discussed earlier to the gear. The second is the statement

```
bounded_by {
    intersection { Z_Disk scale < 14 14 2 > translate < 0 0 -1 > }
```

which serves to speed up the POV Ray Tracer's rendering of the MANTEL.POV file. A bounding object is a simple object that completely encloses a complex shape. In this case, the very complicated gear fits inside a disk. The disk has radius 14, which leaves a little room to spare. A ray tracer has to test many possible ray paths emanating from the camera in order to render the image. Think like a ray-tracing program for a moment and you will understand the value of the bounding shape. The gear is a relatively small part of the overall image, so most rays won't hit it, but the ray tracer doesn't know that in advance. It has to test every possible ray for whether it hits each and every little gear piece, which is very time consuming and wasteful. But the designer of MANTEL.POV guarantees to the ray tracer that the gear is inside the simple shape Z_disk. Therefore the ray tracer can test whether the ray misses Z_Disk. If it does, then it knows that it also misses all those little gear teeth, and it needn't test them. Keep in mind that it is your responsibility to make sure that your bounding shapes really do enclose your objects — if they don't, the results will be unpredictable.

Assembling the Parts

You have now seen a detailed explanation of several parts that make up the mantel clock, but all of them have been in the form of declarations. With the exception of the two light source objects, none of the shapes discussed have yet been placed in the image. The approach used in the design of the POV file MANTEL.POV is to create all the shapes through the use of declarations, and place them in the image all at once. The lines where the clock is assembled come near the bottom of the file. They are the following:

```
#declare CLOCK = composite { //----SOME ASSEMBLY REQUIRED----
   object    { A01                  } //base
   object    { ASS1 translate < 27   16 -19 > } //r.column
   object    { ASS1 translate < -27  16 -19 > } //l.column
   object    { A06  translate < 0    77 -19 > } //support
   object    { A07  translate < 0    70 0.5 > } //pivot sup
   composite { ASS2 translate < 0    16   9 > } //balls
   composite { ASS3 translate < 0    104 -17 > } //crown/box
   object    { G04  translate < -18 120  -3 > } //t.gear
   object    { G04  translate < -22 100  -5 > } //b.gear
   object    { F01  translate < 0   110 -21 > } //face rim
   object    { F02  translate < 0   110 -24 > } //face
   bounded_by {
      intersection { Y_Disk scale < 64 170 64 > translate < 0 -1 0 > }
   }
}

//--------------PLACE CLOCK--------------
composite { CLOCK rotate < 0 -30 0 > }
```

Actually, only this last line places anything in the image. The previous statements use one final declaration of the composite called Clock. In the declaration of Clock, each part is translated into place. For example, consider the gear part G04 that we just disussed. The gear was originally defined centered on the origin, where it had to be for all the teeth to be rotated into place. In the final assembly, two gears are created as two separate objects in the statements:

```
object { G04 translate    < -18 120  -3 >  }   //t.gear
object { G04 translate    < -22 100  -5 >  }   //b.gear
```

The two objects are identical in every respect except the final position within the whole clock. Each part is placed in its proper position according to the calculated coordinates read off the blueprint in this one declaration.

After the Clock declaration, the parts have been assembled, but this statement was yet another mere declaration, and the clock has still not been placed in the image! One simple line accomplishes that. The line is:

```
//--------------PLACE CLOCK--------------
composite { CLOCK rotate < 0 -30 0 > }
```

This statement is *not* a declaration. It causes the ray tracer to render all the pieces in the final image. If you cut out this one line from MANTEL.POV, the whole clock would disappear from the image! When the clock is finally placed, it can also be positioned. Recall that the camera in the Viewpoint block was aimed directly at the x-y plane. Without the Rotate statement, the clock would be viewed straight on. By turning the clock 30 degrees about the vertical y axis, a more attractive angle is achieved.

Variations

The POV data file MANTEL.POV is complex and full of illustrations of the capabilities of the POV-Ray language. At the same time, the file is carefully structured and systematically built so that it is very easy to understand. Even without your mastering all the details, you can make a number of interesting modifications to this file.

1. As with the Mt. Mandel image discussed earlier in this chapter, you can replace the fractal that forms the backdrop of this image. The final few lines of the data file cause the file ST.GIF to be read in and placed in the image. All you have to do is try a different file for ST.GIF and it will be used.

2. You can create a sequence of files that show the mantel clock being built. To do this, add // in front of all the lines that add parts to the CLOCK declaration except the last one. The "//" characters act as comment delimiters in POV, causing the rest of the line to be ignored by the input parser. Then when you render the file, only the uncommented object will show. One by one, uncomment additional parts by deleteing the "//" characters, and re-render the image.

Similarly, you can isolate and render any of the parts by themselves by commenting out all the parts in the CLOCK declaration except the parts you want. For example, to show only the gears, the CLOCK declaration would look like:

```
#declare CLOCK = composite { //----SOME ASSEMBLY REQUIRED----
//    object { A01 }                          //base
//    object { ASS1 translate    < 27  16 -19 >  }   //r.colum
//    object { ASS1 translate    < -27 16 -19 >  }   //l.colum
//    object { A06 translate     < 0   77 -19 >  }   //support
//    object { A07 translate     < 0   70 0.5 >  }   //pivot sup
//    composite { ASS2 translate < 0   16   9 >  }   //balls
//    composite { ASS3 translate < 0  104 -17 >  }   //crown/box
      object { G04 translate     < -18 120  -3 >  }   //t.gear
      object { G04 translate     < -22 100  -5 >  }   //b.gear
//    object { F01 translate     < 0  110 -21 >  }   //face rim
//    object { F02 translate     < 0  110 -24 >  }   //face
      bounded_by {
        intersection { Y_Disk scale < 64 170 64 > translate < 0 -1 0 > }
      }
  }
```

Figure 9-11 shows a sequence of mantel clocks built from the bottom up by successively un-commenting additional objects and adding them to the composite.

Figure 9-11 Building up the mantel clock

MOONRISE

About the Image

The next image contains the shimmering reflection of a rising moon over an ocean, with rugged volcanic cliffs rising above the water. The creation of this image makes use of the synergy between several of the Image Lab tools. Compared to the mantel clock POV data file, the Moonrise data file is very simple, but it contains some advanced uses of POV's features.

Image Credits

Doug Muir used the moonrise image to test out the Height_Field feature of POV-Ray, which he wrote. Therefore Doug is responsible both for the artistry of this image as well as the technical wizardry that makes it possible!

Image Lab Tools and Files Needed

The moonrise image requires the protected-mode version of the POV Ray Tracer, Fractint, and Piclab. All of these programs come with this book except Fractint. You can get Fractint with the book *Fractal Creations*, or from CompuServe; see Chapter 6 for more information. You will also need the data

Figure 9-12 Moonrise

file named NIGHT.POV that is found in the \IMLAB\EXAMPLES directory on your hard disk.

Procedure

The moonrise image requires a plasma fractal created by Fractint to make both the mountains and the moon. You can use the same file for both.

Step 1. Create the Plasma Fractal

You can create a 640x480 plasma fractal from the command line by typing:

```
C:>fractint type=plasma video=sf5 savename=mountain batch=yes ⏎
```

This creates the file MOUNTAIN.GIF which is used to create the mountains in the moonrise image, shown in Figure 9-12.

Step 2. Make the Moon Colors

You can use the same plasma image for the moon, but for this purpose the colors have to be changed to be more moonlike. Start Piclab and load the file MOUNTAIN.GIF.

```
C:>PL (ENTER)
PL>GLOAD MOUNTAIN (ENTER)
PL>GRAY (ENTER)
PL>SHOW (ENTER)
```

The Gray command changes the plasma colors to grayscale. If the colors are light, and there are not many dark shades in the image, there is no need to further change the colors. However, in all probability the shades of gray are too dark to look moonlike. Keep brightening the image until it has many nearly white shades, but is not so bright that all the cloudlike details are washed out. To do this, type:

```
PL>BRIGHT 20 (ENTER)
PL>SHOW (ENTER)
```

As soon as the result looks good to you, type:

```
PL>TRANSFORM (ENTER)
PL>GSAVE MOON (ENTER)
```

Step 3. Generate the Image in POV

The data file NIGHT.POV is shown in Listing 9-6.

· ·

```
// Moonrise by Doug Muir

#include "colors.inc"
#include "shapes.inc"

camera {
  location <10.0  50.0  30.0>
  direction <0.0  0.0  0.7>
  up <0.0  1.0  0.0>
  right <1.333333 0.0 0.0>
  look_at <0.0  0.0  200.0>
}

#declare Mountain = color red 0.8 green 0.37 blue 0.14

object { // The mountain
  height_field {
    gif "mountain.gif"
    water_level 101
    scale <640 128 480>
  }
```

Listing 9-6 The POV-Ray data file NIGHT.POV (*continued on the next page*)

. . . .

```
 texture { color Mountain }
   translate <-100.0 -63.5 -130.0>
   rotate <0.0 -40.0 0.0>
}

object { // The water
   sphere { <0.0  -6400010.0  0.0> 6400000.0 }
   texture {
      turbulence 0.17
      color SeaGreen
      ripples 0.35
      frequency 100.0
      ambient 0.1
      diffuse 0.1
      reflection 0.7
      specular 0.5
      roughness 0.03
      scale <700.0 700.0 700.0>
   }
}

object { // Deep Water
   sphere { <0.0  -6400010.0  0.0> 6399999.0 }
   texture {
      color SeaGreen
      ambient 0.7
      diffuse 0.0
   }
}

object { //Sky
   sphere { <0.0 -1000.0 0.0> 9999000 }
   texture {
      gradient < 0 1 0 >
      color_map {
        [0.0 0.5 color BlueViolet color Navy]
        [0.5 1.01 color Navy color Navy]
      }
      ambient 0.7
      diffuse 0.0
      scale <10 10000000 10>
   }
}

object { // Light source
   light_source { <1000 1400 -4000> color MediumGoldenrod }
}
```

Listing 9-6 The POV-Ray data file NIGHT.POV (*continued on the next page*)

```
object { // Moon
  union {
    quadric { Sphere }
    light_source { <0 0 0> color Grey }
  }
  texture {
    image_map { gif "moon.gif" map_type 1 once }
    diffuse 0.5
    ambient 0.5
  }
  scale <1000000 1000000 1000000>
  translate <0 0 9000000>
  rotate <-12.0 -15.0 0.0>
  no_shadow
}
```

Listing 9-6 The POV-Ray data file NIGHT.POV (*continued*)

Make sure that the two files MOUNTAIN.GIF and MOON.GIF are present in the current directory, and run the protected-mode version of POV from the batch file. To make sure everything is working, start off with a very low resolution. To do this, type:

`C:>POV NIGHT -w80 -h60` (ENTER)

Since the plasma fractal is created randomly each time Fractint is run, there is no way to predict just exactly how high the mountains will be or whether you can see the reflection of the moon on the water. If the mountains block the moon's reflection, you can lower them by adding the line

`translate <0 -50 0>`

right after the line

`scale <640 128 480>`

in the Height_Field block in NIGHT.POV. You can also repeat step 1 and generate a new plasma fractal. The result does not have to look identical to Figure 9-12, but the aesthetic qualities of the image are enhanced if you can see the moon on the water. The random element of the plasma fractal generation makes Doug's original image impossible to exactly duplicate, but it also gives you the opportunity to create similar images based on completely different landscapes.

Step 4. Convert the Targa Output File to GIF

You can use Piclab to convert the file NIGHT.TGA to a GIF file so that you can view it using VGA video hardware. The Piclab commands are:

```
C:>PL (ENTER)
PL>TLOAD NIGHT (ENTER)
PL>MAKEPAL (ENTER)
PL>MAP (ENTER)
PL>GSAVE NIGHT (ENTER)
```

These commands convert the file NIGHT.TGA to NIGHT.GIF.

Discussion of the POV-Ray Data File

The mountain is created by reading in the plasma fractal MOUNTAIN.GIF and interpreting the colors as heights. The colors of the original are not used to color the mountain.

```
#declare Mountain = color red 0.8 green 0.37 blue 0.14

object { // The mountain
  height_field {
    gif "mountain.gif"
    water_level 101
    scale <640 128 480>
  }
  texture { color Mountain }
  translate <-100.0 -63.5 -130.0>
  rotate <0.0 -40.0 0.0>
}
```

The image is mapped into a 1x1x1 cube, so a Scale statement expands the landscape to a larger size. If the mountains block the view of the reflected moon, another strategy for lowering the mountains would be to reduce the y scale value of 128 to a lower value. The Rotate statement swings the mountain range around the y axis; you can adjust the rotation angle for the most pleasing effect.

The way the water is created is very interesting. The sea consists of two giant spheres generated by this portion of the POV input file:

```
object { // The water
  sphere { <0.0  -6400010.0  0.0> 6400000.0 }
  texture {
    turbulence 0.17
    color SeaGreen
    ripples 0.35
    frequency 100.0
    ambient 0.1
    diffuse 0.1
    reflection 0.7
    specular 0.5
    roughness 0.03
    scale <700.0 700.0 700.0>
  }
}
```

```
object { // Deep Water
  sphere { <0.0  -6400010.0  0.0> 6399999.0 }
  texture {
    color SeaGreen
    ambient 0.7
    diffuse 0.0
  }
}
```

The spheres have a radius of 640000, but the *y* coordinate of the center has a large negative value, so the surface of the sphere is visible. The second sphere has a slightly smaller radius. The lower sphere provides deep water color that shows through the surface layer. The waves are created by the Turbulence, Ripple, and Frequency keywords. The Scale command

```
scale <700.0 700.0 700.0>
```

inside the Texture block affects the size of the waves.

The sky is an even larger sphere. It makes use of a color map that smoothly changes from BlueViolet to Navy, and then remains a constant Navy color.

```
object { //Sky
  sphere { <0.0 -1000.0 0.0> 9999000 }
  texture {
    gradient < 0 1 0 >
    color_map {
      [0.0 0.5 color BlueViolet color Navy]
      [0.5 1.01 color Navy color Navy]
    }
    ambient 0.7
    diffuse 0.0
    scale <10 10000000 10>
  }
}
```

There are two light sources. One of them is hidden inside the moon, so that the moonlight can cast shadows on the landscape. The moon is scaled to a very large size, but is also very far away because it is translated 9 million units in the *z* direction. The combination of large size and far distance makes the moon appear small, just as it appears in real life. Even at that large distance, the moon is located inside the giant sky sphere which has a radius of 9,999,000; if the moon were outside the sky sphere, it would be invisible.

```
object { // Light source
  light_source { <1000 1400 -4000> color MediumGoldenrod }
}

object { // Moon
  union {
    quadric { Sphere }
    light_source { <0 0 0> color Grey }
  }
```

```
texture {
   image_map { gif "moon.gif" map_type 1 once }
   diffuse 0.5
   ambient 0.5
}
scale <1000000 1000000 1000000>
translate <0 0 9000000>
rotate <-12.0 -15.0 0.0>
no_shadow
}
```

The texture for the moon uses the Image_Map facility to color the moon with the MOON.GIF file. The Image_Map wraps the GIF file around the sphere, using the original colors. This action is different from the Height_Field which translates the colors to heights and does not use them as colors.

Variations

The elements of the moonrise image are few: moon, mountain, and water. You can experiment with different positions of the moon, the height of the mountains, and try different fractals for both the moon and the mountains.

RAY TRACING 3-D IMAGES

About the Image

You can create stereoscopic images with POV-Ray. Many variables affect the visual result, such as the size of the image, the angle of view, and method of viewing the result. All of these variables boil down to this idea: You make two images, one for the left eye and one for the right eye. The location of the camera is shifted in the two images to simulate the separation of your physical eyes.

Our 3-D example is a beautiful image with a crystal ball, and shiny torus, and some very convincing wooden objects.

Image Credits

This POV data file was created by Dan Farmer.

Image Lab Tools and Files Needed

You will need the POV data file WLEFT.POV that is in the \IMLAB\EXAMPLES directory on your hard disk. You will also need Piclab.

Procedure

Making a stereo image involves rendering the POV data file twice, with two different Camera Location vectors.

Step 1. Create the WLEFT.TGA File

The file WLEFT.POV is shown in Listing 9-7. This is the data file for the left-eye image.

. . . .

```
// Persistence of Vision Ray Tracer
// A couple of wood textures for Aaron Caba, by Dan Farmer
// NOTE: These look much different at 640x480 and above!  Better still
// with some anti-aliasing.
// Takes about 32 minutes &640x480 on 486/33
// (a little longer on an XT)

#include "colors.inc"
#include "shapes.inc"
// #include "shapes3.inc"
#include "textures.inc"

#declare Glass3 = texture {
   specular 1.0
   roughness 0.005
   phong 1
   phong_size 100
   color red 1.0 green 1.0 blue 1.0  alpha 0.7
   ambient 0.0
   diffuse 0.0
   reflection 0.2
   refraction 1.0
   ior 1.95
}

#declare Torus = quartic {
//   Torus specs:
//      Major radius: 7.000000      Minor radius: 3.000000
//      Outer radius: 10.000000     Inner radius: 4.000000

   <   1.000000 0.000000 0.000000 0.000000 2.000000
       0.000000 0.000000 2.000000 0.000000 -116.000000
       0.000000 0.000000 0.000000 0.000000 0.000000
       0.000000 0.000000 0.000000 0.000000 0.000000
       1.000000 0.000000 0.000000 2.000000 0.000000
       80.000000 0.000000 0.000000 0.000000 0.000000
       1.000000 0.000000 -116.000000 0.000000 1600.000000 >
}

// Scaled to fit properly on a unit object,
// with the grain along the X axis (as opposed
// to the Z axis default). Scale and tranform the
// object AFTER applying the texture!
```

Listing 9-7 WLEFT.POV *(continued on the next page)*

. . . .

```
#declare Mahogany = texture {
    wood
    turbulence 0.05
    color_map {
        [0.0 0.5  color red 0.20  green 0.03   blue 0.03
                  color red 0.35  green 0.15   blue 0.08 ]
        [0.5 1.01 color red 0.27  green 0.10   blue 0.10
                  color red 0.20  green 0.03   blue 0.03 ]
    }
    ambient 0.2
    diffuse 0.8
    scale <0.05 0.05 1>
    rotate <0 0 0.5>     // Tilt the grain just a wee
    rotate <0 90 0>      // Put major axis on X
    translate <-0.5 0 0>
}

#declare LightOak =  texture {
    wood
    turbulence 0.05
    color_map {
        [0.0 0.1  color red 0.42 green 0.26 blue 0.15
                  color red 0.42 green 0.26 blue 0.15 ]
        [0.1 0.9  color red 0.42 green 0.26 blue 0.15
                  color red 0.52 green 0.37 blue 0.26 ]
        [0.9 1.0  color red 0.52 green 0.37 blue 0.26
                  color red 0.52 green 0.37 blue 0.26 ]
    }
    ambient 0.2
    diffuse 0.8
    scale <0.05 0.05 1>
    rotate <0 0 0.5>     // Tilt the grain just a wee
    rotate <0 90 0>      // Put major axis on X
    translate <-0.5 0 0>
}

camera {
    location <-1.25  45  -85>
    direction <0.0 0.0  1.25>
    up  <0.0  1.0  0.0>
    right <1.33333 0.0 0.0>
    look_at <0 0 0>
}

// Light source
object { light_source { <100 100 0  > color White } }
object { light_source { <10 100 -150> color White } }
```

Listing 9-7 WLEFT.POV *(continued on the next page)*

. . . .

```
composite {
   object {
      // intersection { Cube }
      box { <-1 -1 -1> <1 1 1> }
      color White
      texture {
         Mahogany
         ambient 0.4        // (Overriding the previous value)
         reflection 0.35
      }
      scale <36 3 21>
   }

   object {
      sphere { <0 0 0> 1 }
      color Red
      texture {
         LightOak
         rotate <0 15 0>
      }
      scale <12 12 12>
      translate <-10 15 60>
   }

   object {
      sphere {<0 0 0> 0.85 }
      color Blue
      texture {
         Glass3
         color green 0.85 blue 0.8 alpha 0.95
      }
      scale <7 7 7>
      translate <15 30 -50>
   }

   // Chrome torus
   object {
      quartic { Torus }
      color Yellow
      texture {
         phong 1 phong_size 10
         diffuse 0.003
         ambient 0.125
         reflection 1
         color White
      }
```

Listing 9-7 WLEFT.POV (*continued on the next page*)

· ·

```
        scale <1.5 1.5 1.5>
        translate <20 14 10>
        rotate <-15 0 10>
    }
    rotate <0 20 0>
}
```

Listing 9-7 WLEFT.POV (*continued*)

Render this file at 160x120 pixels. To do this, use a batch file that invokes either version of POV (the regular memory version works fine with this input file).

```
C:>POV WLEFT -W160 -H120 (ENTER)
```

This will create the file WLEFT.TGA.

Step 2. Create the WRIGHT.TGA File

Now copy WLEFT.POV to the file WRIGHT.POV. Change the Location statement in the Camera block from

```
location <-1.25  45  -85>
```

to

```
location <1.25  45  -85>
```

The only change is to move the camera 2.5 units to the right. In this case a data file unit represents about 1 inch; 2.5 inches is approximately the separation of your two eyes. Now render the WRIGHT.POV file the same way.

Step 3. Create the STEREO.GIF File

You can combine the files WLEFT.TGA and WRIGHT.TGA into a single file that you can view on the screen with the following Piclab script.

```
PL>TLOAD WLEFT (ENTER)
PL>EXPAND 640 480 (ENTER) ; expand dimensions of WLEFT image
PL>TLOAD WRIGHT (ENTER)
PL>OVERLAY 160 0 (ENTER)   ; overlay image to the right of wleft
PL>MAKEPAL (ENTER)
PL>MAP (ENTER)       ; reduce colors to 256
PL>SET DISPLAY SVGA1 (ENTER)      ; 640x480 256 color
PL>GSAVE STEREO (ENTER)
PL>SHOW (ENTER)
```

The result should look like Figure 9-13. In order for you to see the 3-D effect, the corresponding features in the two images should be a little closer together than your eye separation, or about 2 1/4 inches. Try viewing the image through the 3-D glasses that can be ordered using a coupon in the back of

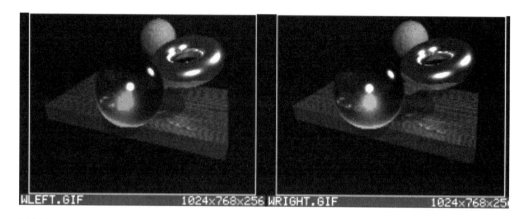

WLEFT.GIF   1024x768x256 WRIGHT.GIF   1024x768x25

Figure 9-13 3-D example

this book. If you have trouble seeing the 3-D, try viewing the file STEREO.GIF produced by these instructions using CompuShow. You can make the image larger or smaller by viewing with different video modes. On a 14-inch monitor, the 640x480x256 mode should be just right.

Variations

The advantage of using the 3-D lenses is that you can view images in full color. You will find some examples to view on the poster. This method only works with small images, because the two images must be separated no more than about two and a half inches.

An alternative approach is to use red/blue glasses. With red/blue glasses you can view much larger images, but only in grayscale. If you have the book *Fractal Creations,* you can use the red/blue glasses that came with it. If you don't have red/blue glasses, you might try your local comic book store.

The commands in Listing 9-8 will combine WLEFT.TGA and WRIGHT.TGA into a red/blue 3-D image. You can type these commands directly into Piclab, but it is better to run them as a Piclab program. You can use your text editor to place these commands in a file called 3-D.

. . . .

```
tload wright
dark 255
trans
rsave stereo
shell copy stereo.r8 stereo.g8
tload wright
gray
rsave stereo
shell copy stereo.r8 stereo.b8
tload wleft
gray
rsave stereo
rload stereo 160 120 color
makepal
map
gsave stereorb
show
```

Listing 9-8 Piclab command file 3-D to create a red/blue image

This Piclab program uses the RAW file format. The WLEFT image is saved to a RAW file named STEREO.R8, the WRIGHT image is saved to STEREO.B8, and a black image is saved to STEREO.G8. These three files are read back into Piclab as a red/blue true-color file, and converted to GIF. The Rload command must be given the image dimensions, in this case 160x120. You should try regenerating WLEFT and WRIGHT using POV at a higher resolution such as 640x480, and when you convert to red/blue, modify the Rload line to

```
rload stereo 640 480 color
```

To run the Piclab command script in the file 3-D, type:

```
C:>PL (ENTER)
PL>RUN 3D (ENTER)
```

When it finishes, try viewing the result with red/blue 3-D glasses. The 3-D script also saves the red/blue image in the file STEREORB.GIF.

INDEX

Books have a substantial influence on the destruction of the forests of the Earth. For example, it takes 17 trees to produce one ton of paper. A first printing of 30,000 copies of a typical 480 page book consumes 108,000 pounds of paper which will require 918 trees!

Waite Group Press™ is against the clear-cutting of forests and supports reforestation of the Pacific Northwest of the United States and Canada, where most of this paper comes from. As a publisher with several hundred thousand books sold each year, we feel an obligation to give back to the planet. We will therefore support and contribute a percentage of our proceeds to organizations which seek to preserve the forests of planet Earth.

FRACTAL CREATIONS
Explore the Magic of Fractals on Your PC
by Timothy Wegner and Mark Peterson

Over 40,000 computer enthusiasts who've purchased this book/software package are creating and exploring the fascinating world of fractals on their computers. **Fractal Creations** includes a full color fractal art poster, 3-D glasses, and *Fractint*, the revolutionary software that makes fractals accessible to anyone with a PC. *Fractint* lets you zoom in on any part of a fractal image, rotate it, do color-cycle animation, and even choose accompanying sound effects and a 3-D mode. PC Magazine said "**Fractal Creations**...is a magical ride...guaranteed to blow your eyes out." Winner of the 1991 Computer Press Association Award for "Best Non-Fiction Computer Book." For MS/PC DOS machines; best with a VGA video board and a 286/386 processor.

ISBN 1-878739-05-0, 315 pp., 1 5.25" disk, color poster, 3-D glasses, $34.95 US/$44.95 Can., Available now

VIRTUAL REALITY PLAYHOUSE
by Nick Lavroff

Jack-in to the world of Virtual Reality with this playful new book and disk package. Virtual Reality is a new interactive technology which creates the convincing illusion that you are completely immersed in worlds existing only inside your computer. **Virtual Reality Playhouse** lets you enter those worlds and even create your own personal digital dimension. Expand the parameters of your mind as you move rapidly from an introduction of virtual reality's basic concepts to visual explorations illustrating real-life applications. Demo programs include a 3-D simulation that puts you inside a robot which travels through a computer-generated city. Or, you can play a game in a 3-D room that can be tilted, spun, and twisted in near impossible ways. Put on the enclosed 3-D glasses and jump right into any one of 8 startling VR simulations. There are even plans for building your own LCD shuttering VR glasses and power glove to manipulate objects in a VR world. For MS/PC DOS machines.

ISBN 1-878739-19 -0, 146 pp., 1 3.5" disk, 3-D glasses, $22.95 US/$29.95 Can., Available June 1992

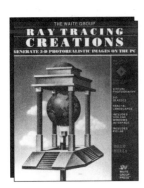

RAY TRACING CREATIONS
Create 3-D Photorealistic Images on the PC
by Drew Wells

With the **Ray Tracing Creations** book/disk combination, you can immediately begin rendering perfect graphic objects like the ones in computer movies. Using the bundled powerful shareware *POV-Ray* program, you'll learn to control the location, shape, light, shading, and surface texture of all kinds of 3-D objects. *POV-Ray*'s C-like language is used to describe simple objects, planes, spheres, and more complex polygons. Over 100 incredible pre-built scenes are included that can be generated, studied, and modified any way you choose. This book provides a complete course in the fundamentals of ray tracing that will challenge and entice you. Contains 386 and 286 versions of *POV-Ray*; VGA display required. For MS/PC DOS machines.

ISBN 1-878739-27-1, 400 pp., 1 HD 3.5" disk, 3-D glasses, $39.95 US/$49.95 Can., Available December 1992

Send for our unique catalog to get more information about these books, as well as our outstanding and award-winning programming titles, including:

Master C: Let the PC Teach You C and **Master C++:** Let the PC Teach You Object-Oriented Programming. Both are book/disk software packages that turn your computer into an infinitely patient C and C++ professor.

Workout C: Hundreds of C projects and exercises and a full-featured C compiler make this an unbeatable training program and value.

C++ Primer Plus: Written by Stephen Prata in the same style as his C Primer Plus, which won the Computer Press Association's coveted "Best How-To Computer Book" award and sold over 400,000 copies.

Object Oriented Programming in Turbo C++: Robert Lafore, master teacher of the programming art, takes the prospective C++ programmer from the basics to the most complex concepts, and

provides anyone with C++ programming experience a comprehensive reference.

Windows API Bible: The only comprehensive guide to the 800 instructions and messages in the Windows Application Programming Interface.

Visual Basic How-To and **Visual Basic Super Bible.** Both books cover the unique Microsoft language that makes Windows programming much more accessible. **How-To** covers tricks, tips, and traps of VB programming. **Super Bible** is the ultimate compendium of reference information on VB.

Turbo Pascal How-To: Everything you need to know to begin writing professional Turbo Pascal programs.

If you love playing with images and ray tracing, and want to be able to build more sophisticated shapes than those shown in the book, you'll want the Image Lab Accessory Disk. The disk also contains some of the best ray-tracing accessories, beautiful POV-Ray source files from ray-tracing experts Mike Miller and Truman Brown, and conversion utilities that let you convert from Autodesk to POV-Ray formats.

All of the source files and utilities on the Accessory Disk are supported by their authors in the Computer Art Forum on Compuserve (GO COMART). Here is a sampling of the best of the Image Lab Accessory Disk:

IMAGE LAB ACCESSORY DISK

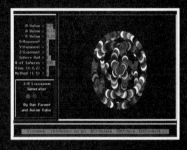

C Render

Ray tracers allow you to define textures that describe how the surfaces of the objects in your scenes will look. A texture interface program like C Render lets you change the surface of a sphere and the plane it sits on by moving bars. These bars control texture attributes like color, reflection, phong highlighting, diffuse lighting, and refraction. Being able to "preview" the textures on screen instead of waiting for POV-Ray to render them is extremely efficient. When you have created a texture you like, you can save it as a texture definition that you can add to your ray-tracing input files.

Ray-Tracing Files

The disk contains a collection of POV-Ray input files of spectacular images by Mike Miller and Truman Brown. You can render these yourself using the POV-Ray program.

Connect the Dots

Many mathematically inspired ray tracings are made from series of dots or spheres strung together. For example, you can make a face, a leg, a plane, and so on out of spheres. The Connect the Dots program smooths these together by making bridging shapes such as ellipsoids and cones. This program is particularly fascinating because it can take as input the output of still other programs. For example, you can smooth the spheres that are created by the Lissajous program to make tubes tied in impossible knots!

Torus Generator

Truman's Torus Generator lets you design inner-tube-shaped geometric figures for your ray tracings. You specify the inner and outer diameter and other Torus parameters, and TTG will create a ray tracing input file.

Other Utilities

In addition to these utilties you'll find programs for converting images made with 3D Studio (or in Autodesk's DXF format) to the POV-Ray format. This lets you design shapes in 3D Studio and then ray trace them with POV-Ray.

Worm

A 3-D editor that you can use to create strings of spheres, or "worms". Output of the program can be used with the Connect the Dots program.

Lissajous

Generates 3-D "Lissajous" figures—complex donut-like patterns formed by mixing waves of different frequencies. With this utility you alter the parameters that determine the shape of the Lissajous curves, and see its colorful shape drawn before your eyes on the screen. When you are done, you can save the result as a ray-tracing data file and use it in your renderings.

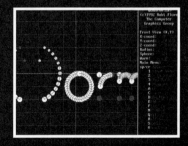

To order this eclectic array of stimulating ray-tracing miscellania, fill out the handy order card at the back of the book.

Image Lab Accessories Order Form

You've explored the programs of Image Lab and you want more! You can't stop! You want to build more sophisticated ray-tracings and you want to make them into full color stereo holographic images. Fill out this post-paid card today and get ready to delve even deeper into the beautiful world of ray-tracing.

To order by phone call 800-368-9369 or 415-924-2576 (FAX)

Name

Company

Address
Street Address Only, No P.O. Box

City   State   ZIP

Daytime Phone

Quantity and Type

Image Lab Accesory Disk	IML-1	Quantity ☐	x $19.95 =	
Stereopticon 707 Stereo Viewing Glasses	SG-707	Quantity ☐	x $6.95 =	

Sub Total	
Sales Tax	
Shipping	
Total Due	

Sales Tax—California residents add 7.25% sales tax.
Shipping:
Glasses: are postpaid first class US Mail in USA.
International: Add $3.00 Canada, $10.00 foreign.

Disk: add $5 USA, $10 Canada, or $20 Foreign for shipping and handling. Standard shipping is UPS Ground. Allow 3 to 4 weeks. Prices are subject to change. Purchase orders subject to credit approval, and verbal purchase orders will not be accepted.

Combined: same as disk alone

Disk Type: ☐ 5.25-inch   ☐ 3.5-inch

Method of Payment

Checks or money orders, payable to The Waite Group. To pay by credit card, complete the following:

☐ Visa   ☐ Mastercard   Card Number

Cardholder's Name _____   Exp. Date ☐☐ ☐☐

Cardholder's Signature _____

StereoOpticon 707

Stereo Viewing Glasses

You've played with the programs in Image Lab and now you want to make some great stereo image pairs for full color 3-D viewing. But wait, you need a special viewer to do that! Well, here is where to get it. Step up to the Waite Group counter and purchase your incredible, full-featured, portable StereoOpticon 707 viewing glasses!

This marvel of western ingenuity can slice, dice, chop, magnify, resolve, and otherwise fuse a left and right image into one very handsome stereo picture with rich color and depth. You use the glasses to view slides made from GIFs, to view the printed stereo images on the poster in this book, or to view holographic stereo images on the screen of your PC.

What is this like? Remember the ViewMaster? You put a circular card in a binocular-like affair and look into it and see beautiful color slides of Donald Duck being cooked on the stove or Goofy falling down the stairs. Well the StereoOpticon 707 does this same thing, only you make your own images using programs like the POV-Ray ray tracer. The StereoOpticon does the rest.

So don't miss out on watching full-color stereo holographic images on your PC screen today. Only $6.95 postpaid (first class US Mail).

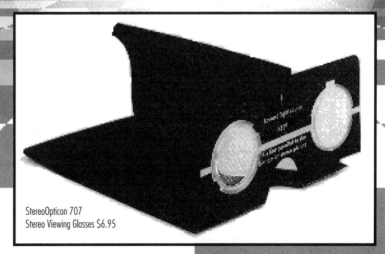

StereoOpticon 707
Stereo Viewing Glasses $6.95

WAITE GROUP PRESS™

This is a legal agreement between you, the end user and purchaser, and The Waite Group®, Inc., and the authors of the shareware programs contained in the disk. By opening the sealed disk package, you are agreeing to be bound by the terms of this Agreement. If you do not agree with the terms of this Agreement, promptly return the unopened disk package and the accompanying items (including the related book and other written material) to the place you obtained them for a refund.

SOFTWARE LICENSE

1.   The Waite Group, Inc. grants you the right to use one copy of the enclosed software programs (the programs) on a single computer system (whether a single CPU, part of a licensed network, or a terminal connected to a single CPU). Each concurrent user of the program must have exclusive use of the related Waite Group, Inc. written materials.

2.   Each of the programs, including the copyrights in each program, is owned by the respective author and the copyright in the entire work is owned by The Waite Group, Inc. and they are therefore protected under the copyright laws of the United States and other nations, under international treaties. You may make only one copy of the disk containing the programs exclusively for backup or archival purposes, or you may transfer the programs to one hard disk drive, using the original for backup or archival purposes. You may make no other copies of the programs, and you may make no copies of all or any part of the related Waite Group, Inc. written materials.

3.   You may not rent or lease the programs, but you may transfer ownership of the programs and related written materials (including any and all updates and earlier versions) if you keep no copies of either, and if you make sure the transferee agrees to the terms of this license.

4.   You may not decompile, reverse engineer, disassemble, copy, create a derivative work, or otherwise use the programs except as stated in this Agreement.

GOVERNING LAW

This Agreement is governed by the laws of the State of California.

Image Lab Accessories Order Form

You've explored the programs of Image Lab and you want more! You can't stop! You want to build more sophisticated ray-tracings and you want to make them into full color stereo holographic images. Fill out this post-paid card today and get ready to delve even deeper into the beautiful world of ray-tracing.

To order by phone call 800-368-9369 or 415-924-2576 (FAX)

Name

Company

Address
Street Address Only, No P.O. Box

City   State   ZIP

Daytime Phone

Quantity and Type

Image Lab Accesory Disk	IML-1	Quantity ☐	x $19.95 =	
Stereopticon 707 Stereo Viewing Glasses	SG-707	Quantity ☐	x $6.95 =	

Sub Total

Sales Tax

Shipping

Total Due

Sales Tax—California residents add 7.25% sales tax.
Shipping:
Glasses: are postpaid first class US Mail in USA.
International: Add $3.00 Canada, $10.00 foreign.

Disk: add $5 USA, $10 Canada, or $20 Foreign for shipping and handling. Standard shipping is UPS Ground. Allow 3 to 4 weeks. Prices are subject to change. Purchase orders subject to credit approval, and verbal purchase orders will not be accepted.

Combined: same as disk alone

Disk Type: ☐ 5.25-inch   ☐ 3.5-inch

Method of Payment

Checks or money orders, payable to The Waite Group. To pay by credit card, complete the following:

☐ Visa   ☐ Mastercard   Card Number

Cardholder's Name _____   Exp. Date

Cardholder's Signature _____

Please fill out this card if you wish to know of future updates to
Image Lab, or to receive our catalog.

Institution Name:

Division/Department

Mail Stop:

Last Name: First Name: Middle Initial:

Street Address:

City: State: Zip:

Daytime telephone: (   )

Date product was acquired: Month   Day   Year   Your Occupation:

Overall, how would you rate *The Waite Group's Image Lab*

☐ Excellent   ☐ Very Good   ☐ Good
☐ Fair   ☐ Below Average   ☐ Poor

What did you like MOST about this product? _____

_____

What did you like LEAST about this product? _____

_____

Please describe any problems you may have encountered with installing or using Image Lab: _____

_____

How do you use this book (tutorial, reference, problem-solver...)?

_____

How did you find the pace of this book? _____

What computer languages are you familiar with?

_____

_____

What is your level of computer expertise?

☐ New   ☐ Dabbler   ☐ Hacker
☐ Power User   ☐ Programmer   ☐ Experienced professional

Is there any program or subject you would like to see The Waite Group cover in a similar approach?

_____

Please describe your computer hardware:

Computer _____   Hard disk _____
5.25" disk drives _____   3.5" disk drives _____
Video card _____   Monitor _____
Printer _____   Peripherals _____

Where did you buy this book?

☐ Bookstore (name: _____)
☐ Discount store (name: _____)
☐ Computer store (name: _____)
☐ Catalog (name: _____)
☐ Direct from WGP   ☐ Other _____

What price did you pay for this book? _____
What influenced your purchase of this book?

_____

☐ Recommendation   ☐ Advertisement
☐ Magazine review   ☐ Store display
☐ Mailing   ☐ Book's format
☐ Reputation of The Waite Group   ☐ Topic

How many computer books do you buy each year? _____
How many other Waite Group books do you own? _____
What is your favorite Waite Group book?

_____

Additional comments? _____

_____

_____

☐ **Check here for a free Waite Group Press catalog**

The Waite Group's Image Lab

NO POSTAGE
NECESSARY
IF MAILED
I IN THE
UNITED STATES

BUSINESS REPLY MAIL

FIRST CLASS MAIL   PERMIT NO. 9   CORTE MADERA, CA

POSTAGE WILL BE PAID BY ADDRESSEE

Waite Group Press, Inc.
Attention: *Image Lab*
200 Tamal Plaza
Corte Madera, CA 94925

- **FOLD HERE** - - - - - - - - - - - - - - - - - - -